Maenads, Martyrs, Matrons, Monastics

A SOURCEBOOK ON WOMEN'S RELIGIONS
IN THE GRECO-ROMAN WORLD

Maenads
Martyrs
Matrons
Monastics

Edited by ROSS S. KRAEMER

FORTRESS PRESS   PHILADELPHIA

Library of Congress Cataloging-in-Publication Data

Maenads, martyrs, matrons, monastics.

Bibliography: p.
Includes index.
1. Women—Mediterranean Region—Religious life—
History—Sources.   2. Women and religion—History—
Sources.   3. Women in Judaism—History—Sources.
4. Women in Christianity—History—Early church, ca.
30–600—Sources.   I. Kraemer, Ross Shepard, 1948–
BL625.7.M34   1988   291'.088042   87–45899
ISBN 0–8006–0855–0
ISBN 0–8006–2071–2 (pbk.)

3213C88   Printed in the United States of America   1–855(C)   1–2071(P)

In memory of
Harriet Dolores Plager Shepard
and
Jochanan H. A. Wijnhoven

ἐν εἰρήνῃ ἡ κοίμησις αὐτῶν

Contents

Section Two. Researching Real Women: Documents to, from, and by Women

Contents   xi

Section Three. Religious Office

Section Four. New Religious Affiliation and Conversion

Preface

The idea for this sourcebook arose thirteen years ago, when I taught my first course on women and religion. The texts I wished to present my students were disparate in many ways, not least in their scattered location (or absence) in the library of a small liberal-arts college in central Pennsylvania. In 1974, women's studies in religion was in its infancy. Rosemary Radford Ruether's anthology of articles on attitudes toward women in Jewish and Christian tradition appeared in print just at the end of the semester. My students spent a lot of time in the reserve room of the library reading fifteen pages of one text and four pages of another.

From inception to implementation was a long process. Along the way, the project acquired and lost coeditors, altered its scale, and changed its format several times. It was preempted by several more pressing projects, among them a dissertation on women's religious activities in the Greco-Roman world and a study of women in Greek-speaking Jewish communities in the Greco-Roman world funded by the National Endowment for the Humanities. Work on this sourcebook has been constrained (and sometimes postponed) by the time limitations inevitable for one who has mostly earned a living not in the conventional manner of a college professor but as a year-round academic administrator without summers off or midwinter breaks. As is perhaps fitting for a collection of piecemeal documents, the sourcebook has been put together piecemeal over the years.

I would never have completed it without the help and support of others. First, I wish to thank Allaire Chandor Brumfield, with whom I first developed a cohesive model for the book and who withdrew as coeditor only when other responsibilities allowed her insufficient time to share in the project. Patty Beebe-Wilson, a student of mine at Stockton State College, spent many hours in the library looking up references and assembling the necessary volumes. The librarians at the Stockton library were their usual generous and cheerful selves in procuring numerous obscure books from other institutions. I am especially grateful to three people for personally providing me with their translations of texts: Janet Timbie for her rendering of the Coptic letter of Shenoute to Tachom; Cynthia Osiek for her translation of several sections of Epiphanius; and Richard Lim for his translation of the Domitiana-Urbanus papyrus. Several colleagues graciously offered critiques of the proposed organization and contents of the book and made helpful suggestions, including Elizabeth Clark, Deirdra Good, Martha Himmelfarb, Susan Niditch, Carolyn Osiek, Kathleen McVey, and Rosemary Radford Ruether. There are no adequate words to describe my debt to my colleague and friend Bernadette J. Brooten, whose work continues to amaze and inspire me and whose encouragement constantly nourishes my own work.

I owe very special thanks to John G. Gager, Jr., and to the entire Department of Religion at Princeton University; they supported my research on women's religion from my early days as a graduate student and have continued to provide me with moral and practical support ever since. In 1982–83, that support took the concrete form of an appointment as Visiting Fellow. The National Endowment for the Humanities provided me with a Fellowship that same year to study women in Greek-speaking Jewish communities in the Greco-Roman period, during which I worked on some of the materials included in this volume, particularly the inscriptions. I also wish to express my appreciation to my colleagues in the Department of Religious Studies at the University of Pennsylvania, who welcomed me into their community while I was still a graduate student, who included me as a member of the department while I held administrative positions at the University, and who have since extended to me the courtesy of an appointment as a Visiting Scholar since 1982. Without the privileges which that entails, especially access to the rich resources of the University's library collections, my work on this sourcebook would have been much more difficult.

At age nine, my daughter, Jordan, who knows about mothers who are doctors of medicine, has not quite figured out mothers who are doctors of philosophy but has figured out that different people must have written the two creation accounts in Genesis and that a third party, probably the publisher, put them together. Without her, everything would be harder. My special thanks are due to John A. Hollar, my editor at Fortress Press, who has in fact put together all these different accounts, and to the entire staff at Fortress. Finally, I wish to thank my husband, Michael, for minding only a little all those nights and weekends I spend in the library or in my study; for understanding, for all the twenty-one years we have known each other, the unrelenting hold the study of religion in antiquity has had on me; and for finding, together and not always easily, the compromises that make possible our work and our life together.

Ross S. Kraemer
October 28, 1987

Abbreviations

ACW	Ancient Christian Writers (Westminster, Md., 1946–)
ANCL	Ante-Nicene Christian Library
ANF	Ante-Nicene Christian Fathers
ANT	M. R. James, *Apocryphal New Testament* (Oxford, 1924; revised, 1955)
Ant. Fluch.	R. Wunsch, *Antike Fluchtafeln* (Bonn, 1912)
AOT	H. D. Sparks, *The Apocryphal Old Testament* (Oxford, 1984)
BHO	*Bibliotheca Hagiographica Orientalis* (Brussels, 1910)
BJS	Brown Judaic Studies
Budé	Collection des universités de France, publiée sur le patronage de l'Association Guillaume Budé
Bull. épig.	*Bulletin épigraphique* (1938–), extracted from *Revue des études grecques*
CCSL	Corpus Christianorum Series Latina (Paris, 1953–)
CIJ	J.-B. Frey, *Corpus of Jewish Inscriptions* I, with prolegomenon by B. Lifshitz (New York, 1975); II (Rome, 1936)
CIL	*Corpus Inscriptionum Latinarum* (Berlin, 1863–)
CPJ	*Corpus Papyrorum Judaicarum*, 3 vols. (Cambridge, Mass., 1957–64)

CSCO	Corpus Scriptorum Christianorum Orientalis (Louvain, 1903–)
CSEL	Corpus Scriptorum Ecclesiasticorum Latinorum (Vienna, 1866–)
CTS	Cambridge Texts and Studies (Cambridge, 1891–)
EPRO	Etudes préliminaires aux religions orientales dans l'Empire Romain (Leiden: E. J . Brill)
FC	Fathers of the Church (1947–)
FENHC	*Facsimile Edition of the Nag Hammadi Codices* (Leiden: E. J. Brill)
GCS	Die griechische christliche Schriftsteller der ersten drei Jahrhunderte (Leipzig, 1897–1941; Berlin and Leipzig, 1953; Berlin, 1954–)
Gibson 1975	E. Gibson, "Montanist Inscriptions at Usak," *Greek, Roman, and Byzantine Studies* 16:433–42
Gibson 1978	E. Gibson, *The "Christians for Christians" Inscriptions of Phrygia* (Cambridge, Mass., 1978)
GRBS	*Greek, Roman, and Byzantine Studies*
Guarducci	M. Guarducci, *Epigrafia Graeca*, 4 vols. (Rome, 1967–78)
HSCP	*Harvard Studies in Classical Philology*
HTR	*Harvard Theological Review*
IG	*Inscriptiones Graecae* (Berlin, 1873–)
ILS	H. Dessau, *Inscriptiones Latinae Selectae*, 3 vols. (Berlin, 1892–1916)
I. Magn.	O. Kern, *Die Inschriften von Magnesia am Meander* (Berlin, 1900)
I. Syrie	*Inscriptions grecques et latines de la Syrie*, 6 vols. (Paris, 1929–59)
L'Ann. épig.	*L'Année épigraphique*
LCC	Library of Christian Classics (Philadelphia and London, 1953–)
LCL	Loeb Classical Library
Lifshitz	B. Lifshitz, *Donateurs et fondateurs dans les synagogues juives* (Paris, 1967)
LSAM	F. Sokolowski, *Lois sacrées de l'Asie Mineure* (Paris, 1955)
LSCG suppl.	F. Sokolowski, *Lois sacrées des cités grecques, supplement* (Paris, 1962)

MAMA	*Monumenta Asiae Minoris Antiqua*, 8 vols. (Manchester, 1928–29)
NewDocs	G. H. R. Horsley, *New Documents Illustrating Early Christianity* (North Ryde, 1976 [1981]–)
NHS	Nag Hammadi Studies (Leiden: E. J. Brill)
NPNFC	A Select Library of Nicene and Post-Nicene Fathers of the Christian Church (Buffalo and New York, 1886–1900; reprinted, Grand Rapids, 1952–)
NTA	E. Hennecke and W. Schneemelcher, *New Testament Apocrypha*, 2 vols. (Philadelphia: Westminster Press, 1963–65)
OCD	*Oxford Classical Dictionary*
OCT	Oxford Classical Texts
OTP	J. H. Charlesworth, *The Old Testament Pseudepigrapha*, 2 vols. (Garden City, N.Y.: Doubleday & Co., 1983–85)
PG	J. Migne, *Patrologia Graeca*
PGM	K. Preisendanz et al., *Papyri Graecae Magicae: Die griechischen Zauberpapyri*, 2 vols. (Stuttgart: Teubner, 1973–74)
P. Hibeh	B. P. Grenfell and A. S. Hunt, *The Hibeh Papyri*, 1906
PL	J. Migne, *Patrologia Latina*
Pleket	H. W. Pleket, *Epigraphica II: Texts on the Social History of the Greek World* (Leiden, 1969)
P. Oxy.	B. P. Grenfell and A. S. Hunt, *The Oxyrhynchus Papyri* (1898–)
PVTG	Pseudepigraphia Veteris Testamenti Graece (Leiden: E. J. Brill)
Ritti	Tullia Ritti, *Inscrizioni e riveli greci nel Museo Maffeiano di Verona* (Rome, 1981)
SBLMS	Society of Biblical Literature Monograph Series
SBLSBS	Society of Biblical Literature Sources for Biblical Study
SBLSP	*Society of Biblical Literature Seminar Papers*
SBLTT	Society of Biblical Literature Texts and Translations
SC	Sources chrétiennes (Paris, 1941–)

SEG	Supplementum Epigraphicum Graecum (Leiden, 1923–)
SJLA	Studies in Judaism in Late Antiquity (Leiden: E. J. Brill)
SWR	Studies in Women and Religion (Lewiston, N.Y.: Edwin Mellen Press)
TAM	Tituli Asiae Minoris (Vienna)
Teubner	Bibliotheca Scriptorum Graecorum et Romanorum Teubneriana (1949–)

Acknowledgments

All excerpts from The Loeb Classical Library are reprinted by permission of Harvard University Press and The Loeb Classical Library.

Excerpts from Bernadette Brooten, *Women Leaders in the Ancient Synagogues*, Brown Judaic Studies 36 (Atlanta: Scholars Press, 1982), reprinted by permission of the author and the copyright holder.

Excerpts from *The Old Testament Pseudepigrapha*, edited by J. H. Charlesworth, copyright © 1985 by James H. Charlesworth. Reprinted by permission of Doubleday, a division of Bantam, Doubleday, Dell Publishing Group, Inc.

Excerpts from John Chrysostom, *Against Judaizing Christians* are from *Fathers of the Church*, vol. 68 (Washington, D.C.: Catholic Univ. of America Press, 1977), and are reprinted by permission of the publisher.

Excerpt from Elizabeth Clark, *Jerome, Chrysostom, and Friends*, Studies in Women and Religion 2 (Lewiston, N.Y.: Edwin Mellen Press, 1979), reprinted by permssion of the publisher and the author.

Translation of BT *Rosh Hashanah* and of excerpts from BT *Kiddushin* are from I. Epstein, ed., 35 vols. of the Babylonian Talmud (London: Soncino Press, 1935–52).

Excerpts from Euripides, "The Bacchae," trans. William Arrowsmith, from David Grene and Richmond Lattimore, eds., *The Complete Greek Tragedies*, vol. 3 (Chicago: Univ. of Chicago Press, 1960), reprinted by permission of the publisher.

Excerpts from *A New Eusebius*, ed. J. Stevenson, rev. W. H. C.

Frend (London: SPCK, 1987), reprinted by permission of the publisher.

Translations of "The Titles of Isis," "Praises of Isis," and "Isis Restores Lucius" are reprinted with permission of Macmillan Publishing Company from *Hellenistic Religions: The Age of Syncretism* by Frederick C. Grant. Copyright 1953 by Library of Liberal Arts, renewed 1981 by Estate of Frederick C. Grant.

Excerpts from Moses Hadas, *The Third and Fourth Books of Maccabees* (New York: Ktav, 1953), reprinted by permission of Dropsie College.

Excerpt from Daryl Hine, *Theocritus: Idylls and Epigrams* (New York: Atheneum, 1983), copyright © 1982 Daryl Hine. Reprinted with the permission of Atheneum Publishers, Inc.

Excerpts from R. A. Kraft, et al., *The Testament of Job: Greek Text and English Translation*, Society of Biblical Literature Texts and Translations 5, Pseudepigrapha Series 4 (Missoula, Mont.: Scholars Press, 1974), reprinted by permission of the authors and the copyright holder.

Excerpts from Mary R. Lefkowitz and Maureen B. Fant, eds., *Women's Life in Greece and Rome* (Baltimore: Johns Hopkins Univ. Press; London: Gerald Duckworth, 1982) are reprinted by permission of the publishers.

Excerpt from Harry J. Leon, *The Jews of Ancient Rome* (Philadelphia: Jewish Publication Society, 1960) copyright © The Jewish Publication Society. Reprinted by permission of the publisher.

Excerpts from *The Acts of the Christian Martyrs*, translated by Herbert Musurillo © 1972 Oxford University Press. Reprinted by permission of Oxford University Press.

Translations by Jacob Neusner of the Mishnah *Niddah* from his *History of the Mishnaic Law of Women*, Studies in Judaism in Late Antiquity 33 (Leiden: E. J. Brill, 1980), and of the Babylonian Talmud *Sotah* and Babylonian Talmud *Sukkah* from his *Talmud of Babylonia: An American Translation*, Brown Judaic Studies 72, 74 (Chico, Calif.: Scholars Press, 1984), reprinted by permission of the translator and copyright holder.

Excerpt from David G. Rice and John E. Stambaugh, *Sources for the Study of Greek Religion*, Sources for Biblical Study 14 (Atlanta: Scholars Press, 1979), reprinted by permission of the authors and the copyright holder.

Excerpts from pp. 152–60, 271–77, 180–87, and 404–5 of *The*

Maenads, Martyrs, Matrons, Monastics

Introduction

My intentions for this sourcebook are fairly straightforward: to assemble in one place in English translation major texts and documents relating to women's religious activities in the various religions of Greco-Roman antiquity, including Judaism and Christianity. Sourcebooks on the religions of Greco-Roman antiquity (many designed as background to the study of the New Testament and early Christianity) are already available,[1] as are anthologies of texts on women's lives in Greek and Roman society,[2] and on women in Christian sources.[3] Attitudes toward women in Judaism and Christianity have been surveyed[4] and there is even a collection of sources for new

1. E.g., J. Stevenson, ed., *A New Eusebius* (London: SPCK, 1957), revised with additional documents by W. H. C. Frend (London: SPCK, 1987); Howard Clark Kee, *The Origins of Christianity: Sources and Documents* (Englewood Cliffs, N.J.: Prentice-Hall, 1973), revised as *The New Testament in Context: Sources and Documents* (Englewood Cliffs, N.J.: Prentice-Hall, 1984); F. F. Bruce, *Jesus and Christian Origins outside the New Testament* (Grand Rapids: Wm. B. Eerdmans, 1974); and David R. Cartlidge and David L. Dungan, eds., *Documents for the Study of the Gospels* (Philadelphia: Fortress Press, 1980). Three anthologies not compiled as background to the New Testament and early Christianity are F. C. Grant, *Hellenistic Religions: The Age of Syncretism* (Indianapolis and New York: Bobbs-Merrill, 1953); idem, *Ancient Roman Religion* (Indianapolis and New York: Bobbs-Merrill, 1957); and G. W. E. Nickelsburg and M. Stone, eds., *Faith and Piety in Early Judaism: Texts and Documents* (Philadelphia: Fortress Press, 1983).

2. Maureen Fant and Mary K. Lefkowitz, eds., *Women's Lives in Greece and Rome* (Baltimore: Johns Hopkins Univ. Press, 1982).

3. Elizabeth A. Clark and Herbert Richardson, eds., *Women in Religion: A Feminist Sourcebook of Christian Thought* (New York: Harper & Row, 1977); and Elizabeth A. Clark, *Women in the Early Church* (Wilmington, Del.: Michael Glazier, 1983).

4. E.g., Rosemary Radford Ruether, ed., *Religion and Sexism: Images of Women in Jewish and Christian Tradition* (New York: Simon & Schuster, 1974); and Leonard

feminist Christian theology.[5] But to date no one has assembled the texts relevant to women's religion in Western antiquity.

Since all collections are selective, there are many materials from Greco-Roman antiquity that shed light on women's religion which are not included here. In choosing sources, I have used several criteria. For the most part, I have chosen to restrict myself chronologically to materials from the fourth century B.C.E. to the early fifth century C.E. A few of the selections from Greek religion are earlier (Euripides' *Bacchae* was written in 405 B.C.E., and the *Hymn to Demeter* dates to the seventh century B.C.E.); these continue to play such a significant role in our understanding of women's religion that I decided to include them. Other sources, such as Jewish and Christian inscriptions and some Christian and Jewish texts, cannot be dated precisely and may be somewhat later than the early fifth century C.E., but their significance is such that I felt they should be included.

Accessibility and familiarity to the modern reader were significant considerations. I deliberately excluded any excerpts from the Bible, either Jewish or Christian Scriptures, because these are readily available. For the same reason, I excluded the Book of Judith, which is included in all editions of the Revised Standard Version Apocrypha. Many of the sources included here are available elsewhere in translation, but often they are not available in undergraduate libraries or are widely scattered even in the best library. A few selections are not available elsewhere in English translation that I know of, including many of the inscriptions, Shenoute's letter to Tachom, and excerpts from Epiphanius.

I did not deliberately set linguistic restrictions, but in fact the materials collected here are translated from six major languages of the Greco-Roman world: Greek, Latin, Aramaic, Hebrew, Syriac, and Coptic. There are undoubtedly sources in other languages which bear on women's religion in Greco-Roman antiquity, but since such materials have not been adequately identified, they are not represented here.

Intentionally I chose wherever possible not to retranslate sources already available in readable English translations, although these are not always altogether free of gender bias. In the majority of cases, I

Swidler, *Women in Judaism: The Status of Women in Formative Judaism* (Metuchen, N.J.: Scarecrow Press, 1976).

5. Rosemary Radford Ruether, *Womanguides: Readings toward a Feminist Theology* (Boston: Beacon Press, 1985).

have sought to reproduce those translations which I thought most fairly reflect the ancient texts in contemporary English. Occasionally, however, the intricacies and costs of obtaining permission to reprint other scholars' translations obliged me to select alternative translations. For those texts I translated myself, especially *The Acts of Thecla* and *The Conversion and Marriage of Aseneth*, I tried to provide a fairly close translation, with attention to issues of gender bias. For the most part, I did not try to resolve issues of textual criticism unless I felt it absolutely necessary. For those readers not skilled in the original languages of the sources, I believe these translations, whether mine or not, present a sufficient representation, while those able to read the originals will not rely wholly on the translations of others in any case.

The texts themselves are accompanied by only a limited apparatus. A final section, "About the Authors and Sources," provides fuller information, including references to the primary sources and translations, and selected bibliography. Through this format, I wish to encourage the reader to pursue the sources themselves and not to rely too heavily on my assessments of them.

I have also chosen to group my selections thematically. The specific groupings were determined in part by the texts themselves and in part by the kinds of issues on which they bear: religious leadership, religious change, feminine aspects of the divine, and so forth. The allocation of a particular selection to its category was sometimes difficult, as many texts could easily have been included in one or more other categories. By organizing the texts into thematic groups rather than chronologically or by religious tradition or by some other principle, I hope to illustrate both the similarities and differences across chronological boundaries and cultural and religious contexts. Within sections, selections are usually arranged in approximately chronological order. Occasionally I deviated from this to group together closely related material, such as the epitaphs of Jewish women called priestess. The dates given are for the source in its written form. In those cases where we know that a text describes a substantially earlier time period, that earlier period is also mentioned.

It was not possible to standardize the use of brackets and parentheses, since permission to reprint previously published translations allows virtually no changes to be made. In most cases, material in square brackets is physically missing from the manuscript or inscription and represents an educated conjecture on the part of scholars. Material in parentheses usually makes explicit what is only implicit in the original, but material in square brackets serves this function in Neusner's translations of rabbinic materials. Occasionally, parentheses contain alternative translations and explanatory material. In the *Testament of Job* (selection 119), pointed brackets identify material absent from a Greek manuscript designated S but present in other sources. In selections from the Nag Hammadi Library (selections 134 and 135) square brackets signify a lacuna in the manuscript, pointed brackets identify corrections of the original scribes' omissions or errors, and parentheses contain material supplied by the modern editors and translators.

Because I intended only to present evidence for women's religious activities, I need to explain my reasons for including (in the section entitled "Researching Real Women: Documents to, from, and by Women") some selections on Jewish women that have no specific religious content. First, we know so little about actual Jewish women from other sources that it seemed worth making an exception to my organizational structure. Second, these texts do in fact shed indirect light on the religious lives of Jewish women, which I discuss briefly in the introduction to that section.

My expectations for this collection are modest in some ways and grandiose in others. They are modest in that I have deliberately not sought to offer the reader much interpretation or analysis of the texts (although many of them have figured prominently in my own research), reserving that for a companion volume. They are grandiose in that I hope the sourcebook will facilitate and stimulate study and research by others, whether undergraduate or graduate students, historians, theologians, other scholars, or simply interested laypersons, into the nature of women's religious activities. Such study and research will, I hope, enrich our understanding not only of women's religion but also of men's religion and perhaps ultimately of human religion as well.

Finally, my intention in collecting these materials was not guided by any particular theological motivation. Unlike Rosemary Radford Ruether, I do not see the texts here as necessarily appropriate to the current theological concerns of contemporary women, whether Jewish, Christian, or other.[6] I approach the sources primarily as a feminist historian of religion: I seek to recover and understand the religious activities and beliefs of women and to integrate that knowl-

6. Ibid.

edge into a revised, enriched appreciation of human religion. From my perspective the vast preponderance of research on religion in my own field, and probably in all others as well, has really been research on men's religion which has been content to equate that with human religion. The texts here, although mostly written and transmitted by men, are where we must begin to reconstruct women's religion in antiquity, to inquire about the differences between women's religion and men's as well as about the similarities, and to revise our models and theories accordingly.

I am not naive about the difficulties of these tasks. I realize full well that these sources can rarely if ever be taken at face value as evidence about women in antiquity. But they, together with other materials I did not include, are all we have. Until we have exhausted our analysis of them, we cannot reject them out of hand, tentative though our conclusions may be.

I am also not naive about another fact: while I approach these sources as a historian, others will approach them for their contemporary theological value. Texts have a habit of taking on lives of their own far beyond what is envisioned by their authors, and this anthology is not likely to be an exception. I only wish to reiterate that there are no theological implications intended by the inclusion of sources in or the exclusion of sources from this collection.

Observances, Rituals, and Festivals

What women do in religious contexts has not received much attention. The texts in this section are primarily descriptive and almost
always filtered to us through a male observer. How accurate these
reports are continues to be an unresolved issue.

How, for example, shall we evaluate accounts by men who claim to
know the details of women's rites from which men are supposedly
excluded? The classical Athenian playwright Euripides, obviously
needing to explain his source even within the confines of drama,
solves the problem by hidden male observers. In his *Bacchae,* excerpted in this section, a herdsman concealed behind the trees reports
back to the king Pentheus, who himself then spies on the women to
his ultimate detriment. What Euripides' real source was we do not
know, and consequently we are not altogether sure that his descriptions are accurate or are even intended to be.

The fourth-century orator Demosthenes, on the other hand, was
able to describe the women's activities for two apparent reasons: at
least one male is said to have participated in them, and at least some
of the activities took place in public, where any observer could see
them.

With many of these texts, the problem of "historical" accuracy
extends further. In the case of some Christian texts in particular, the
authors report activities they wish to discredit, whether it is Epiphanius's description of women functioning as priests and baking cakes to
the virgin Mary or John Chrysostom's disapproval of the attendance
of Christian women at synagogue festivals. On the one hand, we may

wish to apply the so-called criterion of dissimilarity, which says basically that an author who reports undesirable evidence must feel that such evidence is accurate or else it could be omitted. Reports of victory by the victorious are to be scrutinized carefully; reports of defeat by the defeated are more likely to be accurate! In this case, the criterion of dissimilarity would favor the accuracy of these reports, for Epiphanius considers such activities heretical.

On the other hand, authors such as Epiphanius may not have had access to reliable sources or any means of verifying their sources, if the thought of verification even occurred to them. They may have believed their sources accurate, but we must be more suspicious. When Origen of Alexandria reports that the pagan critic of Christianity, Celsus, denigrated Christianity by calling it a religion of women and slaves,[1] it is difficult for us to tell whether this is standard polemic with little historical value or an accurate report providing Celsus grist for his anti-Christian mill. Someone like John Chrysostom, who undeniably had strong feelings about what was and was not appropriate behavior for Christian women and men, may still be a more accurate reporter when he describes the activities of women in his own community rather than some faraway land.

Most of the texts in this section are taken from Greek, Roman, and Hellenistic religions other than Judaism and Christianity. Perhaps this results from the fact that such religions differentiated ritual activities more clearly on the basis of gender. We know, for example, that certain rituals and cults were primarily, if not exclusively, performed by one gender or the other, although certainly other religious rites involved the participation of both women and men.

Within extant Jewish sources, it is difficult to discern much evidence for ritual activities specific to women. Although we know that Jewish women participated in some of the same religious activities as Jewish men, we cannot easily say for certain which. Some Jewish religious activities were restricted to certain men (e.g., priestly sacrifices in the temple), and the rabbis considered women exempt from certain obligations binding on men. The use of rabbinic texts as evidence for the practice of real Jewish women is problematic for a number of reasons, not the least of which is the fact that scholars do not have a firm grasp on the extent to which rabbinic regulations describe the social reality of Jewish communities. Here I have in-

---

1. Origen *Against Celsus* 3.49.

cluded a few selections from rabbinic sources, with this caveat in mind.

Similarly for Christian sources, we possess little in the way of evidence that allows us to see whether men and women shared all ritual activity or whether gender distinctions affected Christian praxis. It is tempting to speculate on a relationship here between the gender distinctions of divinity which polytheism affords and the denial of such distinctions which monotheism seems to require. That is, if divinity can take both male and female forms, men and women can practice separate religious rites, whereas if divinity can have at best only male and female aspects, perhaps the theory of monopraxis, if not the reality, prevails.

In any case, the key point is that these texts offer a range of reports of women's activities without attempting to answer the hard questions of whether and to what extent they accurately depict the religious activities and practices of women in Western antiquity.

1

WHY WOMEN ARE COMPELLED TO WORSHIP DIONYSUS

Euripides *Bacchae* 23–42   405 B.C.E.

Thebes here was the first in this Hellenic land
that I made shriek in ecstasy, that I clothed with the
    fawnskin,
and gave the thyrsus into their hand, the ivy spear;   25
since my mother's sisters, who least should have done so,
denied that Dionysus was son of Zeus—
said that Semele was brided by some mortal man
and then attributed to Zeus the error of her bed,
by a clever idea of Cadmus. For this reason, they were always
    proclaiming,   30
Zeus slew her, because she falsely said he was her lover.

So them I stung in madness from their homes
and they dwell on the mountain stricken in their wits;
I compelled them to wear the apparel proper to my rites,
and all the female seed of the Cadmeians, all   35
of the women, I maddened from their homes;
together with the children of Cadmus, mingled with them,
under the green firs they sit on rocks, with no roof above.
For this land must learn to the full, even against its will,
that it is uninitiated in my bacchic rites;   40
and I must speak in defence of my mother Semele
by appearing to mortals as the god she bore to Zeus.

2

THE RITES OF THE FIRST
BACCHIC WORSHIPERS

Euripides *Bacchae* 677–768   405 B.C.E.

Messenger

The grazing herds of cattle were just ascending
toward the uplands, at the time when the sun
sends out his rays to warm the earth;
and I see three bands of women dancers,   680
of which Autonoe was leader of one, of the second
your mother Agaue, and Ino of the third.
All were sleeping with bodies relaxed,
some leaning their backs against a fir tree's foliage,
others among oak leaves resting their heads on the ground,   685
carelessly, but decently—it is not as you say,
that drunken from the mixing bowl and to the skirl of the
      flute
they hunt in the woods for the Cyprian's pleasure, going off
      one by one.
Then your mother gave a ritual shriek, standing up
in the midst of the bacchants, for them to shake their bodies
      out of sleep,   690
when she heard the lowing of the horned cattle.
And they cast off luxuriant sleep from their eyes
and leapt to their feet, a miracle of discipline to behold,
women young and old and girls still unmarried.
And first they let down their hair on their shoulders   695
and pulled up their fawnskins—as many as had undone
the knots that held them—and the dappled skins
they girdled with snakes that licked their cheeks.
Some of the women held in their arms a roe
or wild wolf cubs, and gave them white milk—   700
those who had newly given birth, whose breasts were still
      swollen,
and who had left behind their babies. On their heads they put
      garlands
of ivy and oak and flowering bryony.
Someone grasped a thyrsus and struck it into a rock

from which a dewy stream of water leaps out;   705
another struck her rod on the ground
and for her the god sent up a spring of wine;
and those who had a desire for the white drink
scraped the ground with their fingertips
and had jets of milk; and from out of the ivied   710
thyrsi, sweet streams of honey dripped.
So that, had you been there, the god you now condemn
you would have courted with prayers because of these sights.
    We cowherds and shepherds gathered together
to vie with each other in sharing our own account   715
of what strange and marvellous things they were doing.
And one who frequented the town and was glib with words
addressed us all: "O you who on the holy plateaus
of the mountains dwell, is it your wish that we hunt
Pentheus' mother Agaue away from the bacchic dances   720
and so oblige our lord?" His suggestion seemed to us
a good one, and we lie in ambush hiding ourselves
in the bushes' foliage. The women, at the appointed
hour, began to move the thyrsus into bacchic dances,
calling in unison on Bromios as Iacchus,   725
the offspring of Zeus; and all the mountain and its wild
    creatures
joined in bacchic worship, and nothing remained unmoved
    by their running.
    Agaue chances to jump close by me
and I leaped out, wanting to seize her,
deserting the ambush place where I was hiding myself.   730
She shouted out, "O my coursing hounds,
we are hunted by these men; but follow me,
follow, armed with your thyrsi in your hands!"
So we took to our heels and escaped
being torn to pieces by the bacchants; but they attacked the
    grazing   735
heifers, with hand that bore no steel.
And one you could have seen holding asunder in her hands
a tight-uddered, young, bellowing heifer;
while others were tearing full-grown cows to pieces.
You could have seen ribs, or a cloven hoof,   740
being hurled to and fro; and these hung

dripping under the fir trees, all mixed with blood.
Bulls that were arrogant before, with rage
in their horns, stumbled to the ground,
borne down by the countless hands of girls.   745
The garments of flesh were drawn apart more quickly
than you could close the lids over your royal eyes.
    The women move like birds lifted by their flight
over the plains stretched out below, which by the streams of
    Asopus
send forth the Thebans' fertile corn crop;   750
and on Hysiae and Erythrae, which lie on the lower slopes
of Cithaeron, like enemies
they fell, and turned everything
upside down. They snatched children from their homes;
and whatever they set on their shoulders stuck there   755
without being tied, and did not fall to the dark ground—
not bronze, not iron; and upon their locks
they carried fire and it did not burn them. The villagers, in
    rage
at being plundered by the bacchants, rushed to arms.
The sight that followed was strange to see, lord;   760
for the men's pointed spears drew no blood,
but the women, discharging thyrsi from their hands,
wounded the men and made them turn their backs in flight:
women did this to men—some god must have helped them!
Back they went to the place they had started from,   765
to the very springs the god sent up for them;
they washed off the blood, while the drops from their cheeks
the snakes cleansed from the skin with their tongues.

3

WOMEN WORSHIPERS OF A
DIONYSIAN DEITY, SABOS

Demosthenes *On the Crown* 259–60   4th century B.C.E.

On attaining manhood, you abetted your mother in her initiations
and the other rituals, and read aloud from the cultic writings. At
night, you mixed the libations, purified the initiates and dressed them
in fawnskins. You cleansed them off with clay and cornhusks, and
raising them up from the purification, you led the chant, "The evil I
flee: the better I find." . . . In the daylight, you led the fine thiasos
through the streets, wearing their garlands of fennel and white poplar.
You rubbed the fat-cheeked snakes and swung them above your head
crying "Euoi Saboi" and dancing to the tune of "hues attes, attes
hues." Old women hailed you "Leader," "mysteries instructor," "ivy-
bearer," "liknon carrier" and the like.

4

RITUALS FOR BRIDES AND PREGNANT WOMEN
IN THE WORSHIP OF ARTEMIS

LSCG suppl. 15   Cyrene, 4th century B.C.E.

13. [If a bride comes to the dormi]tory, she must sacrifice as a penalty to Artemis. She must not share a roof with her husband and must not be polluted; she must purify the temple of Artemis and as penalty sacrifice a full-grown victim, and then she should go to the dormitory. If she pollutes involuntarily, she must purify the temple.

14. A bride must make a ceremonial visit to the bride-room at the temple of Artemis at the festival of Artemis, whenever she wishes, but the sooner the better. If she does not make her ceremonial visit, she must make the regular sacrifice to Artemis at the festival of Artemis as one who has made no visit, and she must purify the temple and sacrifice a victim as penalty.

15. [A pregnant woman] shall make a ceremonial visit [before birth] to the bride-room in the precinct of Artemis and give the Bear priestess feet and head and skin of the sacrifice. If she does not make a ceremonial visit before giving birth she must make a visit afterwards with a full-grown victim. If she makes a ceremonial visit to the temple she must observe ritual purity on the seventh, eighth, and ninth day, and if she does not make a visit, she must perform the rites on these days. If she is polluted, she must purify herself and the temple and sacrifice a full-grown victim as penalty.

16. If a woman miscarries, if the foetus is fully formed, they are polluted as if by a death; if it is not fully formed, the household is polluted as if from childbirth.

5

OBJECTS DEDICATED TO
ARTEMIS BRAURONIA

IG II² 1514   Brauron, 4th century B.C.E.

Archipe [dedicated] a dotted, sleeved tunic in a box during the year Callimachus was archon. Callippe a short tunic, scalloped and embroidered; it has letters woven in. Chaerippe and Eucoline, a dotted tunic in a box. Philumene a silken tunic, in the year Theophilus was archon. Pythias a dotted robe in the year Themistocles was archon. There is an embroidered purple tunic; Thyaene and Malthace dedicated it. Phile [dedicated] a woman's girdle; Pheidylla a white woman's cloak in a box. Mneso a frog-green garment. Nausis a woman's cloak, with a broad purple border in a wave design.

6

WOMEN PARTICIPANTS AT A
FESTIVAL OF ADONIS

Theocritus *Idyll* 15   3d century B.C.E.

Gorgo

Quiet, Praxinoa, someone is going to sing the Adonis
Hymn. It's that woman of Argos's daughter, an elegant singer
Who was supreme in the dirge at last year's competition. I'm certain
She will recite something wonderful. Hush, she is clearing her throat
   now.

Singer

Mistress delighting in Golgo as well as Idalium and the
Heights of Mount Eryx, delighted with playthings of gold,
   Aphrodité,
Lo how the soft-footed Hours have brought your beloved Adonis
Back from torrential Acheron with the return of the twelfth month,
Slowest of those that are blest, the dear Hours, yet awaited with
   longing,
Coming to every man and invariably bringing something.
Cyprian child of Dioné, according to popular legend
You it was made Berenicé, who used to be mortal, immortal,
Pouring ambrosia into the breast of that queen among women.
Gratefully, lady of numerous titles and numerous temples,
For you the daughter of Queen Berenicé, Arsinoé, Helen's
Double, indulges Adonis with every beautiful object.
By him are piled all the seasonal dainties that grow upon fruit trees,
Near him are delicate bouquets protected in baskets of silver,
Also elaborate vessels of gold filled with Syrian scent and
Edible delicacies such as women confect in the pantry
Mixing all manner of herbal ingredients, bleached semolina
With liquid shortening into a pastry that's sweetened with honey.
Every wingèd and creeping and four-footed creature is present.
Green shady bowers abundantly laden with delicate dill-weed
Have been constructed, above which are fluttering juvenile cupids
Just like diminutive nightingales fluttering high in the tree tops,
Trying their newly-fledged wings as they flit to and fro in the
   branches.

O, but the ebony! Yes, and the gold! and the ivory white of
Eagles conveying his cup-bearing boy up to Zeus son of Cronos!
Counterpanes there are on top, all of purple and softer than slumber,
So that Miletus will say, and the shepherd that grazes on Samos,
"See how the couch of attractive Adonis is covered with our wool."
Cypris embraces him, rosy Adonis embraces the goddess;
Eighteen or nineteen at most the approximate age of the bridegroom,
Still with the delicate down round his lips, so his kiss doesn't tickle.
Now let us bid Aphrodite farewell as she clings to her lover.
First thing at dawn, with the dew, all together we'll take him outside
    and
Carry him down to the breakers that throw themselves up on the
    seashore.
There, with our hair all undone and our dresses in folds at our ankles,
Baring our breasts we shall shrilly begin the funereal music.
Dearest Adonis, you go to and fro, both up here and in Hades,
As they relate, most unique among demigods. Not Agamemnon
Bore such a fate, nor did Ajax that mighty but bad-tempered hero,
Neither did Hector, the eldest of Hecuba's sons—there were
    twenty—
Nor did Patroclus, nor Pyrrhus returning from Troy to his homeland;
Nor did the earlier Lapiths, indeed, nor Deucalion's offspring,
Nor the descendants of Pelops, Pelasgian masters of Argos.
O dear Adonis, be gracious as well in the New Year. Your coming
Gladdened us. When you come back your return will be welcome,
    Adonis.

Gorgo

Very ingenious creature that woman, Praxinoa, ain't she?
Lucky to know such a lot, really lucky to have such a sweet voice.
Still, it is time to go home. Diocleidas has not had his dinner
Yet, and the man is like gall, unapproachable when he is hungry.
Farewell, beloved Adonis, and may your return find us happy.

RITUAL REGULATIONS IN A
DIONYSIAC *THIASOS*

LSAM 48   Miletus, 276/5 B.C.E.

Whenever the priestess performs the holy rites on behalf of the
city . . . , it is not permitted for anyone to throw pieces of raw meat
[anywhere], before the priestess has thrown them on behalf of the
city, nor is it permitted for anyone to assemble a band of maenads
[*thiasos*] before the public *thiasos* [has been assembled]. . . .

. . . to provide [for the women] the implements for initiation in all
the orgies . . .

And whenever a woman wishes to perform an initiation for Dionysus Bacchius in the city, in the countryside, or on the islands, she must
pay a piece of gold to the priestess at each biennial celebration.

8

EPITAPH OF ALCMEONIS, A PRIESTESS
OF DIONYSUS

Henrichs, *HSCP* 82 (1978): 148   Miletus, 3d/2d century B.C.E.

Bacchae of the City, say "Farewell you holy priestess." This is what
a good woman deserves. She led you to the mountain and carried all
the sacred objects and implements, marching in procession before
the whole city. Should some stranger ask for her name: Alcmeonis,
daughter of Rhodius, who knew her share of the blessings.

THE ESTABLISHMENT OF DIONYSIAC RITES
IN MAGNESIA

I. Magn. 215a:24–40   Delphi, 3d century B.C.E.?

Go to the holy plain of Thebes to fetch maenads from the race of
Cadmean Ino. They will bring you maenadic rites and noble customs
and will establish troops of Bacchus in your city.

In accordance with the oracle, and through the agency of the envoys, three maenads were brought from Thebes: Cosco, Baubo and
Thettale. And Cosco organised the thiasus named after the plane tree,
Baubo the thiasus outside the city, and Thettale the thiasus named
after Cataebates. After their death they were buried by the Magne-
sians, and Cosco lies buried in the area called Hillock of Cosco, Baubo
in the area called Tabarnis, and Thettale near the theatre.

10

RITUAL EQUIPMENT FOR A WOMEN'S FESTIVAL
IN HELLENISTIC EGYPT

P. Hibeh 54   Egypt, 3d century B.C.E.

Demophon to Ptolemaeus, greetings. Send us at your earliest opportunity the flautist Petoun with the Phrygian flutes, plus the other
flutes. If it's necessary to pay him, do so, and we will reimburse you.
Also send us the eunuch Zenobius with a drum, cymbals and casta-
nets. The women need them for their festival. Be sure he is wearing
his most elegant clothing. Get the special goat from Aristion and send
it to us. . . . Send us also as many cheeses as you can, a new jug, and
vegetables of all kinds, and fish if you have it. Your health! Throw in
some policemen at the same time to accompany the boat.

11

ROMAN MATRONS WHO CELEBRATE
THE MATRALIA: A FESTIVAL TO
THE MOTHER MATUTA

Ovid *Fasti* VI.473–568   1st century B.C.E./C.E.

Now, Phrygian Tithonus, thou dost complain that thou art abandoned by thy spouse, and the watchful Morning Star comes forth
from the eastern waters. Go, good mothers (the Matralia is your festival), and offer to the Theban goddess the yellow cakes that are her
due. Adjoining the bridges and the great Circus is an open space of far
renown, which takes its name from the statue of an ox: there, on this
day, it is said, Servius consecrated with his own sceptered hands a
temple to Mother Matuta. Who the goddess is, why she excludes (for
exclude she does) female slaves from the threshold of her temple, and
why she calls for toasted cakes, do thou, O Bacchus, whose locks are
twined with clustered grapes and ivy, (explain and) guide the poet's
course, if the house of the goddess is also thine. Through the compliance of Jupiter with her request Semele was consumed with fire: Ino
received thee, young Bacchus, and zealously nursed thee with the
utmost care. Juno swelled with rage that Ino should rear the son who
had been snatched from his leman mother; but that son was of the
blood of Ino's sister. Hence Athamas was haunted by the furies and
by a delusive vision, and, little Learchus, thou didst fall by thy father's
hand. His sorrowful mother committed the shade of Learchus to the
tomb and paid all the honours due to the mournful pyre. She, too,
after tearing her rueful hair, leaped forth and snatched thee, Meli-
certes, from thy cradle. A land there is, shrunk with narrow limits,
which repels twin seas, and, single in itself, is lashed by twofold
waters. Thither came Ino, clasping her son in her frenzied embrace,
and hurled herself and him from a high ridge into the deep. Panope
and her hundred sisters received them scatheless, and smoothly glid-
ing bore them through their realms. They reached the mouth of thick-
eddying Tiber before Ino had yet received the name of Leucothea and
before her boy was called Palaemon. There was a sacred grove; it is
doubtful whether it should be called the grove of Semele or the grove
of Stimula: they say that it was inhabited by Ausonian Maenads. Ino
inquired of them what was their nation; she learned that they were
Arcadians and that Evander was king of the place. Dissembling her

godhead, the daughter of Saturn slily incited the Latian Bacchanals by glozing words: "Too easy souls! O blinded hearts! This stranger comes no friend to our assemblies. Her aim is treacherous, she would learn our sacred rites. Yet she has a pledge by which we can ensure her punishment." Scarce had she ended, when the Thyads, with their locks streaming down their necks, filled the air with their howls, and laid hands on Ino, and strove to pluck the boy from her. She invoked the gods whom still she knew not: "Yet gods and men of the land, succour a wretched mother!" The cry reached the neighbouring rocks of the Aventine. The Oetaean hero had driven the Iberian kine to the river bank; he heard and hurried at full speed towards the voice. At the approach of Hercules the women, who but a moment before had been ready to use violence, turned their backs shamefully in womanish flight. "What would'st thou here, O sister of Bacchus' mother?" quoth Hercules, for he recognized her; "doth the same deity who harasses me harass thee also?" She told him her story in part, but part the presence of her son induced her to suppress; for she was ashamed to have been goaded into crime by the furies. Rumour—for she is fleet—flew far on pulsing wings, and thy name, Ino, was on many lips. It is said that as a guest thou didst enter the home of loyal Carmentis and there didst stay thy long hunger. The Tegean priestess is reported to have made cakes in haste with her own hand and to have quickly baked them on the hearth. Even to this day she loves cakes at the festival of the Matralia. Rustic civility was dearer to her than the refinements of art. "Now," said Ino, "reveal to me, O prophetess, my future fate, so far as it is lawful; I pray thee, add this favour to the hospitality I have already received." A brief pause ensued, and then the prophetess assumed her heavenly powers, and all her bosom swelled with majesty divine. Of a sudden you could hardly know her again; so holier, so taller far was she than she had been but now. "Glad tidings I will sing: rejoice, Ino, thy labours are over," said she. "O come propitious to this people evermore! Thou shalt be a divinity of the sea: thy son, too, shall have his home in ocean. Take ye both different names in your own waters. Thou shalt be called Leucothea by the Greeks and Matuta by our people: thy son will have all authority over harbours; he whom we name Portunus will be named Palaemon in his own tongue. Go, I pray ye, be friendly, both of ye, to our country!" Ino bowed assent, she gave her promise. Their troubles ceased: they changed their names: he is a god and she a goddess.

You ask why she forbids female slaves to approach her? She hates

12

ROMAN MATRONS WHO WASH THE STATUE OF VENUS ON APRIL 1

Ovid *Fasti* IV.133–62   1st century B.C.E./C.E.

Duly do ye worship the goddess, ye Latin mothers and brides, and ye, too, who wear not the fillets and long robe. Take off the golden necklaces from the marble neck of the goddess; take off her gauds; the goddess must be washed from top to toe. Then dry her neck and restore to it her golden necklaces; now give her other flowers, now give her the fresh-blown rose. Ye, too, she herself bids bathe under the green myrtle, and there is a certain reason for her command; learn what it is. Naked, she was drying on the shore her oozy locks, when the satyrs, a wanton crew, espied the goddess. She perceived it, and screened her body by myrtle interposed: that done, she was safe, and she bids you do the same. Learn now why ye give incense to Virile Fortune in the place which reeks of warm water. All women strip when they enter that place, and every blemish on the naked body is plain to see; Virile Fortune undertakes to conceal the blemish and to hide it from the men, and this she does for the consideration of a little incense. Nor grudge to take poppy pounded with snowy milk and liquid honey squeezed from the comb; when Venus was first escorted to her eager spouse, she drank that draught: from that time she was a bride. Propitiate her with supplications; beauty and virtue and good fame are in her keeping. In the time of our forefathers Rome had fallen from a state of chastity, and the ancients consulted the old woman of Cumae. She ordered a temple to be built to Venus, and when that was duly done, Venus took the name of Changer of the Heart (*Verticordia*) from the event. Fairest of goddesses, ever behold the sons of Aeneas with look benign, and guard thine offspring's numerous wives.

13

WOMEN'S RITES OF DIONYSUS
IN GREEK CITIES

Diodorus Siculus IV.3.2–5   1st century B.C.E.

And the Boetians and other Greeks and the Thracians, in memory of the campaign in India, have established sacrifices every other year to Dionysus, and believe that at that time the god reveals himself to human beings. Consequently in many Greek cities every other year Bacchic bands of women gather, and it is lawful for the maidens to carry the thyrsus and to join in the frenzied revelry, crying out "Euai!" and honouring the god; while the matrons, forming in groups, offer sacrifices to the god and celebrate his mysteries and, in general, extol with hymns the presence of Dionysus, in this manner acting the part of the Maenads who, as history records, were of old the companions of the god. He also punished here and there throughout all the inhabited world many men who were thought to be impious, the most renowned among the number being Pentheus and Lycurgus. And since the discovery of wine and the gift of it to human beings were the source of such great satisfaction to them, both because of the pleasure which derives from the drinking of it and because of the greater vigour which comes to the bodies of those who partake of it, it is the custom, they say, when unmixed wine is served during a meal to greet it with the words, "To the Good Deity!" but when the cup is passed around after the meal diluted with water, to cry out "To Zeus Saviour!" For the drinking of unmixed wine results in a state of madness, but when it is mixed with the rain from Zeus the delight and pleasure continue, but the ill effect of madness and stupor is avoided. And, in general, the myths relate that the gods who receive the greatest approval at the hands of human beings are those who excelled in their benefactions by reason of their discovery of good things, namely, Dionysus and Demeter, the former because he was the discoverer of the most pleasing drink, the latter because she gave to the race of men the most excellent of the dry foods.

14

WOMEN MEMBERS OF A MONASTIC
JEWISH COMMUNITY OUTSIDE
ALEXANDRIA

Philo *On the Contemplative Life*   1st century C.E.

12. The vocation of these philosophers is at once clear from their title of Therapeutae [m. pl.] and Therapeutrides [f. pl].

32–33. This common sanctuary in which they meet every seventh day is a double enclosure, one portion set apart for the use of the men, the other for the women. For women too regularly make part of the audience with the same ardour and the same sense of their calling. The wall between the two chambers rises up from the ground to three or four cubits built in the form of a breast work, while the space above up to the roof is left open. This arrangement serves two purposes; the modesty becoming to the female sex is preserved, while the women sitting within ear-shot can easily follow what is said since there is nothing to obstruct the voice of the speaker.

68–69. The feast is shared by women also, most of them aged virgins, who have kept their chastity not under compulsion, like some of the Greek priestesses, but of their own free will in their ardent yearning for wisdom. Eager to have her for their life mate they have spurned the pleasures of the body and desire no mortal offspring but those immortal children which only the soul that is dear to God can bring to the birth unaided because the Father has sown in her spiritual rays enabling her to behold the verities of wisdom.

The order of reclining is so apportioned that the men sit by themselves on the right and the women by themselves on the left.

83–88. After the supper they hold the sacred vigil which is conducted in the following way. They rise up all together and standing in the middle of the refectory form themselves first into two choirs, one of men and one of women, the leader and precentor chosen for each being the most honoured amongst them and also the most musical. Then they sing hymns to God composed of many measures and set to many melodies, sometimes chanting together, sometimes taking up the harmony antiphonally, hands and feet keeping time in accompaniment, and rapt with enthusiasm reproduce sometimes the lyrics of the procession, sometimes of the halt and of the wheeling and counter-wheeling of a choric dance. Then when each choir has separately done its own part in the feast, having drunk as in the Bacchic rites of the strong wine of God's love they mix and both together become a single choir, a copy of the choir set up of old beside the Red Sea in honour of the wonders there wrought. For at the command of God the sea became a source of salvation to one party and of perdition to the other. This wonderful sight and experience, an act transcending word and thought and hope, so filled with ecstasy both men and women that forming a single choir they sang hymns of thanksgiving to God their savior, the men led by the prophet Moses and the women by the prophetess Miriam.

It is on this model above all that the choir of the Therapeutae and Therapeutrides, note in response to note, the treble of the women blending with the bass of the men, create an harmonious concert, music in the truest sense.

JEWISH WOMEN IN ALEXANDRIAN PUBLIC LIFE

Philo *The Special Laws* III.169–75   1st century C.E.

Market-places and council-halls and law-courts and gatherings and meetings where a large number of people are assembled, and open-air life with full scope for discussion and action—all these are suitable to men both in war and peace. The women are best suited to the indoor life which never strays from the house, within which the middle door is taken by the maidens as their boundary, and the outer door by those who have reached full womanhood. Organized communities are of two sorts, the greater which we call cities and the smaller which we call households. Both of these have their governors; the government of the greater is assigned to men under the name of statesmanship, that of the lesser, known as household management, to women. A woman, then, should not be a busybody, meddling with matters outside her household concerns, but should seek a life of seclusion. She should not shew herself off like a vagrant in the streets before the eyes of other men, except when she has to go to the temple, and even then she should take pains to go, not when the market is full, but when most people have gone home, and so like a free-born lady worthy of the name, with everything quiet around her, make her oblations and offer her prayers to avert the evil and gain the good. The audacity of women who when men are exchanging angry words or blows hasten to join in, under the pretext of assisting their husbands in the fray, is reprehensible and shameless in a high degree. And so in wars and campaigns and emergencies which threaten the whole country they are not allowed to take their place according to the judgement of the law, having in view the fitness of things, which it was resolved to keep unshaken always and everywhere and considered to be in itself more valuable than victory or liberty or success of any kind. If indeed a woman learning that her husband is being outraged is overcome by the wifely feeling inspired by her love for him and forced by the stress of the emotion to hasten to his assistance, she must not unsex herself by a boldness beyond what nature permits but limit herself to the ways in which a woman can help. For it would be an awful catastrophe if any woman in her wish to rescue her husband from outrage should outrage herself by befouling her own life with

Observances, Rituals, and Festivals   29

the disgrace and heavy reproaches which boldness carried to an extreme entails. What, is a woman to wrangle in the market-place and utter some or other of the words which decency forbids? Should she not when she hears bad language stop her ears and run away? As it is, some of them go to such a length that, not only do we hear amid a crowd of men a woman's bitter tongue venting abuse and contumelious words, but see her hands also used to assault—hands which were trained to weave and spin and not to inflict blows and injuries like pancratiasts and boxers. And while all else might be tolerable, it is a shocking thing, if a woman is so lost to a sense of modesty, as to catch hold of the genital parts of her opponent. The fact that she does so with the evident intention of helping her husband must not absolve her. To restrain her over-boldness she must pay a penalty which will incapacitate herself, if she wishes to repeat the offence, and frighten the more reckless members of her sex into proper behaviour. And the penalty shall be this—that the hand shall be cut off which has touched what decency forbids it to touch.

16

THE WOMEN'S COURT OF THE
JERUSALEM TEMPLE

Josephus *The Jewish War* V.198–200   1st century C.E.

From this again other flights of five steps led up to the gates. Of these there were eight on the north and south, four on either side, and two on the east—necessarily; since in this quarter a special place of worship was walled off for the women, rendering a second gate requisite; this approach opened opposite to the first. On the other sides there was one gate on the south and one on the north giving access to the women's court; for women were not permitted to enter by the others nor yet to pass by way of their own gate beyond the partition wall. This court was, however, thrown open for worship to all Jewish women alike, whether natives of the country or visitors from abroad. The west end of the building had no gate, the wall there being unbroken. The porticoes between the gates, on the inner side of the wall in front of the treasury chambers, were supported by exceedingly beautiful and lofty columns; these porticoes were single, but, except in point of size, in no way inferior to those in the lower court.

Josephus *Against Apion* II.102–4   1st century C.E.

All who ever saw our temple are aware of the general design of the building, and the inviolable barriers which preserved its sanctity. It had four surrounding courts, each with its special statutory restrictions. The outer court was open to all, foreigners included; women during their impurity were alone refused admission. To the second court all Jews were admitted and, when uncontaminated by any defilement, their wives; to the third male Jews, if clean and purified; to the fourth the priests robed in their priestly vestments. The sanctuary was entered only by the high-priests, clad in the raiment peculiar to themselves.

DEVOTEES OF DIONYSUS PROTECTED BY WOMEN FROM THE TOWN OF AMPHISSA

Plutarch *Bravery of Women* 13   1st/2d century C.E.

When the despots in Phocis had seized Delphi, and the Thebans were waging war against them in what has been called the Sacred War, the women devotees of Dionysus, to whom they give the name of Thyads, in Bacchic frenzy wandering at night unwittingly arrived at Amphissa. As they were tired out, and sober reason had not yet returned to them, they flung themselves down in the market-place, and were lying asleep, some here, some there. The wives of the men of Amphissa, fearing, because their city had become allied with the Phocians, and numerous soldiers of the despots were present there, that the Thyads might be treated with indignity, all ran out into the market-place, and, taking their stand round about in silence, did not go up to them while they were sleeping, but when they arose from their slumber, one devoted herself to one of the strangers and another to another, bestowing attentions on them and offering them food. Finally, the women of Amphissa, after winning the consent of their husbands, accompanied the strangers, who were safely escorted as far as the frontier.

THE DIONYSIAC PROCLIVITIES OF OLYMPIAS, MOTHER OF ALEXANDER THE GREAT

Plutarch *Life of Alexander* II.1–5   1st/2d century C.E.

But concerning these matters there is another story to this effect: all the women of these parts were addicted to the Orphic rites and the orgies of Dionysus from very ancient times (being called Klodones and Mimallones), and imitated in many ways the practices of the Edonian women and the Thracian women about Mount Haemus, from whom, as it would seem, the word "threskeuein" came to be applied to the celebration of extravagant and superstitious ceremonies. Now Olympias, who affected these divine possessions more zealously than other women, and carried out these divine inspirations in wilder fashion, used to provide the revelling companies with great tame serpents, which would often lift their heads from out the ivy and the mystic winnowing-baskets, or coil themselves about the wands and garlands of the women, thus terrifying the men.

19

THE PUBLIC AND SECRET RITES TO DEMETER
PERFORMED BY ELDER WOMEN
IN CORINTH

Pausanias *Description of Greece,* Corinth 35.6–8   2d century C.E.

Those who form the procession are followed by men leading from the herd a full-grown cow, fastened with ropes, and still untamed and frisky. Having driven the cow to the temple, some loose her from the ropes that she may rush into the sanctuary, others, who hitherto have been holding the doors open, when they see the cow within the temple, close to the doors. Four old women, left behind inside, are they who dispatch the cow. Whichever gets the chance cuts the throat of the cow with a sickle. Afterwards the doors are opened, and those who are appointed drive up a second cow, and a third after that, and yet a fourth. All are dispatched in the same way by the old women, and the sacrifice has yet another strange feature. On whichever of her sides the first cow falls, all the others must fall on the same. Such is the manner in which the sacrifice is performed by the Hermionians. Before the temple stand a few statues of the women who have served Demeter as her priestess, and on passing inside you see seats on which the old women wait for the cows to be driven in one by one, and images, of no great age, of Athena and Demeter. But the thing itself that they worship more than all else, I never saw, nor yet has any other man, whether stranger or Hermionian. The old women may keep their knowledge of its nature to themselves.

20

THE ATHLETIC CONTESTS FOR WOMEN
IN HONOR OF HERA
AT ELIS

Pausanias *Description of Greece*, Elis I.16.2–8   2d century C.E.

Every fourth year there is woven for Hera a robe by the Sixteen women, and the same also hold games called Heraea. The games consist of foot-races for maidens. These are not all of the same age. The first to run are the youngest; after them come the next in age, and the last to run are the oldest of the maidens. They run in the following way: their hair hangs down, a tunic reaches to a little above the knee, and they bare the right shoulder as far as the breast. These too have the Olympic stadium reserved for their games, but the course of the stadium is shortened for them by about one-sixth of its length. To the winning maidens they give crowns of olive and a portion of the cow sacrificed to Hera. They may also dedicate statues with their names inscribed upon them. Those who administer to the Sixteen are, like the presidents of the games, married women. The games of the maidens too are traced back to ancient times; they say that, out of gratitude to Hera for her marriage with Pelops, Hippodameia assembled the Sixteen Women, and with them inaugurated the Heraea. They relate too that a victory was won by Chloris, the only surviving daughter of the house of Amphion, though with her they say survived one of her brothers. As to the children of Niobe, what I myself chanced to learn about them I have set forth in my account of Argos. Besides the account already given they tell another story about the Sixteen Women as follows. Damophon, it is said, when tyrant of Pisa did much grievous harm to the Eleans. But when he died, since the people of Pisa refused to participate as a people in their tyrant's sins, and the Eleans too became quite ready to lay aside their grievances, they chose a woman from each of the sixteen cities of Elis still inhabited at that time to settle their differences, this woman to be the oldest, the most noble, and the most esteemed of all the women. The cities from which they chose the women were Elis, . . . The women from these cities made peace between Pisa and Elis. Later on they were entrusted with the management of the Heraean games, and with the weaving of the robe for Hera. The Sixteen Women also arrange two choral dances, one called that of Physcoa and the other that of

Hippodameia. This Physcoa they say came from Elis in the Hollow, and the name of the parish where she lived was Orthia. She mated they say with Dionysus, and bore him a son called Narcaeus. When he grew up he made war against the neighbouring folk, and rose to great power, setting up moreover a sanctuary of Athena surnamed Narcaea. They say too that Narcaeus and Physcoa were the first to pay worship to Dionysus. So various honours are paid to Physcoa, especially that of the choral dance, named after her and managed by the Sixteen Women. The Eleans still adhere to the other ancient customs, even though some of the cities have been destroyed. For they are now divided into eight tribes, and they choose two women from each. Whatever ritual it is the duty of either the Sixteen Women or the Elean umpires to perform, they do not perform before they have purified themselves with a pig meet for purification and with water. Their purification takes place at the spring Piera. You reach this spring as you go along the flat road from Olympia to Elis.

21

WOMEN'S WORSHIP OF EILEITHYIA
AND SOSIPOLIS AT ELIS

Pausanias *Description of Greece,* Elis I.20.2–3   2d century C.E.

At the foot of Mount Cronius, on the north . . . , between the treasuries and the mountain, is a sanctuary of Eileithyia, and in it Sosipolis, a native Elean deity, is worshipped. Now they surname Eileithyia Olympian, and choose a priestess for the goddess every year. The old woman who tends Sosipolis herself too by an Elean custom lives in chastity, bringing water for the god's bath and setting before him barley cakes kneaded with honey. In the front part of the temple, for it is built in two parts, is an altar of Eileithyia and an entrance for the public; in the inner part Sosipolis is worshipped, and no one may enter it except the woman who tends the god, and she must wrap her head and face in a white veil. Maidens and matrons wait in the sanctuary of Eileithyia chanting a hymn; they burn all manner of incense to the god, but it is not the custom to pour libations of wine.

22

WOMEN'S RITES TO DEMETER
AT ACHAIA

Pausanias *Description of Greece,* Achaia 27.9–10   2d century C.E.

About sixty stades distant from Pellene is the Mysaeum, a sanctuary of the Mysian Demeter. It is said that it was founded by Mysius, a man of Argos, who according to Argive tradition gave Demeter a welcome in his home. There is a grove in the Mysaeum, containing trees of every kind, and in it rises a copious supply of water from springs. Here they also celebrate a seven days' festival in honour of Demeter. On the third day of the festival the men withdraw from the sanctuary, and the women are left to perform on that night the ritual that custom demands. Not only men are excluded, but even male dogs. On the following day the men come to the sanctuary, and the men and the women laugh and jeer at one another in turn.

23

THE FESTIVAL LAPHRIA,
IN HONOR OF ARTEMIS

Pausanias *Description of Greece*, Achaia 18.11–12   2d century C.E.

Every year too the people of Patrae celebrate the festival Laphria in honour of their Artemis, and at it they employ a method of sacrifice peculiar to the place. Round the altar in a circle they set up logs of wood still green, each of them sixteen cubits long. On the altar within the circle is placed the driest of their wood. Just before the time of the festival they construct a smooth ascent to the altar, piling earth upon the altar steps. The festival begins with a most splendid procession in honour of Artemis, and the maiden officiating as priestess rides last in the procession upon a car yoked to deer. It is, however, not till the next day that the sacrifice is offered, and the festival is not only a state function but also quite a popular general holiday. For the people throw alive upon the altar edible birds and every kind of victim as well; there are wild boars, deer and gazelles; some bring wolf-cubs or bear-cubs, others the full-grown beasts. They also place upon the altar fruit.

24

WOMEN ATTACKED DURING A FESTIVAL TO
DEMETER WHO DEFEND THEMSELVES WITH
SACRIFICIAL IMPLEMENTS

Pausanias *Description of Greece*, Messenia 17   2d century C.E.

There is a place Aegila in Laconia, where is a sanctuary sacred to Demeter. Aristomenes and his men knowing that the women were keeping festival there . . . the women were inspired by the goddess to defend themselves, and most of the Messenians were wounded with the knives with which the women sacrificed the victims and the spits on which they pierced and roasted the meat. Aristomenes was struck with the torches and taken alive. Nevertheless he escaped to Messenia during the same night. Archidameia, the priestess of Demeter, was charged with having released him, not for a bribe but because she had been in love with him before; but she maintained that Aristomenes had escaped by burning through his bonds.

25

THE RELIGIOUS ACTIVITIES OF ROMAN WOMEN, AS VIEWED BY A SKEPTICAL SATIRIST

Juvenal *Satire* VI   1st/2d century C.E.

314–41.

The secret rites of the Good Goddess
  are pretty well known,
When a flute stirs their loins and
  the Maenads of Priapus groan
And howl in frenzy from music and
  wine and toss their hair.
Oh, how they burn for intercourse,
  what cries declare
Their throbbing lust, how wet their
  legs with streaming juices!
Saufeia challenges the pimps'
  slave girls and produces
Such bouncing hips she wins the prize,
  but in turn must yield;
Medullina's copious flow is sure to
  carry the field.
The women share honors: technique's
  as good as breeding at this.
They're not pretending, as in a game,
  and each caress
Is genuine, such as would heat a
  Priam's cold blood and fire
A Nestor's testicles. Then impatient
  with chafing desire,
They're females without veneer, and
  around the ritual den
Rings a cry from every corner: "We're
  ready! Bring in the men!"
And if the stud is sleeping, the
  young man's ordered to wrap
Himself in a robe and hurry over.
  If he's not on tap,
A raid is made on the slaves; remove
  the hope of a slave,

They'll hire a water carrier. If
   they can't find a man, to save
The day they'll get a donkey to
   straddle their itchy behinds.
Oh, would that our ancient rites,
   at least in public shrines,
Were purged of these filthy acts!
   But every Hindu and Moor
Knows who that lady lute player was
   who, so cocksure,
Took a penis bigger than both the
   scrolls that Caesar wrote
Against Cato into a place that boy mice,
   taking note
Of their own testicles, flee; where
   every picture of males,
That opposite sex, is ordered covered
   well with veils.

511–47.

The priests of mad Bellona and Cybele
   come, led through
By a huge half-man, a form that his
   obscene minor crew
Must revere, who cut off his tender
   genitals long ago
With a broken shell. To him the
   noisy crowds bow low,
To him the drummers yield; a Phrygian
   turban adorns
His plebeian features. The lady in
   solemn tones he warns
Of September hurricanes coming, unless
   she will purify
Herself with a gift of a hundred eggs,
   and add a supply
Of old dark-red clothes, so that into
   them any sudden, severe
Forthcoming danger may pass and at
   once expiate the whole year.

On a winter morning she'll go to the
   river, break the ice,
Plunge into the Tiber, and dip her
   timorous head in it thrice,
In the eddies themselves; then, naked
   and shivering, crawl right
Across the whole Field of Mars on
   bleeding knees. If the white
Io commands it, she'll go to the ends
   of Egypt and fetch
From the Nile at tropic Meroë the
   sought-for water with which
To sprinkle Isis' temple that stands
   near the old sheepfolds.
For she thinks the voice of the goddess
   herself gave the word: what a soul,
What a mind, for the gods to be
   conversing with in the night!
Therefore the chief and highest honor
   is given by right
To Anubis who, surrounded by a
   linen-clad troop
And priests with shaven heads, runs
   along deriding the group
Of people bewailing Osiris. It's he
   who for pardon prays
Each time a wife won't abstain from
   copulation on days
That must be observed as holy, and
   huge penalties he takes
Whenever her sheets have been defiled,
   and the silver snake
Has been seen to nod its head. His
   tears and studied singsong
Make sure that Osiris won't deny pardon
   for the wrong,
Bribed, of course, by a thin holy
   cake and a big fat goose.
When he has taken his leave, a
   trembling Jewess, whose

Reed basket and hay are left behind,
   is begging her,
Whispering in her ear—this one's
   an interpreter
Of the laws of Jerusalem, high
   priestess with a tree
As temple, a trusty go-between of
   high heaven. And she
Fills her palm, but much less full, for
   at bargain prices a Jew
Sells you the answer to any dream
   you'd like to come true.

26

ADMONITIONS AGAINST THE PARTICIPATION OF MENSTRUATING CHRISTIAN WOMEN IN THE EUCHARIST AND AGAINST THE PARTICIPATION BY MEN WHO HAVE HAD A NOCTURNAL EMISSION

Dionysius of Alexandria *Epistle to the Bishop Basilides*   3d century C.E.

Canon II

The question touching women in the time of their separation, whether it is proper for them when in such a condition to enter the house of God, I consider a superfluous inquiry. For I do not think that, if they are believing and pious women, they will themselves be rash enough in such a condition either to approach the holy table or to touch the body and blood of the Lord. Certainly the woman who had the issue of blood of twelve years' standing did not touch (the Lord) Himself, but only the hem of His garment, with a view to her cure. For to pray, however a person may be situated, and to remember the Lord, in whatever condition a person may be, and to offer up petitions for the obtaining of help, are exercises altogether blameless. But the individual who is not perfectly pure both in soul and in body, shall be interdicted from approaching the holy of holies.

Canon IV

As to those who are overtaken by an involuntary flux in the night-time, let such follow the testimony of their own conscience, and consider themselves as to whether they are doubtfully minded in this matter or not. And he that doubteth in the matter of meats, the apostle tells us, "is damned if he eat." In these things, therefore, let every one who approaches God be of a good conscience, and of a proper confidence, so far as his own judgment is concerned. And, indeed, it is in order to show your regard for us (for you are not ignorant, beloved) that you have proposed these questions to us, making us of one mind, as indeed we are, and of one spirit with yourself. And I, for my part, have thus set forth my opinions in public, not as a teacher, but only as it becomes us with all simplicity to confer with each other. And when you have examined this opinion of mine, my most intelligent son, you will write back to me your notion of these matters, and let me know whatever may seem to you to be just and preferable, and whether you approve of my judgment in these things. That it may fare well with you, my beloved son, as you minister to the Lord in peace, is my prayer.

27

RABBINIC PURITY REGULATIONS CONCERNING MENSTRUATION AND OTHER BLOOD FLOW

Mishnah *Niddah*   3d century C.E.

1:1

A.   Shammai says, "[For] all women [it is] sufficient for them [to reckon uncleanness from] their time [of discovering a flow]."

B.   Hillel says, "[They are deemed unclean retroactively] from the [time of examination, at which the flow of blood was discovered] to the [last] examination [she made beforehand].

C.   "And even for many days."

D.   And sages say not in accord with the opinion of this one nor in accord with the opinion of that one, but:

E.   [the woman is held to have been unclean only] during [the preceding] twenty-four hours [when] this lessens the period from the examination to the [last] examination,

F.   [and she is held to have been unclean only] during the period from examination to examination [when] this lessens the period of twenty-four hours.

G.   Every woman who has a fixed period—sufficient for her is her time.

H.   She who makes use of test-rags, lo, this is equivalent to an examination,

I.   which lessens either the period of the twenty-four hours or the period from examination to examination.

1:2

A.   How [is the case in which] her time suffices for her?

B.   [If] she was sitting on the bed and engaged in things requiring cleanness and arose and saw [a drop of blood],

C.   she is unclean,

D.   but all of those [things requiring cleanness] are clean.

E.   Even though they have said, "She renders unclean [whatever she touched during the preceding] twenty-four hour period," she takes count [of the days prescribed in the Torah] only from the time that she saw a drop of blood.

1:3

A. R. Eliezer says, "Four women [fall into the category of those for whom the] time [of first seeing blood] suffices:

B. "(1) the virgin, (2) the pregnant woman, (3) the nursing mother, and (4) the old lady."

C. Said R. Joshua, "I heard only [that this rule applies to] the virgin."

D. But the law is in accord with the opinion of R. Eliezer.

1:4

E. Who is (1) the virgin?

F. Any girl who never in her life saw a drop of blood, even though she is married.

G. (2) A pregnant woman?

H. Once it is known that the foetus is present.

I. (3) A nursing mother?

J. Until she will wean her son.

K. [If] she gave her son to a wet-nurse, weaned him, or he died—

L. R. Meir says, "She conveys uncleanness [to everything she touched] during the preceding twenty-four hours."

M. And sages say, "Sufficient for her is her time."

1:5

N. (4) Who is an old woman?

O. Any woman for whom three periods have gone by without a flow near to the time of her old age.

P. R. Eliezer says, "Any woman for whom three periods have passed without her suffering a flow—sufficient for her is her time."

Q. R. Yosé says, "A pregnant woman and a nursing mother for whom three periods have passed—sufficient for them is their time."

1:6

A. And of what case did they speak when they said, "Sufficient for her is her time"?

B. In the case of the first appearance of a drop of blood.

C. But in the case of the second appearance of such a drop of blood, she conveys uncleanness to whatever she touched during the preceding twenty-four hours.

D. But if she saw the first flow by reason of constraint [through abnormal causes], even in the case of the second drop of blood, sufficient for her is her time.

1:7

A.   Even though they have said, "Sufficient for her is her time," (1) she must nonetheless examine herself,

B.   except for (a) the menstruating woman,

C.   and (b) the woman who is sitting in the blood of her purifying [after having given birth].

D.   And (2) she makes use of test rags,

E.   except for (a) the one who is sitting in the blood of her purifying,

F.   and (b) a virgin, whose drops of blood are clean.

G.   And (3) twice must she [who has a fixed period] examine herself:

H.   (a) in the morning and (b) at twilight,

I.   and (c) when she prepares for sexual relations.

J.   Beyond these examinations, women of the priestly caste [must examine themselves] when they eat heave-offering.

K.   R. Judah says, "Also: when they finish eating heave-offering."

2:1

A.   Any hand which makes many examinations—in the case of women is to be praised and in the case of men is to be cut off.

B.   The deaf-mute, and the imbecile, and the blind, and the unconscious woman—

C.   if there are women of sound sense, they care for them, and they eat heave-offering.

D.   It is the way of Israelite women to make use of two test-rags, one for him and one for her.

E.   The pious prepare yet a third, to take care of the house.

2:2

A.   If it [a drop of blood] is found on his, they are unclean and liable for a sacrifice.

B.   If it is found on hers at the time itself, they are unclean [for seven days] and liable for a sacrifice.

C.   If it is found on hers after a while, their uncleanness remains in doubt, and they are exempt from an offering.

D. What is meant by "after a while"?

E. Sufficient time that the woman may descend from the bed and wash her face [sexual organs].

F. And afterward [if a drop of blood appears], she imparts uncleanness [to objects she touched] during the preceding twenty-four-hour period but does not impart uncleanness [as a menstruant for seven days] to him who has had sexual relations with her.

G. R. 'Aqiva says, "Also: she imparts uncleanness to him who has sexual relations with her."

H. And sages agree with R. 'Aqiva in the case of one who sees a bloodstain, that she imparts uncleanness to him who has sexual relations with her.

2:4

A. All women are assumed to be clean for their husbands.

B. Those that come home from a trip—their wives are assumed to be clean for them.

C. The House of Shammai say, "She requires two test-rags for each act of sexual relations.

D. "Or she should have intercourse in the light of a lamp."

E. And the House of Hillel say, "It suffices for her [to make use of] two test-rags for the entire night."

28

RABBINIC ARGUMENTS AGAINST A
MISOGYNIST TRADITION

Babylonian Talmud *Sotah* 22b   5th century C.E.

MISHNAH:

A. She hardly sufficed to drink it before her face turns yellow, her eyes bulge out, and her veins swell.

B. And they say, "Take her away! Take her away!"

C. so that the Temple-court will not be made unclean [by her corpse].

D. [But if nothing happened], if she had merit, she would attribute [her good fortune] to it.

E. There is the possibility that merit suspends the curse for one year, and there is the possibility that merit suspends the curse for two years, and there is the possibility that merit suspends the curse for three years.

F. On this basis Ben Azzai says, "A man is required to teach Torah to his daughter.

G. "For if she should drink the water, she should know that [if nothing happens to her], merit is what suspends [the curse from taking effect]."

H. R. Eliezer says, "Whoever teaches Torah to his daughter teaches her sexual satisfaction."

I. R. Joshua says, "A woman wants a qab [of food] with sexual satisfaction more than nine qabs with abstinence."

J. He would say, "A foolish saint, a smart knave, an abstemious woman,

K. "and the blows of abstainers (perushim)—

L. "lo, these wear out the world."

GEMARA:

A. An abstemious woman [M. 3:4J]:

B. Our rabbis have taught on Tannaite authority:

C. A virgin who prays a great deal, a widow who runs hither and yon, and a minor whose months are not complete—lo, these destroy the world.

D. Is that so? And has not R. Yohanan stated, "We learn fear of heaven from a virgin, [certainty of] receiving a reward from a widow.

E. "Fear of sin from a virgin:" For R. Yohanan heard a virgin fall on her face [in prayer] and say, "Lord of the world, you have created the Garden of Eden and you have created Gehenna, you have created righteous men and you have created wicked men. May it be pleasing to you that no men should stumble through me."

F. "[Certainty of] receiving a reward from a widow:" A widow has a synagogue in her neighborhood, but she used every day to come and pray in the study house of R. Yohanan. He said to her, "My daughter, isn't there a synagogue in your neighborhood?"

G. She said to him, "My lord, is there no reward accruing for the steps that I take [in walking a great distance to pray with you]?"

H. When it is stated [that the virgin and the widow destroy the world], it is, for example, such as Yohani, daughter of Retibi [a widow who by witchcraft made childbirth difficult for a woman and then offered prayer for her].

29

ARABIAN CHRISTIAN WOMEN OF THRACIAN DESCENT WHO BAKE CAKES TO THE VIRGIN MARY AND FUNCTION AS PRIESTS

Epiphanius *Medicine Box* 78.23   4th century C.E.

For it is related that some women in Arabia, who come from the region of Thrace, put forward this silly idea: they prepare a kind of cake in the name of the ever-Virgin, assemble together, and in the name of the holy Virgin they attempt to undertake a deed that is irreverent and blasphemous beyond measure—in her name they function as priests for women. Now all this is godless and irreverent, a degeneration from the proclamation of the Holy Spirit, all of it a diabolic device and the teaching of an unclean spirit. In their regard the saying is fulfilled: "Some will separate themselves from the sound teaching, clinging to myths and demonic teachings" [1 Tim. 4:1]. They will be worshipers of the dead, even as they (the dead) were worshiped in Israel. But the glory given to God by the Saints each in his proper time has become as good as error to those who do not see the truth.

30

A HERESIOLOGIST'S ATTEMPTS TO REFUTE THE TEACHINGS OF CHRISTIAN WOMEN WITH REGARD TO MARY AND TO DISPARAGE THE RITUALS AND RELIGIOUS OFFICES OF WOMEN

Epiphanius *Medicine Box* 79   4th century C.E.

1. Next a heresy has appeared, about which I made mention just above, because of the letter written to Arabia, namely, the one about Mary. This heresy was once more taken up in Arabia from Thrace and the upper parts of Scythia, and has come to our attention. It is quite a ridiculous joke to those who know better. Let us begin to search out and describe what is connected with it. For it will be thought of as silly rather than intelligent, just like others similar to it. For just as those mentioned above, because of an insulting attitude regarding Mary, sow harmful fantasies in human minds by many conjectures, so too these who incline to the opposite extreme are seized by such consummate foolhardiness. Thus what is sung about by some outside (i.e., pagan) philosophers is fulfilled in them, namely, opposite extremes are the same. The harm is equal in both these heresies, of those who disparage the holy Virgin, and again of those who glorify her beyond what is necessary. Are not those who teach this merely women? The female sex is easily mistaken, fallible, and poor in intelligence. It is apparent that through women the devil has vomited this forth. As previously the teaching associated with Quintilla, Maximilla, and Priscilla was utterly ridiculous, so also is this one. For some women prepare a certain kind of little cake with four indentations, cover it with a fine linen veil on a solemn day of the year, and on certain days they set forth bread and offer it in the name of Mary. They all partake of the bread; this is part of what we refuted in the letter written to Arabia. But now we shall clearly set forth everything about it and the refutations against it, and beseeching God, we will give an explanation to the best of our ability, so that by cutting off the roots of this idol-making heresy we may be able, in God, to destroy such madness.

2. Come now, servants of God, let us put on a manly mind and disperse the mania of these women. The whole of this deception is female; the disease comes from Eve who was long ago deceived.

Observances, Rituals, and Festivals   51

Rather it is from the serpent, that seductive beast who spoke to her in the deceptive promise, bringing nothing out into the open and not accomplishing what was promised, but rather bringing about only death by calling real what was unreal, and through the appearance of the tree causing disobedience and turning away from the truth to many diversions. Consider what kind of seed the deceiver sowed by saying, "You will be like gods." Even so the lightheadedness of these women fits well the nature of this beast, by which nature death was produced a long time ago, as I have often said. By looking quickly through the ages until now to whom is it not obvious that this teaching and the form it takes is of the devil and that the undertaking is perverted? Never in any way did a woman function as priest to God, not even Eve herself who had indeed fallen into transgression. But she did not dare to perform such an irreverent thing, nor did one of her daughters, even though Abel was a priest to God, and Cain offered sacrifices before the Lord though they were not acceptable, and Enoch was found pleasing and was taken away, and Noah presented offerings of thanksgiving to the Lord from the surplus of the ark, thus giving a sure sign of a willing disposition and giving thanks to his savior. Abraham the just one performed priestly service to God, and Melchisedech was the priest of the most high God; Isaac was found pleasing to God, and Jacob offered what he could upon the rock, by pouring oil upon the stone of his sons; Levi received the priesthood next in succession; from his descendants are those who received the priestly order, such as Moses, the prophet and revealer of sacred things; Aaron and his sons, Eleazer and Phineas; and Ithamar, his offspring. But why must I tell of the multitude of the priests of God in the Old Covenant? Achitob was a priest; the Korites, the Gersonites, the Memaritai were entrusted with the levitical order, the house of Eli, those after him who were his relatives in the house of Abimelech, Abiathar, Chelkias, and Bouzei, all the way up to Jesus the great priest, Esdras the priest, and the others. And never did a woman exercise priesthood.

3. I go now to the New Testament. If women were assigned to be priests to God or to do anything official in the church, it would certainly have been fitting for Mary herself to exercise priesthood in the New Testament, she who was considered worthy to take to her breasts the heavenly King of all, Son of God, she whose womb became a temple and was prepared as a dwelling place for the incarnate activity of the Lord according to God's love for humanity and the amazing mystery. But it did not please him to do so, nor was she entrusted with the administering of baptism, since Christ could have been baptized by her instead of by John. But John son of Zachary was commissioned to perform a baptism of repentance of sins in the desert, and his father was a priest of God who had a vision at the hour when he offered incense. Peter and Andrew, James and John, Philip and Bartholomew, Thomas, Thaddeus, James the son of Alpheus, Judas son of James, Simon the Canaanite, and Matthias, who was chosen to complete the Twelve—all these were chosen as apostles, who perform the priesthood of the gospel throughout the earth together with Paul and Barnabas and others, as leaders of the mysteries with James the brother of the Lord and first bishop of Jerusalem. From this bishop and the above-mentioned apostles a succession of bishops and presbyters was established in the house of God. There was no woman established among them. There were four daughters of Philip the evangelist who prophesied, but they were not priests. There was Anna the prophetess, daughter of Phanuel, but she was not entrusted with priesthood. It was fitting that the prophecy be fulfilled, that "your sons shall prophesy and your daughters shall dream dreams, and your young men shall see visions." Now there is an order of deaconesses in the church, but not to perform priestly functions nor to be allowed any official work but because of the modesty of the female sex, whether at the time of washing (i.e., baptism), medical examination, or labor, and whenever a woman's body must be undressed. Thus the body need be seen not by a male officiant but by a deaconess who is directed as needed by the priest to care for a woman in need when her body is undressed; in this way the good order and ecclesiastical harmony have been well and sensibly safeguarded according to good measure. Thus neither does the divine word allow a woman to speak in church, nor to have authority over men. There is much to say about this.

4. It is to be observed that only the ecclesiastical rank of deaconesses was required, though he (Paul) named widows, yet as the most elderly and revered, not as presbyteresses or priestesses. Neither are deacons in the ecclesiastical order entrusted with performing any of the sacraments, but only with assisting at services. Whence comes this new myth to us? Whence this female conceit and womanish madness? Whence this evil nourished again by the female element pouring out upon us who know better the effeminacy of deceit, working its own way of luxury, setting upon wretched human nature to drive it out of itself? But let us take on the solid thinking of Job, the skilled fighter, let us arm ourselves by putting the right answer upon our lips, let them say, "You have spoken like one of the silly women." Why will such a thing not appear totally stupid to anyone who has some sense and who has laid hold of God? How is this business not the making of idols and a diabolic undertaking? Under the guise of righteousness the devil always sneaks into the human mind, divinizes mortal nature in human estimation, and skillfully delineates idols after human fashion. Those who worship them have died, but they bring in their idols to be worshiped—though they were never alive (nor can they die which were never alive)—by minds that are adulterous toward the one and only God, like the promiscuous prostitute who is aroused to indiscriminate intercourse while casting off the sobriety of being ruled by a single man.

Now certainly the body of Mary was holy, but she was not God. Indeed she was a virgin and is reverenced as such, but is not given to us to be worshiped; rather she worships him who was born of her flesh, he who came from heaven from the paternal bosom. Because of this we are safeguarded by the gospel saying spoken by the Lord himself, namely, "What is it to me and to you, woman? My hour has not yet come." Or the saying, "Woman, what is it to me and to you?" Lest some think that the holy Virgin is something special, he called her woman, as if prophesying that there would in the future be schisms on earth and heresies, lest any be too much in awe of the holy Virgin and therefore fall prey to this ridiculous heresy.

5. The whole narrative of this heresy is, as I have said, utter nonsense, an old wives' tale. What part of Scripture speaks of it? Which of the prophets allowed a human being to be worshiped, to say nothing of a woman? The vessel is select (even though a woman), in no way corrupted in nature, and is to be held in respect regarding judgment and feeling just like the bodies of the saints—and if I might say anything in excessive praise, like Elias who was a virgin from the womb, who remained so permanently, was taken up, and did not see death; like John who reclined on the breast of the Lord and whom Jesus loved; like holy Thecla; and Mary is to be more honored than the last-named because of the divine plan of which she was found worthy. But neither is Elias to be worshiped, even though he is among the living; nor is John to be worshiped although through his own prayers he achieved a wondrous passing, or rather obtained it as a gift of God. Neither Thecla nor any of the saints is worshiped. The

ancient error will not rule over us, that error of abandoning the Living One and adoring what was made by him. "For they adored and reverenced the creature above the creator," and acted like fools. If he does not wish angels to be worshiped, how much more her who was born of Anna, bestowed on Anna through Joachim, given to her father and mother according to a promise because of their prayer and full devotion, not born any differently from the usual human way but like everyone else from the seed of a man and the womb of a woman? If the account of and traditions about Mary have it that it was said to her father Joachim in the desert, "Your wife has conceived," it did not happen without sexual union, nor without male seed, but the angel was sent to foretell what was to come, lest anyone doubt that she was truly born to that just man and already appointed by God.

6. Let us look at what the Scriptures have to say. Isaiah foretold what was to be fulfilled in the Son of God, saying, "Behold the virgin will conceive and bear a son and they will name him Emmanuel." Now she who conceived was a virgin and he whose name means "God with us" was conceived in a woman. Lest the true event be in doubt in the mind of the prophet, he sees (it) in a vision under the impulse of the Holy Spirit and speaks thus: "And he went in to the prophetess," speaking of the gospel account of the entrance of Gabriel, who was sent from God to tell of the arrival of the only begotten Son of God into the world and his birth from Mary. "And she conceived," he says, "and bore a son. And the Lord said to me, call him 'Take the spoils quickly, despoliate brutally.' Before the child knows how to call father or mother, he will receive the power of Damascus, the spoils of Samaria," etc. All this was not yet completed. It was to happen in the Son of God and be fulfilled after about sixteen hundred years. The prophet saw what was to come many generations after that as already happening. Was it then false? Far from it. But what is arranged by God is trustworthy. It is proclaimed, as if already completed, so that the truth might not be disbelieved, so that the amazing and wondrous mystery to come might not fall in doubt in the mind of the prophet. Do you not see how what was proclaimed does indeed follow, as the holy Isaiah himself says, "He was led as a sheep to the slaughter, like a lamb speechless before his shearer, so did he not open his mouth; who will tell of his generation? For his life is taken up from the earth," and, "I will give (him) evil men for his grave," and the rest? See how the first things are recounted later, and the later things he interprets as having happened, saying, "He was led as a sheep to the slaughter." It is said as if completed. He did not say, "He *is* led," though the one mentioned by Isaiah had not yet been led. It was said by the prophet as if the event had already been accomplished. The mysterious way of God is unchangeable. As he went on, he no longer spoke as if what he said had already happened, lest he give rise to error. "But," he says, "his life is taken up from the earth." From the two prophecies together he shows the truth because "he was led" is already accomplished and "he is taken up" is still to be fulfilled, so that from what has happened you might know the truthfulness and reliability of God's promise, while from what is still to come you will be able to recognize the mysteries as they are revealed.

7. Thus the angel foretold about Mary what her father was to receive from God when he entered into his own house: that which had been requested through the prayers and supplications of father and mother, namely, "Behold, your wife has conceived," so that the mind of the faithful man might be strongly confirmed in the promise. But this seemed foolish to some. Such a birth was considered impossible on earth according to human nature. It was fitting for him alone; nature yielded for him alone. Thus as sculptor and director of the enterprise he fashioned himself from a virgin as from the earth, God who came from heaven, the Word who clothed himself with flesh from the holy Virgin. But this did not happen so that women should be appointed priests after so many generations. God did not wish that in the case of Salome, nor even for Mary herself. He did not permit her to baptize or bless disciples. He did not assign her authority over the earth, but only to be holy, and to be worthy of his kingdom. Neither to the woman called the mother of Rufus, nor to those who followed him from Galilee, nor to Martha the sister of Lazarus and Mary, nor to any of the holy women found worthy to be saved by his coming, who ministered to him out of their own goods, nor to the Canaanite woman, nor to the woman with the hemorrhage even though she was saved, not to any woman on earth did he give the privilege of doing this.

Whence are the twisted designs renewed? Let Mary be held in reverence, but let the Father, Son, and Holy Spirit be worshiped—let no one worship Mary. I say that not to a woman, nor to a man, but to God is the holy mystery directed; not even angels can receive this kind of glorification. May what was written deceitfully in the heart of the deceived be blotted out; let the lust of the tree be dimmed in our eyes; let the creature turn back again to the master; let Eve along with

Adam reverence God alone; may she not be led by the voice of the serpent but may she remain obedient to the command of God: "Do not eat of the tree." The tree itself was not error, but through the tree came erroneous disobedience. Let no one eat of the error related to holy Mary. Even if the tree was blossoming, it was not meant for food, and even if Mary is beautiful and holy and to be honored, she is not to be worshiped.

8. These women revive the old mixed cup of Fortuna and prepare their table for the devil, not for God, as it is written, "The food of ungodliness was eaten," as the divine word says, and, "The women threshed flour and the children collected firewood to make cakes to the heavenly army." Such women were silenced by Jeremiah so that they might not disturb the world—lest they say, "Let us honor the queen of heaven." Taphnas knew that these would be punished; the regions of the Magdulians knew that they would receive the bodies of these women to have them rot there. Do not listen to a woman, O Israel. Raise your head above the evil designs of a woman, for a woman hunts for the noble souls of men. But her feet lead to hell those who consort with death. Do not associate with a common woman. "Honey drips from the lips of a promiscuous woman, which for a short time is smooth in your throat but later you will find it more bitter than bile and sharper than a two-edged sword." Do not believe such a vulgar woman. For every heresy is a vulgar woman, but this female heresy is more—it is that of the one who deceived the first woman. Our mother Eve is to be honored as having been formed by God, but let her not be heeded, lest she persuade her children to eat from the tree and transgress the commandment. Let her repent from useless talk, let her turn back in shame covered with a fig leaf. Let Adam observe her well and no longer obey her. For the persuasion of error and the contrary counsel of a woman bring death to her own husband—not only to him but also to her children. Eve subverted creation through her transgression when she was aroused by the speech and promise of the serpent, and she pulled away from God's teaching and wandered into a strange way of thinking.

9. That is why the Master and Savior of all, wanting to heal the suffering, rebuild what had been razed, and rectify what had been altered, since death had come into the world through a woman, was himself born of a virginal woman so that he might lock up death, restore what was lacking, and perfect what had been altered. Evil returns again to us, so that what is inferior might enter the world. But neither young nor old men listen to the woman because of the good sense given from above. The Egyptian woman did not succeed in her game with the sensible Joseph nor corrupt him even though she pursued her wicked intentions toward the young man through many machinations. Neither can the man who receives his counsel from the Holy Spirit be manipulated, nor does he hide his discretion, so that he might not disgrace his nobility. He abandons his garments and does not destroy the body. He flees the place so as not to fall into the snare. He is afflicted for a time but reigns forever. He is thrown into prison, but it is preferable to remain in prison or in "the corner of a roof" than with a contentious and loquacious woman. Now what is all this saying? Either these idle women offer the cake to Mary as if worshiping her or they undertake to offer on her behalf the above-mentioned rotten fruit. The whole thing is silly and strange, from diabolic activity, all arrogance and deceit.

So as not to prolong these remarks, let what has been said suffice for us. Let Mary be honored and the Lord worshiped. The just ones contrive error for no one. God has no experience of evil and does not tempt anyone to error, nor do the servants of God. Everyone is tempted by being drawn away and baited by his own lusts. Then "lust brings forth sin and sin acted upon gives birth to death."

We have considered all this sufficiently, beloved, so let us proceed, as I have said, crushing with the word of truth the beetle that is golden to the sight but really feathered and winged, having a poisonous sting within itself; let us proceed against this one that still remains, beseeching God to stand by us as we search out the way of truth and to be a perfect defender against the opposition.

31

CHRISTIAN WOMEN IN ANTIOCH PARTAKING
OF JEWISH FESTIVALS AND
ATTENDING SYNAGOGUE

John Chrysostom *Against Judaizing Christians*   4th century C.E.

II.3. If God, then, showed us such honor, will we not deem him deserving of equal honor? Will we let him be outraged by our wives? Will we permit this even though we realize that the greatest punishment and vengeance will be stored up for us when we neglect the salvation of our wives?

II.4. This is why he made you to be head of the wife. This is why Paul gave the order: "If wives wish to learn anything, let them ask their own husbands at home," so that you, like a teacher, a guardian, a patron, might urge her to godliness. Yet when the hour set for the services summons you to the church, you fail to rouse your wives from their sluggish indifference. But now that the devil summons your wives to the feast of Trumpets and they turn a ready ear to his call, you do not restrain them. You let them entangle themselves in accusations of ungodliness, you let them be dragged off into licentious ways. For, as a rule, it is the harlots, the effeminates, and the whole chorus from the theater who rush to that festival.

II.5. And why do I speak of the immorality that goes on there? Are you not afraid that your wife may not come back from there after a demon has possessed her soul? Did you not hear in my previous discourse the argument which clearly proved to us that demons dwell in the very souls of the Jews and in the places in which they gather? Tell me, then. How do you Judaizers have the boldness, after dancing with demons, to come back to the assembly of the apostles? After you have gone off and shared with those who shed the blood of Christ, how is it that you do not shudder to come back and share in the sacred banquet, to partake of his precious blood? Do you not shiver, are you not afraid when you commit such outrages? Have you so little respect for that very banquet?

II.6. I have spoken these words to you. You will speak them to those Judaizers, and they to their wives. "Fortify one another." If a catechumen is sick with this disease, let him be kept outside the church doors. If the sick one be a believer and already initiated, let him be driven from the holy table. For not all sins need exhortation and counsel; some sins, of their very nature, demand cure by a quick and sharp excision. The wounds we can tolerate respond to more gentle cures; those which have festered and cannot be cured, those which are feeding on the rest of the body, need cauterization with a point of steel. So is it with sins. Some need long exhortation; others need sharp rebuke.

IV.3. Whenever your brother needs correction, even if you must lay down your life, do not refuse him. Follow the example of your Master. If you have a servant or if you have a wife, be very careful to keep them at home. If you refuse to let them go to the theater, you must refuse all the more to let them go to the synagogue. To go to the synagogue is a greater crime than going to the theater. What goes on in the theater is, to be sure, sinful; what goes on in the synagogue is godlessness. When I say this I do not mean that you let them go to the theater, for the theater is wicked; I say it so that you will be all the more careful to keep them away from the synagogue.

32

A CHRISTIAN MATRON FROM ROME VISITING
THE HERMITIC ABBOT ARSENIUS

Sayings of the Desert Fathers II.7   5th century C.E.

At one time when the abbot Arsenius was living in Canopus, there
came from Rome in hope to see him a lady, a virgin, of great wealth,
and one that feared God: and Theophilus the archbishop received her.
And she prayed him to use his good offices with the old man, that she
might see him. And the archbishop came to him and asked him,
saying, "A certain lady hath come from Rome, and would see thee."
But the old man would not consent to have her come to him. So
when this was told the lady, she commanded her beasts to be saddled,
saying, "I trust in God, that I shall see him. For in my own city there
are men to spare: but I am come to see the prophets." And when she
came to the old man's cell, by the ordering of God it chanced that he
was found outside his cell. And when the lady saw him, she cast
herself at his feet. But with indignation did he raise her up; and
gazing upon her, said, "If thou dost desire to look upon my face, here
am I: look." But she for shame did not lift her eyes to his face. And
the old man said to her, "Hast thou not heard what I do? To see the
work is enough. How didst thou dare to take upon thee so great a
voyage? Dost thou not know that thou art a woman, and ought not
to go anywhere? And wilt thou now go to Rome and say to the other
women, 'I have seen Arsenius,' and turn the sea into a high road of
women coming to me?" But she said, "If God will that I return to
Rome, I shall let no woman come hither. But pray for me, and always
remember me." He answered and said, "I pray God that He will wipe
the memory of thee from my heart." And hearing this, she went away
troubled. And when she had come back into the city, she fell into a
fever for sorrow. And it was told the archbishop that she was sick:
and he came to comfort her, and asked her what ailed her. And she
said to him, "Would that I had not come hither! For I said to the old
man, 'Remember me.' And he said to me, 'I pray God that He will
wipe the memory of thee from my heart,' and behold I am dying of
that sorrow." And the archbishop said to her, "Knowest thou not that
thou art a woman, and through women doth the Enemy lay siege to
holy men? For this reason did the old man say it, but he doth ever
pray for thy soul." And so her mind was healed. And she departed
with joy to her own place.

33

A PACHOMIAN WOMEN'S MONASTERY IN
FOURTH-CENTURY C.E. EGYPT

Palladius *Lausiac History* 33   5th century C.E.

They also have a monastery of about four hundred women, with the same constitution and the same way of life, except for the goat skin. The women are across the river and the men opposite them. When a virgin dies, the other virgins prepare her body for the burial; they carry it and place it on the bank of the river. The brothers cross over on a ferry, with palm leaves and olive branches and carry the body across with psalmody. Then they bury it in their own tombs.

No one goes over to the women's monastery. A tailor from the world crossed over through ignorance, looking for work. A young [sister] who had come out—for the place is deserted—met him involuntarily and gave him this answer, "We have our own tailors."

Another [sister] saw them talking. Some time later, on the occasion of a quarrel, she accused falsely that [sister] before the community, by a diabolical insinuation [and moved by] great wickedness and boiling temper. A few others joined her in this nasty act. The other was so grieved at undergoing such an accusation, of a thing that had not even come to her mind, that not being able to bear it, she threw herself secretly into the river and died.

Then the slanderer realized that she had slandered out of wickedness and committed that crime. She also could stand it no longer; she went and hanged herself.

When the priest came, the other sisters told him what had happened. Then he ordered that the Eucharist should not be offered for either of them. Those who had not effected a reconciliation between the two, he excommunicated and deprived them from the Eucharist for a period of seven years for their complicity with the slanderer and for having believed what was said.

34

WOMEN BLOWING THE SHOFAR
ON ROSH HASHANAH

Babylonian Talmud *Rosh Hashanah* 32b   5th century C.E.

MISHNAH: [For the sake of] the shofar of New Year it is not allowed to disregard the distance limit nor to remove debris nor to climb a tree nor to ride on an animal nor to swim on the water. It must not be shaped either with an implement the use of which is forbidden on account of Shebuth or with one the use of which is forbidden by express prohibition. If one, however, desires to pour wine or water into it he may do so. Children need not be stopped from blowing; on the contrary, they may be helped till they learn how to blow. One who blows merely to practise does not thereby fulfill his religious obligation, nor does one who hears the blast made by another when practising.

GEMARA: **Children need not be stopped from blowing.** This would imply that women are stopped. [But how can this be], seeing that it has been taught: 'Neither children nor women need be stopped from blowing the *shofar* on the Festival'?—Abaye replied: There is no discrepancy; the one statement follows R. Judah, the other R. Jose and R. Simeon, as it has been taught: '*Speak unto the children* [bene] *of Israel*: [this indicates that] the "*sons*" [bene] of Israel lay on hands but not the "daughters" of Israel. So R. Judah, R. Jose and R. Simeon say that women also have the option of laying on hands'.

35

EXEMPTING WOMEN FROM THE OBLIGATION
TO EAT IN THE SUKKAH DURING THE
JEWISH FESTIVAL OF SUKKOTH

Babylonian Talmud *Sukkah* 28a–b   5th/6th century C.E.

A. Women, slaves, and minors are exempt from the religious requirement of dwelling in a sukkah.

B. A Minor who can take care of himself is liable to the religious requirement of dwelling in a sukkah.

C. M'SH W: Shammai the Elder's daughter-in-law gave birth, and he broke away some of the plaster and covered the hole with sukkah-roofing over her bed, on account of the infant. (Mishnah 2:8)

A. How do we know on that basis of Scripture [the rule at M. 2:8A]?

B. It is in accord with that which our rabbis have taught:

C. "Homeborn" (Lev. 23:42) by itself [without "the" and "every"] would have included every homeborn [encompassing women and minors].

D. [Since it says,] "**The** homeborn," it means to exclude women, and "**Every** . . ." serves to encompass minors. [That explains M. 2:8A, B.]

E. A master has said, "'**The** homeborn' (Lev. 23:42) serves to exclude women."

F. Does this then imply that the word, "homeborn" [without **the**] applies both to women and to men?

G. And has it not been taught, "The homeborn" (Lev. 16:29) [in regard to observance of the Day of Atonement] serves to encompass homeborn women, indicating that they are liable to undertake the distress [of the fast]?

H. Therefore when the word "homeborn" is used [without the "the"] it means to refer only to males.

I. Said Rabbah, "[In fact] these are matters of received law, and the purpose of rabbis was simply to find scriptural support for the received law."

J. Which [of the two laws, the one referring to the *sukkah* or the one about the fasting on the Day of Atonement then] is based on Scripture and which is a received law?

K. And further, what need do I have to make reference either to a received law or to Scripture? In the case of the requirement to dwell in a *sukkah*, that is a religious duty calling for an act of commission and based upon a particular time, and any religious duty calling for an act of commission and based upon a particular time leaves women exempt. [They do not have to keep a law which requires them to do something at a particular time, since they have prior obligations to their families.]

L. As to the Day of Atonement, it derives from a teaching in accord with that which R. Judah said R. Rab said.

M. For R. Judah said Rab said, and so too did a Tannaite authority of the house of R. Ishmael state, "Scripture has said, 'Man or woman' (Num. 5:6), so treating men and women as equal in regard to all those acts subject to penalty that are listed in the Torah." [Accordingly, both matters—*sukkah*, Day of Atonement, derive from secondary exegesis of the law. In no way do they depend upon either a received tradition or a primary exegesis or proof text.]

N. Said Abayye, "Under all circumstances, the *sukkah* [rule concerning women] is a received law, and it is necessary [to make the matter explicit as a received law].

O. "[Why so?] I might have thought to argue as follows: 'You shall dwell' (Lev. 23:42) in the manner in which you ordinarily dwell. Just as, in the case of an ordinary dwelling, a man and his wife [live together], so in the case of a *sukkah*, a man and his wife must live together. [Thus I might have reached the conclusion that a woman is liable to dwell in the *sukkah*.] So we are informed [that that is not the case.]"

P. Said Raba, "It indeed was necessary to provide such a proof [but it is different from Abayye's argument in the same regard]. For I might have said that we shall derive the rule governing the fifteenth [of Tishri, that is, *Sukkot*] from the fifteenth [of Nisan,] that is the festival of the unleavened bread.

Q. "Just as, in the latter case, women are liable [to eat unleavened bread], so in the present case, women are liable [to dwell in a *sukkah*]. So we are informed [that that is not the case]."

R. Now that you have maintained that the rule about women's exemption from the *sukkah* is a received law, what need do I have for a Scriptural proof-text?

S.   It is to encompass proselytes [within the requirement to dwell in a *sukkah*].

T.   You might have said, "The homeborn in Israel" (Lev. 23:34) is what the All-Merciful has said, thus excluding proselytes.

U.   So we are informed that that is not the case, [and proselytes come under the obligation].

V.   As to the Day of Atonement, since what R. Judah said what Rab said has provided an adequate proof, [that women must fast on the Day of Atonement, what need do we have for further proof]?

W.   The proof-text encompasses additional affliction [on the eve of the Day of Atonement, prior to nightfall. The fast begins even before sunset. That additional time is added to the fast, and it applies to women as much as to men.]

X.   You might have thought that since the All-Merciful has excluded the additional affliction from the penalties of punishment and admonition [so that, if one does not observe that additional period of fasting, he is not punished on that account], women are not obligated to observe that additional period at all.

Y.   Accordingly, we are informed [that that is not the case, and women are obligated as much as are men].

36

RABBINIC DISCUSSION ON THE DIFFERENCES IN RABBINIC LAW BETWEEN A MAN AND A WOMAN

Babylonian Talmud *Kiddushin*   5th century C.E.

MISHNAH: What [differences are there in law] between a man and a woman? A man rends his clothes and loosens his hair, but a woman does not rend her clothes and loosen her hair. A man may vow that his son will become a Nazirite, but a woman may not vow that her son will become a Nazirite. A man may be shaved on account of the Naziriteship of his father, but a woman cannot be shaved on account of the Naziriteship of her father. A man may sell his daughter, but a woman may not sell her daughter. A man may give his daughter in betrothal, but a woman may not give her daughter in betrothal. A man is stoned naked, but a woman is not stoned naked. A man is hanged, but a woman is not hanged. A man is sold for his theft, but a woman is not sold for her theft.

29a–b

MISHNAH: All obligations of the son upon the father, men are bound, but women are exempt. But all obligations of the father upon the son, both men and women are bound. All affirmative precepts limited to time, men are liable and women are exempt. But all affirmative precepts not limited to time are binding upon both men and women. And all negative precepts, whether limited to time or not limited to time, are binding upon both men and women; excepting, Ye shall not round [the corners of your heads], neither shalt thou mar [the corner of thy beard], and, He shall not defile himself to the dead.

GEMARA: What is the meaning of **all obligations of the son upon the father?** Shall we say, all obligations which the son is bound to perform for his father? Are then women [i.e., daughters] exempt? But it was taught: [*Every man, his mother and his father ye shall fear:*] *"every man:"* I know this only of a man; whence do I know it of a woman? When it is said, *"Every man, his mother and father ye shall fear"*— behold, two are [mentioned] here.—Said Rab Judah: This is the meaning: **all obligations of the son, [which lie] upon the father** to

do to his son, **men are bound, but women [mothers] are exempt.**
We thus learnt [here] what our Rabbis taught: The father is bound in
respect of his son, to circumcise, redeem, teach him Torah, take a wife
for him, and teach him a craft. Some say, to teach him to swim too.
R. Judah said: He who does not teach his son a craft, teaches him
brigandage, "Brigandage"! can you really think so!—But it is as
though he taught him brigandage.

"To circumcise him." How do we know it?—Because it is written,
And Abraham circumcised his son Isaac. And if his father did not
circumcise him, Beth din is bound to circumcise him, for it is written,
Every male among you shall be circumcised. And if Beth din did not
circumcise him, he is bound to circumcise himself, for it is written,
*And the uncircumcised male who will not circumcise the flesh of his foreskin,
that soul shall be cut off.*

How do we know that she [the mother] has no such obligation?—
Because it is written, [*"And Abraham circumcised his son . . .*] *as God
had commanded him": "him,"* but not *"her"* [the mother]. Now, we
find this so at that time; how do we know it for all times?—The
School of R. Ishmael taught: whenever *"command"* is stated, its only
purpose is to denote exhortation for then and all time. Exhortation, as
it is written. *But charge Joshua, and encourage him, and strengthen him.*
Then and for all time, as it is written, *from the day that the Lord gave
commandment, and onward throughout your generations.*

"To redeem him." How do we know it?—Because it is written, *and
all the firstborn of man among thy sons shalt thou redeem.* And if his
father did not redeem him, he is bound to redeem himself, for it is
written, [*nevertheless the firstborn of man*] *thou shalt surely redeem.* And
how do we know that she [his mother] is not obliged [to redeem
him]?—Because it is written, *thou shalt redeem* [*tifdeh*] [which may
also be read] *thou shalt redeem thyself* [*tippadeh*]: one who is charged
with redeeming oneself is charged to redeem others; whereas one who
is not charged to redeem oneself is not charged to redeem others. And
how do we know that she is not bound to redeem herself?—Because
it is written, *thou shalt redeem* [*tifdeh*], [which may be read] *thou shalt
redeem thyself:* the one whom others are commanded to redeem, is
commanded to redeem oneself: the one whom others are not commanded to redeem is not commanded to redeem oneself. And how do
we know that others are not commanded to redeem her?—Because
the Writ saith, *"and all the firstborn of man among thy sons shalt thou
redeem": "thy sons",* but not thy daughters.

"To teach him Torah." How do we know it?—Because it is written, *And ye shall teach them your sons*. And if his father did not teach him, he must teach himself, for it is written, *and ye shall study*. How do we know that she [the mother] has no duty [to teach her children]?—Because it is written, *we-limaddetem* [*and ye shall teach*], [which also reads] *u-lemadetem* [*and ye shall study*]: [hence] whoever is commanded to study, is commanded to teach; whoever is not commanded to study, is not commanded to teach. And how do we know that she is not bound to teach herself?—Because it is written, *we-limaddetem* [*and ye shall teach*]—*u-lemadetem* [*and ye shall learn*]: the one whom others are commanded to teach is commanded to teach oneself; and the one whom others are not commanded to teach, is not commanded to teach oneself. How then do we know that others are not commanded to teach her?—Because it is written, *"And ye shall teach them your sons"*—but not your daughters.

34a—36a

All affirmative precepts limited to time etc. Our Rabbis taught: Which are affirmative precepts limited to time? *Sukkah, lulab, shofar,* fringes, and phylacteries. And what are affirmative precepts not limited to time? *Mezuzah, "battlement",* [returning] lost property, and the *"dismissal of the nest."*

Now, is this a general principle? But unleavened bread, rejoicing [on Festivals], and "assembling", are affirmative precepts limited to time, and yet incumbent upon women. Furthermore, study of the Torah, procreation, and the redemption of the son, are not affirmative precepts limited to time, and yet women are exempt [therefrom]?—R. Johanan answered: We cannot learn from general principles, even where exceptions are stated. For we learnt: An *"erub"* and a partnership, may be made with all comestibles, excepting water and salt. Are there no more [exceptions]: lo, there are mushrooms and truffles! But [we must answer that] we cannot learn from general principles, even where exceptions are stated.

And affirmative precepts limited to time, women are exempt. Whence do we know it?—It is learned from phylacteries: just as women are exempt from phylacteries, so are they exempt from all affirmative precepts limited to time. Phylacteries [themselves] are derived from the study of the Torah: just as women are exempt from the study of the Torah, so are they exempt from phylacteries. But let us [rather] compare phylacteries to *mezuzah?*—Phylacteries are assimilated to the study of the Torah in both the first section and the second; whereas they are not assimilated to *mezuzah* in the second section. Then let *mezuzah* be assimilated to the study of the Torah?— You cannot think so, because it is written, [*And thou shalt write them upon the* mezuzah *of thine house. . . .*] *That your days may be multiplied:* do then men only need life, and not women!

But what of *sukkah,* which is an affirmative precept limited to time, as it is written, *ye shall dwell in booths seven days,* yet the reason [of woman's exemption] is that Scripture wrote *ha-ezrah,* to exclude women, but otherwise women would be liable?—Said Abaye, It is necessary: I would have thought, since it is written, *ye shall dwell in booths seven days,"* *"ye* shall dwell" [meaning] even as ye [normally] dwell [in a house]: just as [normal] dwelling [implies] a husband and wife [together], so must the *sukkah* be [inhabited by] husband and wife!—But Raba said, It is necessary [for another reason]: I might have thought, we derive [identity of law from the employment of] *"fifteen"* here and in connection with the Feast of unleavened bread: just as there, women are liable, so here too. Hence it is necessary.

But what of pilgrimage, which is an affirmative command limited to time, yet the reason [of woman's exemption] is that Scripture wrote, [*Three times in the year all*] *thy males* [*shall appear before the Lord thy God*], thus excluding women; but otherwise women would be liable?—It is necessary: I would have thought, we learn the meaning of "appearance" from "assembling".

Now, instead of deriving an exemption from phylacteries, let us deduce an obligation from [the precept of] rejoicing?—Said Abaye: As for a woman, her husband must make her rejoice. Then what can be said of a widow?—It refers to her host.

Now, let us learn [liability] from [the precept of] "assembling"?— Because unleavened bread and "assembling" are two verses [i.e., precepts] with the same purpose, and wherever two verses have the same purpose, they cannot throw light [upon other precepts]. If so, phylacteries and pilgrimage are also two verses with one purpose, and cannot illumine [other precepts]?—They are both necessary: for had the Divine Law stated phylacteries but not pilgrimage, I would have thought, let us deduce the meaning of "appearance" from "assembling". While had the Divine Law written pilgrimage but not phylacteries, I would have reasoned, Let phylacteries be assimilated to *mezuzah.* Thus both are necessary. If so, unleavened bread and "assembling" are also necessary?—For what are they necessary? Now, if the Divine Law stated "assembling" but not unleavened bread, it were well: for I would argue, let us deduce "fifteen", "fifteen", from the feast of Tabernacles. But let the Divine Law write unleavened bread, and "assembling" is unnecessary, for I can reason, If it is incumbent upon children, how much more so upon women! Hence it is a case of two verses with the same purpose, and they cannot throw light [upon other precepts].

Now, that is well on the view that they do not illumine [other cases]. But on the view that they do, what may be said? Furthermore, [that] affirmative precepts not limited to time are binding upon women; how do we know it? Because we learn from fear: just as fear is binding upon women, so are all affirmative precepts not limited to time incumbent upon women. But let us [rather] learn from the study of the Torah?—Because the study of the Torah and procreation are two verses which teach the same thing, and wherever two verses teach the same thing, they do not illumine [others]. But according to R. Johanan b. Beroka, who maintained, Concerning *both* [Adam and Eve] it is said, *And God blessed them: and God said unto them, Be fruitful and multiply,* what can be said?—Because the study of the Torah and redemption of the first born are two verses with one purpose, and such do not illumine [others]. But according to R. Johanan b. Beroka too, let procreation and fear be regarded as two verses with one purpose, which do not illumine [other cases]?—Both are necessary. For if the Divine Law wrote fear and not procreation, I would argue, The Divine Law stated, [*Be fruitful, and multiply, and replenish the earth,*] *and conquer it:* only a man, whose nature it is to conquer, but not a woman, as it is not her nature to conquer. And if Scripture wrote procreation and not fear, I would reason: A man, who has the means to do this [*sc.* to shew fear to his parents] is referred to, but not a woman, seeing that she lacks the means to fulfil this; and that being so, she has no obligation at all. Thus both are necessary. Now, that is well on the view that two verses with the same teaching do not illumine [others]: but on the view that they do, what can be said?— Said Raba, The Papunians know the reason of this thing, and who is it? R. Aha b. Jacob. Scripture saith, *And it shall be for a sign unto thee upon thine hand, and for a memorial between thine eyes, that the Torah of the Lord may be in thy mouth:* hence the whole Torah is compared to phylacteries: just as phylacteries are an affirmative command limited to time, and women are exempt, so are they exempt from all positive commands limited to time. And since women are exempt from affirmative precepts limited to time, it follows that they are subject to those not limited to time. Now, that is well on the view that phylacteries are a positive command limited to time; but what can be said on the view that they are not?—Whom do you know to maintain that phylacteries are an affirmative precept not limited to time? R. Meir. But he holds that there are two verses with the same teaching, and such do not illumine [others]. But according to R. Judah, who maintains that two verses with the same teaching illumine [others], and [also] that phylacteries are a positive command limited to time, what can be said?—Because unleavened bread, rejoicing [on Festivals], and "assembling" are three verses with the same teaching, and such do not illumine [others].

And all negative precepts etc. Whence do we know it?—Said Rab Judah in Rab's name, and the School of R. Ishmael taught likewise, Scripture saith, *When a man or a woman shall commit any sin that men commit [. . . then that soul shall be guilty]*: thus the Writ equalised woman and man in respect of all penalties [decreed] in the Torah. The School of R. Eliezer taught, Scripture saith, [*Now these are the judgments*] *which thou shalt set before them:* The Writ equalised woman and man in respect of all civil laws in Scripture. The School of Hezekiah taught, Scripture saith, [*but if the ox were wont to gore . . .*] *and he kill a man or woman* [*the ox shall be stoned, and his owner also shall be put to death*]; the Writ placed woman on a par with man in respect of all death sentences [decreed] in Scripture. Now, it is necessary [that all three should be intimated]. For if the first [only] were stated, [I would say] that the All-Merciful had compassion upon her [woman], for the sake of atonement; but as for civil law, I might argue that it applies only to man, who engages in commerce, but not to woman, who does not. While if the second [alone] were intimated, that is because one's livelihood depends thereon; but as for ransom, I might argue, it applies only to man, who is subject to precepts, but not to woman, who is not subject to them. And if the last [alone] were intimated,—since there is loss of life, the All-Merciful had compassion upon her; but in the first two I might say that it is not so. Thus they are [all] necessary.

Excepting, ye shall not round [the corner of your heads] neither shalt thou mar, etc. As for defiling oneself to the dead, that is well, because it is written, *Speak unto the priests the sons of Aaron:* [*There shall none defile himself for the dead among his people*]: [hence], the sons of Aaron, but not the daughters of Aaron. But how do we know [that she is exempt from] the injunction against rounding [etc.] and marring [etc.]?—Because it is written, *ye shall not round the corner of your heads, neither shalt thou mar the corners of thy beard:* whoever is included in [the prohibition of] marring is included in [that of] rounding; but women, since they are not subject to [the prohibition of] marring, are not subject to [that of] rounding. And how do we know that they are not subject to [the injunction against] marring?—Either by common sense, for they have no beard. Or, alternatively, [from] Scripture. For Scripture saith, *ye shall not round the corner of your* heads, *neither shalt thou mar the corner of thy* beard; since Scripture varies its speech, for otherwise the Divine Law should write, "*the corner of your* beards"; why, "*thy beard*"? [To intimate], "thy *beard*," but not thy wife's beard. Is it then not? But it was taught: The beard of a woman and that of a *saris* who grew hair, are like a [man's] beard in all matters. Surely that means in respect to marring?—Said Abaye: You cannot say that it is in respect to marring, for we learn "*corner*" "*corner*" from the sons of Aaron: just as there, women are exempt; so here too, women are exempt. But if we hold that "*the sons of Aaron*" is written with reference to the whole section, let the Writ refrain from it, and it follows *a fortiori.* For I can argue, If [of] priests, upon whom Scripture imposes additional precepts, [we say] "*the* sons *of Aaron*" but not the daughters of Aaron, how much more so of Israelites!—But for the *gezerah shawah* I would reason that the connection is broken. Then now too let us say that the connection is broken; and as for the *gezerah shawah,*—that is required for what was taught: "*They shall not shave*": I might think that if he shaves it with scissors, he is liable [for violating the injunction]: therefore it is stated, *thou shalt not mar.* I might think that if he plucks it [his hair] out with pincers or a remover, he is liable: therefore it is stated, "*they shall not shave*". How then is it meant? Shaving which involves marring, viz., with a razor. If so, let Scripture write, ["*ye shall not round the corner of your heads, neither shalt thou mar*] that of thy beard"? why [repeat] "*the* corner *of thy beard*"? Hence both are inferred.

Then when it was taught, "The beard of a woman and that of a *saris* who grew hair, are like a [man's] beard in all respects": to what law [does it refer]?—Said Mar Zuṭra: To the uncleanliness of leprosy. "The uncleanliness of leprosy!" But that is explicitly stated, *If a man or a woman have a plague upon the head or the beard?*—But, said Mar Zuṭra, [it is] in respect of purification from leprosy. But purification from leprosy too is obvious; since she is liable to uncleanliness

[through her beard], she needs [the same] purification!—It is necessary: I might have assumed, it is written with separate subjects:
[thus:] *"If a man or a woman have a plague upon the head"*: while *"or
the beard"* reverts to the man [alone]; therefore we are informed
[otherwise].

Issi taught: Women are exempt from the injunction against baldness too. What is Issi's reason?—Because he interprets thus: *Ye are
sons of the Lord your God: ye shall not cut yourselves, nor make any
baldness between your eyes for the dead. For thou art an holy people unto
the Lord thy God;* [the implied limitation] *"sons"* but not daughters [is]
in respect of baldness. You say, in respect of baldness; yet perhaps it is
not so, but rather in respect of cutting? When it is said, *"For thou art
an holy people unto the Lord thy God,"* cutting is referred to; hence, how
can I interpret [the implication] *"sons"* but not daughters? In respect
to baldness. And why do you prefer to include cutting and exclude
baldness? I include cutting which is possible both where there is hair
and where there is no hair, and I exclude baldness which is possible
only in the place of hair. Yet perhaps *"sons"* but not daughters applies
to both baldness and cutting, while *"For thou art an holy people unto
the Lord thy God"* relates to incision!—Issi holds that incision [*seriṭah*]
and cutting [*gedidah*] are identical.

Abaye said: This is Issi's reason, viz., he learns "baldness", "baldness", from the sons of Aaron: just as there, women are exempt, so
here too, women are exempt. But if we hold that the phrase [*"the sons
of Aaron"*] relates to the whole section, let Scripture refrain from it,
and it [woman's exemption] follows *a fortiori*. For I may argue, If [of]
priests, upon whom the Writ imposes additional precepts, [we say]
"the sons of *Aaron"* but not the daughters of Aaron, how much more
so of Israelites!—But for the *gezerah shawah* I would think the
connection is broken. Then now too, let us say that the connection is
broken; and as for the *gezerah shawah*, that is required for what was
taught, *They shall not make a baldness:* I might think that even if one
makes four or five bald patches he is liable for only one [transgres-
sion]; therefore it is stated, *ḳarḥah* [*a baldness*], intimating liability for
each separate act. What is taught by, *"upon their head"*? Because it is
said, *"Ye shall not cut yourselves, nor make any baldness between your eyes
for the dead"*: I might think that one is liable only for between the
eyes. Whence do I know to include the whole head? Therefore it is
stated, *"upon their head,"* to teach liability for the [whole] head as

for between the eyes. Now, I know this only of priests, upon whom Scripture imposes additional precepts; whence do we know it of Israelites?—*Karḥah* [baldness] is stated here, and *karḥah* is also stated below; just as there, one is liable for every act of making baldness, and for the [whole] head as for between the eyes, so here too, one is liable for every act of baldness and in respect of the whole head as for between the eyes. And just as below, [baldness] for the dead [is meant], so here too it is for the dead! If so, let Scripture write *keraḥ* [baldness]: why *karḥah*? That both may be inferred.

Raba said: This is Issi's reason, viz., he learns [the applicability of] *"between your eyes"* from phylacteries: just as there, women are exempt, so here too, women are exempt.

Now, why does Raba not say as Abaye?—[The distinction between] *keraḥ* and *karḥah* is not acceptable to him. And why does Abaye reject Raba's reason?—He can tell you. Phylacteries themselves are learnt from this: just as there, [*"between the eyes"* means] the place where a baldness can be made [viz.,] on the upper part of the head, so here too, the place for wearing [phylacteries] is the upper part of the head.

Now, according to both Abaye and Raba, how do they interpret this [verse], *"Ye are sons* [etc."]?—That is wanted for what was taught: *"Ye are sons of the Lord your God";* when you behave as sons you are designated sons; if you do not behave as sons, you are not designated sons: this is R. Judah's view. R. Meir said: In both cases you are called sons, for it is said, *they are sottish children,* and it is also said, *They are children in whom is no faith,* and it is also said, *a seed of evil-doers, sons that deal corruptly,* and it is said, *and it shall come to pass that, in the place where it was said unto them, Ye are not my people, it shall be said unto them, Ye are the sons of the living God.* Why give these additional quotations?—For should you reply, only when foolish are they designated sons, but not when they lack faith—then come and hear: And it is said, *"They are sons in whom is no faith."* And should you say, when they have no faith they are called sons, but when they serve idols they are not called sons—then come and hear: And it is said, *"a seed of evil-doers, sons that deal corruptly."* And should you say, they are indeed called sons that act corruptly, but not good sons—then come and hear: And it is said, *and it shall come to pass that, in the place where it was said unto them, Ye are not my people, it shall be said unto them, Ye are the sons of the living God.*

Researching Real Women: Documents to, from, and by Women

If the evidence for the religious activities of women in the Greco-Roman world is limited, the evidence for the religious activities of specific historical women, those for whom we have some concrete personal data, is even more limited. This section assembles some of that evidence, including sayings attributed to named female Christian ascetics from Egypt, letters written by men to an individual woman or women, and inscriptions and papyri that shed light on specific Jewish and Christian women.

Regrettably, we possess no ancient literary religious texts known to have been written by women before the fourth century C.E.[1] A significant proportion of Jewish and Christian texts from the Greco-Roman period have come down to us either with author unknown (anonymous) or with an ascription we consider patently impossible (pseudonymous). Scholars routinely used to assume male authorship for all these texts, but a heightened sensitivity due to feminist scholarship has led many scholars to rethink those assumptions and to question whether women authors are hidden behind the labels of anonymous and pseudonymous. Among works possibly composed by women are some portions of the various Apocryphal Acts of the Apostles,[2] *The*

---

1. The few writings by Christian women have been collected in English translation in *A Lost Tradition: Women Writers in the Early Church,* ed. Patricia Wilson-Kastner et al. (Lanham, Md.: Univ. Press of America, 1981); these include *The Martyrdom of Saints Perpetua and Felicitas* and the writings of Proba and Egeria.

2. See Stevan L. Davies, *The Revolt of the Widows: The Social World of the Apocryphal Acts* (Carbondale: Southern Illinois Univ. Press, 1980). See also Dennis R. Mac-

Conversion and Marriage of Aseneth (usually referred to as *Joseph and Aseneth*), and several texts in the Nag Hammadi Library such as the *Hypostasis of the Archons*.[3] At present, however, I consider the evidence to substantiate female authorship of these texts insufficient to warrant their inclusion here; instead, I have included them in appropriate sections elsewhere in the book.

I have made one exception, an excerpt from *The Martyrdom of Saints Perpetua and Felicitas*. In the form in which we now have the martyrdom account, it has been edited and a narrative framework provided, possibly by the North African church writer of the late second and early third centuries C.E. Tertullian. Many scholars currently accept, though, that the first-person portion of the account was composed by Perpetua herself while she was imprisoned awaiting her death in the arena, as the text itself relates.

Some of the selections in this section, particularly those on Jewish women and a few on Christian women, do not bear explicitly on the religious activities of these women. I have included them anyway for two reasons: We know so little especially about specific Jewish women that it has seemed helpful to include some of the relevant papyri and inscriptions here. Second and perhaps more important, these sources may shed indirect light on the religious lives of Jewish women. For example, texts that help us assess the degree to which Jewish women were or were not relatively cloistered may enable us to reevaluate our perceptions of what women did in synagogues: if we have evidence that Jewish women were active participants in the economic and social lives of their communities, playing various public roles, we must take that evidence seriously when we try to assess what roles women might have played in synagogues.[4] Evidence for social relationships between Jewish and non-Jewish women may require us to reconsider our understanding of the nature of Jewish-gentile relationships generally in the Greco-Roman period and may offer insight into the extent to which individual Jewish women observed regula-

---

Donald, *The Legend and the Apostle: The Battle for Paul in Story and Canon* (Philadelphia: Westminster Press, 1983).

3. This possibility was the subject of extended discussion at the conference "Images of the Feminine in Gnosticism," at Claremont, Calif., in 1985, and at the subsequent annual meeting of the Society of Biblical Literature in Anaheim. The proceedings of this conference may be found in *Images of the Feminine in Gnosticism*, ed. Karen L. King (Philadelphia: Fortress Press, 1988).

4. E.g., the work of Bernadette J. Brooten in *Women Leaders in the Ancient Synagogues*, BJS 36 (Chico, Calif.: Scholars Press, 1982).

tions concerning food (Kashrut) or menstrual purity (Niddah), and so forth.

In short, though much of the evidence for actual Jewish women sheds little light on their religious lives (the same is true for actual Jewish men, at least in the papyri and inscriptions), what we know or learn from these sources may enable us to rethink some of the assumptions we hold when we ask questions about Jewish practice and belief in the Greco-Roman period.

Most of the sources in this section are papyri and inscriptions, or letters written by men to women, notably by Jerome and John Chrysostom. We know from Jerome and others that correspondence such as this was not onesided: women wrote to men. It is significant and ironic that the letters by women have by and large not been preserved. We should also keep in mind that correspondence by men and women need not imply the actual ability on the part of either correspondent to write. Professional scribes were available in antiquity to any who could pay for their services, and were employed both by those who could write and those who could not. In most of the letters included here, it is clear that the recipients as well as the writers were highly literate.[5]

Finally, I want to mention a set of sources I would very much like to have included, if only they were available. In 1962, Israeli archaeologists reported the discovery of a cache of papers belonging to a Jewish woman living in the time of Bar Kochba (early second century C.E.). The archive of Babata apparently contains important personal and family documents, but twenty-five years later they have still not been published or made available to interested scholars. Although the discoveries of the Dead Sea Scrolls and the Nag Hammadi Library might make it seem otherwise, the discovery of new ancient sources is a relatively rare event, and it is hard not to wonder whether the archives of Babata might not have been published sooner if they had been the archives of a man. In any case, I trust that they will be available in the near future and that scholarship on Jewish women in late antiquity will benefit from their publication.[6]

5. For a discussion of women's literacy in antiquity, see Susan Guettel Cole, "Could Greek Women Read and Write?" in *Reflections of Women in Antiquity*, ed. Helene P. Foley (New York: Gordon & Breach, 1981), 219–46; and Sarah B. Pomeroy, "Technikai kai Mousikai: The Education of Women in the Fourth Century and in the Hellenistic Period," *American Journal of Ancient History* 2 (1977): 51–68.

6. Brief descriptions of the discovery may be found in H. J. Polotsky's "The Greek Papyri from the Cave of Letters," *Israel Exploration Journal* 12 (1962): 258–62; and in Yigael Yadin's "Expedition D—The Cave of the Letters," ibid., 227–57.

37

THE DISPOSITION OF A LAWSUIT BETWEEN
A JEWISH WOMAN AND A JEWISH MAN
LIVING IN EGYPT

CPJ 19   Egypt, 226 B.C.E.

In the 22nd year of the reign of Ptolemy, son of Ptolemy and
Arsinoe, gods Adelphoi, the priest of Alexander and the gods Adelphoi and the gods Euergetai and the kanephoros of Arsinoe Philadelphos being those officiating in Alexandria, the 22nd of the month
Dystros, at Krokodilopolis in the Arsinoite nome, under the presi-
dency of Zenothemis, the judges being Diomedes, Polykles, Andron,
Theophanes, Maiandrios, Sonikos, Diotrephes. Polydeukes, the clerk
of the court, having constituted us in accordance with the order sent
to him by Aristomachos, appointed strategos of the Arsinoite nome,
of which this is a copy:

"To Polydeukes greeting. Herakleia has requested the king in her
petition to form and swear in a court for her of all the judges except
such as either party may challenge in accordance with the regulations.
Year 21, Dystros 16, Pachon 19."

We have given judgment as below in the action brought by Dositheos against Herakleia according to the following indictment:

"Dositheos son of . . . , Jew of the Epigone, to Herakleia daughter
of Diosdotos, Jewess, as you in your . . . of yourself declared(?), (I
state) that on Peritios 22 of year 21, as I with other persons was
entering the . . . of Apion . . . from the so-called house of Pasytis
which is in Krokodilopolis in the Arsinoite nome opposite the so-
called house of Pasytis the . . . , you came to that place with Kallippos
the . . . and abused me saying that I had told certain persons that (you
are a . . .) woman, and on my abusing you in return you not only spat
on me but seizing the loop of my mantle . . . me and . . . until . . . and
the said Kallippos . . . as the people present rebuked you and Kallippos . . . you ceased your insults . . . to which I have borne witness.
Wherefore I bring an action of assault against you for 200 drachmai,
the assessment of damages being . . . drachmai. And as the assaulted
party I by this indictment . . . The 21st year, the priest of Alexander
and the gods Adelphoi and the gods Euergetai being Galestes son of
Philistion, the kanephoros of Arsinoe Philadelphos being Berenike
daughter of Sosipolis, the 26th of the month Peritios. The case will

be presented against you in the court sitting in the Arsinoite nome, of which Polydeukes is the clerk, on Peritios . . . of the 21st year, and you have received the indictment and have been personally summoned, the witnesses of the summons being . . . phanes son of Nikias, Thracian, official employee, Zopyros son of Symmachos, Persian of the Epigone."

Whereas this was the indictment, and Dositheos neither appeared in person nor put in a written statement nor was willing to plead his case; and whereas Herakleia appeared with her guardian Aristides son of Proteas, Athenian of the Epigone, and put in both a written statement and justificatory documents, and was also willing to defend her case; and whereas the code of regulations which was handed in by Herakleia among the justificatory documents directs us to give judgment in a . . . manner on all points which any person knows or shows us to have been dealt with in the regulations of king Ptolemy, in accordance with the regulations, and on all points which are not dealt with in the regulations, but in the civic laws, in accordance with the laws, and on all other points to follow the most equitable view; but when both parties have been summoned before the court and one of them is unwilling to put in a written statement or plead his case or acknowledge defeat(?) . . . he shall be judged guilty of injustice; we have dismissed the case.

38

A JEWISH WOMAN'S ATTACKS ON A PREGNANT NEIGHBOR

CPJ 133   Egypt, 2d century B.C.E.

To . . . , scribe of the village of . . . , from Sabbataios son of . . . , a Jew, one of the hired labourers of the same village. On Payni 20 in the 28th year, when I was . . .

In consequence of the blows and fall she is suffering severely; she has had to take to her bed and her child is in danger of miscarriage and death. I present you this petition in order that, when you have visited the spot and observed her (?) condition, Johanna may be secured until the result is apparent and that it may not happen that Johanna in case of any untoward event go scot-free. The 28th year, Payni 21.

Registered Payni 25.

39

EPITAPH OF A JEWISH WOMAN WHO DIED ON THE DAY OF HER WEDDING

CIJ/CPJ 1508   Egypt, 1st century B.C.E.

Weep for me, stranger, a maiden ripe for marriage, who formerly shone in a great house. For, decked in fair bridal garments, I, untimely, have received this hateful tomb as my bridal chamber. For when a noise of revellers already at my doors told that I was leaving my father's house, like a rose in a garden nurtured by fresh rain, suddenly Hades came and snatched me away. And I, stranger, who had accomplished twenty revolving years (?) . . .

40

EPITAPH OF HORAIA, WHOSE HUSBAND AND DAUGHTER DIED ONLY DAYS BEFORE HER

CIJ/CPJ 1509   Egypt, 1st century B.C.E.

This is the tomb of Horaia, wayfarer. Shed a tear. The daughter of Nikolaos, who was unfortunate in all things in her thirty years. Three of us are here, husband, daughter, and I whom they struck down with grief.

(My husband died) on the 3rd, then on the 5th my daughter Eirene, to whom marriage was not granted. I then with no place or joy was laid here after them under the earth on the 7th of Choiak. But stranger, you have clearly all there is to know from us to tell all men of the swiftness of death. In the 10th year, Choiak 7.

41

EPITAPH OF A JEWISH WOMAN FROM EGYPT WHO DIED IN CHILDBIRTH

CIJ/CPJ 1510   Egypt, 1st century B.C.E.

This is the grave of Arsinoe, wayfarer. Stand by and weep for her, unfortunate in all things, whose lot was hard and terrible. For I was bereaved of my mother when I was a little girl, and when the flower of my youth made me ready for a bridegroom, my father married me to Phabeis, and Fate brought me to the end of my life in bearing my firstborn child. I had a small span of years, but great grace flowered in the beauty of my spirit. This grave hides in its bosom my chaste body, but my soul has flown to the holy ones. Lament for Arsinoe. In the 25th year, Mechir 2.

42

EPITAPH OF A JEWISH WOMAN
FROM EGYPT

CIJ/CPJ 1513   Egypt, 1st century B.C.E.

Citizens and strangers, all weep for Rachelis, chaste, friend of all, about thirty years old. Do not weep vainly empty (tears?) for me. If I did live but a short allotted span, nevertheless I await a good hope of mercy. And Agathokles, about 38 years old.

43

EPITAPH OF A JEWISH WOMAN
"FROM THE LAND OF ONIAS"
IN EGYPT

CIJ/CPJ 1530   Egypt, 1st century B.C.E.

The speaking stele.
"Who are you who lie in the dark tomb? Tell me your country and birth."
"Arsinoe, daughter of Aline and Theodosios. The famous land of Onias reared me."
"How old were you when you slipped down the dark slope of Lethe?"
"At twenty I went to the sad place of the dead."
"Were you married?"
"I was."
"Did you leave him a child?"
"Childless I went to the house of Hades."
"May earth, the guardian of the dead, be light on you."
"And for you, stranger, may she bear fruitful crops."
In the 16th year, Payni 21.

44

A JEWISH WET NURSE'S
CONTRACT

CPJ 146   Egypt, 13 B.C.E.

(1st hand) To Protarchos in charge of the court. (2d hand) From Marcus Aemilius son of Marcus of the Claudian tribe and from Theodote daughter of Dositheos, a Persian, acting with her guardian and guarantor of the terms of this agreement, her husband, Sophron the son of . . . archos, a Persian of the Epigone. With regard to this matter, Theodote agrees that she will for 18 months from Phamenoth of the present 17th year of Caesar (Augustus) bring up and suckle in her own house in the city with her own milk pure and uncontaminated the foundling slave baby child Tyche which Marcus has entrusted to her, receiving from him each month as payment for her milk and care 8 drachmai of silver besides olive-oil, and Theodote has duly received from Marcus by her guarantor Sophron for the agreed 18 months wages for 9 months adding up to 72 drachmai; and if the child chances to die within this time, Theodote will take up another child and nurse it and suckle it and restore it to Marcus for the same 9 months, receiving no wages, since she has undertaken to nurse continually, providing her monthly care honestly and taking fitting thought for the child, not damaging her milk, not lying with a man, not conceiving, not taking another child to suckle. Whatever she takes or is entrusted with, she will keep safe and restore when it is asked or will pay the value of each thing, except in the case of a manifest loss, which will release her if it is proved. She will not give up her nursing before the time. If she defaults, she and Sophron may be seized and held until they pay back her wages and whatever else she receives and half as much again and the damages and the costs and another 300 drachmai of silver. The distraint may be made on either or both of them, since they guarantee each other, and on their property as if a judgement had been made against them, and whatever guarantees they give and all resort to protection shall be invalid. But if she duly performs everything, Marcus Aemilius will give her the monthly wages for the remaining 9 months and will not take the child away within the time or will himself pay the same penalty. Theodote shall bring the child to Marcus for inspection each month. Surety . . .

Theodote daughter of Dositheos and her husband Sophron for a slave child Tyche for 18 months, for which they have received 8 drachmai for 9 months, in the city.

45

A JEWISH DIVORCE AGREEMENT
FROM EGYPT

CPJ 144   Egypt, 13 B.C.E.

To Protarchos, from Apollonia daughter of Sambathion with her guardian, her mother's brother, Herakleides son of Herakleides, and from Hermogenes son of Hermogenes an Archistrateian. Apollonia and Hermogenes agree that they have dissolved their marriage by an agreement made through the same court in the 13th year of Caesar (Augustus) in the month Pharmouthi. Apollonia agrees that she has duly received back from Hermogenes the dowry of 60 drachmai which he had on her account from her parents Sambathion and Eirene according to the marriage-agreement. They agree therefore that the marriage-agreement is void, and that neither Apollonia nor anyone proceeding on her behalf will proceed against Hermogenes to recover the dowry, and that neither of them will proceed against the other on any matter arising from the marriage or from any other matter arising up to the present day, and that from this day it shall be lawful for Apollonia to marry another man and Hermogenes to marry another woman without penalty, and that whosoever transgresses this agreement shall be liable to the appointed penalty. The 17th year of Caesar (Augustus), Phamenoth 14.

46

A JEWISH WOMAN SETTLING
HER SHARE OF A DEBT

CPJ 148   Egypt, 10 B.C.E.

To Protarchos, from Apollonios the son of Theon and from Martha
(the freedwoman) of Protarchos, acting with her guardian, Herakleides the son of Herakleides. Whereas Apollonios presented to the
archidikastes Artemidoros in the present 20th year of Caesar (Augustus) in the month Hathyr a petition demanding from Martha and also
from Protarchos son of Protarchos 200 drachmai of silver with interest which he submitted to be owing to him from the deceased Protarchos son of Polemon, the patron of Martha and the father of
Protarchos, on the evidence of the promissory note he produced and
of the agreements made by Protarchos; now, since he has been satisfied by Martha in respect of her half share and has duly received from
her her half share, Apollonios agrees that neither he himself nor anyone acting on his behalf will proceed in any way against the property
left by her deceased patron Protarchos with respect to Martha's half
share of the principal and the interest . . . , nor with respect to the . . .
nor to any other loan or demand whatsoever, written or unwritten,
arising from that time to the present day. . . . (And whosoever transgresses) this agreement, shall be liable to damages and the fine legally
established. This shall not prejudice Apollonios' right to proceed
against Protarchos for the remaining half of the principal, 100 drachmai and the interest on them. . . .

SALE OF A HOUSE BETWEEN TWO WOMEN, THE BUYER PROBABLY JEWISH, THE SELLER PROBABLY NOT

CPJ 483   Egypt, 45 C.E.

(I, Thases daughter of Panephremmis . . . acknowledge that I have sold) to Herieus daughter of Sambathiôn, mother Thases, the two-storied house and all its appurtenances which I own at . . . , where the neighbours of the entire house are: south and west, a public street; north, house . . . of Tesenuphis . . . ; east, house of Herieus daughter of Sambathiôn. And I have forthwith received, in cash on the spot, the whole agreed price in full, and I will guarantee (the transaction) with every form of guarantee from the present day for all time, and I will carry out the other provisions stated above, and I have ordered . . . the clerk at the record-office to endorse (this deed) and to . . . Papais son of Pa . . ses wrote for her because she is illiterate.

(2d hand) I, Herieus daughter of Sambathiôn, mother Thases, have bought it as stated above. Leontas son of Eirenaios wrote for her because she is illiterate.

(1st hand?) Sale and cession of house and all its appurtenances at Soknopaiou Nesos in the division of Herakleides, where the neighbours of the entire house are: south and west, public street; north, house . . . of Tesenuphis in the possession of his children; east, house of Herieus daughter of Sambathiôn; and she has received the price and guarantees (the sale): which sale is made by Thases daughter of Panephremmis . . . with a mole on her forehead to the left, and Herieus daughter of Sambathiôn, mother Thases, about 38 years old, likewise with a mole on her forehead to the left. Signatory for the seller, Papais son of Pa . . ses . . . ; for the other party, Leontas son of Eirenaios, about 20 years old, without markings. Fifth year of Tiberius Claudius Caesar Augustus Germanicus Imperator, Pachon 20. Registered through the record-office at Soknopaiou Nesos.

48

JEWISH WOMEN ENUMERATED IN A
TAX DOCUMENT FROM EGYPT

CPJ 421   Egypt, 73 C.E.

The report of Herakleides *amphodarches* of the quarter of "Apollonios' Camp". The liability for the Jewish tax for the fifth year of the
Emperor Caesar Vespasian Augustus being an abstract according to
the statement of the fourth year. The number of Jews taken up by
previous accounts are 5 adult males, 6 adult females, of whom one is
over age and was adjudged as such being 59 years of age in the fourth
year, one minor, being four years of age in the fourth year, total of
names 12. And those taken up through a transcript of the preceding
epikrisis shown to be three years of age in the fourth year, being one
year old in the second year. Males: Philiskos, son of Ptollas, grandson
of Philiskos, mother Erotion. Females: Protous, daughter of Simon,
son of Ptolemaios, mother Dosarion, total 2, 14 in all, of these adult
males 5, minor male 1, who in the fifth year was four years old, adult
females 6, minor female 1, who in the fifth year was five years old,
likewise 1 minor female four years old . . . total of names 14. In
addition there is enrolled in the Jewish tax in the fifth year of the
Emperor Caesar Vespasian Augustus, of minors who in the third year
were one year old and so in the fifth year three years old, of males
taken up, Seuthes, son of Theodoros, grandson of Ptolemaios, mother
Philous found to be two years old in the fourth year, in the *epikrisis* of
the fourth year; total of names 15; of which adult males 5, 1 minor
male who in the fifth year is five years old, adult females 6, 1 female
minor who in the fifth year is five years old, likewise 1 four years old,
total 15. Of these 5 adult males being of those in the list as liable to
the maximum rate of the *laographia,* 5 names, and the remaining
names 10. These individually are: adult females: Tryphaina, daughter
of . . . spas, granddaughter of Kales, mother Dosarion, of those who
are over age, having been adjudged in the fourth year to be 59 years
old, now 61 years old. Dosarion, daughter of Jakoubos, son of Jakoubos, mother Sambous, the wife of Simon, 22 years old, Philous
(daughter of) . . . , mother Ptollous, wife of Theodoros, 20 years old.
Sambathion, daughter of Sabinos, mother Herais, wife of Thegenes,
18 years old. S . . . daughter of . . . mother Theudous, wife of Sambathion . . . years old. Erotion, daughter of . . . on, mother Euterpe,

wife of Ptollas, 22 years old, total 6. Minor males, four years old in the fifth year: Philiskos, son of Ptollas, grandson of Philiskos, mother Erotion, 1 name, likewise those three years old in the fifth year: Seuthes, son of Theodoros, grandson of Ptolemaios, mother Philous, 1. Females five years old in the fifth year. Protous, daughter of Theodoros, mother Philous, 1. Likewise those four years old in the fifth year: Protous, daughter of Simon, son of Ptolemaios, mother Dosarion, 1. Total of names 10. Together with the 5 names of those liable to the maximum rate of the *laographia,* total as above 15 names, at 8 drachmai and 2 oboloi each, 125 drachmai, for the *aparchai* 15 drachmai, total 140 drachmai. A similar copy has been deposited with the royal scribe through Amoutio . . . the scribe, in the fifth year of Vespasian on the 20th of Germanikios.

49

MANUMISSION OF A JEWISH FEMALE SLAVE BY A WOMAN FROM OXYRHYNCHOS AND HER BROTHER

CPJ 473   Egypt, 291 c.e.

Translation of manumission. We, Aurelius . . . of the illustrious and most illustrious city of Oxyrhynchos, and his sister by the same mother Aurelia . . . daughter of . . . the former *exegetes* and senator of the same city, with her guardian . . . the admirable . . . , have manumitted and discharged *inter amicos* our house-born slave Paramone, aged 40 years, and her children . . . with a scar on the neck, aged 10 years, and Jakob, aged 4 years, . . . from all the rights and powers of the owner: fourteen talents of silver having been paid to us for the manumission and discharge by the community of the Jews through Aurelius Dioskoros . . . and Aurelius Justus, senator of Ono in Syrian Palestine, father of the community. . . . And, the question being put, we have acknowledged that we have manumitted and discharged them, and that for the said manumission and discharge of them we have paid the above-mentioned sum, and that we have no rights at all and no powers over them from the present day, because we have been paid and have received for them the above-mentioned money, once and for all, through Aurelius Dioskoros and Aurelius Justus. Transacted in the illustrious and most illustrious city of Oxyrhynchos . . . , in the second consulship of Tiberianus and the first of Dion, year 7 of Imperator Caesar Gaius Aurelius Valerius Diocletianus and year 6 of Imperator Caesar Marcus Aurelius Valerius Maximianus, Germanici, Maximi, Pii, Felices, Augusti: Pharmouthi . . . nineteenth day.

(2d hand) . . . Paramone and her children . . . and Jakob . . . (I witness) the agreement as stated above. I, Aurelius . . . (wrote for him) as he is illiterate.

(3d hand) Aurelius Theon also called . . . of the money . . . piety (Eusebia?) . . . rights . . . of Dioskoros . . . Justus . . . the (talents) of silver . . . manumit . . . illiterate.

50

SOME WOMEN EXPLICITLY CALLED JEW
IN INSCRIPTIONS

CIJ 678   Soklos, Hungary, 3d century C.E.

To the Spirits of the Dead
To Septimia Maria, *Iudea*,
who lived 18 years.
Actia Sabinilla (her) mother.

CIJ 77*   Brescia, Italy, date uncertain

To the *Iunones* (female spirits associated with Juno). Annia *Iuda*,
freedperson of Lucius, fulfilled a vow on behalf of her household.

CIL 8.7530   Cirta, North Africa, date uncertain

To the Spirits of the Dead. To Julia Victoria, *Judea*.

51

A WOMAN SEEKING TO ATTRACT THE LOVE
OF ANOTHER WOMAN WITH
A MAGICAL SPELL

PGM 32.1–19   Egypt, date uncertain

I adjure you, Evangelos, by Anubis and Hermes and all the rest down below; attract and bind Sarapias whom Helen bore, to this Herais, whom Thermoutharin bore, now, now; quickly, quickly. By her soul and heart attract Sarapias herself, whom [Helen] bore from her own womb. MAEI OTE ELBŌSATOK ALAOUBĒTO ŌEIO . . . AĒN. Attract and [bind the soul and heart of Sarapias], whom [Helen bore, to this] Herais, [whom] Thermoutharin [bore] from her womb [now, now; quickly, quickly].

52

A WOMAN WHO IMPLORES OSERAPIS TO AVENGE
HER AGAINST HER DAUGHTER'S FATHER

PGM 40.1–18   Egypt, date uncertain

O master Oserapis and the gods who sit with Oserapis, I [pray] to you, I Artemisie, daughter of Amasis, against my daughter's father, [who] robbed [her] of the funeral gifts and tomb. So if he has not acted justly toward me and his own children—as indeed he has acted unjustly toward me and his own children—let Oserapis and the gods grant that he not approach the grave of his children, nor that he bury his own parents. As long as my cry for help is deposited here, he and what belongs to him should be utterly destroyed badly, both on earth and on sea, by Oserapis and the gods who sit together with Oserapis, nor should he attain propitiation from Oserapis nor from the gods who sit with Oserapis.

Artemisie has deposited this supplication, supplicating Oserapis and the gods who sit with Oserapis to punish justly. As long as my supplication [is deposited] here, the father of this girl should not by any means attain propitiation from the gods.

A CHRISTIAN WOMAN'S ACCOUNT OF
HER PERSECUTION

The Martyrdom of Saints Perpetua and Felicitas   Early 3d century C.E.

1. The deeds recounted about the faith in ancient times were a proof of God's favour and achieved the spiritual strengthening of men as well; and they were set forth in writing precisely that honour might be rendered to God and comfort to men by the recollection of the past through the written word. Should not then more recent examples be set down that contribute equally to both ends? For indeed these too will one day become ancient and needful for the ages to come, even though in our own day they may enjoy less prestige because of the prior claim of antiquity.

Let those then who would restrict the power of the one Spirit to times and seasons look to this: the more recent events should be considered the greater, being later than those of old, and this is a consequence of the extraordinary graces promised for the last stage of time. For *in the last days, God declares, I will pour out my Spirit upon all flesh and their sons and daughters shall prophesy and on my manservants and my maidservants I will pour my Spirit, and the young men shall see visions and the old men shall dream dreams.* So too we hold in honour and acknowledge not only new prophecies but new visions as well, according to the promise. And we consider all the other functions of the Holy Spirit as intended for the good of the Church; for the same Spirit has been sent to distribute all his gifts to all, as the Lord apportions to everyone. For this reason we deem it imperative to set them forth and to make them known through the word for the glory of God. Thus no one of weak or despairing faith may think that supernatural grace was present only among men of ancient times, either in the grace of martyrdom or of visions, for God always achieves what he promises, as a witness to the non-believer and a blessing to the faithful.

And so, my brethren and little children, *that which we have heard and have touched with our hands we proclaim also to you, so that* those of *you* that were witnesses may recall the glory of the Lord and those that now learn of it through hearing *may have fellowship* with the holy martyrs and, through them, *with* the Lord *Christ Jesus,* to whom belong splendour and honour for all ages. Amen.

2. A number of young catechumens were arrested, Revocatus and his fellow slave Felicitas, Saturninus and Secundulus, and with them Vibia Perpetua, a newly married woman of good family and upbringing. Her mother and father were still alive and one of her two brothers was a catechumen like herself. She was about twenty-two years old and had an infant son at the breast. (Now from this point on the entire account of her ordeal is her own, according to her own ideas and in the way that she herself wrote it down.)

3. While we were still under arrest (she said) my father out of love for me was trying to persuade me and shake my resolution. "Father," said I, "do you see this vase here, for example, or waterpot or whatever?"

"Yes, I do", said he.

And I told him: "Could it be called by any other name than what it is?"

And he said: "No."

"Well, so too I cannot be called anything other than what I am, a Christian."

At this my father was so angered by the word "Christian" that he moved towards me as though he would pluck my eyes out. But he left it at that and departed, vanquished along with his diabolical arguments.

For a few days afterwards I gave thanks to the Lord that I was separated from my father, and I was comforted by his absence. During these few days I was baptized, and I was inspired by the Spirit not to ask for any other favour after the water but simply the perseverance of the flesh. A few days later we were lodged in the prison; and I was terrified, as I had never before been in such a dark hole. What a difficult time it was! With the crowd the heat was stifling; then there was the extortion of the soldiers; and to crown all, I was tortured with worry for my baby there.

Then Tertius and Pomponius, those blessed deacons who tried to take care of us, bribed the soldiers to allow us to go to a better part of the prison to refresh ourselves for a few hours. Everyone then left that dungeon and shifted for himself. I nursed my baby, who was faint from hunger. In my anxiety I spoke to my mother about the child, I tried to comfort my brother, and I gave the child in their charge. I was in pain because I saw them suffering out of pity for me. These were the trials I had to endure for many days. Then I got permission for my baby to stay with me in prison. At once I recovered my health, relieved as I was of my worry and anxiety over the child. My prison had suddenly become a palace, so that I wanted to be there rather than anywhere else.

4. Then my brother said to me: "Dear sister, you are greatly privileged; surely you might ask for a vision to discover whether you are to be condemned or freed."

Faithfully I promised that I would, for I knew that I could speak with the Lord, whose great blessings I had come to experience. And so I said: "I shall tell you tomorrow." Then I made my request and this was the vision I had.

I saw a ladder of tremendous height made of bronze, reaching all the way to the heavens, but it was so narrow that only one person could climb up at a time. To the sides of the ladder were attached all sorts of metal weapons: there were swords, spears, hooks, daggers, and spikes; so that if anyone tried to climb up carelessly or without paying attention, he would be mangled and his flesh would adhere to the weapons.

At the foot of the ladder lay a dragon of enormous size, and it would attack those who tried to climb up and try to terrify them from doing so. And Saturus was the first to go up, he who was later to give himself up of his own accord. He had been the builder of our strength, although he was not present when we were arrested. And he arrived at the top of the staircase and he looked back and said to me: "Perpetua, I am waiting for you. But take care; do not let the dragon bite you."

"He will not harm me," I said, "in the name of Christ Jesus."

Slowly, as though he were afraid of me, the dragon stuck his head out from underneath the ladder. Then, using it as my first step, I trod on his head and went up.

Then I saw an immense garden, and in it a grey-haired man sat in shepherd's garb; tall he was, and milking sheep. And standing around him were many thousands of people clad in white garments. He raised his head, looked at me, and said: "I am glad you have come, my child."

He called me over to him and gave me, as it were, a mouthful of the milk he was drawing; and I took it into my cupped hands and consumed it. And all those who stood around said: "Amen!" At the sound of this word I came to, with the taste of something sweet still in my mouth. I at once told this to my brother, and we realized that we would have to suffer, and that from now on we would no longer have any hope in this life.

5. A few days later there was a rumour that we were going to be given a hearing. My father also arrived from the city, worn with worry, and he came to see me with the idea of persuading me.

"Daughter," he said, "have pity on my grey head—have pity on me your father, if I deserve to be called your father, if I have favoured you above all your brothers, if I have raised you to reach this prime of your life. Do not abandon me to be the reproach of men. Think of your brothers, think of your mother and your aunt, think of your child, who will not be able to live once you are gone. Give up your pride! You will destroy all of us! None of us will ever be able to speak freely again if anything happens to you."

This was the way my father spoke out of love for me, kissing my hands and throwing himself down before me. With tears in his eyes he no longer addressed me as his daughter but as a woman. I was sorry for my father's sake, because he alone of all my kin would be unhappy to see me suffer.

I tried to comfort him saying: "It will all happen in the prisoner's dock as God wills; for you may be sure that we are not left to ourselves but are all in his power."

And he left me in great sorrow.

6. One day while we were eating breakfast we were suddenly hurried off for a hearing. We arrived at the forum, and straight away the story went about the neighbourhood near the forum and a huge crowd gathered. We walked up to the prisoner's dock. All the others when questioned admitted their guilt. Then, when it came my turn, my father appeared with my son, dragged me from the step, and said: "Perform the sacrifice—have pity on your baby!"

Hilarianus the governor, who had received his judicial powers as the successor of the late proconsul Minucius Timinianus, said to me: "Have pity on your father's grey head; have pity on your infant son. Offer the sacrifice for the welfare of the emperors."

"I will not", I retorted.

"Are you a Christian?" said Hilarianus.

And I said: "Yes, I am."

When my father persisted in trying to dissuade me, Hilarianus ordered him to be thrown to the ground and beaten with a rod. I felt sorry for father, just as if I myself had been beaten. I felt sorry for his pathetic old age.

Then Hilarianus passed sentence on all of us: we were condemned to the beasts, and we returned to prison in high spirits. But my baby had got used to being nursed at the breast and to staying with me in prison. So I sent the deacon Pomponius straight away to my father to ask for the baby. But father refused to give him over. But as God willed, the baby had no further desire for the breast, nor did I suffer any inflammation; and so I was relieved of any anxiety for my child and of any discomfort in my breasts.

7. Some days later when we were all at prayer, suddenly while praying I spoke out and uttered the name Dinocrates. I was surprised; for the name had never entered my mind until that moment. And I was pained when I recalled what had happened to him. At once I realized that I was privileged to pray for him. I began to pray for him and to sigh deeply for him before the Lord. That very night I had the following vision. I saw Dinocrates coming out of a dark hole, where there were many others with him, very hot and thirsty, pale and dirty. On his face was the wound he had when he died.

Now Dinocrates had been my brother according to the flesh; but he had died horribly of cancer of the face when he was seven years old, and his death was a source of loathing to everyone. Thus it was for him that I made my prayer. There was a great abyss between us: neither could approach the other. Where Dinocrates stood there was a pool full of water; and its rim was higher than the child's height, so that Dinocrates had to stretch himself up to drink. I was sorry that, though the pool had water in it, Dinocrates could not drink because of the height of the rim. Then I woke up, realizing that my brother was suffering. But I was confident that I could help him in his trouble; and I prayed for him every day until we were transferred to the military prison. For we were supposed to fight with the beasts at the military games to be held on the occasion of the emperor Geta's birthday. And I prayed for my brother day and night with tears and sighs that this favour might be granted me.

8. On the day we were kept in chains, I had this vision shown to me. I saw the same spot that I had seen before, but there was Dinocrates all clean, well dressed, and refreshed. I saw a scar where the wound had been; and the pool that I had seen before now had its rim lowered to the level of the child's waist. And Dinocrates kept drinking

water from it, and there above the rim was a golden bowl full of water. And Dinocrates drew close and began to drink from it, and yet the bowl remained full. And when he had drunk enough of the water, he began to play as children do. Then I awoke, and I realized that he had been delivered from his suffering.

9. Some days later, an adjutant named Pudens, who was in charge of the prison, began to show us great honour, realizing that we possessed some great power within us. And he began to allow many visitors to see us for our mutual comfort.

Now the day of the contest was approaching, and my father came to see me overwhelmed with sorrow. He started tearing the hairs from his beard and threw them on the ground; he then threw himself on the ground and began to curse his old age and to say such words as would move all creation. I felt sorry for his unhappy old age.

10. The day before we were to fight with the beasts I saw the following vision. Pomponius the deacon came to the prison gates and began to knock violently. I went out and opened the gate for him. He was dressed in an unbelted white tunic, wearing elaborate sandals. And he said to me: "Perpetua, come; we are waiting for you."

Then he took my hand and we began to walk through rough and broken country. At last we came to the amphitheatre out of breath, and he led me into the centre of the arena.

Then he told me: "Do not be afraid. I am here, struggling with you." Then he left.

I looked at the enormous crowd who watched in astonishment. I was surprised that no beasts were let loose on me; for I knew that I was condemned to die by the beasts. Then out came an Egyptian against me, of vicious appearance, together with his seconds, to fight with me. There also came up to me some handsome young men to be my seconds and assistants.

My clothes were stripped off, and suddenly I was a man. My seconds began to rub me down with oil (as they are wont to do before a contest). Then I saw the Egyptian on the other side rolling in the dust. Next there came forth a man of marvellous stature, such that he rose above the top of the amphitheatre. He was clad in a beltless purple tunic with two stripes (one on either side) running down the middle of his chest. He wore sandals that were wondrously made of gold and silver, and he carried a wand like an athletic trainer and a green branch on which there were golden apples.

And he asked for silence and said: "If this Egyptian defeats her he will slay her with the sword. But if she defeats him, she will receive this branch." Then he withdrew.

We drew close to one another and began to let our fists fly. My opponent tried to get hold of my feet, but I kept striking him in the face with the heels of my feet. Then I was raised up into the air and I began to pummel him without as it were touching the ground. Then when I noticed there was a lull, I put my two hands together linking the fingers of one hand with those of the other and thus I got hold of his head. He fell flat on his face and I stepped on his head.

The crowd began to shout and my assistants started to sing psalms. Then I walked up to the trainer and took the branch. He kissed me and said to me: "Peace be with you, my daughter!" I began to walk in triumph towards the Gate of Life. Then I awoke. I realized that it was not with wild animals that I would fight but with the Devil, but I knew that I would win the victory. So much for what I did up until the eve of the contest. About what happened at the contest itself, let him write of it who will.

11. But the blessed Saturus has also made known his own vision and he has written it out with his own hand. We had died, he said, and had put off the flesh, and we began to be carried towards the east by four angels who did not touch us with their hands. But we moved along not on our backs facing upwards but as though we were climbing up a gentle hill. And when we were free of the world, we first saw an intense light. And I said to Perpetua (for she was at my side): "This is what the Lord promised us. We have received his promise."

While we were being carried by these four angels, a great open space appeared, which seemed to be a garden, with rose bushes and all manner of flowers. The trees were as tall as cypresses, and their leaves were constantly falling. In the garden there were four other angels more splendid than the others. When they saw us they paid us homage and said to the other angels in admiration: "Why, they are here! They are here!"

Then the four angels that were carrying us grew fearful and set us down. Then we walked across to an open area by way of a broad road, and there we met Jucundus, Saturninus, and Artaxius, who were burnt alive in the same persecution, together with Quintus who had actually died as a martyr in prison. We asked them where they had been. And the other angels said to us: "First come and enter and greet the Lord."

12. Then we came to a place whose walls seemed to be constructed of light. And in front of the gate stood four angels, who entered in and put on white robes. We also entered and we heard the sound of voices in unison chanting endlessly: *"Holy, holy, holy!"* In the same place we seemed to see an aged man with white hair and a youthful face, though we did not see his feet. On his right and left were four elders, and behind them stood other aged men. Surprised, we entered and stood before a throne: four angels lifted us up and we kissed the aged man and he touched our faces with his hand. And the elders said to us: "Let us rise." And we rose and gave the kiss of peace. Then the elders said to us: "Go and play."

To Perpetua I said: "Your wish is granted."

She said to me: "Thanks be to God that I am happier here now than I was in the flesh."

13. Then we went out and before the gates we saw the bishop Optatus on the right and Aspasius the presbyter and teacher on the left, each of them far apart and in sorrow. They threw themselves at our feet and said: "Make peace between us. For you have gone away and left us thus."

And we said to them: "Are you not our bishop, and are you not our presbyter? How can you fall at our feet?"

We were very moved and embraced them. Perpetua then began to speak with them in Greek, and we drew them apart into the garden under a rose arbour.

While we were talking with them, the angels said to them: "Allow them to rest. Settle whatever quarrels you have among yourselves." And they were put to confusion.

Then they said to Optatus: "You must scold your flock. They approach you as though they had come from the games, quarrelling about the different teams."

And it seemed as though they wanted to close the gates. And there we began to recognize many of our brethren, martyrs among them. All of us were sustained by a most delicious odour that seemed to satisfy us. And then I woke up happy.

14. Such were the remarkable visions of these martyrs, Saturus and Perpetua, written by themselves. As for Secundulus, God called him from this world earlier than the others while he was still in prison, by a special grace that he might not have to face the animals. Yet his flesh, if not his spirit, knew the sword.

15. As for Felicitas, she too enjoyed the Lord's favour in this wise.

She had been pregnant when she was arrested, and was now in her eighth month. As the day of the spectacle drew near she was very distressed that her martyrdom would be postponed because of her pregnancy; for it is against the law for women with child to be executed. Thus she might have to shed her holy, innocent blood afterwards along with others who were common criminals. Her comrades in martyrdom were also saddened; for they were afraid that they would have to leave behind so fine a companion to travel alone on the same road to hope. And so, two days before the contest, they poured forth a prayer to the Lord in one torrent of common grief. And immediately after their prayer the birth pains came upon her. She suffered a good deal in her labour because of the natural difficulty of an eight months' delivery.

Hence one of the assistants of the prison guards said to her: "You suffer so much now—what will you do when you are tossed to the beasts? Little did you think of them when you refused to sacrifice."

"What I am suffering now", she replied, "I suffer by myself. But then another will be inside me who will suffer for me, just as I shall be suffering for him."

And she gave birth to a girl; and one of the sisters brought her up as her own daughter.

16. Therefore, since the Holy Spirit has permitted the story of this contest to be written down and by so permitting has willed it, we shall carry out the command or, indeed, the commission of the most saintly Perpetua, however unworthy I might be to add anything to this glorious story. At the same time I shall add one example of her perseverance and nobility of soul.

The military tribune had treated them with extraordinary severity because on the information of certain very foolish people he became afraid that they would be spirited out of the prison by magical spells.

Perpetua spoke to him directly. "Why can you not even allow us to refresh ourselves properly? For we are the most distinguished of the condemned prisoners, seeing that we belong to the emperor; we are to fight on his very birthday. Would it not be to your credit if we were brought forth on the day in a healthier condition?"

The officer became disturbed and grew red. So it was that he gave the order that they were to be more humanely treated; and he allowed her brothers and other persons to visit, so that the prisoners could dine in their company. By this time the adjutant who was head of the gaol was himself a Christian.

17. On the day before, when they had their last meal, which is called the free banquet, they celebrated not a banquet but rather a love feast. They spoke to the mob with the same steadfastness, warned them of God's judgement, stressing the joy they would have in their suffering, and ridiculing the curiosity of those that came to see them. Saturus said: "Will not tomorrow be enough for you? Why are you so eager to see something that you dislike? Our friends today will be our enemies on the morrow. But take careful note of what we look like so that you will recognize us on the day." Thus everyone would depart from the prison in amazement, and many of them began to believe.

18. The day of their victory dawned, and they marched from the prison to the amphitheatre joyfully as though they were going to heaven, with calm faces, trembling, if at all, with joy rather than fear. Perpetua went along with shining countenance and calm step, as the beloved of God, as a wife of Christ, putting down everyone's stare by her own intense gaze. With them also was Felicitas, glad that she had safely given birth so that now she could fight the beasts, going from one blood bath to another, from the midwife to the gladiator, ready to wash after childbirth in a second baptism.

They were then led up to the gates and the men were forced to put on the robes of priests of Saturn, the women the dress of the priestesses of Ceres. But the noble Perpetua strenuously resisted this to the end.

"We came to this of our own free will, that our freedom should not be violated. We agreed to pledge our lives provided that we would do no such thing. You agreed with us to do this."

Even injustice recognized justice. The military tribune agreed. They were to be brought into the arena just as they were. Perpetua then began to sing a psalm: she was already treading on the head of the Egyptian. Revocatus, Saturninus, and Saturus began to warn the onlooking mob. Then when they came within sight of Hilarianus, they suggested by their motions and gestures: "You have condemned us, but God will condemn you" was what they were saying.

At this the crowds became enraged and demanded that they be scourged before a line of gladiators. And they rejoiced at this that they had obtained a share in the Lord's sufferings.

19. But he who said, *Ask and you shall receive,* answered their prayer by giving each one the death he had asked for. For whenever they would discuss among themselves their desire for martyrdom, Saturninus indeed insisted that he wanted to be exposed to all the different beasts, that his crown might be all the more glorious. And so at the outset of the contest he and Revocatus were matched with a leopard, and then while in the stocks they were attacked by a bear. As for Saturus, he dreaded nothing more than a bear, and he counted on being killed by one bite of a leopard. Then he was matched with a wild boar; but the gladiator who had tied him to the animal was gored by the boar and died a few days after the contest, whereas Saturus was only dragged along. Then when he was bound in the stocks awaiting the bear, the animal refused to come out of the cages, so that Saturus was called back once more unhurt.

20. For the young women, however, the Devil had prepared a mad heifer. This was an unusual animal, but it was chosen that their sex might be matched with that of the beast. So they were stripped naked, placed in nets and thus brought out into the arena. Even the crowd was horrified when they saw that one was a delicate young girl and the other was a woman fresh from childbirth with the milk still dripping from her breasts. And so they were brought back again and dressed in unbelted tunics.

First the heifer tossed Perpetua and she fell on her back. Then sitting up she pulled down the tunic that was ripped along the side so that it covered her thighs, thinking more of her modesty than of her pain. Next she asked for a pin to fasten her untidy hair: for it was not right that a martyr should die with her hair in disorder, lest she might seem to be mourning in her hour of triumph.

Then she got up. And seeing that Felicitas had been crushed to the ground, she went over to her, gave her her hand, and lifted her up. Then the two stood side by side. But the cruelty of the mob was by now appeased, and so they were called back through the Gate of Life.

There Perpetua was held up by a man named Rusticus who was at the time a catechumen and kept close to her. She awoke from a kind of sleep (so absorbed had she been in ecstasy in the Spirit) and she began to look about her. Then to the amazement of all she said: "When are we going to be thrown to that heifer or whatever it is?"

When told that this had already happened, she refused to believe it until she noticed the marks of her rough experience on her person and her dress. Then she called for her brother and spoke to him together with the catechumens and said: "You must all *stand fast in the faith* and love one another, and do not be weakened by what we have gone through."

21. At another gate Saturus was earnestly addressing the soldier

Pudens. "It is exactly", he said, "as I foretold and predicted. So far not one animal has touched me. So now you may believe me with all your heart: I am going in there and I shall be finished off with one bite of the leopard." And immediately as the contest was coming to a close a leopard was let loose, and after one bite Saturus was so drenched with blood that as he came away the mob roared in witness to his second baptism: "Well washed! Well washed!" For well washed indeed was one who had been bathed in this manner.

Then he said to the soldier Pudens: "Good-bye. Remember me, and remember the faith. These things should not disturb you but rather strengthen you."

And with this he asked Pudens for a ring from his finger, and dipping it into his wound he gave it back to him again as a pledge and as a record of his bloodshed.

Shortly after he was thrown unconscious with the rest in the usual spot to have his throat cut. But the mob asked that their bodies be brought out into the open that their eyes might be the guilty witnesses of the sword that pierced their flesh. And so the martyrs got up and went to the spot of their own accord as the people wanted them to, and kissing one another they sealed their martyrdom with the ritual kiss of peace. The others took the sword in silence and without moving, especially Saturus, who being the first to climb the stairway was the first to die. For once again he was waiting for Perpetua. Perpetua, however, had yet to taste more pain. She screamed as she was struck on the bone; then she took the trembling hand of the young gladiator and guided it to her throat. It was as though so great a woman, feared as she was by the unclean spirit, could not be dispatched unless she herself were willing.

Ah, most valiant and blessed martyrs! Truly are you called and chosen for the glory of Christ Jesus our Lord! And any man who exalts, honours, and worships his glory should read for the consolation of the Church these new deeds of heroism which are no less significant than the tales of old. For these new manifestations of virtue will bear witness to one and the same Spirit who still operates, and to God the Father almighty, to his Son Jesus Christ our Lord, to whom is splendour and immeasurable power for all the ages. Amen.

54

A TABLET INSCRIBED BY A YOUNG WOMAN, COMPELLING A DIVINE SPIRIT TO BRING HER THE MAN SHE DESIRES TO MARRY, USING LANGUAGE REMINISCENT OF THE SEPTUAGINT

Ant. Fluch. V   Date uncertain

I bind you by oath, divine spirit who is present here, in the holy name.
Aoth Abaoth, the god of Abraam, (Abraan), Iao of Jacob (Iakos), Iao
Aoth Abaoth, the god of Israel (Israma). Hear the honored, the
fearful and great name and lead him to *and to depart from and [to go]
to Urbanus, whom Urbana bore,* Domitiana, whom Candida bore,
bring him to her, full of love, raging with jealousy and without sleep
over his love and passion for her, and make him ask her to return to
his house as wife. I bind you by oath, great, eternal, ever-eternal,
all-powerful god who is superior to the gods above. I bind you by
oath, creator of heaven and sea. I bind you by oath, the one who has
passed through the pious. I bind you by oath, the one who has separated the sea with the staff, to lead and yoke Urbanus, whom Urbana
bore, to Domitiana, whom Candida bore, full of love, tormented and
sleepless on account of his passion and desire for her, in order that he
may lead her back to his house as his wife. I bind you by oath, the
one who made the ass stop giving birth. I bind you by oath, the one
who separated light from darkness. I bind you by oath, the one who
shattered the rocks. I bind you by oath, the one who broke the mountains asunder. I bind you by oath, the one who formed the earth upon
her foundations.

I bind you by oath in the holy name which is not to be uttered. I
shall call it by name with an equal number and the daimons will be
raised and become astonished and exceedingly fearful, to lead and
yoke the husband Urbanus, whom Urbana bore, to Domitiana, whom
Candida bore, full of love, and to beg her. Now Quickly.

I bind you by oath, the one who made the luminaries and stars in
heaven through the voice of command so as to bring light to all men.
I bind you by oath, the one who shook the entire world, who both
over-turned and spewed out the mountains, the one who made all the
earth tremble and renewed all the inhabitants. I bind you by oath, the
one who made the signs in heaven, on earth and in the sea, to lead

and yoke Urbanus the husband, whom Urbana bore, to Domitiana, whom Candida bore, full of love, raging with passion for her, begging and asking her to come back to his house as his wife. I bind you by oath, the eternal god, the great god, the all-powerful, whom all the mountains and valleys in all the world feared, you through whom the lion releases his prey, the mountains, the earth and the sea tremble . . . "appear each fear which he has" (meaning unclear) of the eternal, immortal, all-watching, evil-hating one who knows all good and evil things in the sea, in the rivers, in the mountains and on land, Aoth Abaoth, the god of Abraam and the Iao of Jacob, Iao Aoth Abaoth, the god of Israel. Lead, yoke Urbanus, whom Urbana bore, to Domitiana, whom Candida bore, and bring him back full of love, sleepless and tormented by his love, his desire and his passion for Domitiana, whom Candida bore. Yoke them in marriage and [make them] live together in love for the rest of their lives. Make him her obedient slave, desiring no other woman or maiden, but Domitiana alone, whom Candida bore, and to have her as his wife for the rest of their lives. Now, Now, Quickly, Quickly.

55

A FAMILY TOMB ERECTED BY A WOMAN IN ASIA MINOR, UNDER THE PROTECTION OF THE MOTHER OF THE GODS, SIPULENES

Ritti, 158   Smyrna, late 2d/early 3d century C.E.

Aurelia Tryphaina, daughter of Alexandros, erected the ancestral *heröon* for herself and for her heirs and freedpersons, and for Antonios Melitinos with his wife, Omoia, and their children, and Pamphilos only, having purchased the new sarcophagus of Prokonnesian marble by the sundial. No one has the authority to put another into the new sarcophagus, except only Tryphaina—similarly neither to [put her] into another ancestral sarcophagus nor to give the *heröon* over to strangers. Anyone who shall dare to do this shall give twenty-five hundred denaria to the Mother of the Gods Sipulenes. A copy of this inscription has been placed in the archive, Ailios Bionos being stephanophoros, in the third month.

56

SARCOPHAGUS INSCRIPTION OF A JEWISH WOMAN, HER HUSBAND, AND THEIR CHILDREN

CIJ 775   Hierapolis, 2d/3d century C.E.

This *soros* and the area surrounding it belong to Aurelia Augusta, daughter of Zotikos, in which she is to be buried, and her husband Glukonianos, also called Apros, and their children. Anyone else who buries [someone] in it shall give ——— denaria to the community of Jews resident in Hierapolis as reparation, and 2000 denaria to the plaintiff. A copy [of this inscription] has been deposited in the archive of the Jews.

59

A CHRISTIAN WOMAN ESTABLISHES
A FAMILY TOMB

son 1978, 32   Akmonia, 296/97 C.E.

urelia Julia for her father . . . and her mother, Beroneikiane and
my sweetest child Severus and Moundane, (my) daughter-in-law,
nemory. Christians.

60

A WOMAN IN IONIA WHO IS HONORED BY
THE JEWISH COMMUNITY FOR HER
SUBSTANTIAL DONATIONS

tz 13 (*CIJ* 738)   Phocea, probably 3d century C.E.

ion, daughter of Straton, son of Empedon, having erected the
bly hall and the enclosure of the open courtyard with her own
, gave them as a gift to the Jews. The synagogue of the Jews
ed Tation, daughter of Straton, son of Empedon, with a golden
and the privilege of sitting in the seat of honor.

Following Louis Robert, I have here and elsewhere translated the gen-
a man's name, when it follows a woman's name, as "daughter of . . ."
han as "wife of . . ." Although either translation is possible, Robert
cogent evidence that "daughter of . . ." is the far more likely reading
majority of cases. In this inscription, I have translated *hē synagogē tōn*
as "the synagogue of the Jews," but it might equally be translated as
mmunity of the Jews," which is the meaning it bears in a number of
er inscriptions.

57

BURIAL INSCRIPTION FROM ASIA I
A WOMAN AND HER MOTHER, WIT
IMPRECATIONS AGAINST VIOI
THE TOMB

MAMA 6, 231

I, Aurelios Zosimos, erected the *heröon* to A
called Tatia, my wife, in which I am also to be
Flavia, daughter of Skymnos, my mother-in-la
No one has the right to put another in. Anyon
shall give 2000 [denaria] to the most holy tre:
reckon with the hand of God.

NOTE: I have left untranslated some of the Greek
receptacle and the burial site. In Asia Minor, in p
terminology was employed for the vessel into whic
burial monument, and the burial site, and it is n
were the differences between some of these. For c
may not be crucial. A useful glossary occurs in Gi
"Anyone who dares . . ." more literally reads, "If
pay . . ." I have chosen my translation to avoid t
tion of ". . . he or she shall pay . . ." This reflects i
prohibitions are not intended to be read as gend
as men could set up tombs, presumably they cou
violating them, and thus culpable.

58

A FATHER'S INSCRIPTION OF T
OF HIS JEWISH DAI

TAM 3(1941), 448

Marcus Aurelios Ermaios, son of Keue
funerary urn for his daughter, Aurelia A
has the right to bury anyone else. Any
1000 denaria to the most sacred treasui
ing into graves.

Gil

for
in i

Lifshi

Ta
asser
funds
hono
crow

NOTE:
itive o
rather
present
in the
Ioudaiö
"the co
our oth

61

A WOMAN FULFILLING A VOW FOR HERSELF, HER CHILDREN, AND HER GRANDCHILDREN

Lifshitz 30 (*IG* 2924)   Tralles, Caria, 3d century C.E.

I, Capitolina, the most revered and pious one, having made the entire dais, made the revetment of the stairs, in fulfillment of a vow for myself, and (my) children and (my) grandchildren. Blessings.

62

A BURIAL MONUMENT FUNDED BY A WOMAN FROM HER DOWRY FOR HER HUSBAND, HERSELF, AND HER SON AND DAUGHTER-IN-LAW

CIJ 763   Akmonia, 3d/4th century C.E.?

Ammia, daughter of Eutyches, prepared a monument for her husband, Salimachos, and herself, from her own dowry. Let there be a curse unto the children's children lest anyone entomb anyone except my son Eutyches and his wife.

63

EPITAPHS BY THREE CHRISTIAN WOMEN, POSSIBLY MONTANISTS, SET UP FOR THEIR FAMILIES

Gibson 1978   Akça, ca. 305 C.E.

8. Aurelia Domna for her husband, Meles, and for herself (while still) alive; and their children Kyrillos and Alexandros and Istratonikes and Eythycheianes and Tationos and Alexandria and Auxanon and Kyriakes and Eusebis and Domnos for their father and mother, who is (still) alive, Christians for Christians.

12. Aurelia Appes for her sweetest husband, Trophimos, called also Krasos, and their children Trophimos and Nikomachos and Domna and Appes for their father and their mother, who is (still) alive, Christians for Christians.

13. Aurelia Tation, daughter of Philomelos, for her child Mikos, and Hermiones for her husband, Mikos, and Mikalos for his father, Christians for Christians in memory.

64

THE EPITAPH OF A MARRIED COUPLE, PROBABLY CHRISTIAN, WITH THE HUSBAND'S BEQUESTS TO HIS WIFE AND OTHERS

Gibson 1978, 15   Akça, ca. 305 C.E.

Aurelios Onesimos and Stratonikos and Trophimas took possession of the portions (of land) which were bequeathed to them; and let no one ever make any claim, either himself or through another.

Aurelios Papylos son of Onesimos, and Appes, for their children Eugenious and Amias; and for their grandchild Epiktetos and Eugenia; and for themselves (while still) alive; and their children Papylos and Amianos for their father and mother; and Ardemas and Amias and Trophimos for their sweetest parents-in-law and their sweetest brother-in-law, in memory. I, Aurelios Papylos, leave my (tool) chest and tools and the portions (of land) which were bequeathed to me, to Papylos and Amianos. Then I leave to Euthychiane and Appe(s) 30 measures of barley mixed with wheat and to my wife I leave 30 measures and a sheep.

65

TEN INSCRIPTIONS FROM A SYNAGOGUE, COMMEMORATING CONTRIBUTIONS FOR THE PAVING OF A MOSAIC FLOOR

Lifshitz (*I. Syrie* 1322–27, 1329, 1332,
1335, 1336; also, incomplete in *CIJ*)　　　　Apamea, Syria, ca. 391 C.E.

41. Alexandra, in fulfillment of a vow, gave 100 feet for the welfare of (her) whole household.

42. Ambrosia, in fulfillment of a vow, gave 50 feet for the welfare of (her) whole household.

43. Domnina, in fulfillment of a vow, gave 100 feet for the welfare of all (her) household.

44. Eupithis, in fulfillment of a vow, gave 100 feet for the welfare of all (her) household.

45. Diogenis, in fulfillment of a vow, gave 100 feet for the welfare of all (her) household.

46. Saprikia, in fulfillment of a vow, gave 150 feet for the welfare of all (her) household.

48. Thaumasis, together with Hesychion (his) wife, and children, and Eustathis (his) mother-in-law, gave 100 feet.

51. Colonis, in fulfillment of a vow, gave 75 feet for her welfare and that of her children.

54. So-and-so, for her welfare and that of [her children] and of (her) grandchildren, gave . . .

55. Eupithis, in fulfillment of a vow, for the welfare of herself and that of (her) husband, and of (her) children and all her household, gave this place.

NOTE: Literally, we should translate, ". . . made . . . feet . . . ," but since the clear sense is of a donation, I have chosen the English ". . . gave . . . feet . . ."

66

SAYINGS OF THE ASCETIC DESERT MOTHER
SARAH

Sayings of the Desert Fathers   5th century C.E.

1. It was related of Amma Sarah that for thirteen years she waged warfare against the demon of fornication. She never prayed that the warfare should cease but she said, "O God, give me strength."

2. Once the same spirit of fornication attacked her more intently, reminding her of the vanities of the world. But she gave herself up to the fear of God and to asceticism and went up onto her little terrace to pray. Then the spirit of fornication appeared corporally to her and said, "Sarah, you have overcome me." But she said, "It is not I who have overcome you, but my master, Christ."

3. It was said concerning her that for sixty years she lived beside a river and never lifted her eyes to look at it.

4. Another time, two old men, great anchorites, came to the district of Pelusia to visit her. When they arrived one said to the other, "Let us humiliate this old woman." So they said to her, "Be careful not to become conceited thinking of yourself: 'Look how anchorites are coming to see me, a mere woman.'" But Amma Sarah said to them, "According to nature I am a woman, but not according to my thoughts."

5. Amma Sarah said, "If I prayed God that all men should approve of my conduct, I should find myself a penitent at the door of each one, but I shall rather pray that my heart may be pure towards all."

6. She also said, "I put out my foot to ascend the ladder, and I place death before my eyes before going up it."

7. She also said, "It is good to give alms for men's sake. Even if it is only done to please men, through it one can begin to seek to please God."

8. Some monks of Scetis came one day to visit Amma Sarah. She offered them a small basket of fruit. They left the good fruit and ate the bad. So she said to them, "You are true monks of Scetis."

9. She also said to the brothers, "It is I who am a man, you who are women."

67

SAYINGS OF THE ASCETIC DESERT MOTHER
SYNCLETICA

Sayings of the Desert Fathers   5th century C.E.

1. Amma Syncletica said, "In the beginning there are a great many battles and a good deal of suffering for those who are advancing towards God and afterwards, ineffable joy. It is like those who wish to light a fire; at first they are choked by the smoke and cry, and by this means obtain what they seek (as it is said: 'Our God is a consuming fire' [Heb. 12.24]): so we also must kindle the divine fire in ourselves through tears and hard work."

2. She also said, "We who have chosen this way of life must obtain perfect temperance. It is true that among seculars, also, temperance has the freedom of the city, but intemperance cohabits with it, because they sin with all the other senses. Their gaze is shameless and they laugh immoderately."

3. She also said, "Just as the most bitter medicine drives out poisonous creatures so prayer joined to fasting drives evil thoughts away."

4. She also said, "Do not let yourself be seduced by the delights of the riches of the world, as though they contained something useful on account of vain pleasure. Worldly people esteem the culinary art, but you, through fasting and thanks to cheap food, go beyond their abundance of food. It is written: 'He who is sated loathes honey.' (Prov. 27.7) Do not fill yourself with bread and you will not desire wine."

5. Blessed Syncletica was asked if poverty is a perfect good. She said, "For those who are capable of it, it is a perfect good. Those who can sustain it receive suffering in the body but rest in the soul, for just as one washes coarse clothes by trampling them underfoot and turning them about in all directions, even so the strong soul becomes much more stable thanks to voluntary poverty."

6. She also said, "If you find yourself in a monastery do not go to another place, for that will harm you a great deal. Just as the bird who abandons the eggs she was sitting on prevents them from hatching, so the monk or the nun grows cold and their faith dies, when they go from one place to another."

7. She also said, "Many are the wiles of the devil. If he is not able to disturb the soul by means of poverty, he suggests riches as an attraction. If he has not won the victory by insults and disgrace, he suggests praise and glory. Overcome by health, he makes the body ill. Not having been able to seduce it through pleasures, he tries to overthrow it by involuntary sufferings. He joins to this, very severe illness, to disturb the faint-hearted in their love of God. But he also destroys the body by very violent fevers and weighs it down with intolerable thirst. If, being a sinner, you undergo all these things, remind yourself of the punishment to come, the everlasting fire and the sufferings inflicted by justice, and do not be discouraged here and now. Rejoice that God visits you and keep this blessed saying on your lips: 'The Lord has chastened me sorely but he has not given me over unto death.' (Ps. 118.18) You were iron, but fire has burnt the rust off you. If you are righteous and fall ill, you will go from strength to strength. Are you gold? You will pass through fire purged. Have you been given a thorn in the flesh? (2 Cor. 12.1) Exult, and see who else was treated like that; it is an honour to have the same sufferings as Paul. Are you being tried by fever? Are you being taught by cold? Indeed Scripture says: 'We went through fire and water; yet thou hast brought us forth to a spacious place.' (Ps. 66.12) You have drawn the first lot? Expect the second. By virtue offer holy words in a loud voice. For it is said: 'I am afflicted and in pain.' (Ps. 69.29) By this share of wretchedness you will be made perfect. For he said: 'The Lord hears when I call him.' (Ps. 4.3) So open your mouth wider to be taught by these exercises of the soul, seeing that we are under the eyes of our enemy."

8. She also said, "If illness weighs us down, let us not be sorrowful as though, because of the illness and the prostration of our bodies we could not sing, for all these things are for our good, for the purification of our desires. Truly fasting and sleeping on the ground are set before us because of our sensuality. If illness then weakens this sensuality the reason for these practices is superfluous. For this is the great asceticism: to control oneself in illness and to sing hymns of thanksgiving to God."

9. She also said, "When you have to fast, do not pretend illness. For those who do not fast often fall into real sicknesses. If you have begun to act well, do not turn back through constraint of the enemy, for through your endurance, the enemy is destroyed. Those who put out to sea at first sail with a favourable wind; then the sails spread, but later the winds become adverse. Then the ship is tossed by the waves and is no longer controlled by the rudder. But when in a little while there is a calm, and the tempest dies down, then the ship sails on again. So it is with us, when we are driven by the spirits who are against us; we hold to the cross as our sail and so we can set a safe course."

10. She also said, "Those who have endured the labours and dangers of the sea and then amass material riches, even when they have gained much desire to gain yet more and they consider what they have at present as nothing and reach out for what they have not got. We, who have nothing of that which we desire, wish to acquire everything through the fear of God."

11. She also said, "Imitate the publican, and you will not be condemned with the Pharisee. Choose the meekness of Moses and you will find your heart which is a rock changed into a spring of water."

12. She also said, "It is dangerous for anyone to teach who has not first been trained in the 'practical' life. For if someone who owns a ruined house receives guests there, he does them harm because of the dilapidation of his dwelling. It is the same in the case of someone who has not first built an interior dwelling; he causes loss to those who come. By words one may convert them to salvation, but by evil behaviour, one injures them."

13. She also said, "It is good not to get angry, but if this should happen, the Apostle does not allow you a whole day for this passion, for he says: 'Let not the sun go down.' (Eph. 4.25) Will you wait till all your time is ended? Why hate the man who has grieved you? It is not he who has done the wrong, but the devil. Hate sickness but not the sick person."

14. She also said, "Those who are great athletes must contend against stronger enemies."

15. She also said, "There is an asceticism which is determined by the enemy and his disciples practice it. So how are we to distinguish between the divine and royal asceticism and the demonic tyranny? Clearly through its quality of balance. Always use a single rule of fasting. Do not fast four or five days and break it the following day with any amount of food. In truth lack of proportion always corrupts. While you are young and healthy, fast, for old age with its weakness will come. As long as you can, lay up treasure, so that when you cannot, you will be at peace."

16. She also said, "As long as we are in the monastery, obedience is preferable to asceticism. The one teaches pride, the other humility."

17. She also said, "We must direct our souls with discernment. As long as we are in the monastery, we must not seek our own will, nor follow our personal opinion, but obey our fathers in the faith."

18. She also said, "It is written, 'Be wise as serpents and innocent as doves.' (Matt. 10.16) Being like serpents means not ignoring attacks and wiles of the devil. Like is quickly known to like. The simplicity of the dove denotes purity of action."

19. Amma Syncletica said, "There are many who live in the mountains and behave as if they were in the town, and they are wasting their time. It is possible to be a solitary in one's mind while living in a crowd, and it is possible for one who is a solitary to live in the crowd of his own thoughts."

20. She also said, "In the world, if we commit an offence, even an involuntary one, we are thrown into prison; let us likewise cast ourselves into prison because of our sins, so that voluntary remembrance may anticipate the punishment that is to come."

21. She also said, "Just as a treasure that is exposed loses its value, so a virtue which is known vanishes, just as wax melts when it is near fire, so the soul is destroyed by praise and loses all the results of its labour."

22. She also said, "Just as it is impossible to be at the same moment both a plant and a seed, so it is impossible for us to be surrounded by worldly honour and at the same time to bear heavenly fruit."

23. She also said, "My children, we all want to be saved, but because of our habit of negligence, we swerve away from salvation."

24. She also said, "We must arm ourselves in every way against the demons. For they attack us from outside, and they also stir us up from within; and the soul is then like a ship when great waves break over it, and at the same time it sinks because the hold is too full. We are just like that: we lose as much by the exterior faults we commit as by the thoughts inside us. So we must watch for the attacks of men that come from outside us, and also repel the interior onslaughts of our thoughts."

25. She also said, "Here below we are not exempt from temptations. For Scripture says, 'Let him who thinks that he stands take heed lest he fall.' (1 Cor. 10.12) We sail on in darkness. The psalmist calls our life a sea and the sea is either full of rocks, or very rough, or else it is calm. We are like those who sail on a calm sea, and seculars are like those on a rough sea. We always set our course by the sun of justice, but it can often happen that the secular is saved in tempest and darkness, for he keeps watch as he ought, while we go to the bottom through negligence, although we are on a calm sea, because we have let go of the guidance of justice."

26. She also said, "Just as one cannot build a ship unless one has some nails, so it is impossible to be saved without humility."

27. She also said, "There is grief that is useful, and there is grief that is destructive. The first sort consists in weeping over one's own faults and weeping over the weakness of one's neighbours, in order not to destroy one's purpose, and attach oneself to the perfect good. But there is also a grief that comes from the enemy, full of mockery, which some call *accidie*. This spirit must be cast out, mainly by prayer and psalmody."

68

SAYINGS OF THE ASCETIC DESERT MOTHER THEODORA

Sayings of the Desert Fathers 5th century C.E.

1. Amma Theodora asked Archbishop Theophilus about some words of the apostle saying, "What does this mean, 'Knowing how to profit by circumstances'?" (Col. 4, 5) He said to her, "This saying shows us how to profit at all times. For example, is it a time of excess for you? By humility and patience buy up the time of excess, and draw profit from it. Is it the time of shame? Buy it up by means of resignation and win it. So everything that goes against us can, if we wish, become profitable to us."

2. Amma Theodora said, "Let us strive to enter by the narrow gate. Just as the trees, if they have not stood before the winter's storms cannot bear fruit, so it is with us; this present age is a storm and it is only through many trials and temptations that we can obtain an inheritance in the kingdom of heaven."

3. She also said, "It is good to live in peace, for the wise man practises perpetual prayer. It is truly a great thing for a virgin or a monk to live in peace, especially for the younger ones. However, you should realize that as soon as you intend to live in peace, at once evil comes and weighs down your soul through *accidie*, faintheartedness, and evil thoughts. It also attacks your body through sickness, debility, weakening of the knees, and all the members. It dissipates the strength of soul and body, so that one believes one is ill and no longer able to pray. But if we are vigilant, all these temptations fall away. There was, in fact a monk who was seized by cold and fever every time he began to pray, and he suffered from headaches, too. In this condition, he said to himself, 'I am ill, and near to death; so now I will get up before I die and pray.' By reasoning in this way, he did violence to himself and prayed. When he had finished, the fever abated also. So, by reasoning in this way, the brother resisted, and prayed and was able to conquer his thoughts."

4. The same Amma Theodora said, "A devout man happened to be insulted by someone, and he said to him, 'I could say as much to you, but the commandment of God keeps my mouth shut.'" Again she said this, "A Christian discussing the body with a Manichean expressed himself in these words, 'Give the body discipline and you will see that the body is for him who made it.'"

5. The same amma said that a teacher ought to be a stranger to the desire for domination, vain-glory, and pride; one should not be able to fool him by flattery, nor blind him by gifts, nor conquer him by the stomach, nor dominate him by anger; but he should be patient, gentle and humble as far as possible; he must be tested and without partisanship, full of concern, and a lover of souls.

6. She also said that neither asceticism, nor vigils nor any kind of suffering are able to save, only true humility can do that. There was an anchorite who was able to banish the demons; and he asked them, "What makes you go away? Is it fasting?" They replied, "We do not eat or drink." "Is it vigils?" They replied, "We do not sleep." "Is it separation from the world?" "We live in the deserts." "What power sends you away then?" They said, "Nothing can overcome us, but only humility." "Do you see how humility is victorious over the demons?"

7. Amma Theodora also said, "There was a monk, who, because of the great number of his temptations said, 'I will go away from here.' As he was putting on his sandals, he saw another man who was also putting on his sandals and this other monk said to him, 'Is it on my account that you are going away? Because I go before you wherever you are going.'"

8. The same amma was asked about the conversations one hears; "If one is habitually listening to secular speech, how can one yet live for God alone, as you suggest?" She said, "Just as when you are sitting at table and there are many courses, you take some but without pleasure, so when secular conversations come your way, have your heart turned towards God, and thanks to this disposition, you will hear them without pleasure, and they will not do you any harm."

9. Another monk suffered bodily irritation and was infested with vermin. Now originally he had been rich. So the demons said to him, "How can you bear to live like this, covered with vermin?" But this monk, because of the greatness of his soul, was victorious over them.

10. Another of the old men questioned Amma Theodora saying, "At the resurrection of the dead, how shall we rise?" She said, "As pledge, example, and as prototype we have him who died for us and is risen, Christ our God."

69

A LETTER FROM THE ABBOT SHENOUTE TO
TACHOM, HEAD OF A CONVENT
IN EGYPT

CSCO 42:21–22   5th century C.E.

Shenoute writes to Tachom as one barbarian to another, not as a father to a mother, nor as a brother to a sister.

Though you did not know me until today, I knew you. I did not learn about you recently; I have known about you from the first. If I say, "If I have changed (toward you), what would you have done?" it must mean that if I did not change, you would not have begun to "build the tower."

When did I come to you vengefully since the sound of your folly fills the village where you are, not because I am lord over you, but for the love of God? When the Lord God confused their language, we didn't hear or find it written that they returned and built that tower (again), did we? And I am amazed, for many times God has confused the speech between you and me. I am talking about our false knowledge and our selfish doctrine and our evil thoughts that deceive us. And we turn around and build the tower (again).

At that time, those people made bricks from earth. They had their reward, in accordance with their desires, in the forbearance of God, who is exalted, the one who gave it to them in accordance with their desires. Those, on the other hand, who build the tower now—though I do not speak of everyone—their whole plan comes from the wickedness of Satan. Then, they said senselessly, "We will build it so that the top (of the tower) reaches up to heaven" (Gen. 11:4). Now, those who build this in every place think that they are wise, that their heart reaches the throne and judgment seat of God.

I said, "If you do not know what (message) is proper to send us —namely, 'Forgive me'—even if we sinned against you by not again sending you the one whom you did deem worthy to meet, then you do not understand anything." And if your "father" is not the one we sent in accordance with order and the rules of God, then you yourself are not a "mother." If you say of the one whom we sent, "We are not his," though he is your brother in the flesh, then you have separated yourself from us. If you say, "We are his," then the one who is writing to you is the one you would not meet, nor deem worthy of it.

Or perhaps you have a case at law with him? If you are not a wise mother, what will those who call you "mother" do to become wise without you? If some are wise, even one hundred are not enough to take counsel with you. . . .

70

INSTRUCTION FOR REARING A VIRGIN CHRISTIAN DAUGHTER

Letter 107, Jerome to Laeta   403 C.E.

1. The apostle Paul writing to the Corinthians and instructing in sacred discipline a church still untaught in Christ has among other commandments laid down also this: "The woman which hath an husband that believeth not, and if he be pleased to dwell with her, let her not leave him. For the unbelieving husband is sanctified by the believing wife, and the unbelieving wife is sanctified by the believing husband; else were your children unclean but now are they holy." Should any person have supposed hitherto that the bonds of discipline are too far relaxed and that too great indulgence is conceded by the teacher, let him look at the house of your father, a man of the highest distinction and learning, but one still walking in darkness; and he will perceive as the result of the apostle's counsel sweet fruit growing from a bitter stock and precious balsams exhaled from common canes. You yourself are the offspring of a mixed marriage; but the parents of Paula—you and my friend Toxotius—are both Christians. Who could have believed that to the heathen pontiff Albinus should be born—in answer to a mother's vows—a Christian granddaughter; that a delighted grandfather should hear from the little one's faltering lips Christ's Alleluia, and that in his old age he should nurse in his bosom one of God's own virgins? Our expectations have been fully gratified. The one unbeliever is sanctified by his holy and believing family. For, when a man is surrounded by a believing crowd of children and grandchildren, he is as good as a candidate for the faith. I for my part think that, had he possessed so many Christian kinsfolk when he was a young man, he might then have been brought to believe in Christ. For though he may spit upon my letter and laugh at it, and though he may call me a fool or a madman, his son-in-law did the same before he came to believe. Christians are not born but made. For all its gilding the Capitol is beginning to look dingy. Every temple in Rome is covered with soot and cobwebs. The city is stirred to its depths and the people pour past their half-ruined shrines to visit the tombs of the martyrs. The belief which has not been accorded to conviction may come to be extorted by very shame.

2. I speak thus to you, Laeta my most devout daughter in Christ, to teach you not to despair of your father's salvation. My hope is that the same faith which has gained you your daughter may win your father too, and that so you may be able to rejoice over blessings bestowed upon your entire family. You know the Lord's promise: "The things which are impossible with men are possible with God." It is never too late to mend. The robber passed even from the cross to paradise. Nebuchadnezzar also, the king of Babylon, recovered his reason, even after he had been made like the beasts in body and in heart and had been compelled to live with the brutes in the wilderness. And to pass over such old stories which to unbelievers may well seem incredible, did not your own kinsman Gracchus whose name betokens his patrician origin, when a few years back he held the prefecture of the City, overthrow, break in pieces, and shake to pieces the grotto of Mithras and all the dreadful images therein? Those I mean by which the worshippers were initiated as Raven, Bridegroom, Soldier, Lion, Perseus, Sun, Crab, and Father? Did he not, I repeat, destroy these and then, sending them before him as hostages, obtain for himself Christian baptism?

Even in Rome itself paganism is left in solitude. They who once were the gods of the nations remain under their lonely roofs with horned-owls and birds of night. The standards of the military are emblazoned with the sign of the Cross. The emperor's robes of purple and his diadem sparkling with jewels are ornamented with representations of the shameful yet saving gibbet. Already the Egyptian Serapis has been made a Christian; while at Gaza Marnas mourns in confinement and every moment expects to see his temple overturned. From India, from Persia, from Ethiopia we daily welcome monks in crowds. The Armenian bowman has laid aside his quiver, the Huns learn the psalter, the chilly Scythians are warmed with the glow of the faith. The Getæ, ruddy and yellow-haired, carry tent-churches about with their armies: and perhaps their success in fighting against us may be due to the fact that they believe in the same religion.

3. I have nearly wandered into a new subject, and while I have kept my wheel going, my hands have been moulding a flagon when it has been my object to frame an ewer. For, in answer to your prayers and those of the saintly Marcella, I wish to address you as a mother and to instruct you how to bring up our dear Paula, who has been consecrated to Christ before her birth and vowed to His service before her conception. Thus in our own day we have seen repeated the story told us in the Prophets, of Hannah, who though at first barren afterwards became fruitful. You have exchanged a fertility bound up with sorrow for offspring which shall never die. For I am confident that having given to the Lord your first-born you will be the mother of sons. It is the first-born that is offered under the Law. Samuel and Samson are both instances of this, as is also John the Baptist who when Mary came in leaped for joy. For he heard the Lord speaking by the mouth of the Virgin and desired to break from his mother's womb to meet Him. As then Paula has been born in answer to a promise, her parents should give her a training suitable to her birth. Samuel, as you know, was nurtured in the Temple, and John was trained in the wilderness. The first as a Nazarite wore his hair long, drank neither wine nor strong drink, and even in his childhood talked with God. The second shunned cities, wore a leathern girdle, and had for his meat locusts and wild honey. Moreover, to typify that penitence which he was to preach, he was clothed in the spoils of the hump-backed camel.

4. Thus must a soul be educated which is to be a temple of God. It must learn to hear nothing and to say nothing but what belongs to the fear of God. It must have no understanding of unclean words, and no knowledge of the world's songs. Its tongue must be steeped while still tender in the sweetness of the psalms. Boys with their wanton thoughts must be kept from Paula: even her maids and female attendants must be separated from worldly associates. For if they have learned some mischief they may teach more. Get for her a set of letters made of boxwood or of ivory and called each by its proper name. Let her play with these, so that even her play may teach her something. And not only make her grasp the right order of the letters and see that she forms their names into a rhyme, but constantly disarrange their order and put the last letters in the middle and the middle ones at the beginning that she may know them all by sight as well as by sound. Moreover, so soon as she begins to use the style upon the wax, and her hand is still faltering, either guide her soft fingers by laying your hand upon hers, or else have simple copies cut upon a tablet; so that her efforts confined within these limits may keep to the lines traced out for her and not stray outside of these. Offer prizes for good spelling and draw her onwards with little gifts such as children of her age delight in. And let her have companions in her lessons to excite emulation in her, that she may be stimulated when she sees them praised. You must not scold her if she is slow to learn but must employ praise to excite her mind, so that she may be glad when she excels others and sorry when she is excelled by them. Above all you must take care not to make her lessons distasteful to her lest a dislike for them conceived in childhood may continue into her maturer years. The very words which she tries bit by bit to put together and to pronounce ought not to be chance ones, but names specially fixed upon and heaped together for the purpose, those for example of the prophets or the apostles or the list of patriarchs from Adam downwards as it is given by Matthew and Luke. In this way while her tongue will be well-trained, her memory will be likewise developed. Again, you must choose for her a master of approved years, life, and learning. A man of culture will not, I think, blush to do for a kinswoman or a highborn virgin what Aristotle did for Philip's son when, descending to the level of an usher, he consented to teach him his letters. Things must not be despised as of small account in the absence of which great results cannot be achieved. The very rudiments and first beginnings of knowledge sound differently in the mouth of an educated man and of an uneducated. Accordingly you must see that the child is not led away by the silly coaxing of women to form a habit of shortening long words or of decking herself with gold and purple. Of these habits one will spoil her conversation and the other her character. She must not therefore learn as a child what afterwards she will have to unlearn. The eloquence of the Gracchi is said to have been largely due to the way in which from their earliest years their mother spoke to them. Hortensius became an orator while still on his father's lap. Early impressions are hard to eradicate from the mind. When once wool has been dyed purple who can restore it to its previous whiteness? An unused jar long retains the taste and smell of that with which it is first filled. Grecian history tells us that the imperious Alexander who was lord of the whole world could not rid himself of the tricks of manner and gait which in his childhood he had caught from his governor Leonides. We are always ready to imitate what is evil; and faults are quickly copied where virtues appear inattainable. Paula's nurse must not be intemperate, or loose, or given to gossip. Her bearer must be respectable, and her fosterfather of grave demeanour. When she sees her grandfather, she must leap upon his breast, put her arms round his neck, and, whether he likes it or not, sing Alleluia in his ears. She may be fondled by her grandmother, may smile at her father to shew that she recognizes him, and may so endear herself to everyone, as to make the whole family rejoice in the possession of such a rosebud. She should be told at once whom she has for her other grandmother and whom for her aunt; and she ought also to learn in what army it is that she is enrolled as a recruit, and what Captain it is under whose banner she is called to serve. Let her long to be with the absent ones and encourage her to make playful threats of leaving you for them.

5. Let her very dress and garb remind her to Whom she is promised. Do not pierce her ears or paint her face consecrated to Christ with white lead or rouge. Do not hang gold or pearls about her neck or load her head with jewels, or by reddening her hair make it suggest the fires of gehenna. Let her pearls be of another kind and such that she may sell them hereafter and buy in their place the pearl that is "of great price." In days gone by a lady of rank, Praetextata by name, at the bidding of her husband Hymettius, the uncle of Eustochium, altered that virgin's dress and appearance and arranged her neglected hair after the manner of the world, desiring to overcome the resolution of the virgin herself and the expressed wishes of her mother. But lo in the same night it befell her that an angel came to her in her dreams. With terrible looks he menaced punishment and broke silence with these words, 'Have you presumed to put your husband's commands before those of Christ? Have you presumed to lay sacrilegious hands upon the head of one who is God's virgin? Those hands shall forthwith wither that you may know by torment what you have done, and at the end of five months you shall be carried off to hell. And farther, if you persist still in your wickedness, you shall be bereaved both of your husband and of your children.' All of which came to pass in due time, a speedy death marking the penitence too long delayed of the unhappy woman. So terribly does Christ punish those who violate His temple, and so jealously does He defend His precious jewels. I have related this story here not from any desire to exult over the misfortunes of the unhappy, but to warn you that you must with much fear and carefulness keep the vow which you have made to God.

6. We read of Eli the priest that he became displeasing to God on account of the sins of his children; and we are told that a man may not be made a bishop if his sons are loose and disorderly. On the other hand it is written of the woman that "she shall be saved in childbearing, if they continue in faith and charity and holiness with chastity." If then parents are responsible for their children when these are of ripe age and independent; how much more must they be responsible for them when, still unweaned and weak, they cannot, in the Lord's words, "discern between their right hand and their left:"— when, that is to say, they cannot yet distinguish good from evil? If you take precautions to save your daughter from the bite of a viper, why are you not equally careful to shield her from "the hammer of the whole earth"? to prevent her from drinking of the golden cup of Babylon? to keep her from going out with Dinah to see the daughters of a strange land? to save her from the tripping dance and from the trailing robe? No one administers drugs till he has rubbed the rim of the cup with honey; so, the better to deceive us, vice puts on the mien and the semblance of virtue. Why then, you will say, do we read: — "the son shall not bear the iniquity of the father, neither shall the father bear the iniquity of the son," but "the soul that sinneth it shall die"? The passage, I answer, refers to those who have discretion, such as he of whom his parents said in the gospel: — "he is of age . . . he shall speak for himself." While the son is a child and thinks as a child and until he comes to years of discretion to choose between the two roads to which the letter of Pythagoras points, his parents are responsible for his actions whether these be good or bad. But perhaps you imagine that, if they are not baptized, the children of Christians are liable for their own sins; and that no guilt attaches to parents who withhold from baptism those who by reason of their tender age can offer no objection to it. The truth is that, as baptism ensures the salvation of the child, this in turn brings advantage to the parents. Whether you would offer your child or not lay within your choice, but now that you have offered her, you neglect her at your peril. I speak generally for in your case you have no discretion, having offered your child even before her conception. He who offers a victim that is lame or maimed or marked with any blemish is held guilty of sacrilege. How much more then shall she be punished who makes ready for the embraces of the king a portion of her own body and the purity of a stainless soul, and then proves negligent of this her offering?

7. When Paula comes to be a little older and to increase like her Spouse in wisdom and stature and in favour with God and man, let her go with her parents to the temple of her true Father but let her not come out of the temple with them. Let them seek her upon the world's highway amid the crowds and the throng of their kinsfolk, and let them find her nowhere but in the shrine of the scriptures, questioning the prophets and the apostles on the meaning of that spiritual marriage to which she is vowed. Let her imitate the retirement of Mary whom Gabriel found alone in her chamber and who was frightened, it would appear, by seeing a man there. Let the child emulate her of whom it is written that "the king's daughter is all glorious within." Wounded with love's arrow let her say to her beloved,

"the king hath brought me into his chambers." At no time let her go abroad, lest the watchmen find her that go about the city, and lest they smite and wound her and take away from her the veil of her chastity, and leave her naked in her blood. Nay rather when one knocketh at her door let her say: "I am a wall and my breasts like towers. I have washed my feet; how shall I defile them?"

8. Let her not take her food with others, that is, at her parents' table; lest she see dishes she may long for. Some, I know, hold it a greater virtue to disdain a pleasure which is actually before them, but I think it a safer self-restraint to shun what must needs attract you. Once as a boy at school I met the words: 'It is ill blaming what you allow to become a habit.' Let her learn even now not to drink wine "wherein is excess." But as, before children come to a robust age, abstinence is dangerous and trying to their tender frames, let her have baths if she require them, and let her take a little wine for her stomach's sake. Let her also be supported on a flesh diet, lest her feet fail her before they commence to run their course. But I say this by way of concession not by way of command; because I fear to weaken her, not because I wish to teach her self-indulgence. Besides why should not a Christian virgin do wholly what others do in part? The superstitious Jews reject certain animals and products as articles of food, while among the Indians the Brahmans and among the Egyptians the Gymnosophists subsist altogether on porridge, rice, and apples. If mere glass repays so much labour, must not a pearl be worth more labour still? Paula has been born in response to a vow. Let her life be as the lives of those who were born under the same conditions. If the grace accorded is in both cases the same, the pains bestowed ought to be so too. Let her be deaf to the sound of the organ, and not know even the uses of the pipe, the lyre, and the cithern.

9. And let it be her task daily to bring to you the flowers which she has culled from scripture. Let her learn by heart so many verses in the Greek, but let her be instructed in the Latin also. For, if the tender lips are not from the first shaped to this, the tongue is spoiled by a foreign accent and its native speech debased by alien elements. You must yourself be her mistress, a model on which she may form her childish conduct. Never either in you nor in her father let her see what she cannot imitate without sin. Remember both of you that you are the parents of a consecrated virgin, and that your example will teach her more than your precepts. Flowers are quick to fade and a baleful wind soon withers the violet, the lily, and the crocus. Let her never appear in public unless accompanied by you. Let her never visit a church or a martyr's shrine unless with her mother. Let no young man greet her with smiles; no dandy with curled hair pay compliments to her. If our little virgin goes to keep solemn eves and all-night vigils, let her not stir a hair's breadth from her mother's side. She must not single out one of her maids to make her a special favourite or a confidante. What she says to one all ought to know. Let her choose for a companion not a handsome well-dressed girl, able to warble a song with liquid notes but one pale and serious, sombrely attired and with the hue of melancholy. Let her take as her model some aged virgin of approved faith, character, and chastity, apt to instruct her by word and by example. She ought to rise at night to recite prayers and psalms; to sing hymns in the morning; at the third, sixth, and ninth hours to take her place in the line to do battle for Christ; and, lastly, to kindle her lamp and to offer her evening sacrifice. In these occupations let her pass the day, and when night comes let it find her still engaged in them. Let reading follow prayer with her, and prayer again succeed to reading. Time will seem short when employed on tasks so many and so varied.

10. Let her learn too how to spin wool, to hold the distaff, to put the basket in her lap, to turn the spinning wheel and to shape the yarn with her thumb. Let her put away with disdain silken fabrics, Chinese fleeces, and gold brocades: the clothing which she makes for herself should keep out the cold and not expose the body which it professes to cover. Let her food be herbs and wheaten bread with now and then one or two small fishes. And that I may not waste more time in giving precepts for the regulation of appetite (a subject I have treated more at length elsewhere) let her meals always leave her hungry and able on the moment to begin reading or chanting. I strongly disapprove—especially for those of tender years—of long and immoderate fasts in which week is added to week and even oil and apples are forbidden as food. I have learned by experience that the ass toiling along the high way makes for an inn when it is weary. Our abstinence may turn to glutting, like that of the worshippers of Isis and of Cybele who gobble up pheasants and turtle-doves piping hot that their teeth may not violate the gifts of Ceres. If perpetual fasting is allowed, it must be so regulated that those who have a long journey before them may hold out all through; and we must take care that we do not, after starting well, fall halfway. However in Lent, as I have written before now, those who practise self-denial should spread every stitch of canvas, and the charioteer should for once slacken the reins and increase the speed of his horses. Yet there will be one rule for those who live in the world and another for virgins and monks. The layman in Lent consumes the coats of his stomach, and living like a snail on his own juices makes ready a paunch for rich foods and feasting to come. But with the virgin and the monk the case is different; for, when these give the rein to their steeds, they have to remember that for them the race knows of no intermission. An effort made only for a limited time may well be severe, but one that has no such limit must be more moderate. For whereas in the first case we can recover our breath when the race is over, in the last we have to go on continually and without stopping.

11. When you go a short way into the country, do not leave your daughter behind you. Leave her no power or capacity of living without you, and let her feel frightened when she is left to herself. Let her not converse with people of the world or associate with virgins indifferent to their vows. Let her not be present at the weddings of your slaves and let her take no part in the noisy games of the household. As regards the use of the bath, I know that some are content with saying that a Christian virgin should not bathe along with eunuchs or with married women, with the former because they are still men at all events in mind, and with the latter because women with child offer a revolting spectacle. For myself, however, I wholly disapprove of baths for a virgin of full age. Such an one should blush and feel overcome at the idea of seeing herself undressed. By vigils and fasts she mortifies her body and brings it into subjection. By a cold chastity she seeks to put out the flame of lust and to quench the hot desires of youth. And by a deliberate squalor she makes haste to spoil her natural good looks. Why, then, should she add fuel to a sleeping fire by taking baths?

12. Let her treasures be not silks or gems but manuscripts of the holy scriptures; and in these let her think less of gilding, and Babylonian parchment, and arabesque patterns, than of correctness and accurate punctuation. Let her begin by learning the psalter, and then let her gather rules of life out of the proverbs of Solomon. From the Preacher let her gain the habit of despising the world and its vanities. Let her follow the example set in Job of virtue and of patience. Then let her pass on to the gospels never to be laid aside when once they have been taken in hand. Let her also drink in with a willing heart the Acts of the Apostles and the Epistles. As soon as she has enriched the storehouse of her mind with these treasures, let her commit to memory the prophets, the heptateuch, the books of Kings and of Chronicles, the rolls also on Ezra and Esther. When she has done all these she may safely read the Song of Songs but not before: for, were she to read it at the beginning, she would fail to perceive that, though it is written in fleshly words, it is a marriage song of a spiritual bridal. And not understanding this she would suffer hurt from it. Let her avoid all apocryphal writings, and if she is led to read such not by the truth of the doctrines which they contain but out of respect for the miracles contained in them; let her understand that they are not really written by those to whom they are ascribed, that many faulty elements have been introduced into them, and that it requires infinite discretion to look for gold in the midst of dirt. Cyprian's writings let her have always in her hands. The letters of Athanasius and the treatises of Hilary she may go through without fear of stumbling. Let her take pleasure in the works and wits of all in whose books a due regard for the faith is not neglected. But if she reads the works of others let it be rather to judge them than to follow them.

13. You will answer, 'How shall I, a woman of the world, living at Rome, surrounded by a crowd, be able to observe all these injunctions?' In that case do not undertake a burthen to which you are not equal. When you have weaned Paula as Isaac was weaned and when you have clothed her as Samuel was clothed, send her to her grandmother and aunt; give up this most precious of gems, to be placed in Mary's chamber and to rest in the cradle where the infant Jesus cried. Let her be brought up in a monastery, let her be one amid companies of virgins, let her learn to avoid swearing, let her regard lying as sacrilege, let her be ignorant of the world, let her live the angelic life, while in the flesh let her be without the flesh, and let her suppose that all human beings are like herself. To say nothing of its other advantages this course will free you from the difficult task of minding her, and from the responsibility of guardianship. It is better to regret her absence than to be for ever trembling for her. For you cannot but tremble as you watch what she says and to whom she says it, to whom she bows and whom she likes best to see. Hand her over to Eustochium while she is still but an infant and her every cry is a prayer for you. She will thus become her companion in holiness now as well as her successor hereafter. Let her gaze upon and love, let her "from her earliest years admire" one whose language and gait and dress are an education in virtue. Let her sit in the lap of her grandmother, and let this latter repeat to her granddaughter the lessons that she once bestowed upon her own child. Long experience has shewn Paula how to rear, to preserve, and to instruct virgins; and daily inwoven in her crown is the mystic century which betokens the highest chastity. O happy virgin! happy Paula, daughter of Toxotius, who through the virtues of her grandmother and aunt is nobler in holiness than she is in lineage! Yes, Laeta: were it possible for you with your own eyes to see your mother-in-law and your sister, and to realize the mighty souls which animate their small bodies; such is your innate thirst for chastity that I cannot doubt but that you would go to them even before your daughter, and would emancipate yourself from God's first decree of the Law to put yourself under His second dispensation of the Gospel. You would count as nothing your desire for other offspring and would offer up yourself to the service of God. But because "there is a time to embrace, and a time to refrain from embracing," and because "the wife hath not power of her own body," and because the apostle says "Let every man abide in the same calling wherein he was called" in the Lord, and because he that is under the yoke ought so to run as not to leave his companion in the mire, I counsel you to pay back to the full in your offspring what meantime you defer paying in your own person. When Hannah had once offered in the tabernacle the son whom she had vowed to God she never took him back; for she thought it unbecoming that one who was to be a prophet should grow up in the same house with her who still desired to have other children. Accordingly after she had conceived him and given him birth, she did not venture to come to the temple alone or to appear before the Lord empty, but first paid to Him what she owed; and then, when she had offered up that great sacrifice, she returned home and because she had borne her firstborn for God, she was given five children for herself. Do you marvel at the happiness of that holy woman? Imitate her faith. Moreover, if you will only send Paula, I promise to be myself both a tutor and a fosterfather to her. Old as I am I will carry her on my shoulders and train her stammering lips; and my charge will be a far grander one than that of the worldly philosopher; for while he only taught a King of Macedon who was one day to die of Babylonian poison, I shall instruct the handmaid and spouse of Christ who must one day be offered to her Lord in heaven.

71

THE LIFE OF PAULA, LEADER IN WOMEN'S EARLY MONASTICISM

Letter 108, Jerome to Eustochium   404 C.E.

1. If all the members of my body were to be converted into tongues, and if each of my limbs were to be gifted with a human voice, I could still do no justice to the virtues of the holy and venerable Paula. Noble in family, she was nobler still in holiness; rich formerly in this world's goods, she is now more distinguished by the poverty that she has embraced for Christ. Of the stock of the Gracchi and descended from the Scipios, the heir and representative of that Paulus whose name she bore, the true and legitimate daughter of that Martia Papyria who was mother to Africanus, she yet preferred Bethlehem to Rome, and left her palace glittering with gold to dwell in a mud cabin. We do not grieve that we have lost this perfect woman; rather we thank God that we have had her, nay that we have her still. For "all live unto" God, and they who return unto the Lord are still to be reckoned members of his family. We have lost her, it is true, but the heavenly mansions have gained her; for as long as she was in the body she was absent from the Lord and would constantly complain with tears:—"Woe is me that I sojourn in Mesech, that I dwell in the tents of Kedar; my soul hath been this long time a pilgrim." It was no wonder that she sobbed out that even she was in darkness (for this is the meaning of the word Kedar) seeing that, according to the apostle, "the world lieth in the evil one;" and that, "as its darkness is, so is its light;" and that "the light shineth in darkness and the darkness comprehended it not." She would frequently exclaim: "I am a stranger with thee and a sojourner as all my fathers were," and again, I desire "to depart and to be with Christ." As often too as she was troubled with bodily weakness (brought on by incredible abstinence and by redoubled fastings), she would be heard to say: "I keep under my body and bring it into subjection; lest that by any means, when I have preached to others, I myself should be a castaway;" and "It is good neither to eat flesh nor to drink wine;" and "I humbled my soul with fasting;" and "thou wilt make all" my "bed in" my "sickness;" and "Thy hand was heavy upon me: my moisture is turned into the drought of summer." And when the pain which she bore with such wonderful patience darted through her, as if she saw the heavens

opened she would say: "Oh that I had wings like a dove! for then would I fly away and be at rest."

2. I call Jesus and his saints, yes and the particular angel who was the guardian and the companion of this admirable woman to bear witness that these are no words of adulation and flattery but sworn testimony every one of them borne to her character. They are, indeed, inadequate to the virtues of one whose praises are sung by the whole world, who is admired by bishops, regretted by bands of virgins, and wept for by crowds of monks and poor. Would you know all her virtues, reader, in short? She has left those dependent on her poor, but not so poor as she was herself. In dealing thus with her relatives and the men and women of her small household—her brothers and sisters rather than her servants—she has done nothing strange: for she has left her daughter Eustochium—a virgin consecrated to Christ for whose comfort this sketch is made—far from her noble family and rich only in faith and grace.

3. Let me then begin my narrative. Others may go back a long way even to Paula's cradle and, if I may say so, to her swaddling-clothes, and may speak of her mother Blaesilla and her father Rogatus. Of these the former was a descendant of the Scipios and the Gracchi; whilst the latter came of a line distinguished in Greece down to the present day. He was said, indeed, to have in his veins the blood of Agamemnon who destroyed Troy after a ten years' siege. But I shall praise only what belongs to herself, what wells forth from the pure spring of her holy mind. When in the gospel the apostles ask their Lord and Saviour what He will give to those who have left all for His sake, He tells them that they shall receive an hundredfold now in this time and in the world to come eternal life. From which we see that it is not the possession of riches that is praiseworthy but the rejection of them for Christ's sake; that, instead of glorying in our privileges, we should make them of small account as compared with God's faith. Truly the Saviour has now in this present time made good His promise to His servants and handmaidens. For one who despised the glory of a single city is to-day famous throughout the world; and one who while she lived at Rome was known by no one outside it has by hiding herself at Bethlehem become the admiration of all lands Roman and barbarian. For what race of men is there which does not send pilgrims to the holy places? And who could there find a greater marvel than Paula? As among many jewels the most precious shines most brightly, and as the sun with its beams obscures and puts out the paler fires of the stars; so by her lowliness she surpassed all others in virtue and influence and, while she was least among all, was greater than all. The more she cast herself down, the more she was lifted up by Christ. She was hidden and yet she was not hidden. By shunning glory she earned glory; for glory follows virtue as its shadow; and deserting those who seek it, it seeks those who despise it. But I must not neglect to proceed with my narrative or dwell too long on a single point forgetful of the rules of writing.

4. Being then of such parentage, Paula married Toxotius in whose veins ran the noble blood of Aeneas and the Julii. Accordingly his daughter, Christ's virgin Eustochium, is called Julia, as he Julius.

A name from great Iulus handed down.

I speak of these things not as of importance to those who have them, but as worthy of remark in those who despise them. Men of the world look up to persons who are rich in such privileges. We on the other hand praise those who for the Saviour's sake despise them; and strangely depreciating all who keep them, we eulogize those who are unwilling to do so. Thus nobly born, Paula through her fruitfulness and her chastity won approval from all, from her husband first, then from her relatives, and lastly from the whole city. She bore five children; Blaesilla, for whose death I consoled her while at Rome; Paulina, who has left the reverend and admirable Pammachius to inherit both her vows and property, to whom also I addressed a little book on her death; Eustochium, who is now in the holy places, a precious necklace of virginity and of the church; Rufina, whose untimely end overcame the affectionate heart of her mother; and Toxotius, after whom she had no more children. You can thus see that it was not her wish to fulfil a wife's duty, but that she only complied with her husband's longing to have male offspring.

5. When he died, her grief was so great that she nearly died herself: yet so completely did she then give herself to the service of the Lord, that it might have seemed that she had desired his death.

In what terms shall I speak of her distinguished, and noble, and formerly wealthy house; all the riches of which she spent upon the poor? How can I describe the great consideration she shewed to all and her far reaching kindness even to those whom she had never seen? What poor man, as he lay dying, was not wrapped in blankets given by her? What bedridden person was not supported with money from her purse? She would seek out such with the greatest diligence throughout the city, and would think it a misfortune were any hungry or sick person to be supported by another's food. So lavish was her charity that she robbed her children; and, when her relatives remonstrated with her for doing so, she declared that she was leaving to them a better inheritance in the mercy of Christ.

6. Nor was she long able to endure the visits and crowded receptions, which her high position in the world and her exalted family entailed upon her. She received the homage paid to her sadly, and made all the speed she could to shun and to escape those who wished to pay her compliments. It so happened that at that time the bishops of the East and West had been summoned to Rome by letter from the emperors to deal with certain dissensions between the churches, and in this way she saw two most admirable men and Christian prelates, Paulinus bishop of Antioch and Epiphanius, bishop of Salamis or, as it is now called, Constantia, in Cyprus. Epiphanius, indeed, she received as her guest; and, although Paulinus was staying in another person's house, in the warmth of her heart she treated him as if he too were lodged with her. Inflamed by their virtues she thought more and more each moment of forsaking her home. Disregarding her house, her children, her servants, her property, and in a word everything connected with the world, she was eager—alone and unaccompanied (if ever it could be said that she was so)—to go to the desert made famous by its Pauls and by its Antonies. And at last when the winter was over and the sea was open, and when the bishops were returning to their churches, she also sailed with them in her prayers and desires. Not to prolong the story, she went down to Portus accompanied by her brother, her kinsfolk and above all her own children eager by their demonstrations of affection to overcome their loving mother. At last the sails were set and the strokes of the rowers carried the vessel into the deep. On the shore the little Toxotius stretched forth his hands in entreaty, while Rufina, now grown up, with silent sobs besought her mother to wait till she should be married. But still Paula's eyes were dry as she turned them heavenwards; and she overcame her love for her children by her love for God. She knew herself no more as a mother, that she might approve herself a handmaid of Christ. Yet her heart was rent within her, and she wrestled with her grief, as though she were being forcibly separated from parts of herself. The greatness of the affection she had to overcome made all admire her victory the more. Among the cruel hardships which attend prisoners of war in the hands of their enemies, there is none severer than the separation of parents from their children. Though it is against the laws of nature, she endured this trial with unabated faith; nay more she sought it with a joyful heart: and overcoming her love for her children by her greater love for God, she concentrated herself quietly upon Eustochium alone, the partner alike of her vows and of her voyage. Meantime the vessel ploughed onwards and all her fellow-passengers looked back to the shore. But she turned away her eyes that she might not see what she could not behold without agony. No mother, it must be confessed, ever loved her children so dearly. Before setting out she gave them all that she had, disinheriting herself upon earth that she might find an inheritance in heaven.

7. The vessel touched at the island of Pontia ennobled long since as the place of exile of the illustrious lady Flavia Domitilla who under the Emperor Domitian was banished because she confessed herself a Christian; and Paula, when she saw the cells in which this lady passed the period of her long martyrdom, taking to herself the wings of faith, more than ever desired to see Jerusalem and the holy places. The strongest winds seemed weak and the greatest speed slow. After passing between Scylla and Charybdis she committed herself to the Adriatic sea and had a calm passage to Methone. Stopping here for a short time to recruit her wearied frame

> She stretched her dripping limbs upon the shore:
> Then sailed past Malea and Cythera's isle,
> The scattered Cyclades, and all the lands
> That narrow in the seas on every side.

Then leaving Rhodes and Lycia behind her, she at last came in sight of Cyprus, where falling at the feet of the holy and venerable Epiphanius, she was by him detained ten days; though this was not, as he supposed, to restore her strength but, as the facts prove, that she might do God's work. For she visited all the monasteries in the island, and left, so far as her means allowed, substantial relief for the brothers in them whom love of the holy man had brought thither from all parts of the world. Then crossing the narrow sea she landed at Seleucia, and going up thence to Antioch allowed herself to be detained for a little time by the affection of the reverend confessor Paulinus. Then, such was the ardour of her faith that she, a noble lady who had always previously been carried by eunuchs, went her way—and that in mid-winter—riding upon an ass.

8. I say nothing to her journey through Coele-Syria and Phoenicia

(for it is not my purpose to give you a complete itinerary of her wanderings); I shall only name such places as are mentioned in the sacred books. After leaving the Roman colony of Berytus and the ancient city of Zidon she entered Elijah's town on the shore at Zarephath and therein adored her Lord and Saviour. Next passing over the sands of Tyre on which Paul had once knelt she came to Acco or, as it is now called, Ptolemais, rode over the plains of Megiddo which had once witnessed the slaying of Josiah, and entered the land of the Philistines. Here she could not fail to admire the ruins of Dor, once a most powerful city; and Strato's Tower, which though at one time insignificant was rebuilt by Herod king of Judaea and named Caesarea in honour of Caesar Augustus. Here she saw the house of Cornelius now turned into a Christian church; and the humble abode of Philip; and the chambers of his daughters the four virgins "which did prophesy." She arrived next at Antipatris, a small town half in ruins, named by Herod after his father Antipater, and at Lydda, now become Diospolis, a place made famous by the raising again of Dorcas and the restoration to health of Aeneas. Not far from this are Arimathaea, the village of Joseph who buried the Lord, and Nob, once a city of priests but now the tomb in which their slain bodies rest. Joppa too is hard by, the port of Jonah's flight: which also—if I may introduce a poetic fable—saw Andromeda bound to the rock. Again resuming her journey, she came to Nicopolis, once called Emmaus, where the Lord became known in the breaking of bread; an action by which He dedicated the house of Cleopas as a church. Starting thence she made her way up lower and higher Bethhoron, cities founded by Solomon but subsequently destroyed by several devastating wars; seeing on her right Ajalon and Gibeon where Joshua the son of Nun when fighting against the five kings gave commandments to the sun and moon, where also he condemned the Gibeonites (who by a crafty stratagem had obtained a treaty) to be hewers of wood and drawers of water. At Gibeah also, now a complete ruin, she stopped for a little while remembering its sin, and the cutting of the concubine into pieces, and how in spite of all this three hundred men of the tribe of Benjamin were saved that in after days Paul might be called a Benjamite.

9. To make a long story short, leaving on her left the mausoleum of Helena queen of Abiabene who in time of famine had sent corn to the Jewish people, Paula entered Jerusalem, Jebus, or Salem, that city of three names which after it had sunk to ashes and decay was by Aelius Hadrianus restored once more as Aelia. And although the proconsul of Palestine, who was an intimate friend of her house, sent forward his apparitors and gave orders to have his official residence placed at her disposal, she chose a humble cell in preference to it. Moreover, in visiting the holy places so great was the passion and the enthusiasm she exhibited for each, that she could never have torn herself away from one had she not been eager to visit the rest. Before the Cross she threw herself down in adoration as though she beheld the Lord hanging upon it: and when she entered the tomb which was the scene of the Resurrection she kissed the stone which the angel had rolled away from the door of the sepulchre. Indeed so ardent was her faith that she even licked with her mouth the very spot on which the Lord's body had lain, like one athirst for the river which he has longed for. What tears she shed there, what groans she uttered, and what grief she poured forth, all Jerusalem knows; the Lord also to whom she prayed knows. Going out thence she made the ascent of Zion; a name which signifies either "citadel" or "watch-tower." This formed the city which David formerly stormed and afterwards rebuilt. Of its storming it is written, "Woe to Ariel, to Ariel"—that is, God's lion, (and indeed in those days it was extremely strong)—"the city which David stormed:" and of its rebuilding it is said, "His foundation is in the holy mountains: the Lord loveth the gates of Zion more than all the dwellings of Jacob." He does not mean the gates which we see to-day in dust and ashes; the gates he means are those against which hell prevails not and through which the multitude of those who believe in Christ enter in. There was shewn to her upholding the portico of a church the bloodstained column to which our Lord is said to have been bound when He suffered His scourging. There was shewn to her also the spot where the Holy Spirit came down upon the souls of the one hundred and twenty believers, thus fulfilling the prophecy of Joel.

10. Then, after distributing money to the poor and her fellow-servants so far as her means allowed, she proceeded to Bethlehem stopping only on the right side of the road to visit Rachel's tomb. (Here it was that she gave birth to her son destined to be not what his dying mother called him, Benoni, that is the "Son of my pangs" but as his father in the spirit prophetically named him Benjamin, that is "the Son of the right hand.") After this she came to Bethlehem and entered into the cave where the Saviour was born. Here, when she looked upon the inn made sacred by the virgin and the stall where the ox knew his owner and the ass his master's crib, and where the words of the same prophet had been fulfilled "Blessed is he that soweth beside the waters where the ox and the ass trample the seed under their feet:" when she looked upon these things I say, she protested in my hearing that she could behold with the eyes of faith the infant Lord wrapped in swaddling clothes and crying in the manger, the wise men worshipping Him, the star shining overhead, the virgin mother, the attentive foster-father, the shepherds coming by night to see "the word that was come to pass" and thus even then to consecrate those opening phrases of the evangelist John "In the beginning was the word" and "the word was made flesh." She declared that she could see the slaughtered innocents, the raging Herod, Joseph and Mary fleeing into Egypt; and with a mixture of tears and joy she cried: 'Hail Bethlehem, house of bread, wherein was born that Bread that came down from heaven. Hail Ephratah, land of fruitfulness and of fertility, whose fruit is the Lord Himself. Concerning thee has Micah prophesied of old, "Thou Bethlehem Ephratah art not the least among the thousands of Judah, for out of thee shall he come forth unto me that is to be ruler in Israel; whose goings forth have been from of old, from everlasting. Therefore wilt thou give them up, until the time that she which travaileth hath brought forth: then the remnant of his brethren shall return unto the children of Israel." For in thee was born the prince begotten before Lucifer. Whose birth from the Father is before all time: and the cradle of David's race continued in thee, until the virgin brought forth her son and the remnant of the people that believed in Christ returned unto the children of Israel and preached freely to them in words like these: "It was necessary that the word of God should first have been spoken to you; but seeing ye put it from you and judge yourselves unworthy of everlasting life, lo, we turn to the Gentiles." For the Lord hath said: "I am not sent but unto the lost sheep of the house of Israel." At that time also the words of Jacob were fulfilled concerning Him, "A prince shall not depart from Judah nor a lawgiver from between his feet, until He come for whom it is laid up, and He shall be for the expectation of the nations." Well did David swear, well did he make a vow saying: "Surely I will not come into the tabernacle of my house nor go up into my bed: I will not give sleep to mine eyes, or slumber to my eyelids, or rest to the temples of my head, until I find out a place for the Lord, an habitation for the . . . God of Jacob." And immediately he explained the object of his desire, seeing with prophetic eyes that He would come whom we now believe to have come. "Lo we heard of Him at Ephratah: we found Him in the fields of the wood." The Hebrew word *Zo* as I have learned from your lessons means not *her,* that is Mary the Lord's mother, but *him* that is the Lord Himself. Therefore he says boldly: "We will go into His tabernacle: we will worship at His footstool." I too, miserable sinner though I am, have been accounted worthy to kiss the manger in which the Lord cried as a babe, and to pray in the cave in which the travailing virgin gave birth to the infant Lord. "This is my rest" for it is my Lord's native place; "here will I dwell" for this spot has my Saviour chosen. "I have prepared a lamp for my Christ" "My soul shall live unto Him and my seed shall serve him."'

After this Paula went a short distance down the hill to the tower of Edar, that is 'of the flock,' near which Jacob fed his flocks, and where the shepherds keeping watch by night were privileged to hear the words: "Glory to God in the highest and on earth peace, good-will toward men." While they were keeping their sheep they found the Lamb of God; whose fleece bright and clean was made wet with the dew of heaven when it was dry upon all the earth beside, and whose blood when sprinkled on the doorposts drove off the destroyer of Egypt and took away the sins of the world.

11. Then immediately quickening her pace she began to move along the old road which leads to Gaza, that is to the 'power' or 'wealth' of God, silently meditating on that type of the Gentiles, the Ethiopian eunuch, who in spite of the prophet changed his skin and whilst he read the old testament found the fountain of the gospel. Next turning to the right she passed from Bethzur to Eshcol which means "a cluster of grapes." It was hence that the spies brought back that marvellous cluster which was the proof of the fertility of the land and a type of Him who says of Himself: "I have trodden the wine press alone; and of the people there was none with me." Shortly afterwards she entered the home of Sarah and beheld the birthplace of Isaac and the traces of Abraham's oak under which he saw Christ's day and was glad. And rising up from thence she went up to Hebron, that is Kirjath-Arba, or the City of the Four Men. These are Abraham, Isaac, Jacob, and the great Adam whom the Hebrews suppose (from the book of Joshua the son of Nun) to be buried there. But many are of opinion that Caleb is the fourth and a monument at one side is pointed out as his. After seeing these places she did not care to go on to Kirjath-sepher, that is "the village of letters;" because despising the letter that killeth she had found the spirit that giveth life. She admired more the upper springs and the nether springs which Othniel the son of Kenaz the son of Jephunneh received in place of a south land and a waterless possession, and by the conducting of which he watered the dry fields of the old covenant. For thus did he typify the redemption which the sinner finds for his old sins in the waters of baptism. On the next day soon after sunrise she stood upon the brow of Caphar-barucha, that is, "the house of blessing," the point to which Abraham pursued the Lord when he made intercession with Him. And here, as she looked down upon the wide solitude and upon the country once belonging to Sodom and Gomorrah, to Admah and Zeboim, she beheld the balsam vines of Engedi and Zoar. By Zoar I mean that "heifer of three years old" which was formerly called Bela and in Syriac is rendered Zoar that is 'little.' She called to mind the cave in which Lot found refuge, and with tears in her eyes warned the virgins her companions to beware of "wine wherein is excess;" for it was to this that the Moabites and Ammonites owe their origin.

12. I linger long in the land of the midday sun for it was there and then that the spouse found her bridegroom at rest and Joseph drank wine with his brothers once more. I will return to Jerusalem and, passing through Tekoa the home of Amos, I will look upon the glistening cross of Mount Olivet from which the Saviour made His ascension to the Father. Here year by year a red heifer was burned as a holocaust to the Lord and its ashes were used to purify the children of Israel. Here also according to Ezekiel the Cherubim after leaving the temple founded the church of the Lord.

After this Paula visited the tomb of Lazarus and beheld the hospitable roof of Mary and Martha, as well as Bethphage, 'the town of the priestly jaws.' Here it was that a restive foal typical of the Gentiles received the bridle of God, and covered with the garments of the apostles offered its lowly back for Him to sit on. From this she went straight on down the hill to Jericho thinking of the wounded man in the gospel, of the savagery of the priests and Levites who passed him by, and of the kindness of the Samaritan, that is, the guardian, who placed the half-dead man upon his own beast and brought him down to the inn of the church. She noticed the place called Adomim or the Place of Blood, so-called because much blood was shed there in the frequent incursions of marauders. She beheld also the sycamore tree of Zacchaeus, by which is signified the good works of repentance whereby he trod under foot his former sins of bloodshed and rapine, and from which he saw the Most High as from a pinnacle of virtue. She was shewn too the spot by the wayside where the blind men sat who, receiving their sight from the Lord, became types of the two peoples who should believe upon Him. Then entering Jericho she saw the city which Hiel founded in Abiram his firstborn and of which he set up the gates in his youngest son Segub. She looked upon the camp of Gilgal and the hill of the foreskins suggestive of the mystery of the second circumcision; and she gazed at the twelve stones brought thither out of the bed of Jordan to be symbols of those twelve foundations on which are written the names of the twelve apostles. She saw also that fountain of the Law most bitter and barren which the true Elisha healed by his wisdom changing it into a well sweet and fertilising. Scarcely had the night passed away when burning with eagerness she hastened to the Jordan, stood by the brink of the river, and as the sun rose recalled to mind the rising of the sun of righteousness; how the priest's feet stood firm in the middle of the riverbed; how afterwards at the command of Elijah and Elisha the waters were divided hither and thither and made way for them to pass; and again how the Lord had cleansed by His baptism waters which the deluge had polluted and the destruction of mankind had defiled.

13. It would be tedious were I to tell of the valley of Achor, that is, of 'trouble and crowds,' where theft and covetousness were condemned; and of Bethel, 'the house of God,' where Jacob poor and destitute slept upon the bare ground. Here it was that, having set beneath his head a stone which in Zechariah is described as having seven eyes and in Isaiah is spoken of as a corner-stone, he beheld a ladder reaching up to heaven; yes, and the Lord standing high above it holding out His hand to such as were ascending and hurling from on high such as were careless. Also when she was in Mount Ephraim she made pilgrimages to the tombs of Joshua the son of Nun and of Eleazar the son of Aaron the priest, exactly opposite the one to the other; that of Joshua being built at Timnath-serah "on the north side of the hill of Gaash," and that of Eleazar "in a hill that pertained to Phinehas his son." She was somewhat surprised to find that he who had had the distribution of the land in his own hands had selected for himself portions uneven and rocky. What shall I say about Shiloh where a ruined altar is still shewn to-day, and where the tribe of Benjamin anticipated Romulus in the rape of the Sabine women? Passing by Shechem (not Sychar as many wrongly read) or as it is now called Neapolis, she entered the church built upon the side of Mount Gerizim around Jacob's well; that well where the Lord was sitting when hungry and thirsty He was refreshed by the faith of the woman of Samaria. Forsaking her five husbands by whom are in-

tended the five books of Moses, and that sixth not a husband of whom she boasted, to wit the false teacher Dositheus, she found the true Messiah and the true Saviour. Turning away thence Paula saw the tombs of the twelve patriarchs, and Samaria which in honour of Augustus Herod renamed Augusta or in Greek Sebaste. There lie the prophets Elisha and Obadiah and John the Baptist than whom there is not a greater among those that are born of women. And here she was filled with terror by the marvels she beheld; for she saw demons screaming under different tortures before the tombs of the saints, and men howling like wolves, baying like dogs, roaring like lions, hissing like serpents and bellowing like bulls. They twisted their heads and bent them backwards until they touched the ground; women too were suspended head downward and their clothes did not fall off. Paula pitied them all, and shedding tears over them prayed Christ to have mercy on them. And weak as she was she climbed the mountain on foot; for in two of its caves Obadiah in a time of persecution and famine had fed a hundred prophets with bread and water. Then she passed quickly through Nazareth the nursery of the Lord; Cana and Capernaum familiar with the signs wrought by Him; the lake of Tiberias sanctified by His voyages upon it; the wilderness where countless Gentiles were satisfied with a few loaves while the twelve baskets of the tribes of Israel were filled with the fragments left by them that had eaten. She made the ascent of mount Tabor whereon the Lord was transfigured. In the distance she beheld the range of Hermon; and the wide stretching plains of Galilee where Sisera and all his host had once been overcome by Barak; and the torrent Kishon separating the level ground into two parts. Hard by also the town of Nain was pointed out to her, where the widow's son was raised. Time would fail me sooner than speech were I to recount all the places to which the revered Paula was carried by her incredible faith.

14. I will now pass on to Egypt, pausing for a while on the way at Socoh, and at Samson's well which he clave in the hollow place that was in the jaw. Here I will lave my parched lips and refresh myself before visiting Moresbeth; in old days famed for the tomb of the prophet Micah, and now for its church. Then skirting the country of the Horites and Gittites, Mareshah, Edom, and Lachish, and traversing the lonely wastes of the desert where the tracks of the traveller are lost in the yielding sand, I will come to the river of Egypt called Sihor, that is "the muddy river," and go through the five cities of

Egypt which speak the language of Canaan, and through the land of Goshen and the plains of Zoan on which God wrought his marvellous works. And I will visit the city of No, which has since become Alexandria; and Nitria, the town of the Lord, where day by day the filth of multitudes is washed away with the pure nitre of virtue. No sooner did Paula come in sight of it than there came to meet her the reverend and estimable bishop, the confessor Isidore, accompanied by countless multitudes of monks many of whom were of priestly or of Levitical rank. On seeing these Paula rejoiced to behold the Lord's glory manifested in them; but protested that she had no claim to be received with such honour. Need I speak of the Macarii, Arsenius, Serapion, or other pillars of Christ! Was there any cell that she did not enter? Or any man at whose feet she did not throw herself? In each of His saints she believed that she saw Christ Himself; and whatever she bestowed upon them she rejoiced to feel that she had bestowed it upon the Lord. Her enthusiasm was wonderful and her endurance scarcely credible in a woman. Forgetful of her sex and of her weakness she even desired to make her abode, together with the girls who accompanied her, among these thousands of monks. And, as they were all willing to welcome her, she might perhaps have sought and obtained permission to do so; had she not been drawn away by still greater passion for the holy places. Coming by sea from Pelusium to Maioma on account of the great heat, she returned so rapidly that you would have thought her a bird. Not long afterwards, making up her mind to dwell permanently in holy Bethlehem, she took up her abode for three years in a miserable hostelry; till she could build the requisite cells and monastic buildings, to say nothing of a guest house for passing travellers where they might find the welcome which Mary and Joseph had missed. At this point I conclude my narrative of the journeys that she made accompanied by Eustochium and many other virgins.

15. I am now free to describe at greater length the virtue which was her peculiar charm; and in setting forth this I call God to witness that I am no flatterer. I add nothing. I exaggerate nothing. On the contrary I tone down much that I may not appear to relate incredibilities. My carping critics must not insinuate that I am drawing on my imagination or decking Paula, like Aesop's crow, with the fine feathers of other birds. Humility is the first of Christian graces, and hers was so pronounced that one who had never seen her, and who on account of her celebrity had desired to see her, would have believed that he saw not her but the lowest of her maids. When she was surrounded by companies of virgins she was always the least remarkable in dress, in speech, in gesture, and in gait. From the time that her husband died until she fell asleep herself she never sat at meat with a man, even though she might know him to stand upon the pinnacle of the episcopate. She never entered a bath except when dangerously ill. Even in the severest fever she rested not on an ordinary bed but on the hard ground covered only with a mat of goat's hair; if that can be called rest which made day and night alike a time of almost unbroken prayer. Well did she fulfil the words of the psalter: "All the night make I my bed to swim; I water my couch with my tears"! Her tears welled forth as it were from fountains, and she lamented her slightest faults as if they were sins of the deepest dye. Constantly did I warn her to spare her eyes and to keep them for the reading of the gospel; but she only said: 'I must disfigure that face which contrary to God's commandment I have painted with rouge, white lead, and antimony. I must mortify that body which has been given up to many pleasures. I must make up for my long laughter by constant weeping. I must exchange my soft linen and costly silks for rough goat's hair. I who have pleased my husband and the world in the past, desire now to please Christ.' Were I among her great and signal virtues to select her chastity as a subject of praise, my words would seem superfluous; for, even when she was still in the world, she set an example to all the matrons of Rome, and bore herself so admirably that the most slanderous never ventured to couple scandal with her name. No mind could be more considerate than hers, or none kinder towards the lowly. She did not court the powerful; at the same time, if the proud and the vainglorious sought her, she did not turn from them with disdain. If she saw a poor man, she supported him: and if she saw a rich one, she urged him to do good. Her liberality alone knew no bounds. Indeed, so anxious was she to turn no needy person away that she borrowed money at interest and often contracted new loans to pay off old ones. I was wrong, I admit; but when I saw her so profuse in giving, I reproved her alleging the apostle's words: "I mean not that other men be eased and ye burthened; but by an equality that now at this time your abundance may be a supply for their want, that their abundance also may be a supply for your want." I quoted from the gospel the Saviour's words: "he that hath two coats, let him impart one of them to him that hath none"; and I warned her that she might not always have means to do as she would wish. Other arguments I adduced to the same purpose; but with admirable modesty and brevity she overruled them all. "God is my witness," she said, "that what I do I do for His sake. My prayer is that I may die a beggar not leaving a penny to my daughter and indebted to strangers for my winding sheet." She then concluded with these words: "I, if I beg, shall find many to give to me; but if this beggar does not obtain help from me who by borrowing can give it to him, he will die; and if he dies, of whom will his soul be required?" I wished her to be more careful in managing her concerns, but she with a faith more glowing than mine clave to the Saviour with her whole heart and poor in spirit followed the Lord in His poverty, giving back to Him what she had received and becoming poor for His sake. She obtained her wish at last and died leaving her daughter overwhelmed with a mass of debt. This Eustochium still owes and indeed cannot hope to pay off by her own exertions; only the mercy of Christ can free her from it.

16. Many married ladies make it a habit to confer gifts upon their own trumpeters, and while they are extremely profuse to a few, withhold all help from the many. From this fault Paula was altogether free. She gave her money to each according as each had need, not ministering to self-indulgence but relieving want. No poor person went away from her empty handed. And all this she was enabled to do not by the greatness of her wealth but by her careful management of it. She constantly had on her lips such phrases as these: "Blessed are the merciful for they shall obtain mercy:" and "water will quench a flaming fire; and alms maketh an atonement for sins;" and "make to yourselves friends of the mammon of unrighteousness that . . . they may receive you into everlasting habitations;" and "give alms . . . and behold all things are clean unto you;" and Daniel's words to King Nebuchadnezzar in which he admonished him to redeem his sins by almsgiving. She wished to spend her money not upon these stones, that shall pass away with the earth and the world, but upon those living stones, which roll over the earth; of which in the apocalypse of John the city of the great king is built; of which also the scripture tells us that they shall be changed into sapphire and emerald and jasper and other gems.

17. But these qualities she may well share with a few others and the devil knows that it is not in these that the highest virtue consists. For, when Job has lost his substance and when his house and children have been destroyed, Satan says to the Lord: "Skin for skin, yea all that a man hath, will he give for his life. But put forth thine hand now and

touch his bone and his flesh, and he will curse thee to thy face." We know that many persons while they have given alms have yet given nothing which touches their bodily comfort; and while they have held out a helping hand to those in need are themselves overcome with sensual indulgences; they whitewash the outside but within they are "full of dead men's bones." Paula was not one of these. Her self-restraint was so great as to be almost immoderate; and her fasts and labours were so severe as almost to weaken her constitution. Except on feast days she would scarcely ever take oil with her food; a fact from which may be judged what she thought of wine, sauce, fish, honey, milk, eggs, and other things agreeable to the palate. Some persons believe that in taking these they are extremely frugal; and, even if they surfeit themselves with them, they still fancy their chastity safe.

18. Envy always follows in the track of virtue: as Horace says, it is ever the mountain top that is smitten by the lightning. It is not surprising that I declare this of men and women, when the jealousy of the Pharisees succeeded in crucifying our Lord Himself. All the saints have had illwishers, and even Paradise was not free from the serpent through whose malice death came into the world. So the Lord stirred up against Paula Hadad the Edomite to buffet her that she might not be exalted, and warned her frequently by the thorn in her flesh not to be elated by the greatness of her own virtues or to fancy that, compared with other women, she had attained the summit of perfection. For my part I used to say that it was best to give in to rancour and to retire before passion. So Jacob dealt with his brother Esau; so David met the unrelenting persecution of Saul. I reminded her how the first of these fled into Mesopotamia; and how the second surrendered himself to the Philistines, and chose to submit to foreign foes rather than to enemies at home. She however replied as follows:—'Your suggestion would be a wise one if the devil did not everywhere fight against God's servants and handmaidens, and did he not always precede the fugitives to their chosen refuges. Moreover, I am deterred from accepting it by my love for the holy places; and I cannot find another Bethlehem elsewhere. Why may I not by my patience conquer this ill will? Why may I not by my humility break down this pride, and when I am smitten on the one cheek offer to the smiter the other? Surely the apostle Paul says "Overcome evil with good." Did not the apostles glory when they suffered reproach for the Lord's sake? Did not even the Saviour humble Himself, taking the form of a servant and being made obedient to the Father unto death, even the death of the cross, that He might save us by His passion? If Job had not fought the battle and won the victory, he would never have received the crown of righteousness, or have heard the Lord say: "Thinkest thou that I have spoken unto thee for aught else than this, that thou mightest appear righteous." In the gospel those only are said to be blessed who suffer persecution for righteousness' sake. My conscience is at rest, and I know that it is not from any fault of mine that I am suffering; moreover affliction in this world is a ground for expecting a reward hereafter.' When the enemy was more than usually forward and ventured to reproach her to her face, she used to chant the words of the psalter: "While the wicked was before me, I was dumb with silence; I held my peace even from good:" and again, "I as a deaf man heard not; and I was as a dumb man that openeth not his mouth:" and "I was as a man that heareth not, and in whose mouth are no reproofs." When she felt herself tempted, she dwelt upon the words in Deuteronomy: "The Lord your God proveth you, to know whether ye love the Lord your God with all your heart and with all your soul." In tribulations and afflictions she turned to the splendid language of Isaiah: "Ye that are weaned from the milk and drawn from the breasts, look for tribulation upon tribulation, for hope also upon hope: yet a little while must these things be by reason of the malice of the lips and by reason of a spiteful tongue." This passage of scripture she explained for her own consolation as meaning that the weaned, that is, those who have come to full age, must endure tribulation upon tribulation that they may be accounted worthy to receive hope upon hope. She recalled to mind also the words of the apostle, "we glory in tribulations also: knowing that tribulation worketh patience, and patience experience, and experience hope: and hope maketh not ashamed" and "though our outward man perish, yet the inward man is renewed day by day": and "our light affliction which is but for a moment worketh in us an eternal weight of glory; while we look not at the things which are seen but at the things which are not seen: for the things which are seen are temporal but the things which are not seen are eternal." She used to say that, although to human impatience the time might seem slow in coming, yet that it would not be long but that presently help would come from God who says: "In an acceptable time have I heard thee, and in a day of salvation have I helped thee." We ought not, she declared, to dread the deceitful lips and tongues of the wicked, for we rejoice in the aid of the Lord who warns us by His prophet: "fear ye not the reproach of men, neither be ye afraid of their revilings; for the moth shall eat them up like a garment, and the worm shall eat them like wool": and she quoted His own words, "In your patience ye shall win your souls": as well as those of the apostle, "the sufferings of this present time are not worthy to be compared with the glory which shall be revealed in us": and in another place, "we are to suffer affliction" that we may be patient in all things that befall us, for "he that is slow to wrath is of great understanding: but he that is hasty of spirit exalteth folly."

19. In her frequent sicknesses and infirmities she used to say, "when I am weak, then am I strong:" "we have our treasure in earthen vessels" until "this corruptible shall have put on incorruption and this mortal shall have put on immortality" and again "as the sufferings of Christ abound in us, so our consolation also aboundeth by Christ:" and then "as ye are partakers of the sufferings, so shall ye be also of the consolation." In sorrow she used to sing: "Why art thou cast down, O my soul? and why art thou disquieted within me? hope thou in God for I shall yet praise him who is the health of my countenance and my God." In the hour of danger she used to say: "If any man will come after me, let him deny himself and take up his cross and follow me:" and again "whosoever will save his life shall lose it," and "whosoever will lose his life for my sake the same shall save it." When the exhaustion of her substance and the ruin of her property were announced to her she only said: "What is a man profited, if he shall gain the whole world and lose his own soul? or what shall a man give in exchange for his soul:" and "naked came I out of my mother's womb, and naked shall I return thither. The Lord gave, and the Lord hath taken away: blessed be the name of the Lord:" and Saint John's words, "Love not the world neither the things that are in the world. For all that is in the world, the lust of the flesh, and the lust of the eyes and the pride of life, is not of the Father but is of the world. And the world passeth away and the lust thereof." I know that when word was sent to her of the serious illnesses of her children and particularly of Toxotius whom she dearly loved, she first by her self-control fulfilled the saying: "I was troubled and I did not speak," and then cried out in the words of scripture, "He that loveth son or daughter more than me is not worthy of me." And she prayed to the Lord and said: Lord "preserve thou the children of those that are appointed to die," that is, of those who for thy sake every day die bodily. I am aware that a talebearer—a class of persons who do a great deal of harm—once told her as a kindness that owing to her great fervour in virtue some people thought her mad and declared that something should be done for her head. She replied in the words of the apostle, "we are made a spectacle unto the world and to angels and to men," and "we are fools for Christ's sake" but "the foolishness of God is wiser than men." It is for this reason she said that even the Saviour says to the Father, "Thou knowest my foolishness," and again "I am as a wonder unto many, but thou are my strong refuge." "I was as a beast before thee; nevertheless I am continually with thee." In the gospel we read that even His kinsfolk desired to bind Him as one of weak mind. His opponents also reviled him saying "thou art a Samaritan and hast a devil," and another time "he casteth out devils through Beelzebub the chief of the devils." But let us, she continued, listen to the exhortation of the apostle, "Our rejoicing is this, the testimony of our conscience that in simplicity and sincerity . . . by the grace of God we have had our conversation in the world." And let us hear the Lord when He says to His apostles, "If ye were of the world the world would love his own; but because ye are not of the world . . . therefore the world hateth you." And then she turned to the Lord Himself, saying, "Thou knowest the secrets of the heart," and "all this is come upon us; yet have we not forgotten thee, neither have we dealt falsely in thy covenant; our heart is not turned back." "Yea for thy sake are we killed all the day long; we are counted as sheep for the slaughter." But "the Lord is on my side: I will not fear what man doeth unto me." She had read the words of Solomon, "My son, honour the Lord and thou shalt be made strong; and beside the Lord fear thou no man." These passages and others like them she used as God's armour against the assaults of wickedness, and particularly to defend herself against the furious onslaughts of envy; and thus by patiently enduring wrongs she soothed the violence of the most savage breasts. Down to the very day of her death two things were conspicuous in her life, one her great patience and the other the jealousy which was manifested towards her. Now jealousy gnaws the heart of him who harbours it: and while it strives to injure its rival raves with all the force of its fury against itself.

20. I shall now describe the order of her monastery and the method by which she turned the continence of saintly souls to her own profit. She sowed carnal things that she might reap spiritual things; she gave earthly things that she might receive heavenly things; she forewent things temporal that she might in their stead obtain things eternal.

Besides establishing a monastery for men, the charge of which she left to men, she divided into three companies and monasteries the numerous virgins whom she had gathered out of different provinces, some of whom are of noble birth while others belonged to the middle or lower classes. But, although they worked and had their meals separately from each other, these three companies met together for psalm-singing and prayer. After the chanting of the Alleluia—the signal by which they were summoned to the Collect—no one was permitted to remain behind. But either first or among the first Paula used to await the arrival of the rest, urging them to diligence rather by her own modest example than by motives of fear. At dawn, at the third, sixth, and ninth hours, at evening, and at midnight they recited the psalter each in turn. No sister was allowed to be ignorant of the psalms, and all had every day to learn a certain portion of the holy scriptures. On the Lord's day only they proceeded to the church beside which they lived, each company following its own mother-superior. Returning home in the same order, they then devoted themselves to their allotted tasks, and made garments either for themselves or else for others. If a virgin was of noble birth, she was not allowed to have an attendant belonging to her own household lest her maid having her mind full of the doings of the old days and of the license of childhood might by constant converse open old wounds and renew former errors. All the sisters were clothed alike. Linen was not used except for drying the hands. So strictly did Paula separate them from men that she would not allow even eunuchs to approach them; lest she should give occasion to slanderous tongues (always ready to cavil at the religious) to console themselves for their own misdoing. When a sister was backward in coming to the recitation of the psalms or shewed herself remiss in her work, Paula used to approach her in different ways. Was she quick-tempered? Paula coaxed her. Was she phlegmatic? Paula chid her, copying the example of the apostle who said: "What will ye? Shall I come to you with a rod or in love and in the spirit of meekness?" Apart from food and raiment she allowed no one to have anything she could call her own, for Paul had said, "Having food and raiment let us be therewith content." She was afraid lest the custom of having more should breed covetousness in them; an appetite which no wealth can satisfy, for the more it has the more it requires, and neither opulence nor indigence is able to diminish it. When the sisters quarrelled one with another she reconciled them with soothing words. If the younger ones were troubled with fleshly desires, she broke their force by imposing redoubled fasts; for she wished her virgins to be ill in body rather than to suffer in soul. If she chanced to notice any sister too attentive to her dress, she reproved her for her error with knitted brows and severe looks, saying; "a clean body and a clean dress mean an unclean soul. A virgin's lips should never utter an improper or an impure word, for such indicate a lascivious mind and by the outward man the faults of the inward are made manifest." When she saw a sister verbose and talkative or forward and taking pleasure in quarrels, and when she found after frequent admonitions that the offender shewed no signs of improvement; she placed her among the lowest of the sisters and outside their society, ordering her to pray at the door of the refectory instead of with the rest, and commanding her to take her food by herself, in the hope that where rebuke had failed shame might bring about a reformation. The sin of theft she loathed as if it were sacrilege; and that which among men of the world is counted little or nothing she declared to be in a monastery a crime of the deepest dye. How shall I describe her kindness and attention towards the sick or the wonderful care and devotion with which she nursed them? Yet, although when others were sick she freely gave them every indulgence, and even allowed them to eat meat; when she fell ill herself, she made no concessions to her own weakness, and seemed unfairly to change in her own case to harshness the kindness which she was always ready to shew to others.

21. No young girl of sound and vigorous constitution could have delivered herself up to a regimen so rigid as that imposed upon herself by Paula whose physical powers age had impaired and enfeebled. I admit that in this she was too determined, refusing to spare herself or to listen to advice. I will relate what I know to be a fact. In the extreme heat of the month of July she was once attacked by a violent fever and we despaired of her life. However by God's mercy she rallied, and the doctors urged upon her the necessity of taking a little light wine to accelerate her recovery; saying that if she continued to drink water they feared that she might become dropsical. I on my side secretly appealed to the blessed pope Epiphanius to admonish, nay even to compel her, to take the wine. But she with her usual sagacity and quickness at once perceived the stratagem, and with a smile let him see that the advice he was giving her was after all not his but mine. Not to waste more words, the blessed prelate after many exhortations left her chamber; and, when I asked him what he had accomplished, replied, "Only this that old as I am I have been almost persuaded to drink no more wine." I relate this story not because I approve of persons rashly taking upon themselves burthens beyond their strength (for does not the scripture say: "Burden not thyself above thy power"?) but because I wish from this quality of perseverance in her to shew the passion of her mind and the yearning of her believing soul; both of which made her sing in David's words, "My soul thirsteth for thee, my flesh longeth after thee." Difficult as it is always to avoid extremes, the philosophers are quite right in their opinion that virtue is a mean and vice an excess, or as we may express it in one short sentence "In nothing too much." While thus unyielding in her contempt for food Paula was easily moved to sorrow and felt crushed by the deaths of her kinsfolk, especially those of her children. When one after another her husband and her daughters fell asleep, on each occasion the shock of their loss endangered her life. And although she signed her mouth and her breast with the sign of the cross, and endeavoured thus to alleviate a mother's grief; her feelings overpowered her and her maternal instincts were too much for her confiding mind. Thus while her intellect retained its mastery she was overcome by sheer physical weakness. On one occasion a sickness seized her and clung to her so long that it brought anxiety to us and danger to herself. Yet even then she was full of joy and repeated every moment the apostle's words: "O wretched man that I am! who shall deliver me from the body of this death?" The careful reader may say that my words are an invective rather than an eulogy. I call that Jesus whom she served and whom I desire to serve to be my witness that so far from unduly eulogizing her or depreciating her I tell the truth about her as one Christian writing of another; that I am writing a memoir and not a panegyric, and that what were faults in her might well be virtues in others less saintly. I speak thus of her faults to satisfy my own feelings and the passionate regret of us her brothers and sisters, who all of us love her still and all of us deplore her loss.

22. However, she has finished her course, she has kept the faith, and now she enjoys the crown of righteousness. She follows the Lamb whithersoever he goes. She is filled now because once she was hungry. With joy does she sing: "as we have heard, so have we seen in the city of the Lord of hosts, in the city of our God." O blessed change! Once she wept but now laughs for evermore. Once she despised the broken cisterns of which the prophet speaks; but now she has found in the Lord a fountain of life. Once she wore haircloth but now she is

clothed in white raiment, and can say: "thou hast put off my sack-cloth, and girded me with gladness." Once she ate ashes like bread and mingled her drink with weeping; saying "my tears have been my meat day and night;" but now for all time she eats the bread of angels and sings: "O taste and see that the Lord is good;" and "my heart is overflowing with a goodly matter; I speak the things which I have made touching the king." She now sees fulfilled Isaiah's words, or rather those of the Lord speaking through Isaiah: "Behold, my servants shall eat but ye shall be hungry: behold, my servants shall drink but ye shall be thirsty: behold, my servants shall rejoice, but ye shall be ashamed: behold, my servants shall sing for joy of heart, but ye shall cry for sorrow of heart, and shall howl for vexation of spirit." I have said that she always shunned the broken cisterns: she did so that she might find in the Lord a fountain of life, and that she might rejoice and sing: "as the hart panteth after the waterbrooks, so pant-eth my soul after Thee, O God. When shall I come and appear before God?"

23. I must briefly mention the manner in which she avoided the foul cisterns of the heretics whom she regarded as no better than heathen. A certain cunning knave, in his own estimation both learned and clever, began without my knowledge to put to her such questions as these: What sin has an infant committed that it should be seized by the devil? Shall we be young or old when we rise again? If we die young and rise young, we shall after the resurrection require to have nurses. If however we die young and rise old, the dead will not rise again at all: they will be transformed into new beings. Will there be a distinction of sexes in the next world? Or will there be no such distinction? If the distinction continues, there will be wedlock and sexual intercourse and procreation of children. If however it does not continue, the bodies that rise again will not be the same. For, he argued, "the earthy tabernacle weigheth down the mind that museth upon many things," but the bodies that we shall have in heaven will be subtle and spiritual according to the words of the apostle: "it is sown a natural body: it is raised a spiritual body." From all of which considerations he sought to prove that rational creatures have been for their faults and previous sins subjected to bodily conditions; and that according to the nature and guilt of their transgression they are born in this or that state of life. Some, he said, rejoice in sound bodies and wealthy and noble parents; others have for their portion diseased frames and poverty stricken homes; and by imprisonment in the present world and in bodies pay the penalty of their former sins. Paula listened and reported what she heard to me, at the same time pointing out the man. Thus upon me was laid the task of opposing this most noxious viper and deadly pest. It is of such that the Psalmist speaks when he writes: "deliver not the soul of thy turtle dove unto the wild beast," and "Rebuke the wild beast of the reeds;" creatures who write iniquity and speak lies against the Lord and lift up their mouths against the Most High. As the fellow had tried to deceive Paula, I at her request went to him, and by asking him a few questions involved him in a dilemma. Do you believe, said I, that there will be a resurrection of the dead or do you disbelieve? He replied, I believe. I went on: Will the bodies that rise again be the same or different? He said, The same. Then I asked: What of their sex? Will that remain unaltered or will it be changed? At this question he became silent and swayed his head this way and that as a serpent does to avoid being struck. Accordingly I continued, As you have nothing to say I will answer for you and will draw the conclusion from your premises. If the woman shall not rise again as a woman nor the man as a man, there will be no resurrection of the dead. For the body is made up of sex and members. But if there shall be no sex and no members what will become of the resurrection of the body, which cannot exist without sex and members? And if there shall be no resurrection of the body, there can be no resurrection of the dead. But as to your objection taken from marriage, that, if the members shall remain the same, marriage must inevitably be allowed; it is disposed of by the Saviour's words: "ye do err not knowing the scriptures nor the power of God. For in the resurrection they neither marry nor are given in marriage but are as the angels." When it is said that they neither marry nor are given in marriage, the distinction of sex is shewn to persist. For no one says of things which have no capacity for marriage such as a stick or a stone that they neither marry nor are given in marriage; but this may well be said of those who while they can marry yet abstain from doing so by their own virtue and by the grace of Christ. But if you cavil at this and say, how shall we in that case be like the angels with whom there is neither male nor female, hear my answer in brief as follows. What the Lord promises to us is not the nature of angels but their mode of life and their bliss. And therefore John the Baptist is called an angel even before he is beheaded, and all God's holy men and virgins manifest in themselves even in this world the life of angels. When it is said "ye shall be like the angels," likeness only is promised and not a change of nature.

24. And now do you in your turn answer me these questions. How do you explain the fact that Thomas felt the hands of the risen Lord and beheld His side pierced by the spear? And the fact that Peter saw the Lord standing on the shore and eating a piece of a roasted fish and a honeycomb. If He stood, He must certainly have had feet. If He pointed to His wounded side He must have also had chest and belly for to these the sides are attached and without them they cannot be. If He spoke, He must have used a tongue and palate and teeth. For as the bow strikes the strings, so to produce vocal sound does the tongue come in contact with the teeth. If His hands were felt, it follows that He must have had arms as well. Since therefore it is admitted that He had all the members which go to make up the body, He must have also had the whole body formed of them, and that not a woman's but a man's; that is to say, He rose again in the sex in which He died. And if you cavil farther and say: We shall eat then, I suppose, after the resurrection; or How can a solid and material body enter in contrary to its nature through closed doors? you shall receive from me this reply. Do not for this matter of food find fault with belief in the resurrection: for our Lord after raising the daughter of the ruler of the synagogue commanded food to be given her. And Lazarus who had been dead four days is described as sitting at meat with Him, the object in both cases being to shew that the resurrection was real and not merely apparent. And if from our Lord's entering in through closed doors you strive to prove that His body was spiritual and aerial, He must have had this spiritual body even before He suffered; since—contrary to the nature of heavy bodies—He was able to walk upon the sea. The apostle Peter also must be believed to have had a spiritual body for he also walked upon the waters with buoyant step. The true explanation is that when anything is done against nature, it is a manifestation of God's might and power. And to shew plainly that in these great signs our attention is asked not to a change in nature but to the almighty power of God, he who by faith had walked on water began to sink for the want of it and would have done so, had not the Lord lifted him up with the reproving words, "O thou of little faith wherefore didst thou doubt?" I wonder that you can display such effrontery when the Lord Himself said, "reach hither thy finger, and behold my hands; and reach hither thy hand and thrust it into my side: and be not faithless but believing," and in another place, "behold my hands and my feet that it is I myself: handle me and see; for a spirit hath not flesh and bones as ye see me have. And when he had thus spoken he shewed them his hands and his feet." You hear Him speak of bones and flesh, of feet and hands; and yet you want to palm off on me the bubbles and airy nothings of which the stoics rave!

25. Moreover, if you ask how it is that a mere infant which has never sinned is seized by the devil, or at what age we shall rise again seeing that we die at different ages; my only answer—an unwelcome one, I fancy—will be in the words of scripture: "The judgments of God are a great deep," and "O the depth of the riches both of the wisdom and knowledge of God! how unsearchable are his judgments, and his ways past finding out! For who hath known the mind of the Lord? or who hath been his counsellor?" No difference of age can affect the reality of the body. Although our frames are in a perpetual flux and lose or gain daily, these changes do not make us different individuals. I was not one person at ten years old, another at thirty and another at fifty; nor am I another now when all my head is gray. According to the traditions of the church and the teaching of the apostle Paul, the answer must be this; that we shall rise as perfect men in the measure of the stature of the fulness of Christ. At this age the Jews suppose Adam to have been created and at this age we read that the Lord and Saviour rose again. Many other arguments did I adduce from both testaments to stifle the outcry of this heretic.

26. From that day forward so profoundly did Paula commence to loathe the man—and all who agreed with him in his doctrines—that she publicly proclaimed them as enemies of the Lord. I have related this incident less with the design of confuting in a few words a heresy which would require volumes to confute it, than with the object of shewing the great faith of this saintly woman who preferred to subject herself to perpetual hostility from men rather than by friendships hurtful to herself to provoke or to offend God.

27. To revert then to that description of her character which I began a little time ago; no mind was ever more docile than was hers. She was slow to speak and swift to hear, remembering the precept, "Keep silence and hearken, O Israel." The holy scriptures she knew by heart, and said of the history contained in them that it was the foundation of the truth; but, though she loved even this, she still preferred to seek for the underlying spiritual meaning and made this the keystone of the spiritual building raised within her soul. She asked leave that she and her daughter might read over the old and new testaments under my guidance. Out of modesty I at first refused compliance, but as she persisted in her demand and frequently urged me to consent to it, I at last did so and taught her what I had learned not from myself—for self-confidence is the worst of teachers—but from the church's most famous writers. Wherever I stuck fast and honestly confessed myself at fault she would by no means rest content but would force me by fresh questions to point out to her which of many different solutions seemed to me the most probable. I will mention here another fact which to those who are envious may well seem incredible. While I myself beginning as a young man have with much toil and effort partially acquired the Hebrew tongue and study it now unceasingly lest if I leave it, it also may leave me; Paula, on making up her mind that she too would learn it, succeeded so well that she could chant the psalms in Hebrew and could speak the language without a trace of the pronunciation peculiar to Latin. The same accomplishment can be seen to this day in her daughter Eustochium, who always kept close to her mother's side, obeyed all her commands, never slept apart from her, never walked abroad or took a meal without her, never had a penny that she could call her own, rejoiced when her mother gave to the poor her little patrimony, and fully believed that in filial affection she had the best heritage and the truest riches. I must not pass over in silence the joy which Paula felt when she heard her little granddaughter and namesake, the child of Laeta and Toxotius— who was born and I may even say conceived in answer to a vow of her parents dedicating her to virginity—when, I say, she heard the little one in her cradle sing "alleluia" and falter out the words "grandmother" and "aunt." One wish alone made her long to see her native land again; that she might know her son and his wife and child to have renounced the world and to be serving Christ. And it has been granted to her in part. For while her granddaughter is destined to take the veil, her daughter-in-law has vowed herself to perpetual chastity, and by faith and alms emulates the example that her mother has set her. She strives to exhibit at Rome the virtues which Paula set forth in all their fulness at Jerusalem.

28. What ails thee, my soul? Why dost thou shudder to approach her death? I have made my letter longer than it should be already; dreading to come to the end and vainly supposing that by saying nothing of it and by occupying myself with her praises I could postpone the evil day. Hitherto the wind has been all in my favour and my keel has smoothly ploughed through the heaving waves. But now my speech is running upon the rocks, the billows are mountains high, and imminent shipwreck awaits both you and me. We must needs cry out: "Master, save us, we perish:" and "awake, why sleepest thou, O Lord?" For who could tell the tale of Paula's dying with dry eyes? She fell into a most serious illness and thus gained what she most desired, power to leave us and to be joined more fully to the Lord. Eusto-chium's affection for her mother, always true and tried, in this time of sickness approved itself still more to all. She sat by Paula's bedside, she fanned her, she supported her head, she arranged her pillows, she chafed her feet, she rubbed her stomach, she smoothed down the bedclothes, she heated hot water, she brought towels. In fact she anticipated the servants in all their duties, and when one of them did anything she regarded it as so much taken away from her own gain. How unceasingly she prayed, how copiously she wept, how constantly she ran to and fro between her prostrate mother and the cave of the Lord! imploring God that she might not be deprived of a companion so dear, that if Paula was to die she might herself no longer live, and that one bier might carry to burial her and her mother. Alas for the frailty and perishableness of human nature! Except that our belief in Christ raises us up to heaven and promises eternity to our souls, the physical conditions of life are the same for us as for the brutes. "There is one event to the righteous and to the wicked; to the good and to the evil; to the clean and to the unclean; to him that sacrificeth and to him that sacrificeth not: as is the good so is the sinner; and he that sweareth as he that feareth an oath." Man and beast alike are dissolved into dust and ashes.

29. Why do I still linger, and prolong my suffering by postponing it? Paula's intelligence shewed her that her death was near. Her body and limbs grew cold and only in her holy breast did the warm beat of the living soul continue. Yet, as though she were leaving strangers to go home to her own people, she whispered the verses of the psalmist: "Lord, I have loved the habitation of thy house and the place where thine honour dwelleth," and "How amiable are thy tabernacles, O Lord of hosts! My soul longeth yea even fainteth for the courts of the Lord," and "I had rather be an outcast in the house of my God than to dwell in the tents of wickedness." When I asked her why she re-mained silent refusing to answer my call, and whether she was in pain, she replied in Greek that she had no suffering and that all things were to her eyes calm and tranquil. After this she said no more but closed her eyes as though she already despised all mortal things, and kept repeating the verses just quoted down to the moment in which she breathed out her soul, but in a tone so low that we could scarcely hear what she said. Raising her finger also to her mouth she made the sign of the cross upon her lips. Then her breath failed her and she gasped for death; yet even when her soul was eager to break free, she turned the death-rattle (which comes at last to all) into the praise of the Lord. The bishop of Jerusalem and some from other cities were present, also a great number of the inferior clergy, both priests and levites. The entire monastery was filled with bodies of virgins and monks. As soon as Paula heard the bridegroom saying: "Rise up my love my fair one, my dove, and come away: for, lo, the winter is past, the rain is over and gone," she answered joyfully "the flowers appear on the earth; the time to cut them has come" and "I believe that I shall see the good things of the Lord in the land of the living."

30. No weeping or lamentation followed her death, such as are the custom of the world; but all present united in chanting the psalms in their several tongues. The bishops lifted up the dead woman with their own hands, placed her upon a bier, and carrying her on their shoulders to the church in the cave of the Saviour, laid her down in the centre of it. Other bishops meantime carried torches and tapers in the procession, and yet others led the singing of the choirs. The whole population of the cities of Palestine came to her funeral. Not a single monk lurked in the desert or lingered in his cell. Not a single virgin remained shut up in the seclusion of her chamber. To each and all it would have seemed sacrilege to have withheld the last tokens of respect from a woman so saintly. As in the case of Dorcas, the widows and the poor shewed the garments Paula had given them; while the destitute cried aloud that they had lost in her a mother and a nurse. Strange to say, the paleness of death had not altered her expression; only a certain solemnity and seriousness had overspread her features. You would have thought her not dead but asleep.

One after another they chanted the psalms, now in Greek, now in Latin, now in Syriac; and this not merely for the three days which elapsed before she was buried beneath the church and close to the cave of the Lord, but throughout the remainder of the week. All who were assembled felt that it was their own funeral at which they were assisting, and shed tears as if they themselves had died. Paula's daughter, the revered virgin Eustochium, "as a child that is weaned of his mother," could not be torn away from her parent. She kissed her eyes, pressed her lips upon her brow, embraced her frame, and wished for nothing better than to be buried with her.

31. Jesus is witness that Paula has left not a single penny to her daughter but, as I said before, on the contrary a large mass of debt; and, worse even than this, a crowd of brothers and sisters whom it is hard for her to support but whom it would be undutiful to cast off. Could there be a more splendid instance of self-renunciation than that of this noble lady who in the fervour of her faith gave away so much of her wealth that she reduced herself to the last degree of poverty? Others may boast, if they will, of money spent in charity, or large sums heaped up in God's treasury, of votive offerings hung up with cords of gold. None of them has given more to the poor than Paula, for Paula has kept nothing for herself. But now she enjoys the true riches and those good things which eye hath not seen nor ear heard, neither have they entered into the heart of man. If we mourn, it is for ourselves and not for her; yet even so, if we persist in weeping for one who reigns with Christ, we shall seem to envy her her glory.

32. Be not fearful, Eustochium: you are endowed with a splendid heritage. The Lord is your portion; and, to increase your joy, your mother has now after a long martyrdom won her crown. It is not only the shedding of blood that is accounted a confession: the spotless service of a devout mind is itself a daily martyrdom. Both alike are crowned; with roses and violets in the one case, with lilies in the other. Thus in the Song of Songs it is written: "my beloved is white and ruddy;" for, whether the victory be won in peace or in war, God gives the same guerdon to those who win it. Like Abraham your mother heard the words: "get thee out of thy country, and from thy kindred, unto a land that I will shew thee;" and not only that but the Lord's command given through Jeremiah: "flee out of the midst of Babylon, and deliver every man his soul." To the day of her death she never returned to Chaldaea, or regretted the fleshpots of Egypt or its strong-smelling meats. Accompanied by her virgin bands she became a fellow-citizen of the Saviour; and now that she has ascended from her little Bethlehem to the heavenly realms she can say to the true Naomi: "thy people shall be my people and thy God my God."

33. I have spent the labour of two nights in dictating for you this treatise; and in doing so I have felt a grief as deep as your own. I say in 'dictating' for I have not been able to write it myself. As often as I have taken up my pen and have tried to fulfil my promise; my fingers

have stiffened, my hand has fallen, and my power over it has vanished. The rudeness of the diction, devoid as it is of all elegance or charm, bears witness to the feeling of the writer.

34. And now, Paula, farewell, and aid with your prayers the old age of your votary. Your faith and your works unite you to Christ; thus standing in His presence you will the more readily gain what you ask. In this letter "I have built" to your memory "a monument more lasting than bronze," which no lapse of time will be able to destroy. And I have cut an inscription on your tomb, which I here subjoin; that, wherever my narrative may go, the reader may learn that you are buried at Bethlehem and not uncommemorated there.

The Inscription on Paula's Tomb

Within this tomb a child of Scipio lies,
A daughter of the farfamed Pauline house,
A scion of the Gracchi, of the stock
Of Agamemnon's self, illustrious:
Here rests the lady Paula, well-beloved
Of both her parents, with Eustochium
For daughter; she the first of Roman dames
Who hardship chose and Bethlehem for Christ.

In front of the cavern there is another inscription as follows:—

Seest thou here hollowed in the rock a grave,
'Tis Paula's tomb; high heaven has her soul.
Who Rome and friends, riches and home forsook
Here in this lonely spot to find her rest.
For here Christ's manger was, and here the kings
To Him, both God and man, their off'rings made.

35. The holy and blessed Paula fell asleep on the seventh day before the Kalends of February, on the third day of the week, after the sun had set. She was buried on the fifth day before the same Kalends, in the sixth consulship of the Emperor Honorius and the first of Aristaenetus. She lived in the vows of religion five years at Rome and twenty years at Bethlehem. The whole duration of her life was fifty-six years eight months and twenty-one days.

72

DISCORD BETWEEN AN ASCETIC MOTHER AND DAUGHTER, EACH OF WHOM WAS LIVING WITH A MONK

Letter 117, Jerome to the two unnamed women   405 C.E.?

Introduction

1. A certain brother from Gaul has told me that his virgin-sister and widowed mother, though living in the same city, have separate abodes and have taken to themselves clerical protectors either as guests or stewards; and that by thus associating with strangers they have caused more scandal than by living apart. When I groaned and expressed what I felt more by silence than words; "I beseech you," said he, "rebuke them in a letter and recall them to mutual harmony; make them once more mother and daughter." To whom I replied, "a nice task this that you lay upon me, for me a stranger to reconcile two women whom you, a son and brother, have failed to influence. You speak as though I occupied the chair of a bishop instead of being shut up in a monastic cell where, far removed from the world's turmoil, I lament the sins of the past and try to avoid the temptations of the present. Moreover, it is surely inconsistent, while one buries oneself out of sight, to allow one's tongue free course through the world." "You are too fearful," he replied; "where is that old hardihood of yours which made you 'scour the world with copious salt,' as Horace says of Lucilius?" "It is this," I rejoined, "that makes me shy and forbids me to open my lips. For through accusing crime I have been myself made out a criminal. Men have disputed and denied my assertions until, as the proverb goes, I hardly know whether I have ears or feeling left. The very walls have resounded with curses levelled at me, and 'I was the song of drunkards.' Under the compulsion of an unhappy experience I have learned to be silent, thinking it better to set a watch before my mouth and to keep the door of my lips than to incline my heart to any evil thing, or, while censuring the faults of others, myself to fall into that of detraction." In answer to this he said: "Speaking the truth is not detraction. Nor will you lecture the world by administering a particular rebuke; for there are few persons, if any, open to this special charge. I beg of you, therefore, as I have put myself to the trouble of this long journey, that you will not suffer me to have come for nothing. The Lord knows that, after the sight of the holy places, my principal object in coming has been to heal by a letter from you the division between my sister and my mother." "Well," I replied, "I will do as you wish, for after all the letters will be to persons beyond the sea and words written with reference to definite persons can seldom offend other people. But I must ask you to keep what I say secret. You will take my advice with you to encourage you by the way; if it is listened to, I will rejoice as much as you; while if, as I rather think, it is rejected, I shall have wasted my words and you will have made a long journey for nothing."

The Letter

2. In the first place my sister and my daughter, I wish you to know that I am not writing to you because I suspect anything evil of you. On the contrary I implore you to live in harmony, so as to give no ground for any such suspicions. Moreover had I supposed you fast bound in sin—far be this from you—I should never have written, for I should have known that my words would be addressed to deaf ears. Again, if I write to you somewhat sharply, I beg of you to ascribe this not to any harshness on my part but to the nature of the ailment which I attempt to treat. Cautery and the knife are the only remedies when mortification has once set in; poison is the only antidote known for poison; great pain can only be relieved by inflicting greater pain. Lastly I must say this that even if your own consciences acquit you of misdoing, yet the very rumour of such brings disgrace upon you. Mother and daughter are names of affection; they imply natural ties and reciprocal duties; they form the closest of human relations after that which binds the soul to God. If you love each other, your conduct calls for no praise: but if you hate each other, you have committed a crime. The Lord Jesus was subject to His parents. He reverenced that mother of whom He was Himself the parent; He respected the foster-father whom He had Himself fostered; for He remembered that He had been carried in the womb of the one and in the arms of the other. Wherefore also when He hung upon the cross He commended to His disciple the mother whom He had never before His passion parted from Himself.

3. Well, I shall say no more to the mother, for perhaps age, weakness, and loneliness make sufficient excuses for her; but to you the daughter I say: "Is a mother's house too small for you whose womb was not too small? When you have lived with her for ten months in the one, can you not bear to live with her for one day in the other? or are you unable to meet her gaze? Can it be that one who has borne you and reared you, who has brought you up and knows you, is dreaded by you as a witness of your home-life? If you are a true virgin, why do you fear her careful guardianship; and, if you have fallen, why do you not openly marry? Wedlock is like a plank offered to a shipwrecked man and by its means you may remedy what previously you have done amiss. I do not mean that you are not to repent of your sin or that you are to continue in evil courses; but, when a tie of the kind has been formed, I despair of breaking it altogether. However, a return to your mother will make it easier for you to bewail the virginity which you have lost through leaving her. Or if you are still unspotted and have not lost your chastity, be careful of it for you may lose it. Why must you live in a house where you must daily struggle for life and death? Can any one sleep soundly with a viper near him? No; for, though it may not attack him it is sure to frighten him. It is better to be where there is no danger, than to be in danger and to escape. In the one case we have a calm; in the other careful steering is necessary. In the one case we are filled with joy; in the other we do but avoid sorrow.

4. But you will perhaps reply: "my mother is not well-behaved, she desires the things of the world, she loves riches, she disregards fasting, she stains her eyes with antimony, she likes to walk abroad in gay attire, she hinders me from the monastic vow, and so I cannot live with her." But first of all, even though she is as you say, you will have the greater reward for refusing to forsake her with all her faults. She has carried you in her womb, she has reared you; with gentle affection she has borne with the troublesome ways of your childhood. She has washed your linen, she has tended you when sick, and the sickness of maternity was not only borne for you but caused by you. She has brought you up to womanhood, she has taught you to love Christ. You ought not to be displeased with the behaviour of a mother who has consecrated you as a virgin to the service of your spouse. Still if you cannot put up with her dainty ways and feel obliged to shun them, and if your mother really is, as people so often say, a woman of the world, you have others, virgins like yourself, the holy company of chastity. Why, when you forsake your mother, do you choose for companion a man who perhaps has left behind him a sister and mother of his own? You tell me that she is hard to get on with and that he is easy; that she is quarrelsome and that he is amiable. I will ask you one question: Did you go straight from your home to the man or did you fall in with him afterwards? If you went straight to him, the reason why you left your mother is plain. If you fell in with him afterwards, you shew by your choice what you missed under your mother's roof. The pain that I inflict is severe and I feel the knife as much as you. "He that walketh uprightly walketh surely." Only that my conscience would smite me, I should keep silence and be slow to blame others where I am not guiltless myself. Having a beam in my own eye I should be reluctant to see the mote in my neighbour's. But as it is I live far away among Christian brothers; my life with them is honourable as eyewitnesses of it can testify; I rarely see, or am seen by, others. It is most shameless, therefore, in you to refuse to copy me in respect of self-restraint, when you profess to take me as your model. If you say: "my conscience is enough for me too. God is my judge who is witness of my life. I care not what men may say;" let me urge upon you the apostle's words: "provide things honest" not only in the sight of God but also "in the sight of all men." If any one carps at you for being a Christian and a virgin, mind it not; you have left your mother it may be said to live in a monastery among virgins, but censure on this score is your glory. When men blame a maid of God not for self-indulgence but only for insensibility to affection, what they condemn as callous disregard of a parent is really a lively devotion towards God. For you prefer to your mother Him whom you are bidden to prefer to your own soul. And if the day ever comes that she also shall so prefer Him, she will find in you not a daughter only but a sister as well.

5. "What then?" you will say, "is it a crime to have a man of religion in the house with me?" You seize me by the collar and drag me into court either to sanction what I disapprove or else to incur the dislike of many. A man of religion never separates a daughter from her mother. He welcomes both and respects both. A daughter may be as religious as she pleases; still a mother who is a widow is a guaranty for her chastity. If this person whoever he is is of the same age with yourself, he should honour your mother as though she were his own; and, if he is older, he should love you as a daughter and subject you to a mother's discipline. It is not good either for your reputation or for his that he should like you more than your mother: for his affection might appear to be less for you than for your youth. This is what I should say if a monk were not your brother and if you had no relatives able to protect you. But what excuse has a stranger for thrusting himself in where there are both a mother and a brother, the one a widow and the other a monk? It is good for you to feel that you are a daughter and a sister. However, if you cannot manage both, and if your mother is too hard a morsel to swallow, your brother at any rate should satisfy you. Or, if he is too harsh, she that bore you may prove more gentle. Why do you turn pale? Why do you get excited? Why do you blush, and with trembling lips betray the restlessness of your mind? One thing only can surpass a woman's love for her mother and brother; and that is her passion for her husband.

6. I am told, moreover, that you frequent suburban villas and their pleasant gardens in the company of relatives and intimate friends. I have no doubt that it is some female cousin or connexion who for her own satisfaction carries you about with her as a novel kind of attendant. Far be it from me to suspect that you would desire men's society; even though they should be those of your own family. But pray, maiden, answer me this; do you appear alone in your kinsfolk's society? or do you bring your favourite with you? Shameless as you may be, you will hardly venture to flaunt him in the eyes of the world. If you ever do so, your whole circle will cry out about both you and him; every one's finger will be pointed at you; and your cousins who in your presence to please you call him a monk and a man of religion, will laugh at you behind your back for having such an unnatural husband. If on the other hand you go out alone—which I rather suppose to be the case—you will find yourself clothed in sober garb among slave youths, women married or soon to be so, wanton girls, and dandies with long hair and tight-fitting vests. Some bearded fop will offer you his hand, he will hold you up if you feel tired, and the pressure of his fingers will either be a temptation to you, or will shew that you are a temptation to him. Again when you sit down to table with married men and women, you will have to see kisses in which you have no part, and dishes partaken of which are not for you. Moreover it cannot but do you harm to see other women attired in silk dresses and gold brocades. At table also whether you like it or not, you will be forced to eat flesh and that of different kinds. To make you drink wine they will praise it as a creature of God. To induce you to take baths they will speak of dirt with disgust; and, when on second thoughts you do as you are bid, they will with one voice salute you as spotless and open, a thorough lady. Meantime some singer will give to the company a selection of softly flowing airs; and as he will not venture to look at other men's wives, he will constantly fix his eyes on you who have no protector. He will speak by nods and convey by his tone what he is afraid to put into words. Amid induce-ments to sensuality so marked as these, even iron wills are apt to be overcome with desire; an appetite which is the more imperious in virgins because they suppose that sweetest of which they have no experience. Heathen legends tell us that sailors actually ran their ships on the rocks that they might listen to the songs of the Sirens; and that the lyre of Orpheus had power to draw to itself trees and animals and to soften flints. In the banquet-hall chastity is hard to keep. A shining skin shews a sin-stained soul.

7. As a schoolboy I have read of one—and have seen his effigy true to the life in the streets—who continued to cherish an unlawful passion even when his flesh scarcely clung to his bones, and whose malady remained uncured until death cured it. What then will become of you a young girl physically sound, dainty, stout, and ruddy, if you allow yourself free range among flesh-dishes, wines, and baths, not to mention married men and bachelors? Even if when solicited you refuse to consent, you will take the fact of your being asked as evi-dence that you are considered handsome. A sensual mind pursues dishonourable objects with greater zest than honourable ones; and when a thing is forbidden hankers after it with greater pleasure. Your very dress, cheap and sombre as it is, is an index of your secret feel-ings. For it has no creases and trails along the ground to make you appear taller than you are. Your vest is purposely ripped asunder to shew what is beneath and while hiding what is repulsive, to reveal what is fair. As you walk, the very creaking of your black and shiny shoes attracts the notice of the young men. You wear stays to keep your breasts in place, and a heaving girdle closely confines your chest. Your hair covers either your forehead or your ears. Sometimes too you let your shawl drop so as to lay bare your white shoulders; and, as if unwilling that they should be seen, you quickly conceal what you have purposely disclosed. And when in public you for modesty's sake cover your face, like a practised harlot you only shew what is likely to please.

8. You will exclaim "How do you know what I am like, or how, when you are so far away, can you see what I am doing?" Your own brother's tears and sobs have told me, his frequent and scarcely endur-able bursts of grief. Would that he had lied or that his words had been words of apprehension only and not of accusation. But, believe me, liars do not shed tears. He is indignant that you prefer to himself a young man, not it is true clothed in silk or wearing his hair long but

muscular and dainty in the midst of his squalor; and that this fellow holds the purse-strings, looks after the weaving, allots the servants their tasks, rules the household, and buys from the market all that is needed. He is at once steward and master, and as he anticipates the slaves in their duties, he is carped at by all the domestics. Everything that their mistress has not given them they declare that he has stolen from them. Servants as a class are full of complaints; and no matter what you give them, it is always too little. For they do not consider how much you have but only how much you give; and they make up for their chagrin in the only way they can, that is, by grumbling. One calls him a parasite, another an impostor, another a money-seeker, another by some novel appellation that hits his fancy. They noise it abroad that he is constantly at your bed-side, that when you are sick he runs to fetch nurses, that he holds basins, airs sheets, and folds bandages for you. The world is only too ready to believe scandal, and stories invented at home soon get afloat abroad. Nor need you be surprised if your servantmen and servantmaids get up such tales about you, when even your mother and your brother complain of your conduct.

9. Do, therefore, what I advise you and entreat you to do: if possible, be reconciled with your mother; or, if this may not be, at least come to terms with your brother. Or if you are filled with an implacable hatred of relationships usually so dear, separate at all events from the man, whom you are said to prefer to your own flesh and blood, and, if even this is impossible for you, (for, if you could leave him, you would certainly return to your own) pay more regard to appearances in harbouring him as your companion. Live in a separate building and take your meals apart; for if you remain under one roof with him slanderers will say that you share with him your bed. You may thus easily get help from him when you feel you need it, and yet to a considerable degree escape public discredit. Yet you must take care not to contract the stain of which Jeremiah tells us that no nitre or fuller's soap can wash it out. When you wish him to come to see you, always have witnesses present; either friends, or freedmen, or slaves. A good conscience is afraid of no man's eyes. Let him come in unembarrassed and go out at his ease. Let his silent looks, his unspoken words and his whole carriage, though at times they may imply embarrassment, yet indicate peace of mind. Pray, open your ears and listen to the outcry of the whole city. You have already both of you lost your own names and are known each by that of the other. You are spoken of as his, and he is said to be yours. Your mother and your brother have heard this and are ready to take you in between them. They implore you to consent to this arrangement, so that the scandal of your intimacy with this man which is confined to yourself may give place to a glory common to all. You can live with your mother and he with your brother. You can more boldly shew your regard for one who is your brother's comrade; and your mother will more properly esteem one who is the friend of her son and not of her daugher. But if you frown and refuse to accept my advice, this letter will openly expostulate with you. 'Why,' it will say, 'do you beset another man's servant? Why do you make Christ's minister your slave? Look at the people and scan each face as it comes under your view. When he reads in the church all eyes are fixed upon you; and you, using the licence of a wife, glory in your shame. Secret infamy no longer contents you; you call boldness freedom; "you have a whore's forehead and refuse to be ashamed."

10. Once more you exclaim that I am over-suspicious, a thinker of evil, too ready to follow rumours. What? I suspicious? I ill-natured? I, who as I said in the beginning have taken up my pen because I have no suspicions? Or is it you that are careless, loose, disdainful? You who at the age of twenty-five have netted in your embrace a youth whose beard has scarcely grown? An excellent instructor he must be, able no doubt by his severe looks both to warn and frighten you! No age is safe from lust, yet gray hairs are some security for decent conduct. A day will surely come (for time glides by imperceptibly) when your handsome young favourite will find a wealthier or more youthful mistress. For women soon age and particularly if they live with men. You will be sorry for your decision and regret your obstinacy in a day when your means and reputation shall be alike gone, and when this unhappy intimacy shall be happily broken off. But perhaps you feel sure of your ground and see no reason to fear a breach where affection has had so long a time to develop and grow.

11. To you also, her mother, I must say a word. Your years put you beyond the reach of scandal; do not take advantage of this to indulge in sin. It is more fitting that your daughter should learn from you how to part from a companion than that you should learn from her how to give up a paramour. You have a son, a daughter, and a son-in-law, or at least one who is your daughter's partner. Why then should you seek other society than theirs, or wish to kindle anew expiring flames? It would be more becoming in you to screen your daughter's fault than to make it an excuse for your own misdoing. Your son is a monk, and, if he were to live with you, he would strengthen you in your religious profession and in your vow of widowhood. Why should you take in a complete stranger, especially in a house not large enough to hold a son and a daughter? You are old enough to have grand-children. Invite the pair home then. Your daughter went away by herself; let her return with this man. I say 'man' and not 'husband' that none may cavil. The word describes his sex and not his relation to her. Or if she blushes to accept your offer or finds the house in which she was born too narrow for her, then move both of you to her abode. However limited may be its accommodation, it can take in a mother and a brother better than a stranger. In fact, if she lives in the same house and occupies the same room with a man, she cannot long preserve her chastity. It is different when two women and two men live together. If the third person concerned—he, I mean, who fosters your old age—will not make one of the party and causes only dissension and confusion, the pair of you can do without him. But if the three of you remain together, then your brother and son will offer him a sister and a mother. Others may speak of the two strangers as step-father and son-in-law; but your son must speak of them as his foster-father and his brother.

Note

12. Working quickly I have completed this letter in a single night anxious alike to gratify a friend and to try my hand on a rhetorical theme. Then early in the morning he has knocked at my door on the point of starting. I wish also to shew my detractors that like them I too can say the first thing that comes into my head. I have, therefore, introduced few quotations from the scriptures and have not, as in most of my books, interwoven its flowers in my discourse. The letter has been, in fact, dictated off-hand and poured forth by lamp-light so fast that my tongue has outstripped my secretaries' pens and that my volubility has baffled the expedients of shorthand. I have said this much that those who make no allowances for want of ability may make some for want of time.

73

THE LIFE OF MARCELLA, A FOUNDER OF WOMEN'S ASCETIC ENCLAVES

Letter 127, Jerome to Principia   412 C.E.

1. You have besought me often and earnestly, Principia, virgin of Christ, to dedicate a letter to the memory of that holy woman Marcella, and to set forth the goodness long enjoyed by us for others to know and to imitate. I am so anxious myself to do justice to her merits that it grieves me that you should spur me on and fancy that your entreaties are needed when I do not yield even to you in love of her. In putting upon record her signal virtues I shall receive far more benefit myself than I can possibly confer upon others. If I have hitherto remained silent and have allowed two years to go over without making any sign, this has not been owing to a wish to ignore her as you wrongly suppose, but to an incredible sorrow which so overcame my mind that I judged it better to remain silent for a while than to praise her virtues in inadequate language. Neither will I now follow the rules of rhetoric in eulogizing one so dear to both of us and to all the saints, Marcella the glory of her native Rome. I will not set forth her illustrious family and lofty lineage, nor will I trace her pedigree through a line of consuls and praetorian prefects. I will praise her for nothing but the virtue which is her own and which is the more noble, because forsaking both wealth and rank she has sought the true nobility of poverty and lowliness.

2. Her father's death left her an orphan, and she had been married less than seven months when her husband was taken from her. Then as she was young, and highborn, as well as distinguished for her beauty—always an attraction to men—and her self-control, an illustrious consular named Cerealis paid court to her with great assiduity. Being an old man he offered to make over to her his fortune so that she might consider herself less his wife than his daughter. Her mother Albina went out of her way to secure for the young widow so exalted a protector. But Marcella answered: "had I a wish to marry and not rather to dedicate myself to perpetual chastity, I should look for a husband and not for an inheritance;" and when her suitor argued that sometimes old men live long while young men die early, she cleverly retorted: "a young man may indeed die early, but an old man cannot live long." This decided rejection of Cerealis convinced others that they had no hope of winning her hand.

In the gospel according to Luke we read the following passage: "there was one Anna, a prophetess, the daughter of Phanuel, of the tribe of Aser: she was of great age, and had lived with an husband seven years from her virginity; and she was a widow of about fourscore and four years, which departed not from the temple but served God with fastings and prayers night and day." It was no marvel that she won the vision of the Saviour, whom she sought so earnestly. Let us then compare her case with that of Marcella and we shall see that the latter has every way the advantage. Anna lived with her husband seven years; Marcella seven months. Anna only hoped for Christ; Marcella held Him fast. Anna confessed him at His birth; Marcella believed in Him crucified. Anna did not deny the Child; Marcella rejoiced in the Man as king. I do not wish to draw distinctions between holy women on the score of their merits, as some persons have made it a custom to do as regards holy men and leaders of churches; the conclusion at which I aim is that, as both have one task, so both have one reward.

3. In a slander-loving community such as Rome, filled as it formerly was with people from all parts and bearing the palm for wickedness of all kinds, detraction assailed the upright and strove to defile even the pure and the clean. In such an atmosphere it is hard to escape from the breath of calumny. A stainless reputation is difficult nay almost impossible to attain; the prophet yearns for it but hardly hopes to win it: "Blessed," he says, "are the undefiled in the way who walk in the law of the Lord." The undefiled in the way of this world are those whose fair fame no breath of scandal has ever sullied, and who have earned no reproach at the hands of their neighbours. It is this which makes the Saviour say in the gospel: "agree with," or be complaisant to, "thine adversary whilst thou art in the way with him." Who ever heard a slander of Marcella that deserved the least credit? Or who ever credited such without making himself guilty of malice and defamation? No; she put the Gentiles to confusion by shewing them the nature of that Christian widowhood which her conscience and mien alike set forth. For women of the world are wont to paint their faces with rouge and white-lead, to wear robes of shining silk, to adorn themselves with jewels, to put gold chains round their necks, to pierce their ears and hang in them the costliest pearls of the Red Sea, and to scent themselves with musk. While they mourn for the husbands they have lost they rejoice at their own deliverance and freedom to choose fresh partners—not, as God wills, to obey these but to rule over them.

With this object in view they select for their partners poor men who contented with the mere name of husbands are the more ready to put up with rivals as they know that, if they so much as murmur, they will be cast off at once. Our widow's clothing was meant to keep out the cold and not to shew her figure. Of gold she would not wear so much as a seal-ring, choosing to store her money in the stomachs of the poor rather than to keep it at her own disposal. She went nowhere without her mother, and would never see without witnesses such monks and clergy as the needs of a large house required her to interview. Her train was always composed of virgins and widows, and these women serious and staid; for, as she well knew, the levity of the maids speaks ill for the mistress and a woman's character is shewn by her choice of companions.

4. Her delight in the divine scriptures was incredible. She was for ever singing, "Thy words have I hid in mine heart that I might not sin against thee," as well as the words which describe the perfect man, "his delight is in the law of the Lord; and in his law doth he meditate day and night." This meditation in the law she understood not of a review of the written words as among the Jews the Pharisees think, but of action according to that saying of the apostle, "whether, therefore, ye eat or drink or what soever ye do, do all to the glory of God." She remembered also the prophet's words, "through thy precepts I get understanding," and felt sure that only when she had fulfilled these would she be permitted to understand the scriptures. In this sense we read elsewhere that "Jesus began both to do and teach." For teaching is put to the blush when a man's conscience rebukes him; and it is in vain that his tongue preaches poverty or teaches alms-giving if he is rolling in the riches of Croesus and if, in spite of his threadbare cloak, he has silken robes at home to save from the moth.

Marcella practised fasting, but in moderation. She abstained from eating flesh, and she knew rather the scent of wine than its taste; touching it only for her stomach's sake and for her often infirmities. She seldom appeared in public and took care to avoid the houses of great ladies, that she might not be forced to look upon what she had once for all renounced. She frequented the basilicas of apostles and martyrs that she might escape from the throng and give herself to private prayer. So obedient was she to her mother that for her sake she did things of which she herself disapproved. For example, when her mother, careless of her own offspring, was for transferring all her property from her children and grandchildren to her brother's family, Marcella wished the money to be given to the poor instead, and yet could not bring herself to thwart her parent. Therefore she made over her ornaments and other effects to persons already rich, content to throw away her money rather than to sadden her mother's heart.

5. In those days no highborn lady at Rome had made profession of the monastic life, or had ventured—so strange and ignominious and degrading did it then seem—publicly to call herself a nun. It was from some priests of Alexandria, and from pope Athanasius, and subsequently from Peter, who, to escape the persecution of the Arian heretics, had all fled for refuge to Rome as the safest haven in which they could find communion—it was from these that Marcella heard of the life of the blessed Antony, then still alive, and of the monasteries in the Thebaid founded by Pachomius, and of the discipline laid down for virgins and for widows. Nor was she ashamed to profess a life which she had thus learned to be pleasing to Christ. Many years after her example was followed first by Sophronia and then by others, of whom it may be well said in the words of Ennius:

> Would that ne'er in Pelion's woods
> Had the axe these pinetrees felled.

My revered friend Paula was blessed with Marcella's friendship, and it was in Marcella's cell that Eustochium, that paragon of virgins, was gradually trained. Thus it is easy to see of what type the mistress was who found such pupils.

The unbelieving reader may perhaps laugh at me for dwelling so long on the praises of mere women; yet if he will but remember how holy women followed our Lord and Saviour and ministered to Him of their substance, and how the three Marys stood before the cross and especially how Mary Magdalen—called the tower from the earnestness and glow of her faith—was privileged to see the rising Christ first of all before the very apostles, he will convict himself of pride sooner than me of folly. For we judge of people's virtue not by their sex but by their character, and hold those to be worthy of the highest glory who have renounced both rank and wealth. It was for this reason that Jesus loved the evangelist John more than the other disciples. For John was of noble birth and known to the high priest, yet was so little appalled by the plottings of the Jews that he introduced Peter into his court, and was the only one of the apostles bold enough to take his stand before the cross. For it was he who took the Savior's parent to his own home; it was the virgin son who received the virgin mother as a legacy from the Lord.

6. Marcella then lived the ascetic life for many years, and found herself old before she bethought herself that she had once been young. She often quoted with approval Plato's saying that philosophy consists in meditating on death. A truth which our own apostle indorses when he says: "for your salvation I die daily." Indeed according to the old copies our Lord himself says: "whosoever doth not bear His cross daily and come after me cannot be my disciple." Ages before, the Holy Spirit had said by the prophet: "for thy sake are we killed all the day long: we are counted as sheep for the slaughter." Many generations afterwards the words were spoken: "remember the end and thou shalt never do amiss," as well as that precept of the eloquent satirist: "live with death in your mind; time flies; this say of mine is so much taken from it." Well then, as I was saying, she passed her days and lived always in the thought that she must die. Her very clothing was such as to remind her of the tomb, and she presented herself as a living sacrifice, reasonable and acceptable, unto God.

7. When the needs of the Church at length brought me to Rome in company with the reverend pontiffs, Paulinus and Epiphanius—the first of whom ruled the church of the Syrian Antioch while the second presided over that of Salamis in Cyprus,—I in my modesty was for avoiding the eyes of highborn ladies, yet she pleaded so earnestly, "both in season and out of season" as the apostle says, that at last her perseverance overcame my reluctance. And, as in those days my name was held in some renown as that of a student of the scriptures, she never came to see me that she did not ask me some question concerning them, nor would she at once acquiesce in my explanations but on the contrary would dispute them; not, however, for argument's sake but to learn the answers to those objections which might, as she saw, be made to my statements. How much virtue and ability, how much holiness and purity I found in her I am afraid to say; both lest I may exceed the bounds of men's belief and lest I may increase your sorrow by reminding you of the blessings that you have lost. This much only will I say, that whatever in me was the fruit of long study and as such made by constant meditation a part of my nature, this she tasted, this she learned and made her own. Consequently after my departure from

Rome, in case of a dispute arising as to the testimony of scripture on any subject, recourse was had to her to settle it. And so wise was she and so well did she understand what philosphers call *to prepon*, that is, "the becoming," in what she did, that when she answered questions she gave her own opinion not as her own but as from me or some one else, thus admitting that what she taught she had herself learned from others. For she knew that the apostle had said: "I suffer not a woman to teach," and she would not seem to inflict a wrong upon the male sex many of whom (including sometimes priests) questioned her concerning obscure and doubtful points.

8. I am told that my place with her was immediately taken by you, that you attached yourself to her, and that, as the saying goes, you never let even a hair's-breadth come between her and you. You both lived in the same house and occupied the same room so that every one in the city knew for certain that you had found a mother in her and she a daughter in you. In the suburbs you found for yourselves a monastic seclusion, and chose the country instead of the town because of its loneliness. For a long time you lived together, and as many ladies shaped their conduct by your examples, I had the joy of seeing Rome transformed into another Jerusalem. Monastic establishments for virgins became numerous, and of hermits there were countless numbers. In fact so many were the servants of God that monasticism which had before been a term of reproach became subsequently one of honour. Meantime we consoled each other for our separation by words of mutual encouragement, and discharged in the spirit the debt which in the flesh we could not pay. We always went to meet each other's letters, tried to outdo each other in attentions, and anticipated each other in courteous inquiries. Not much was lost by a separation thus effectually bridged by a constant correspondence.

9. While Marcella was thus serving the Lord in holy tranquillity, there arose in these provinces a tornado of heresy which threw everything into confusion; indeed so great was the fury into which it lashed itself that it spared neither itself nor anything that was good. And as if it were too little to have disturbed everything here, it introduced a ship freighted with blasphemies into the port of Rome itself. The dish soon found itself a cover; and the muddy feet of heretics fouled the clear waters of the faith of Rome. No wonder that in the streets and in the market places a soothsayer can strike fools on the back or, catching up his cudgel, shatter the teeth of such as carp at him; when such venomous and filthy teaching as this has found at Rome dupes whom it can lead astray. Next came the scandalous version of Origen's book *On First Principles,* and that 'fortunate' disciple who would have been indeed fortunate had he never fallen in with such a master. Next followed the confutation set forth by my supporters, which destroyed the case of the Pharisees and threw them into confusion. It was then that the holy Marcella, who had long held back lest she should be thought to act from party motives, threw herself into the breach. Conscious that the faith of Rome—once praised by an apostle—was now in danger, and that this new heresy was drawing to itself not only priests and monks but also many of the laity besides imposing on the bishop who fancied others are guileless as he was himself, she publicly withstood its teachers choosing to please God rather than men.

10. In the gospel the Saviour commends the unjust steward because, although he defrauded his master, he acted wisely for his own interests. The heretics in this instance pursued the same course; for, seeing how great a matter a little fire had kindled, and that the flames applied by them to the foundations had by this time reached the housetops, and that the deception practised on many could no longer be hid, they asked for and obtained letters of commendation from the church, so that it might appear that till the day of their departure they had continued in full communion with it. Shortly afterwards the distinguished Anastasius succeeded to the pontificate; but he was soon taken away, for it was not fitting that the head of the world should be struck off during the episcopate of one so great. He was removed, no doubt, that he might not seek to turn away by his prayers the sentence of God passed once for all. For the words of the Lord to Jeremiah concerning Israel applied equally to Rome: "pray not for this people for their good. When they fast I will not hear their cry; and when they offer burnt-offering and oblation, I will not accept them; but I will consume them by the sword and by the famine and by the pestilence." You will say, what has this to do with the praises of Marcella? I reply, She it was who originated the condemnation of the heretics. She it was who furnished witnesses first taught by them and then carried away by their heretical teaching. She it was who showed how large a number they had deceived and who brought up against them the impious books *On First Principles,* books which were passing from hand to hand after being 'improved' by the hand of the scorpion. She it was lastly who called on the heretics in letter after letter to appear in their own defence. They did not indeed venture to come, for they were so conscience-stricken that they let the case go against them by default rather than face their accusers and be convicted by them. This glorious victory originated with Marcella, she was the source and cause of this great blessing. You who shared the honour with her know that I speak the truth. You know too that out of many incidents I only mention a few, not to tire out the reader by a wearisome recapitulation. Were I to say more, ill natured persons might fancy me, under pretext of commending a woman's virtues, to be giving vent to my own rancour. I will pass now to the remainder of my story.

11. The whirlwind passed from the West into the East and threatened in its passage to shipwreck many a noble craft. Then were the words of Jesus fulfilled: "when the son of man cometh, shall he find faith on the earth?" The love of many waxed cold. Yet the few who still loved the true faith rallied to my side. Men openly sought to take their lives and every expedient was employed against them. So hotly indeed did the persecution rage that "Barnabas also was carried away with their dissimulation;" nay more he committed murder, if not in actual violence at least in will. Then behold God blew and the tempest passed away; so that the prediction of the prophet was fulfilled, "thou takest away their breath, they die, and return to their dust. In that very day his thoughts perish," as also the gospel-saying, "Thou fool, this night thy soul shall be required of thee: then whose shall those things be, which thou hast provided?"

12. Whilst these things were happening in Jebus a dreadful rumour came from the West. Rome had been besieged and its citizens had been forced to buy their lives with gold. Then thus despoiled they had been besieged again so as to lose not their substance only but their lives. My voice sticks in my throat; and, as I dictate, sobs choke my utterance. The City which had taken the whole world was itself taken; nay more famine was beforehand with the sword and but few citizens were left to be made captives. In their frenzy the starving people had recourse to hideous food; and tore each other limb from limb that they might have flesh to eat. Even the mother did not spare the babe at her breast. In the night was Moab taken, in the night did her wall fall down. "O God, the heathen have come into thine inheritance; thy holy temple have they defiled; they have made Jerusalem an orchard. The dead bodies of thy servants have they given to be meat unto the fowls of the heaven, the flesh of thy saints unto the beasts of the earth. Their blood have they shed like water round about Jerusalem; and there was none to bury them."

Who can set forth the carnage of that night?
What tears are equal to its agony?
Of ancient date a sovran city falls;
And lifeless in its streets and houses lie
Unnumbered bodies of its citizens.
In many a ghastly shape doth death appear.

13. Meantime, as was natural in a scene of such confusion, one of the bloodstained victors found his way into Marcella's house. Now be it mine to say what I have heard, to relate what holy men have seen; for there were some such present and they say that you too were with her in the hour of danger. When the soldiers entered she is said to have received them without any look of alarm; and when they asked her for gold she pointed to her coarse dress to shew them that she had no buried treasure. However they would not believe in her self-chosen poverty, but scourged her and beat her with cudgels. She is said to have felt no pain but to have thrown herself at their feet and to have pleaded with tears for you, that you might not be taken from her, or owing to your youth have to endure what she as an old woman had no occasion to fear. Christ softened their hard hearts and even among bloodstained swords natural affection asserted its rights. The barbarians conveyed both you and her to the basilica of the apostle Paul, that you might find there either a place of safety or, if not that, at least a tomb. Hereupon Marcella is said to have burst into great joy and to have thanked God for having kept you unharmed in answer to her prayer. She said she was thankful too that the taking of the city had found her poor, not made her so, that she was now in want of daily bread, that Christ satisfied her needs so that she no longer felt hunger, that she was able to say in word and in deed: "naked came I out of my mother's womb, and naked shall I return thither: the Lord gave and the Lord hath taken away; blessed be the name of the Lord."

14. After a few days she fell asleep in the Lord; but to the last her powers remained unimpaired. You she made the heir of her poverty, or rather the poor through you. When she closed her eyes, it was in your arms; when she breathed her last breath, your lips received it; you shed tears but she smiled, conscious of having led a good life and hoping for her reward hereafter.

In one short night I have dictated this letter in honour of you, revered Marcella, and of you, my daughter Principia; not to shew off my own eloquence but to express my heartfelt gratitude to you both; my one desire has been to please both God and my readers.

74

A CONSOLING LETTER FROM THE EXILED CHRYSOSTOM TO HIS FRIEND OLYMPIAS, SEEKING HER POLITICAL SUPPORT

Letter 9, John Chrysostom to Olympias   404 C.E.

1. Why do you lament? why do you belabour yourself, and demand of yourself a punishment which your enemies were not able to demand from you, having thus abandoned your soul to the tyranny of dejection? For the letters which you sent to me by the hands of Patricius have discovered to me the wounds which have been inflicted on your mind. Wherefore also I am very sorrowful and much distressed that when you ought to be using every exertion and making it your business to expel dejection from your soul, you go about collecting distressing thoughts, even inventing things (so you say) which do not exist, and tearing yourself to pieces for no purpose, and to your very great injury. For why are you grieved because you could not remove me from Cucusus? Yet indeed, as far as you were concerned, you did remove me, having made every exertion and endeavour for this purpose. And even if it has not been actually accomplished you ought not to be vexed on that account. For perhaps it seemed good to God that I should be set to run the longer double course, in order that the garland of victory might be rendered more glorious. Why then are you vexed on account of these things, in consequence of which my fame is spread abroad, when you ought to leap and dance for joy and bind wreaths upon your brow, because I have been deemed worthy of so great an honour which far exceeds my merits? Is it the desolation of this place which grieves you? Yet what can be pleasanter than my sojourn here? I have quietness, and tranquillity, plenty of leisure and good bodily health. For although the town has neither market-place nor market that is nothing to me. For all things are poured abundantly upon me as out of a flowing spring. I find my lord the Bishop here and my lord Dioscorus are constantly employed in providing for my refreshment. And the good Patricius will tell you that as far as my sojourn here is concerned I pass my time cheerfully and gladly, surrounded by attention. But if you lament the events which occurred in Caesarea, here again your conduct is unworthy of yourself. For there also bright garlands of victory were woven for me, inasmuch as all were proclaiming and publishing my praises, and expressing won-

der and astonishment at the ill-treatment to which I had been subjected followed by expulsion. Meanwhile however do not let any one know these things, although they are the theme of much gossip. For my lord Poeanius has disclosed to me that the presbyters of Pharetrius himself have arrived on the spot, who declare that they were in communion with me and had no communication or intercourse or partnership with my adversaries. Therefore to avoid upsetting them do not let any one know these things. For certainly the things which befell me were very grievous: and if I had not suffered any other distress the events which happened there would have sufficed to procure innumerable rewards for me: so extreme was the danger which I encountered. Now I beseech you to keep these matters secret, and so I will give you a short account of them, not in order to grieve you but rather to make you glad. For herein consists the material of my gain, herein consists my wealth, herein the means of getting rid of my sins—that my journey is continually encompassed by trials of this kind, and that they are inflicted upon me by persons from whom they were quite unexpected. For when I was about to enter the region of Cappadocia, having escaped from that man of Galatia, who nearly threatened me with death, many persons met me on the way saying "the lord Pharetrius is awaiting you, and going about in all directions for fear of missing the pleasure of meeting you, and making every possible endeavour to see you, and embrace you, and show you all manner of affectionate regard; and he has set the monasteries of men and women in motion for this purpose. Now when I heard these things I did not expect that any of them would really take place, but formed an impression in my own mind precisely the reverse: but of this I said nothing to any of those who brought me this message.

2. Now when I arrived late one evening at Caesarea, in an exhausted and worn-out condition, being in the very height of a burning fever, faint and suffering to the last degree, I lighted upon an inn situated just at the outskirts of the city, and took great pains to find some physicians and allay this fiery fever; for it was now the height of my tertian malady. And in addition to this there was the fatigue of the journey, the toil, the strain, the total absence of attendants, the difficulty of getting supplies, the want of a physician, the wasting effects of toil, and heat and sleeplessness; thus I was well nigh a dead man when I entered the city. Then indeed I was visited by the whole body of the clergy, and the people, monks, nuns, physicians, and I had the benefit of great attention, as all paid me every kind of ministration

and assistance. Yet even thus, being oppressed by the lethargy arising from the feverish heat I was in an extremely distressed condition. At length by degrees the malady was coming to an end and abating. Pharetrius however nowhere appeared; but waited for my departure, I know not with what purpose in view. When then I saw that my disorder had slightly abated I began to form plans for my journey so as to reach Cucusus, and enjoy a little repose after the calamities of the way. And whilst I was thus situated it was suddenly announced that the Isaurians in countless multitudes were overrunning the district of Caesarea, and had burnt a large village, and were most violently disposed. The tribune, having heard this, took the soldiers which he had and went out. For they were afraid lest the enemy should make an assault also upon the city, and all were in terror, and in an agony of alarm the very soil of their country being in jeopardy, so that even the old men undertook the defence of the walls. While affairs were in this condition suddenly towards dawn a rabble of monks (for so I must call them, indicating their frenzy by the expression) rushed up to the house where we were, threatening to set fire to it, and to treat us with the utmost violence unless we turned out of it. And neither the fear of the Isaurians, nor my own infirmity which was so grievously afflicting me, nor anything else made them more reasonable, but they pressed on, animated by such fierce rage that even the proconsular soldiers were terrified. For they kept threatening them with blows and boasted that they had shamefully beaten many of the proconsular soldiers. The soldiers having heard these things, sought refuge with me, and entreated and beseeched me, saying "even if we are to fall into the hands of the Isaurians deliver us from these wild beasts." When the governor heard this he hastened down to the house intending to succour me. But the monks would not pay any heed to his exhortations, and in fact he was powerless. Perceiving the great strait in which affairs were placed and not daring to advise me either to go out to certain death, or on the other hand to stay indoors, owing to the excessive fury of these men, he sent to Pharetrius beseeching him to grant a few days respite on account of my infirmity and the impending danger. But even then nothing was effected, and on the morrow the monks arrived even fiercer than before, and none of the presbyters dared to stand by me and help me, but covered with shame and blushes (for they said that these things were done by the instructions of Pharetrius) they concealed themselves and lay hid, not responding even when I called them. What need to make a long story?

Although such great terrors were imminent, and death well nigh a certainty, and the fever was oppressing me (for I had not yet got relief from the troubles arising from that cause) I flung myself at high noon into the litter, and was carried out thence, all the people shrieking and howling, and imprecating curses on the perpetrator of these deeds, whilst every one wailed and lamented. But when I got outside the city, some of the clergy also gradually came out and escorted me, mourning as they went. And having heard some persons say "Where are you leading him away to manifest death?" one of those who was warmly attached to me said to me "Depart I entreat you; fall into the hands of the Isaurians, provided you get clear away from us. For wherever you may fall, you will fall into a place of security, if only you escape our hands." Having heard and seen these things the good Seleucia, the generous wife of my lord Ruffinus (a most attentive friend she was to me), exhorted and entreated me to lodge at her suburban house which was about five miles from the city and she sent some men to escort me, and so I departed thither.

3. But not even there was this plot against me to come to an end. For as soon as Pharetrius knew what she had done, he published, as she said, many threats against her. But when she received me into her suburban villa I knew nothing of these things; for when she came out to meet me she concealed these things from me, but disclosed them to her steward who was there, and ordered him to afford me every possible means of repose, and if any of the monks should make an assault, wishing to insult or maltreat me, he was to collect the labourers from her other farms, and thus marshal a force against them. Moreover she besought me to take refuge in her house, which had a fortress and was impregnable, that I might escape the hands of the bishop and monks. This however I could not be induced to do, but remained in the villa, knowing nothing of the plans which were devised after these things. For even then they were not content to desist from their fury against me but Pharetrius beset the lady as she says, straitly threatening her, constraining and forcing her to expel me even from the suburbs, so that at midnight, I knowing nothing of these things, the lady being unable to endure his annoyance, announced, without my knowledge, that the barbarians were at hand, for she was ashamed to mention the compulsion which she had undergone. So in the middle of the night Evethius the presbyter came to me, and having roused me from sleep, exclaimed with a loud voice "Get up, I pray you, the barbarians are upon us, they are close at hand." Imagine my condition on hearing

this! Then, when I said to him what must we do? we cannot take refuge in the city lest we suffer worse things than what the Isaurians are going to do to us, he compelled me to go out. It was midnight, a dark, murky night without a moon—a circumstance which filled up the measure of our perplexity—we had no companion, no assistant, for all had deserted us. Nevertheless under the pressure of fear and in the expectation of immediate death, I got up, suffering as I was, having ordered torches to be lit. These however the presbyter ordered to be put out, for fear as he said lest the barbarians should be attracted by the light and attack us; so the torches were extinguished. Then the mule which carried my litter fell on its knees, the road being rugged, and steep and stony, and I who was inside was thrown down and narrowly escaped destruction, after which I dismounted, and was dragged along on foot, being held fast by Evethius the presbyter (for he also had alighted from his mule), and so I plodded on, led, or rather hauled by the hand, for to walk was impossible through such a difficult country, and amongst steep mountains in the middle of the night. Imagine what my sufferings must have been, encompassed as I was by such calamities, and oppressed by the fever, ignorant of the plans which had been made, but in terror of the barbarians and trembling with the expectation of falling into their hands. Do you not think that these sufferings alone, even if nothing else besides had befallen me, would avail to blot out many of my sins, and afford ample material for obtaining praise with God? Now the reason of all this, at least as I suppose, was, that as soon as I arrived in Caesarea, those who were in official positions, the learned men who were ex-vicars, and ex-governors, the ex-tribunes and indeed the whole people visited me every day, paid me great attention, and treated me as the apple of their eye; I suppose these things irritated Pharetrius and that the envy which drove me from Constantinople did not refrain from pursuing me even here. This at least is what I suppose, for I do not positively declare it but only suspect it to be the fact.

And what is one to say about the other events which happened on the way, the fears and the perils? As I recall them day by day, and continually bear them in mind, I am elated with pleasure, I leap for joy as one who has a great treasure laid up in store for him; for such is my position and feeling about them. Wherefore also I beseech your honour to rejoice at these things, to be glad, and leap for joy, and to glorify God who has counted me worthy to suffer these things. And I beseech you to keep these matters to yourself, and not to divulge them to any one, although for the most part the proconsular soldiers can fill all the city (with the story) as they themselves have undergone extreme danger.

4. Nevertheless do not let any one know this from your prudence, but rather put down those who talk about it. But if you are distressed lest the consequences of my ill-treatment should remain, know for certain that I have shaken myself entirely free from them, and that I am in better bodily health than when I was sojourning in Caesarea. And why do you dread the cold? for a suitable dwelling has been prepared for me, and my lord Dioscorus does and arranges everything so as to prevent my having the least sensation of cold. And if I may form a conjecture from the outset of my experience, the climate now seems to me oriental in character, no less than that of Antioch. So great is the warmth, so pleasant is the temperature. But you have grieved me much by saying "perhaps you are annoyed with me as having neglected you," yet I despatched a letter many days ago to your honour begging you not to move me from this place. Now I have had occasion to consider that you need a strong defence and much toil and labour to be able to make a satisfactory apology for this expression. But perhaps you have made a partial apology, by saying "I am generally occupied in thinking how to increase my affliction." But I in my turn reckon it as the greatest accusation that you should say "I take a pride in increasing my sorrow by thinking over it:" for when you ought to make every possible effort to dispel your affliction you do the devil's will, by increasing your despondency and sorrow. Are you not aware how great an evil despondency is?

As to the Isaurians, dismiss your fears in future concerning them: for they have returned into their own country: and the governor has done everything necessary in this respect; and I am in far greater security here than when I was in Caesarea. For in future I have no one to fear so much as the bishops, with a few exceptions. On the account of the Isaurians then fear nothing: for they have retreated, and when winter has set in they are confined to their own homes, although they may possibly come out after Whitsuntide. And what do you mean by saying that you have not the benefit of letters from me? I have already sent you three long letters, one by the proconsular soldiers, one by Antonius, and the third by Anatolius my servant; two of them were a salutary medicine capable of reviving anyone who was desponding or stumbling, and conducting him into a healthy state of serenity. When you have received these letters then go over them constantly and thoroughly, and you will perceive their force and enjoy experience of their healing power, and benefit, and will inform me that you have derived much advantage therefrom. I have also a third letter ready, similar to these, which I do not choose to send at the present time having been exceedingly vexed at your saying "I accumulate sorrowful thoughts, even inventing things which do not exist," an utterance unworthy of yourself, which makes me hide my head for shame. But read those letters which I have sent, and you will no longer say these things, even if you are infinitely bent on being despondent. I at least have not ceased, and will not cease saying that sin is the only thing which is really distressing; and that all other things are but dust and smoke. For what is there grievous in inhabiting a prison and wearing a chain? or in being ill-treated when it is the occasion of so much gain? or why should exile be grievous or confiscation of goods? These are mere words, destitute of any terrible reality, words void of sorrow. For if you speak of death you only mention that which is the debt of nature: a thing which must in any case be undergone even if no one hastens it: and if you speak of exile you mention that which only involves a change of country and the sight of many cities: or if you speak of confiscation of goods you mention what is only freedom and emancipation from care.

5. Do not cease to pay attention to Maruthas the Bishop, as far as it concerns you, so as to lift him up out of the pit. For I have special need of him on account of the affairs in Persia. And ascertain from him, if you can, what has been accomplished there through his agency, and for what purpose he has come home, and let me know whether you have delivered the two epistles which I sent to him: and if he is willing to write to me, I will write to him again: but if he should not be willing let him at least signify to your prudence whether anything more has taken place there, and whether he is likely to accomplish anything by going thither again. For on this account I was anxious to have an interview with him. Nevertheless let all things which depend on you be done, and take care to fulfill your own part, even if all men are rushing headlong to ruin. For your reward will thus be perfected. By all means therefore make friends with him as far as it is possible. I beseech you not to neglect what I am about to say, but to pay diligent heed to it. The Marsian and Gothic monks where the Bishop Serapion has constantly been concealed have informed me that Moduarius the deacon has come bringing word that Unitas, that excellent bishop whom I lately ordained and sent into Gothia, has been laid to rest, after achieving many great exploits: and the deacon was the bearer of a letter from the king of the Goths begging that a bishop might be sent to them. Since then I see no other means of meeting the threatened catastrophe with a view to its correction save delay and postponement (as it is impossible for them to sail into the Bosporus or into those parts at the present time), take measures to put them off for a time on account of the winter season: and do not by any means neglect this: for it is a matter of the greatest importance. For there are two things which would specially distress me if they were to happen, which God forbid: one is that a bishop should be appointed by these men who have wrought such great wickedness, and who have no right to appoint, and the other is that any one should be made without consideration. For you know yourself that they are not anxious to create some worthy man bishop, and if this should take place, which heaven forbid, you are aware what will follow. Use all diligence therefore to prevent either of these things happening: but if it were possible for Moduarius quietly and secretly to hasten out to me it would be of the greatest advantage. But if this is not possible let what is practicable under the circumstances be done. For that which takes place in the case of money, and actually occurred in the case of the widow in the gospel, also holds good in the case of practical affairs. For as that poor woman when she had cast two mites into the treasury surpassed all those who had cast in more, because she used up her whole substance: even so they who devote themselves to the work in hand with all their might discharge it completely, so far as they are concerned, even if nothing results from it, and they have their reward perfected.

I am very grateful to Hilarius the bishop: for he wrote to me asking to be allowed to depart to his own country, and to set things in order there, and then to come back again. As his presence therefore is of great service (for he is a devout, inflexible, and zealous man) I have urged him to depart and to return speedily. Take care then that the letter is quickly and safely delivered to him and not cast on one side: for he eagerly and earnestly begged for letters from me, and his presence is a great benefit. By all means therefore have a care of the letters; and if Herodius the presbyter be not on the spot see that they are delivered to my friends by the hands of some discreet man who has a head on his shoulders.

75

THE LIFE OF OLYMPIAS, ASCETIC AND
SUPPORTER OF JOHN CHRYSOSTOM

Life of Olympias   5th century C.E.

Life or regime and action of the pious, blessed and righteous Olympias, who was deaconess of the very holy cathedral of Constantinople. Bless me, father.

1. The Kingdom of our Savior Jesus Christ, existing before the ages and shining forth to ages without end, confers immortality on those who have served as its shield-bearers, who have completed the race and kept their faith in God spotless and steadfast. There are those who have practiced hospitality, the crown of perfections, such as the holy forefather Abraham and his nephew Lot; others have fought for self-control, as the holy Joseph; others have contended with sufferings to win patience, as the blessed Job; others have delivered their bodies to the fire and to tortures in order to receive the crown of incorruptibility. Not fearing the outrages of tyrants, but as noble combatants they have trampled the devil under foot and have been received as inheritors of the Kingdom of God. Among them was Thecla, a citizen of heaven, a martyr who conquered in many contests, the holy one among women, who despised wealth, hated the sharp and transitory pleasures of this world, refused a pecunious marriage and confessed that she would present herself a chaste virgin to her true Bridegroom. Having followed the teachings of Paul, the blessed apostle, and having taken into her heart the divinely inspired Scriptures, she received the crown of incorruptibility from our Lord and Savior Jesus Christ and to ages without end she rests with all the saints who from eternity have pleased the Lord Jesus Christ. Olympias walked in the footsteps of this saint, Thecla, in every virtue of the divinely-inspired way of life. Olympias, most serious and zealous for the road leading to heaven, followed the intent of the divine Scriptures in everything and was perfected through these things.

2. She was daughter according to the flesh of Seleucus, one of the *comites,* but according to the spirit, she was the true child of God. It is said that she was descended from Ablabius who was governor and she was bride for a few days of Nebridius, the prefect of the city of Constantinople, but in truth she did not grace the bed of anyone. For it is said that she died an undefiled virgin, having become a partner of the divine Word, a consort of every true humility, a companion and servant of the holy, catholic and apostolic church of God. Left an orphan, she was joined in marriage to a husband, but by the goodness of God she was preserved uncorrupted in flesh and in spirit. For God, who watches over everything, who foresees the outcome of humans, did not deem it worthy for the one who was briefly her husband to live with her for a year. The debt of nature was shortly demanded of him and she was preserved a blameless virgin until the end.

3. Again she could have used the apostolic rule which says, "I wish young widows to marry, run a household," but she did not agree to this, although she had birth, wealth, a very expensive education, a naturally good disposition, and was adorned with the bloom of youth; like a gazelle, she leapt over the insufferable snare of a second marriage. "For the law was not laid down for the righteous man, but for the unruly, the impure, and the insatiable." Through a certain demonic jealousy, it transpired that her untimely widowhood became the subject of mischief. She was falsely accused before the emperor Theodosius of having dispensed her goods in a disorderly fashion. Since indeed she was his relation, he took pains to unite her in marriage with a certain Elpidius, a Spaniard, one of his own relatives. He directed many persistent entreaties to her and when he failed to achieve his goal, he was annoyed. The pious Olympias, however, explained her position to the emperor Theodosius: "If my King, the Lord Jesus Christ, wanted me to be joined with a man, he would not have taken away my first husband immediately. Since he knew that I was unsuited for the conjugal life and was not able to please a man, he freed him, Nebridius, from the bond and delivered me of this very burdensome yoke and servitude to a husband, having placed upon my mind the happy yoke of continence."

4. She clarified these things to the emperor Theodosius in this manner, before the plot against the most holy John, patriarch of Constantinople. The emperor, when he had heard the testimony against the pious Olympias, commanded the man then prefect of the city, Clementius, to keep her possessions under guard until she reached her thirtieth year, that is, her physical prime. And the prefect, having received the guardianship from the emperor, oppressed her to such a degree at Elpidius' urging (she did not have the right either to meet with the notable bishops nor to come near the church) so that groaning under the strain, she would meekly bear the option of marriage. But she, even more grateful to God, responded to these events by proclaiming, "You have shown toward my humble person, O sovereign master, a goodness befitting a king and suited to a bishop, when you commanded my very heavy burden to be put under careful guard, for the administration of it caused me anxiety. But you will do even better if you order that it be distributed to the poor and to the churches, for I prayed much to avoid the vainglory arising from the apportionment, lest I neglect true riches for those pertaining to material things."

5. The emperor, upon his return from the battle against Maximus, gave the order that she could exercise control over her own possessions, since he had heard of the intensity of her ascetic discipline. But she distributed all of her unlimited and immense wealth and assisted everyone, simply and without distinction. For the sake of many she surpassed that Samaritan of whom an account is given in the holy Gospels. Once upon a time he found on the road down to Jericho a man who was crushed half-dead by robbers; he raised him onto his own beast, carried him as far as the inn, and having mixed the oil of generosity with strong wine, he healed his wounds.

Then straightway after the distribution and sealing up of all her goods, there was rekindled in her the divine love and she took refuge in the haven of salvation, the great, catholic, and apostolic church of this royal city. She followed to the letter with intelligence the divinely-inspired teachings of the most holy archbishop of this sacred church, John, and gave to him for this holy church (imitating also in this act those ardent lovers and disciples of Christ who in the beginning of salvation's proclamation brought to the feet of the apostles their possessions) ten thousand pounds of gold, twenty thousand of silver and all of her real estate situated in the provinces of Thrace, Galatia, Cappadocia Prima, and Bithynia; and more, the houses belonging to her in the capital city, the one situated near the most holy cathedral, which is called "the house of Olympias"; together with the house of the tribune, complete with baths, and all the buildings near it; a mill; and a house which belonged to her in which she lived near the public baths of Constantinople; and another house of hers which was called the "house of Evander"; as well as all of her suburban properties.

6. Then by the divine will she was ordained deaconess of this holy cathedral of God and she built a monastery at an angle south of it. She owned all the houses lying near the holy church and all the shops which were at the southern angle mentioned. She constructed a path from the monastery up to the narthex of the holy church, and in the first quarter she enclosed her own chambermaids, numbering fifty, all of whom lived in purity and virginity. Next, Elisanthia, her relative who had seen the good work pleasing to God, which God gave to her to carry out, also herself a virgin, emulating the divine zeal, bade farewell to the ephemeral and empty things of life with her sisters Martyria and Palladia, also virgins. Then the three entered with all the others, having made over in advance all of their possessions to the same holy monastery. Likewise, also Olympia, the niece of the afore-said holy Olympias, with many other women of senatorial families, chose the Kingdom of Heaven and disdained these lowly things below which drag us down, in accordance with the grace and good favor of God who wishes all to be saved and who fosters the divine love in them. They entered also with the rest, so that all those who gathered together according to the grace of God in that holy fold of Christ numbered two hundred and fifty, all adorned with the crown of virginity and practicing the most exalted life which befits the saints.

7. When these events had transpired in this manner by divine assist-ance, the noble servant of God Olympias again brought to the above-mentioned hallowed church through the most holy patriarch John the entire remainder of all her real estate, situated in all the provinces, and her interest in the public bread supply. And he also ordained as dea-conesses of the holy church her three relatives, Elisanthia, Martyria, and Palladia, so that the four deaconesses would be able to be to-gether without interruption in the most sacred monastery founded by her.

8. One was struck with amazement at seeing certain things in the holy chorus and angelic institution of these holy women: their inces-sant continence and sleeplessness, the constancy of their praise and thanksgiving to God, their "charity which is the bond of perfection," their stillness. For no one from the outside, neither man nor woman, was permitted to come upon them, the only exception being the most holy patriarch John, who visited continuously and sustained them with his most wise teachings. Thus fortified each day by his divinely-inspired instruction, they kindled in themselves the divine love so that their great and holy love streamed forth to him. The pious and blessed Olympias (who in these matters too imitated the women disciples of Christ who served him from their possessions) prepared for the holy John his daily provisions and sent them to the bishop, for there was not much separation between the episcopal residence and the monas-tery, only a wall. And she did this not only before the plots against

him, but also after he was banished; up to the end of his life she provided for all his expenses as well as for those who were with him in his exile.

9. Then the devil could not bear the great and wondrous way of life of these pious women, the way of life, first of all, consistently made straight by God's grace, and secondly, a way made straight by the uninterrupted teaching of the most holy patriarch. Evil men who were hateful and had enmity to John among the holy men because he was no respecter of persons in his scrutiny of the unrighteous, the devil, the hater of good, suborned and struck with the arrow of calumny and they contrived a diabolical machination against both him, i.e. John, and that holy woman. He was slandered by them not only in respect to her, but also concerning ecclesiastical affairs; according to their whim, they condemned and exiled him. The herald and teacher of truth, however, received the assaults of his antagonists like a noble athlete and carried off the prize of victory, departing the storm of the present life and being transposed to the calm above. And this pious woman after his exile did not give way but made a motion for his recall to every royal and priestly person. The opposition encompassed her with numerous evils; they stitched together slanders and untimely abuse against her until the occasion when they made her appear before the city prefect for interrogation by him.

10. When they saw her openness concerning the truth, they could not bear the nobility and immutability of her love for God. They wished to put a stop to the constant activity in which she was engaged on behalf of the holy John's recall and they sent her as well into exile in Nicomedia, the capital city of the province of Bithynia. But she, strengthened by the divine grace, nobly and courageously, for the sake of love of God, bore the storms of trials and diverse tribulations which came upon her. The whole rest of her life she passed in the capital city of Nicomedia, performing every ascetic act and maintaining her rule of life unchanged there. Victorious in the good fight, she crowned herself with the crown of patience, having turned over her flock by the divine allotment to Marina, among the blessed, who was her relative and spiritual daughter, whom she had received from the undefiled and salvatory baptism; she prayed that she receive in turn the souls unto herself and be preserved in tranquillity in all things. And Marina did this for Olympias, not only for the remaining time which the holy Olympias passed in the metropolis of Nicomedia, but also after her death. For when the pious woman was about to join the holy fathers, both to be set free from the present life and to be with Christ, again she decreed in writing that the aforesaid Marina of divine choice exhibit much care and succor, and committed to her, after God, all the sisters and their care. Having done this, she escaped from the storm of human woes and crossed over to the calm haven of our souls, Christ the God.

11. But before her holy body was buried, she appeared in a dream to the metropolitan of the same city of Nicomedia, saying, "Place my remains in a casket, put it on a boat, let the boat go adrift into the stream, and at the place where the boat stops, disembark onto the ground and place me there." The metropolitan did what had been told him in the vision concerning Olympias and put the casketed body in the boat and let the boat loose into the stream. Toward the hour of midnight the boat reached the shore in front of the gallery of the pure house of the holy apostle Thomas which is in Brochthoi and there it rested without advancing further. At the same hour an angel of the Lord appeared in a dream to the superior and to the sacristan of the same august house, saying, "Rise and put the casket which you have found in the boat which has come to anchor on the shore in front of the gallery in the sanctuary." When they heard this, they saw all the church gates open by themselves, but since they were still asleep, they thought that the event was an illusion. Having secured the gates again, there appeared to them once more the previous vision. Still a third time, the angel pressed them with much earnestness and said, "Go out and take the casket of the holy Olympias, for she has suffered much for the sake of God, and put the casket in the sanctuary." Then they arose, again saw the gates of the church open, and no longer remained disbelieving. Taking the holy Gospels, the cross, the candelabra with candles, along with the incense, they went out praying into the gallery and found her holy remains in the boat. They called together all the female and male ascetics, and holding the candles and making great praise and thanksgiving to God, they deposited her holy remains in the sanctuary of the aforementioned venerable house of the holy apostle Thomas in Brochthoi. People could see numerous cures taking place at her holy tomb; impure spirits were banished and many diverse illnesses departed from those afflicted with them. And the holy, pious blessed servant of God, Olympias, ended her life in the month of July, on the 25th, in the reign of Arcadius, the most divine and pious emperor. She is numbered in the choir of the pious confes-

sors and reigns together with the immortal King, Christ our God, for ages without end.

12. After her death, the truly noble servant of God, Marina, the friend of Christ, Olympias' relative and spiritual daughter, whom, as has been said, she received from the holy, undefiled, salvatory baptism, made clear to everyone the love which she had for that blessed soul. Performing and fulfilling the deposit from Olympias and everything which she had commanded her, she took in her arms, preserved safe, and governed the whole caravan of her flock which Olympias had placed in her hands, after those of God and our Lady, the completely holy Mother of God, so that none of the sisters experienced any deprivation by their separation from that woman Olympias who is among the saints. And after the death of the pious woman Marina, there was chosen as leader of that holy flock of Christ, the very dear friend of God who was mentioned above, the deaconess Elisanthia, her relative, who preserved unchanged the entire rule which she had received from that pious and blessed soul, and she followed all her virtues.

13. Let these things be said. I have deemed it necessary and entirely useful for the profit of many to run over in the narrative one by one the holy virtues of the noble servant of God, Olympias, who is among the saints. For no place, no country, no desert, no island, no distant setting, remained without a share in the benevolence of this famous woman; rather, she furnished the churches with liturgical offerings and helped the monasteries and convents, the beggars, the prisoners, and those in exile; quite simply, she distributed her alms over the entire inhabited world. And the blessed Olympias herself burst the supreme limit in her almsgiving and her humility, so that nothing can be found greater than what she did. She had a life without vanity, an appearance without pretence, character without affectation, a face without adornment; she kept watch without sleeping, she had an immaterial body, a mind without vainglory, intelligence without conceit, an untroubled heart, an artless spirit, charity without limits, unbounded generosity, contemptible clothing, immeasurable self-control, rectitude of thought, undying hope in God, ineffable almsgiving; she was the ornament of all the humble and was in addition worthily honored by the most holy patriarch John. For she abstained from eating meat and for the most part she went without bathing. And if a need for a bath arose through sickness (for she suffered constantly in her stomach), she came down to the waters with her shift on, out of modesty even for herself, so they said.

14. And she looked after the needs of many fathers, as I have said, and of those of the most blessed John the archbishop, proving herself worthy of his virtue. For when he had been plotted against and exiled, as has already been explained, the pious woman provided without distraction for his need and for those with him. This is no small thing for the workers of Christ who are anxious both night and day for Christ's affairs. As Paul greeted Persis, Tryphaena, and Tryphosa, the pious Olympias, imitator of God, perhaps received the same greeting.

And I know that this completely virtuous and divinely-inspired Olympias provided also for the blessed Nectarius, the archbishop of Constantinople, who was completely persuaded by her even in the affairs of the church, and for Amphilochius, bishop of Iconium, and Optimus, and Peter, and Gregory the brother of the holy Basil, and Epiphanius the archbishop of Constantia in Cyprus, and many others of the saints and inspired fathers who lived in the capital city. Why is it necessary to say that she also bestowed upon them property in the country and money? And when the aforesaid Optimus died in Constantinople at this time, she shut the eyes of the great man with her own hands. In addition, she relieved the piteous without measure in all ways. She sustained Antiochus of Ptolemais, and Acacius, the bishop of Beroea, and the holy Severian, the bishop of Gabala, and in a word, all the priests residing there, in addition to innumerable ascetics and virgins.

15. And due to her sympathy for them, she endured many trials by the actions of a willfully evil and vulgar person; contending eagerly in not a few contests on behalf of the truth of God, she lived faultlessly in unmeasured tears night and day, "submitting to every human being for the sake of the Lord," full of every reverence, bowing before the saints, venerating the bishops, honoring the presbyters, respecting the priests, welcoming the ascetics, being anxious for the virgins, supplying the widows, raising the orphans, shielding the elderly, looking after the weak, having compassion on sinners, guiding the lost, having pity on all, pity without stinting anything on the poor. Engaging in much catechizing of unbelieving women and making provision for all the necessary things of life, she left a reputation for goodness throughout her whole life which is ever to be remembered. Having called from slavery to freedom her myriad household servants, she proclaimed them to be of the same honor as her own nobility. Or rather, if it is necessary to speak truthfully, they appeared more noble in their way of dress than that holy woman. For there could be found nothing cheaper than her clothing; the most ragged items were coverings unworthy of her manly courage. And she cultivated in herself a gentleness so that she surpassed even the simplicity of children themselves. Never any blame, not even from her neighbors, was incurred by that image of Christ, but her whole intolerable life was spent in penitence and in a great flood of tears. One was more likely to see the fount run dry in the trenches than her eyes, lowered, always gazing on Christ, leave off crying for a while. Why go on? For to whatever extent I might provide leisure for my mind to recount the contests and virtues of this ardent soul, one will find many and poor the descriptions of the deeds. And does anyone not believe that I speak with restraint concerning the steadfast Olympias, who besides was an entirely precious vessel of the Holy Spirit? There was an eyewitness who also viewed the life of this blessed woman, her angelic regime; since he was her true spiritual friend and related to her family, much was distributed by him in accordance with her intent.

16. Accordingly, the divine and divinely-inspired Olympias herself, no longer having any fleshly thought, submitted herself to the authorities, obedient to the powers, bowed before the churches, venerated the bishops and the presbyters, honored all the clergy, was deemed worthy as a confessor on behalf of the truth and received the many storms of unjust slander; her life was judged to be among the confessors by as many pious people as dwelt in Constantinople. For close to death, she took the risk in the contests for God. Having perfected herself in these, she won the blessed glory and is crowned in an endless age. And she is a member of the chorus in the undefiled mansions where she lives with the pious souls like herself and where she openly demands from the Lord God the recompense for good deeds.

17. Let us ask that her prayers importune the benevolent God who pities everybody, that he give up tortures for our sins and quench the Gehenna kindled by our failures, that we may turn in repentance to the good-hearted God and receive from him abundant pity. And the holy and blessed woman exhorts us who read and hear, she teaches us in Christ Jesus by the voice of St. Paul, the chorus leader of the holy apostles, "Preserve the traditions which you have learned beforehand, and watch, how you walk not as the foolish, but as the wise; redeem the time, for the days are evil, for the battle is not against flesh and blood but against the princes, against the powers, against the world-rulers of this dark age, against the spiritual powers of evil in the heavens," that is, not only does he mean against men but against the unclean spirits, who suggest to each person to continue in errors and destructively subvert those who have their heads in the air. Therefore put on the armor of God, that is, purity of body and spirit, humility, gentleness, continence. Return no one evil for evil, but if you see your brother stumbling in some way, or about to be cast down by the devil, do not remain silent, lest he fall, but just as the divine Scriptures teach us, accuse him, censure him, exhort him, looking out for yourself lest you also be tempted. Then let no one deceive you by persuasiveness and the flattery of empty and idle words, but behave in a seemly fashion to everyone, most of all to those in the household of faith. And watch out also for this: for if a woman married to a mortal and perishable man is found to be corrupted by another, she will be subjected to punishments, torments, and exiles, how much more will the one who is promised in marriage to our ruler and Lord Jesus Christ, if she abandon him and cleave to this vain and transitory life, merit a worse punishment? But may the Lord make us pure and blameless before his face in love, in the embassy of our holy, honored Lady, the Mother of God and ever-virgin Mary, and of the holy Olympias, and both the readers and the hearers with their whole souls. May the Lord give grace and pity on the day of judgment and he will deliver us all completely from the devil's deeds, in Christ Jesus our Lord.

18. And I ask you, I the sinner who also has written this, I adjure you according to the benevolent God, the ruler of all, and to our Lord Jesus Christ and to the Holy Spirit, that you who read in peace and listen in true hope pray on behalf of my poor soul for the remission of sins and that a favorable judgment be offered to me and to all readers by our benevolent Savior Jesus Christ, the true and living God, for to him belong glory, honor, and adoration, with the Father and the Holy Spirit, now and forever, throughout the ages. Amen.

76

EPITAPH OF EUTERPE, A CHRISTIAN WOMAN
CALLED COMPANION OF
THE MUSES

Guarducci 4:525   Sicily, 5th century C.E.

Here lies Euterpe, the companion of the Muses. She lived chastely and piously and blamelessly for 22 years, 3 months. She died on November 27.

77

DONATION BY A CHRISTIAN SHIPOWNER
AND HER DAUGHTER

Guarducci 4:373   Cos, 5th century C.E.

Eustochiane, the most modest shipowner, and Maria her daughter, adorned the portico with mosaic.

Religious Office

A significant portion of the evidence we have for women's religious activities in Greco-Roman antiquity relates to their roles as officiants in religious rites and as holders of office in religious communities. This evidence is often concrete. Various inscriptions and epitaphs identify specific women as officials and leaders, whether in pagan, Jewish, or Christian contexts. An inscription honoring Tata of Aphrodisias informs us that she was a priestess of Hera for life and a *stephanophorus* (literally, crown-bearer) in the imperial cult. It also indicates in some detail the responsibilities she undertook in those capacities.

Testimony to the leadership roles of women in religious contexts has received a mixed response from scholars. Many classicists seem willing to take at face value the evidence for women as priestesses and other cult officials, but scholars of early Judaism and early Christianity have routinely misinterpreted or discounted the sources documenting women as religious leaders in early synagogues and churches. Several generations of scholars have insisted that Jewish inscriptions that attribute titles of synagogue office to women must have been "honorary" in nature, by which they mean that women bore titles only but played no meaningful and official role in their communities. Without any substantiating evidence, women's titles are dismissed as the titles of their husbands or fathers. Or they are explained as a reward for financial contributions, conferring some public recognition but no authority. As Bernadette Brooten has convincingly demonstrated, there is no basis for such interpretations except the unsubstantiated assumptions of scholars that women could not have been holders of legitimate religious office in ancient Jewish synagogues.[1]

Evidence for women leaders in early Christian churches has not fared much better. At the beginning of the third century C.E., Tertullian railed against those who would interpret the Acts of Thecla as evidence that women could baptize and teach,[2] and centuries of commentators have not departed significantly from his assumption that the evidence for there being women in strong leadership positions is not to be taken as authoritative. Ironically, Tertullian's motive was not far different from that of modern interpreters: namely, the fear that an account of a woman baptizing and teaching would be used to legitimate the authority of other women to baptize and teach. Twentieth-century discussions of women's leadership in early Judaism and early Christianity have been undertaken principally in the light of debates about the legitimacy of women priests, ministers, and rabbis in our own time. Both supporters and antagonists of having women hold modern religious office have looked to ancient practice to substantiate their position, a procedure fraught with difficulty not the least because of the thorny question of whether contemporary religious practice must have a legitimation in ancient custom.[3]

Much work remains to be done concerning the exercise of leadership and authority by women in ancient religious contexts. We need to know more about exactly which offices women have held and what activities, authority, prestige, honors, and responsibility went with those offices. We need to know more about how one attained religious offices, including the factors of family connections, financial contributions, and the like.

More attention should also be paid to the correlations between the gender of the deity and the gender of the deity's officiants. In the extremely popular cult of the goddess Isis, which had many women devotees, cult offices were held by both women and men, but the higher offices seem to have been held mostly by men, as Françoise Dunand notes.[4] Still, we need to employ the kind of precise, detailed

1. Bernadette J. Brooten, *Women Leaders in the Ancient Synagogues,* BJS 36 (Chico, Calif.: Scholars Press, 1982).

2. Tertullian *On Baptism* 17.

3. See, e.g., Elaine Pagels, "Paul and Women: A Response to Recent Discussion," *Journal of the American Academy of Religion* 42 (1974): 538–49.

4. Françoise Dunand, "Le Statut des Hiereiai en Egypte Romaine," in *Hommages à Maarten J. Vermaseren,* ed. M. B. de Boer and T. A. Edridge (Leiden: E. J. Brill, 1978), 1:352–74.

approach that Dunand typifies, in order to learn whether women were more likely to hold religious office in the service of goddesses than in the service of gods.

For Judaism and Christianity, such analysis may seem pointless at first. Theological insistence that God has no gender aside, God is routinely presented in early Jewish and Christian materials as male. More and more scholars, though, are beginning to recognize that within early Judaism and early Christianity, significant feminine aspects of divinity may be detected, whether in the figure of Wisdom (which is feminine both in Hebrew and in Greek),[5] in the description of Metanoia in *The Conversion and Marriage of Aseneth,* or in the various gnostic texts from the Nag Hammadi Library. Tantalizing evidence may suggest that women played greater leadership roles in communities that employed such texts, language, and imagery. We need to pursue this possibility further while treating the simplistic correlations with caution.

5. For discussion of the feminine Sophia in early Christianity, see Elisabeth Schüssler Fiorenza, *In Memory of Her: A Feminist Theological Reconstruction of Christian Origins* (New York: Crossroad, 1983), 130–40. See also Rose Horman Arthur, *The Wisdom Goddess: Feminine Motifs in Eight Nag Hammadi Documents* (Lanham, Md.: Univ. Press of America, 1984), and Deirdre J. Good, *Restructuring the Tradition of Sophia in Gnostic Literature,* SBLMS 32 (Atlanta: Scholars Press, 1987). Additional bibliography may be found in the Authors and Sources section, under Nag Hammadi Library.

78

HONORS AND PRIVILEGES BESTOWED ON A
PRIESTESS OF ATHENA AFTER
A PROCESSION TO PYTHIAN APOLLO

IG II^2 1136.   Delphi, 2d century B.C.E.

. . . Greetings. Whereas the people of Athens led a Pythian procession to Pythian Apollo in a grand manner worthy of the god and their
particular excellence: the priestess of Athena, Chrysis daughter of
Nicetes, also was present with the procession; she made the journey
out and the return well, appropriately, and worthily of the people of
Athens and of our own city. With good fortune, it was voted by the
city of Delphi to praise Chrysis, daughter of Nicetes, and to crown
her with the god's crown that is customary among the Delphians. It
was voted also to give *proxenia* to her and to her descendants from the
city, and the right to consult the oracle, priority of trial, safe conduct,
freedom from taxes, and a front seat at all the contests held by the
city, the right to own land and a house and all the other honours
customary for *proxenoi* and benefactors of the city.

79

THE INSTITUTION OF THE
VESTAL VIRGINS

Plutarch *Life of Numa Pompilius* 10   1st century C.E.

In the beginning, then, they say that Gegania and Verenia were consecrated to this office by Numa, who subsequently added to them Canuleia and Tarpeia; that at a later time two others were added by Servius, making the number which has continued to the present time. It was ordained by the king that the sacred virgins should vow themselves to chastity for thirty years; during the first decade they are to learn their duties, during the second to perform the duties they have learned, and during the third to teach others these duties. Then, the thirty years being now passed, any one who wishes has liberty to marry and adopt a different mode of life, after laying down her sacred office. We are told, however, that few have welcomed the indulgence, and that those who did so were not happy, but were a prey to repentance and dejection for the rest of their lives, thereby inspiring the rest with superstitious fears, so that until old age and death they remained steadfast in their virginity.

But Numa bestowed great privileges upon them, such as the right to make a will during the life time of their fathers, and to transact and manage their other affairs without a guardian, like the mothers of three children. When they appear in public, the fasces are carried before them, and if they accidentally meet a criminal on his way to execution, his life is spared; but the virgin must make oath that the meeting was involuntary and fortuitous, and not of design. He who passes under the litter on which they are borne, is put to death. For their minor offences the virgins are punished with stripes, the Pontifex Maximus sometimes scourging the culprit on her bare flesh, in a dark place, with a curtain interposed. But she that has broken her vow of chastity is buried alive near the Colline gate. Here a little ridge of earth extends for some distance along the inside of the city-wall; the Latin word for it is "agger." Under it a small chamber is constructed, with steps leading down from above. In this are placed a couch with its coverings, a lighted lamp, and very small portions of the necessaries of life, such as bread, a bowl of water, milk, and oil, as though they would thereby absolve themselves from the charge of destroying by hunger a life which had been consecrated to the highest services of religion. Then the culprit herself is placed on a litter, over which coverings are thrown and fastened down with cords so that not even a cry can be heard from within, and carried through the forum. All the people there silently make way for the litter, and follow it without uttering a sound, in a terrible depression of soul. No other spectacle is more appalling, nor does any other day bring more gloom to the city than this. When the litter reaches its destination, the attendants unfasten the cords of the coverings. Then the high-priest, after stretching his hands toward heaven and uttering certain mysterious prayers before the fatal act, brings forth the culprit, who is closely veiled, and places her on the steps leading down into the chamber. After this he turns his face, as do the rest of the priests, and when she has gone down, the steps are taken up, and great quantities of earth are thrown into the entrance to the chamber, hiding it away, and making the place level with the rest of the mound. Such is the punishment of those who break their vow of virginity.

80

HOW VESTAL VIRGINS
ARE CHOSEN

Aulus Gellius *Attic Nights* I.12   2d century C.E.

Those who have written about "taking" a Vestal virgin, of whom
the most painstaking is Antistius Labeo, have stated that it is unlawful
for a girl to be chosen who is less than six, or more than ten, years
old; she must also have both father and mother living; she must be
free too from any impediment in her speech, must not have impaired
hearing, or be marked by any other bodily defect; she must not herself
have been freed from paternal control, nor her father before her, even
if her father is still living and she is under the control of her grandfather; neither one nor both of her parents may have been slaves or
engaged in mean occupations. But they say that one whose sister has
been chosen to that priesthood acquires exemption, as well as one
whose father is a flamen or an augur, one of the Fifteen in charge of
the Sibylline Books, one of the Seven who oversee the banquets of the
gods, or a dancing priest of Mars. Exemption from that priesthood is
regularly allowed also to the betrothed of a pontiff and to the daughter of a priest of the tubilustrium. Furthermore the writings of Ateius
Capito inform us that the daughter of a man without residence in
Italy must not be chosen, and that the daughter of one who has three
children must be excused.

Now, as soon as the Vestal virgin is chosen, escorted to the House
of Vesta and delivered to the pontiffs, she immediately passes from
the control of her father without the ceremony of emancipation or
loss of civil rights, and acquires the right to make a will.

But as to the method and ritual for choosing a Vestal, there are,
it is true, no ancient written records, except that the first to be appointed was chosen by Numa. There is, however, a Papian law, which
provides that twenty maidens be selected from the people at the
discretion of the chief pontiff, that a choice by lot be made from that
number in the assembly, and that the girl whose lot is drawn be
"taken" by the chief pontiff and become Vesta's. But that allotment in
accordance with the Papian law is usually unnecessary at present. For
if any man of respectable birth goes to the chief pontiff and offers his
daughter for the priesthood, provided consideration may be given to

her candidacy without violating any religious requirement, the senate grants him exemption from the Papian law.

Now the Vestal is said to be "taken," it appears, because she is grasped by the hand of the chief pontiff and led away from the parent under whose control she is, as if she had been taken in war. In the first book of Fabius Pictor's *History* the formula is given which the chief pontiff should use in choosing a Vestal. It is this: "I take thee, Amata, as one who has fulfilled all the legal requirements, to be priestess of Vesta, to perform the rites which it is lawful for a Vestal to perform for the Roman people, the Quirites."

Now, many think that the term "taken" ought to be used only of a Vestal. But, as a matter of fact, the flamens of Jupiter also, as well as the augurs, were said to be "taken." Lucius Sulla, in the second book of his *Autobiography,* wrote as follows: "Publius Cornelius, the first to receive the surname Sulla, was taken to be flamen of Jupiter." Marcus Cato, in his accusation of Servius Galba, says of the Lusitanians: "Yet they say that they wished to revolt. I myself at the present moment wish a thorough knowledge of the pontifical law; shall I therefore be taken as chief pontiff? If I wish to understand the science of augury thoroughly, shall anyone for that reason take me as augur?"

Furthermore, in the *Commentaries on the Twelve Tables* compiled by Labeo we find this passage: "A Vestal virgin is not heir to any intestate person, nor is anyone her heir, should she die without making a will, but her property, they say, reverts to the public treasury. The legal principle involved is an unsettled question."

The Vestal is called "Amata" when taken by the chief pontiff, because there is a tradition that the first one who was chosen bore that name.

81

THE TITLES, HONORS, AND
OFFICES OF TATA

Pleket 18   Aphrodisias, 2d century c.e.

The council and the people and the senate honour with first-rank honours Tata, daughter of Diodorus son of Diodorus son of Leon, reverend priestess of Hera for life, mother of the city, who became and remained the wife of Attalus son of Pytheas the *stephanephorus*, herself a member of an illustrious family of the first rank, who, as priestess of the imperial cult a second time, twice supplied oil for athletes in hand-bottles, filled most lavishly from basins for the better part of the night as well [as in the day], who became a *stephanephorus*, offered sacrifices throughout the year for the health of the imperial family, who held banquets for the people many times with couches provided for the public, who herself, for dances and plays, imported the foremost performers in Asia and displayed them in her native city (and the neighbouring cities could also come to the display of the performance), a woman who spared no expense, who loved honour, glorious in virtue and chastity.

82

HONORS FOR THE PRIESTESS
BERENICE

Pleket 25   Syros, 2d/3d century C.E.

The resolution of the *prytaneis* approved by the council and the
people: Whereas Berenice, daughter of Nicomachus, wife of Aristocles
son of Isidorus, has conducted herself well and appropriately on all
occasions, and after she was made a magistrate, unsparingly celebrated
rites at her own expense for gods and men on behalf of her native city,
and after she was made priestess of the heavenly gods and the holy
goddesses Demeter and Kore and celebrated their rites in a holy and
worthy manner, has given up her life—meanwhile she had also raised
her own children. Voted to commend the span of this woman's lifetime, to crown her with the gold wreath which in our fatherland is
customarily used to crown good women. Let the man who proposed
this resolution announce at her burial: "The people of Syros crown
Berenice daughter of Nicomachus with a gold crown in recognition of
her virtue and her good will towards them."

83

A PRIESTESS HONORED BY
THE SENATE

Pleket 29   Thasos, 4th century C.E.?

With good fortune. The senate honours Flavia Vibia Sabina, most
noteworthy high priestess, and because of her ancestors uniquely
mother of the council: she is the only woman, first in all time to have
honours equal to those of the senators.

84

EPITAPH OF RUFINA, HEAD OF
THE SYNAGOGUE

CIJ 741   Smyrna, Ionia, 2d century c.e.

Rufina, a Jewess, head of the synagogue, built this tomb for her freed slaves and the slaves raised in her house. No one else has the right to bury anyone (here). Anyone who dares to do (so), will pay 1500 denaria to the sacred treasury and 1000 denaria to the Jewish people. A copy of this inscription has been placed in the (public) archives.

85

EPITAPH OF SOPHIA OF GORTYN, HEAD OF
THE SYNAGOGUE

CIJ 731c   Kastelli Kissamou, Crete, 4th/5th century c.e.

Sophia of Gortyn, elder and head of the synagogue of Kisamos (lies) here. The memory of the righteous one for ever. Amen.

86

INSCRIPTION OF THEOPEMPTE, HEAD OF
THE SYNAGOGUE

CIJ 756   Myndos, Caria, Asia Minor, 4th/5th century c.e.

[From Th]eopempte, head of the synagogue, and her son Eusebios.

87

EPITAPH OF A JEWISH
WOMAN LEADER

CIJ 696b   Thebes in Phthiotis, Thessaly, date uncertain

Tomb of Peristeria, leader.

88

SIX EPITAPHS OF JEWISH WOMEN ELDERS IN THE FIRST SIX CENTURIES C.E.

CIJ 400   Rome

Here lies Sara Ura, elder (or: aged woman).

CIJ 581   Venosa, Italy

Tomb of Beronike, elder and daughter of Ioses.

CIJ 590   Venosa, Italy

Tomb of Mannine, elder; daughter of Longinus, father; grand-daughter of Faustinus, father; (aged) 38 years.

CIJ 597   Venosa, Italy

Tomb of Faustina, elder.

CIJ 692   Bizye, Thrace

Tomb of Rebeka, the elder, who has fallen asleep.

SEG 27 (1977), 1201   Oea, Tripolitania, North Africa

Tomb of Makaria (or: the blessed) Mazauzala, elder. She lived [. . .] years. Rest. God is with the holy and the righteous ones.

89

EPITAPH OF A JEWISH
MARRIED WOMAN ELDER

Kraemer, *HTR* 78 (1985): 431–38   Malta, 4th/5th century C.E.

[. . .], head of the council of elders, lover of the commandments, and Eulogia, the elder, his wife.

90

EPITAPH OF A JEWISH PRIESTESS
FROM EGYPT

CIJ/CPJ 1514   Tel el Yahoudieh, Leontopolis, Egypt, June 7, 28 B.C.E.

O Marin, priestess, worthy one, friend to all, causing pain to no one and friend to your neighbors, farewell. Approximately fifty years old. In the third year of Caesar, on the 13th day of Payni.

91

EPITAPH OF A ROMAN JEWISH WOMAN
CALLED PRIESTESS

CIJ 315   Rome, 3d/4th century C.E.

Here lies Gaudentia, 24, priestess. In peace (be) her sleep.

92

EPITAPH OF THE MOTHER OF A
JEWISH WOMAN CALLED PRIESTESS

CIJ 1007   Beth Shearim, 4th century C.E.

Sara, daughter of Naimia, mother of the priestess Lady Maria, lies here.

93

EPITAPH OF A CHRISTIAN WOMAN ELDER

L'Ann. épig. (1975), 454   Date uncertain

Here lies Kale, the elder. She lived 50 years blamelessly. Her life ended September 14.

94

EPITAPH OF A CHRISTIAN WOMAN ELDER, POSSIBLY MONTANIST

Gibson 1975   Asia Minor, 3d century C.E.

Diogas the bishop to Ammion (fem.) the elder, in memory.

95

EPITAPH OF SOPHIA THE DEACON, THE SECOND PHOEBE

Guarducci 4:445   Jerusalem, late 4th century C.E.

Here lies the servant and bride of Christ
Sophia the deacon, the second Phoebe,
She fell asleep in peace on the 21st of the month of March
in the 11th indiction . . .

NOTE: In selections 95–100, I have tried to show a distinction in the Greek terminology by translating, "deacon," when the Greek uses the feminine article with the masculine form *(hē diakonos)* and, "deaconess," when the Greek uses the feminine article with a feminized form *(hē diakonissa)*. The use both of masculine terms with a feminine article and of feminized forms occurs for the terms "elder" *(presbyter, presbyterissa)* and several other terms of synagogue office.

96

A VOW FULFILLED BY THE DEACON AGRIPPIANE

Bull. épig. 89 (1976), 288   Patrae, Greece

The deacon Agrippiane, most beloved of God, made the mosaic because of her vow.

97

A BURIAL MONUMENT ERECTED BY
A WOMAN DEACON, DAUGHTER OF
AN ELDER

MAMA 7, 471   Bulduk, date uncertain

Domna the deacon, daughter of Theophilos the elder, set up (the monument) to her own father-in-law, Miros, and to her husband, Patroklos, in memory.

98

A VOW FULFILLED BY
A DEACONESS

NewDocs 2 (1977): 194   Stobi, 4th/5th century C.E.

Because of a vow of the matron the most pious deaconess paved the exedra with mosaic.

NOTE: The woman's name may be Matrona.

99

EPITAPH OF THE DEACONESS
ATHANASIA

Guarducci 4:345   Delphi, 5th century C.E.

The most pious deaconess Athanasia
having lived a blameless life modestly
having been ordained a deaconess by the most holy bishop,
Pantamianos, made this monument, in which lie her remains.
If any other dares to open this monument, in which the
deaconess has been deposited, he will have the portion of
Judas, the betrayer of our Lord, Jesus Christ.
No less so those clerics who may be present at this
time, and assent [to the removal of]
the aforementioned deaconess. . . .

100

EPITAPH OF MARIA
THE DEACON

NewDocs 2 (1977), 109   Archelais, Cappadocia, 6th century C.E.

Here lies Maria the deacon, of pious and blessed memory, who in
accordance with the statement of the apostle reared children, practised
hospitality, washed the feet of the saints, distributed her bread to the
afflicted. Remember her, Lord, when you come in your kingdom.

A MONTANIST VISIONARY WHO SUBMITS
HER REVELATION TO
CAREFUL SCRUTINY

Tertullian *On the Soul* 9   2d/3d century c.e.

We have now amongst us a sister whose lot it has been to be favoured with gifts of revelation, which she experiences in the Spirit by
ecstatic vision amidst the sacred rites of the Lord's Day in the church;
she converses with angels, and sometimes even with the Lord; she
both sees and hears mysterious communications; some men's hearts
she discerns, and she obtains directions for healing for such as need
them. Whether it be in the reading of the Scriptures, or in the chanting of psalms, or in the preaching of sermons, or in the offering up of
prayers, in all these religious services matter and opportunity are
afforded her of seeing visions. Perchance, while this sister of ours was
in the Spirit, we had discoursed on some topic about the soul. After
the people are dismissed at the conclusion of the sacred services, she is
in the regular habit of reporting to us whatever things she may have
seen in vision; for all her communications are examined with the most
scrupulous care, in order that their truth may be probed. "Amongst
other things," she says, "there was shown to me a soul in bodily
shape, and a spirit appeared to me; not, however, a void and empty
illusion, but such as would offer itself to be even grasped by the hand,
clear and transparent and of an ethereal colour, and in form resembling that of a human being in every respect." This was her vision,
and for her witness there was God; and the apostle is a fitting surety
that there were to be Spiritual gifts in the Church.

THE MONTANIST PROPHETS
MAXIMILLA AND PRISCILLA

Hippolytus *Refutation of All Heresies* VIII.12　　　　　2d/3d century C.E.

But there are others who themselves are even more heretical in nature [than the foregoing], and are Phrygians by birth. These have been rendered victims of error from being previously captivated by [two] wretched women, called a certain Priscilla and Maximilla, whom they supposed [to be] prophetesses. And they assert that into these the Paraclete Spirit had departed; and antecedently to them, they in like manner consider Montanus as a prophet. And being in possession of an infinite number of their books, [the Phrygians] are overrun with delusion; and they do not judge whatever statements are made by them, according to [the criterion of] reason; nor do they give heed unto those who are competent to decide; but they are heedlessly swept onwards, by the reliance which they place on these [impostors]. And they allege that they have learned something more through these, than from law, and prophets, and the Gospels. But they magnify these wretched women above the Apostles and every gift of Grace, so that some of them presume to assert that there is in them a something superior to Christ. These acknowledge God to be the Father of the universe, and Creator of all things, similarly with the Church, and [receive] as many things as the Gospel testifies concerning Christ. They introduce, however, the novelties of fasts, and feasts, and meals of parched food, and repasts of radishes, alleging that they have been instructed by women.

WOMEN BISHOPS, PRESBYTERS, AND PROPHETS AMONG THE FOLLOWERS OF QUINTILLA AND PRISCILLA

Epiphanius *Medicine Box* 49   4th century C.E.

1. The Quintillians, who are also called Pepuzians, Artotyritai, and Priscillians, are all Cataphrygians and originate from them but differ somewhat among themselves. These Cataphrygians or Priscillians say that in Pepuza either Quintilla or Priscilla, I am not sure which, but one of them, was, as they said, sleeping in Pepuza when Christ came to her and lay beside her in the following fashion, as that deluded woman recounted. "In a vision," she said, "Christ came to me in the form of a woman in a bright garment, endowed me with wisdom, and revealed to me that this place is holy, and it is here that Jerusalem is to descend from heaven." Because of this they say that even to this day some women and men engage in incubation on the spot waiting to see Christ. Some women among them are called prophetesses, but I do not clearly know whether among them or among the Cataphrygians. They are alike and have the same way of thinking.

2. They use both the Old and New Testament and also speak in the same way of a resurrection of the dead. They consider Quintilla together with Priscilla as founder, the same as the Cataphrygians. They bring with them many useless testimonies, attributing a special grace to Eve because she first ate of the tree of knowledge. They acknowledge the sister of Moses as a prophetess as support for their practice of appointing women to the clergy. Also, they say, Philip had four daughters who prophesied. Often in their assembly seven virgins dressed in white enter carrying lamps, having come in to prophesy to the people. They deceive the people present by giving the appearance of ecstasy; they pretend to weep as if showing the grief of repentance by shedding tears and by their appearance lamenting human life. Women among them are bishops, presbyters, and the rest, as if there were no difference of nature. "For in Christ Jesus there is neither male nor female." These are the things we have learned. They are called Artotyritai because in their mysteries they use bread and cheese and in this fashion they perform their rites.

3. It is totally laughable among human beings to separate from the correct belief and turn to vanity and the variety of ecstasies and frenzies. Deranged minds follow those who do not hold fast to the anchor of truth and those who yield themselves to anyone who would lead them after any cause whatsoever. Even if women among them are ordained to the episcopacy and presbyterate because of Eve, they hear the Lord saying: "Your orientation will be toward your husband and he will rule over you." The apostolic saying escaped their notice, namely that: "I do not allow a woman to speak or have authority over a man." And again: "Man is not from woman but woman from man"; and "Adam was not deceived, but Eve was first deceived into transgression." Oh, the multifaceted error of this world!

Passing this judgment as on a toothless lizard full of madness, I will go on to the next things, beloved, calling upon God to help our inadequacy and to enable us to fulfill our promise [i.e., to write the book].

104

THE MONTANIST PROPHETS
MAXIMILLA AND PRISCILLA

Eusebius *History of the Church* V.16   4th century C.E.
                                        in reference to 2d century C.E.

7—10. In Phrygian Mysia there is said to be a village called Arda-
bav. There they say that a recent convert called Montanus, when
Gratus was proconsul of Asia, in the unbounded lust of his soul for
leadership gave access to himself to the adversary, became obsessed,
and suddenly fell into frenzy and convulsions. He began to be ecstatic
and to speak and to talk strangely, prophesying contrary to the custom which belongs to the tradition and succession of the church from
the beginning. Of those who at that time heard these bastard utterances some were vexed, thinking that he was possessed by a devil
and by a spirit of error, and was disturbing the populace; they rebuked him, and forbade him to speak, remembering the distinction
made by the Lord, and his warning to keep watchful guard against the
coming of the false prophets; but others, as though elevated by a holy
spirit and a prophetic gift, and not a little conceited, forgot the Lord's
distinction, and encouraged the mind-injuring and seducing and
people-misleading spirit, being cheated and deceived by it so that he
could not be kept silent. But by some art, or rather by such an evil
scheme of artifice, the devil wrought destruction for the disobedient,
and receiving unworthy honours from them stimulated and inflamed
their understanding which was already dead to the true faith; so that
he raised up two more women and filled them with the bastard spirit
so that they spoke madly and improperly and strangely, like Montanus. The spirit gave blessings to those who rejoiced and were proud
in him, and puffed them up by the greatness of its promises. Yet
sometimes it flatly condemned them completely, wisely, and faithfully,
that it might seem to be critical, though but few of the Phrygians
were deceived. But when the arrogant spirit taught to blaspheme the
whole Catholic church throughout the world, because the spirit of
false prophecy received from it neither honour nor entrance, for the
Christians of Asia after assembling for this purpose many times and in
many parts of the province, tested the recent utterances, pronounced
them profane, and rejected the heresy,—then at last the Montanists
were driven out of the church and excommunicated.

17–19. . . . and he writes thus: "And let not the spirit which speaks through Maximilla say, in the same work according to Asterius Orbanus, 'I am driven away like a wolf from the sheep. I am not a wolf, I am word and spirit and power.' But let him show clearly and prove the power in the spirit, and let him through the spirit force to recognize him those who were then present for the purpose of testing and conversing with the spirit as it spoke,—eminent men and bishops, Zoticus from the village Cumane, and Julian from Apamea, whose mouths the party of Themiso muzzled, and did not allow the false spirit which deceived the people to be refuted by them."

In the same book, again, after other refutations of the false prophecies of Maximilla, in a single passage he both indicates the time at which he wrote this, and quotes her predictions, in which she foretold future wars and revolutions, and he corrects the falsehood of them as follows: "Has it not been made obvious already that this is another lie? For it is more than thirteen years to-day since the woman died, and there has been in the world neither local nor universal war, but rather by the mercy of God continuing peace even for Christians."

105

SAYINGS OF THE MONTANIST MAXIMILLA, FROM THE 2D CENTURY C.E.

Epiphanius *Medicine Box* 48   4th century C.E.

2.4. After me, there will be no prophet, but the completion.

12.4. Hear not me; rather, hear Christ [through me].

13.1. The Lord sent me to be partisan, informer, interpreter of this task, and of the covenant and of the pronouncement; compelled, willingly or unwillingly, to learn the knowledge of God.

106

SAYINGS OF THE MONTANIST PRISCILLA, FROM THE 2D CENTURY C.E.

Epiphanius *Medicine Box* 49.1.3   4th century C.E.

Appearing in the form of a woman, radiantly robed, Christ came to me and implanted wisdom within me and revealed to me that this place [Pepuza] is holy, and that here Jerusalem is to come down from heaven.

Eusebius *History of the Church* V.16.17   4th century C.E.

I am driven away as a wolf from sheep. I am not a wolf. I am Word and Spirit and Power.

107

REGULATIONS FOR
DEACONESSES

Constitutions of the Holy Apostles II.26   4th century C.E.?

Let the Bishop, therefore, preside over you as one honored with the authority of God, which he is to exercise over the clergy, and by which he is to govern all the people. But let the deacon minister to him as Christ doth to his Father, and let him serve him unblamably in all things, as Christ doeth nothing of himself, but doeth always those things that please his Father. Let also the deaconess be honored by you in the place of the Holy Ghost, and not do nor say any thing without the deacon; as neither doth the Comforter say nor do any thing of himself, but giveth glory to Christ by waiting for his pleasure. And as we cannot believe on Christ without the teaching of the Spirit, so let not any woman address herself to the deacon or to the Bishop without the deaconess. Let the presbyters be esteemed by you to represent us the apostles, and let them be the teachers of divine knowledge; since our Lord, when he sent us, said, *Go ye, and make disciples of all nations, baptizing them in the name of the Father, and of the Son, and of the Holy Ghost; teaching them to observe all things whatsoever I have commanded you.* Let the widows and orphans be esteemed as representing the altar of burnt-offering; and let the virgins be honored as representing the altar of incense, and the incense itself.

108

REGULATIONS FOR
CHRISTIAN WIDOWS

Constitutions of the Holy Apostles III   4th century C.E.?

3. Of What Character the Widows Ought to Be,
and How They Ought to Be Supported by the Bishop

But the true widows are those who have had only one husband, having a good report among the generality for good works; *widows indeed,* sober, chaste, faithful, pious, who have brought up their children well, and have *entertained strangers* unblamably; who are to be supported, as devoted to God.

Besides, do thou, O Bishop, be mindful of the needy, both reaching out thy helping hand, and making provision for them, as the steward of God, distributing seasonably the oblations to every one of them, to the widows, the orphans, the friendless, and those who are tried with affliction.

4. That We Ought to Be Charitable to
All Sorts of Persons in Want

For what if some are neither widows nor widowers, but stand in need of assistance, either through poverty, or some disease, or the maintenance of a great number of children? It is thy duty to oversee all people, and to take care of them all. For they that bestow gifts do not immediately, and without the use of discretion, give them to the widows, but barely bring them in, calling them *free-will offerings,* that so thou, who knowest those that are in affliction, mayest, as a good steward, give them their portion of the gift. For God knoweth the giver, though thou distributest it to those in want, when he is absent. And he hath the reward of well-doing, but thou the blessedness of a just distribution of it. But do thou tell them who was the giver, that they may pray for him by name. For it is our duty to do good to all men, not fondly preferring one or another, whoever they may be. For the Lord saith, *Give to every one that asketh thee.* It is evident that it is meant of every one that is really in want, whether he be friend or foe, whether he be a kinsman or a stranger, whether he be single or married.

For in all the Scripture the Lord giveth us exhortations in respect to the needy, saying, first by Isaiah, *Deal thy bread to the hungry, and bring the poor who have no covering into thy house. If thou seest the naked, do thou cover him; and thou shalt not overlook those who are of thine own family and seed.* And then by Daniel he saith to the potentate, *Wherefore, O king, let my counsel please thee, and purge thy sins by acts of mercy, and thine iniquities by bowels of compassion to the needy.* And he saith by Solomon, *By acts of mercy and of faith, iniquities are purged.* And he saith again by David, *Blessed is he that hath regard to the poor and needy; the Lord shall deliver him in the evil day.* And again, *He hath dispersed abroad; he hath given to the needy; his righteousness remaineth for ever.* And Solomon saith, *He that hath mercy on the poor lendeth to the Lord; according to his gift it shall be paid him again.* And afterwards, *He that stoppeth his ear, that he may not hear him that is in want, he also himself shall call, and there shall be none to hear him.*

5. That the Widows Are to Be Very Careful of Their Deportment

Let every widow be meek, quiet, gentle, sincere, free from anger; not talkative, not clamorous, not hasty of speech, not given to evil-speaking, not captious, not double-tongued, not a busy-body. If she see or hear any thing that is not right, let her be as one that doth not see, and as one that doth not hear; and let the widow mind nothing but to pray for those that give, and for the whole church; and when she is asked any thing by any one, let her not easily answer, except questions concerning faith, and righteousness, and hope in God; remitting to the rulers those that desire to be instructed in the doctrines of godliness. Let her answer only so as may tend to subvert the error of polytheism, and demonstrate the doctrine concerning the monarchy of God. But of the remaining doctrines, let her not answer any thing rashly, lest, by saying any thing unlearnedly, she should cause the Word to be blasphemed.

For the Lord hath taught us, that the Word is like *a grain of mustard seed,* which is of a fiery nature; and, if any one useth it unskilfully, he will find it bitter. For in the mystical points we ought not to be rash, but cautious. For the Lord exhorteth us, saying, *Cast not your pearls before swine, lest they trample them with their feet, and turn again and rend you.* For unbelievers, when they hear the doctrine concerning Christ not explained as it ought to be, but defectively, and especially that concerning his incarnation or his passion, will rather reject it with scorn, and laugh at it as false, than praise God for it. And so the aged women will be guilty of rashness, and of causing blasphemy, and will inherit a woe. For, saith he, *Woe to him by whom my name is blasphemed among the Gentiles.*

6. That Women Ought Not to Teach, Because It Is Unseemly; and What Women Followed Our Lord

We do not permit our *women to teach in the church,* but only to pray, and to hear those that teach. For our Master and Lord, Jesus Christ himself, when he sent us, the twelve, to make disciples of the people and of the nations, did nowhere send out women to preach, although he did not want such; for there were with us the mother of our Lord, and his sisters; also Mary Magdalen; and Mary, the mother of James; and Martha and Mary, the sisters of Lazarus; Salome, and certain others. For, had it been necessary for women to teach, he himself would have first commanded these also to instruct the people with us. For, if *the head of the wife be the man,* it is not reasonable that the rest of the body should govern the head.

Let the widow, therefore, own herself to be the *altar of God,* and let her sit in her house, and not enter into the houses of the faithful, under any pretence, to receive any thing; for the altar of God never runneth about, but is fixed in one place. Let, therefore, the virgin and the widow be such as do not run about, or gad to the houses of those who are alien from the faith. For such as these are gadders and impudent; they do not make their feet to rest in one place, because they are not widows, but purses ready to receive, triflers, evil speakers, counsellors of strife, without shame, impudent; who, being such, are not worthy of him that called them. For they do not come to the common resting place of the congregation on the Lord's day, as those that are watchful. But they either slumber, or trifle, or allure men, or beg, or ensnare others, bringing them to the evil one; not suffering them to be watchful in the Lord; but taking care that they go out as vain as they came in, because they do not hear the Word of the Lord either taught or read. For of such as these the prophet Isaiah saith, *Hearing ye shall hear, and shall not understand; and seeing ye shall see, and not perceive; for the heart of this people is waxen gross.*

7. What Are the Characters of Widows, Falsely So Called

In the same manner, therefore, the ears of the hearts of such widows as these are stopped, so that they will not sit within in their cottages to speak to the Lord, but will run about with the design of getting, and, by their foolish prattling, fulfil the desires of the adversary. Such widows, therefore, are not affixed to the altar of Christ.

For there are some widows who esteem gain their business; and, since they ask without shame, and receive without being satisfied, they render the generality more backward in giving. For when they ought to be content with their subsistence from the church, as having moderate desires; on the contrary, they run from the house of one of their neighbors to that of another, and disturb them, heaping up to themselves plenty of money, and lend at bitter usury; and are solicitous only about Mammon, whose bag is their god; who prefer eating and drinking before all virtue, saying, *Let us eat and drink, for to-morrow we die;* who esteem these things as if they were durable, and not transitory. For she that useth herself to nothing but talking of money, worshippeth Mammon instead of God; that is, she is a servant to gain, but cannot be pleasing to God, nor resigned to his worship; not being able to intercede with him, because her mind and disposition run after money; for *where the treasure is, there will the heart be also.* For she is thinking in her mind whither she may go to receive, or that a certain woman, her friend, hath forgotten her, and she hath somewhat to say to her. She that thinketh of such things as these will no longer attend to her prayers, but to that thought which offereth itself; so that, although sometimes she may wish to pray for some one, she will not be heard, because she doth not offer her petition to the Lord with the whole heart.

But she that will attend to God will sit within, and mind the things of the Lord, day and night, offering her sincere petition with a mouth ready to utter the same without ceasing. As, therefore, Judith, most famous for her wisdom, and of a good report for her modesty, *prayed to God night and day for Israel;* so also the widow who is like her, will offer her intercession, without ceasing, for the church of God; and he will hear her, because her mind is fixed on this thing alone, and is disposed to be neither insatiable nor expensive; when her eye is pure, and her hearing clean, and her hands undefiled, and her feet quiet, and her mouth prepared for neither gluttony nor trifling, but speaking the things that are fit, and partaking of only such things as are necessary for her maintenance. So being grave, and giving no disturbance, she will be pleasing to God; and, as soon as she asketh any thing, the gift will anticipate her; as he saith, *While thou art speaking, I will say, Behold I am here.* Let such a one also be free from the love of money,

free from arrogance, not given to filthy lucre, not insatiable nor glut-
tonous; but continent, meek, giving nobody disturbance, pious, modest, sitting at home, singing, and praying, and reading, and watching,
and fasting; speaking to God continually in songs and hymns. And let
her take wool, and assist others, rather than herself be in need of any
thing; being mindful of that widow who is honored with the Lord's
testimony, who, coming into the temple, *cast into the treasury two
mites, which make a farthing*. And Christ our Lord and Master, and
Searcher of hearts, saw her, and said, *Verily I say unto you, that this
widow hath cast into the treasury more than they all. For all they have cast
in of their abundance; but this woman of her penury hath cast in all the
living that she had.*

The widows, therefore, ought to be grave, obedient to their Bishops, and their Presbyters, and their Deacons, and besides these to the
Deaconesses, with piety, reverence, and fear; not usurping authority,
nor desiring to do any thing beyond the constitution, without the
consent of the Deacon; as suppose the going to any one to eat or
drink with him, or to receive any thing from any body; but, if without
direction she do any one of these things, let her be punished with
fasting, or else let her be separated on account of her rashness.

8. That a Widow Ought Not to Accept of Alms
from the Unworthy; nor Ought a Bishop,
nor Any Other of the Faithful

For how doth such a one know of what character the person is
from whom she receiveth; or from what sort of ministration he sup-
plieth her with food,—whether it doth not arise from rapine, or some
other ill course of life? while the widow is unmindful, that, if she
receive in a way unworthy of God, she must give an account for every
one of these things. For neither will the priests at any time receive a
free-will offering from such a one, as suppose from a rapacious person, or from a harlot. For it is written, *Thou shalt not covet* those
things that are *thy neighbor's;* and, *Thou shall not offer the hire of a harlot
to the Lord God.* From such as these no offerings ought to be accepted,
nor indeed from those that are separated from the church.

Let the widows also be ready to obey the commands given them by
their superiors, and let them do according to the appointment of the
Bishop, being obedient to him as to God. For he that receiveth from
one so deserving of blame, or from one excommunicated, and prayeth
for him while he purposeth to go on in a wicked course, and while he

is not willing at any time to repent, holdeth communion with him in prayer, and grieveth Christ, who rejecteth the unrighteous; and he confirmeth them by means of the unworthy gift, and is defiled with them, not suffering them to come to repentance, so as to fall down before God with lamentation, and pray to him.

9. That Women Ought Not to Baptize; Because It Is Impious, and Contrary to the Doctrine of Christ

Now as to women's baptizing, we let you know, that there is no small peril to those that undertake it. Therefore we do not advise you to do it; for it is dangerous, or, rather, wicked and impious. For if the *man* be *the head of the woman,* and he be originally ordained for the priesthood, it is not just to abrogate the order of the creation, and, leaving the ruler, to come to the subordinate body. For the woman is the body of the man, taken from his side, and subject to him, from whom also she was separated for the procreation of children. For the Scripture saith, *He shall rule over thee.* For the man is ruler of the woman, as being her head. But if in the foregoing *Constitutions* we have not permitted them to teach, how will any one allow them, contrary to nature, to perform the office of a priest? For this is one of the ignorant practices of the Gentile atheism, to ordain women priests to the female deities; not one of the constitutions of Christ.

But, if baptism were to be administered by women, certainly our Lord would have been baptized by his own mother, and not by John; or, when he sent us to baptize, he would have sent along with us women also for this purpose. But now he hath nowhere, either by constitution or by writing, delivered to us any such thing; as knowing the order of nature and the decency of the action; as being the Creator of nature, and the Legislator of the constitution.

13. How the Widows Are to Pray for Those Who Supply Their Necessities

Thou art blessed, O God, who hast refreshed my fellow-widow. Bless, O Lord, and glorify him who hath bestowed these things upon her; and let his good work ascend in truth to thee; and remember him for good in the day of his visitation. And as for my Bishop, who hath so well performed his duty to thee, and hath ordered such a reasonable alms to be bestowed on my fellow-widow, in need of clothing, do thou increase his glory, and give him a crown of rejoicing in the day when thy visitation shall be revealed.

In the same manner, let the widow who hath received the favor join with the other in praying for him who bestowed it.

14. That She Who Hath Been Kind to the Poor Ought Not to Boast, and Tell Abroad Her Name, according to the Constitution of the Lord

But if any woman hath done a kindness, let her, as a prudent person, conceal her own name, not sounding a trumpet before her, that her alms may be with God in secret, as the Lord saith, *When thou doest thine alms, let not thy left hand know what thy right hand doeth, that thine alms may be in secret.* And let the widow pray for him that gave her the alms, whosoever he be, as she is the holy altar of Christ; and the Father, who seeth in secret, will reward openly him that did good.

But those widows who will not live according to the command of God, are solicitous and inquisitive what Deaconess it is that hath administered the charity, and what widows have received it. And when such a one hath learned those things, she murmureth at the Deaconess who distributed the charity, saying, Dost not thou see that I am in more distress and in greater want of thy charity? Why, therefore, hast thou preferred her before me? She saith these things foolishly, not understanding that this doth not depend on the will of man, but on the appointment of God. For if she is herself a witness that she was nearer, and proved herself in greater want and more in need of clothing, than the other, she ought to understand who it is that made this constitution, and to hold her peace, and not to murmur at the Deaconess who distributed the charity, but to enter into her own house, and to cast herself prostrate on her face, to make supplication to God that her sin may be forgiven her. For God commanded her who did the kindness not to proclaim it; and this widow murmured, because proclamation was not made, so that she might know, and run to receive; nay, did not only murmur, but also cursed her, forgetting him that said, *He that blesseth thee is blessed, and he that curseth thee is cursed.* But the Lord saith, *When ye enter into a house, say, Peace be to this house; and if the son of peace be there, your peace shall rest upon it. But if it be not worthy, your peace shall return to you.*

15. That It Doth Not Become Us to Revile Our Neighbors, Because Cursing Is Contrary to Christianity

If, therefore, peace returneth upon those that sent it, nay, upon those that before had actually given it, because it did not find persons fit to receive it, much rather will a curse return upon the head of him that unjustly sent it, because he to whom it was sent was not worthy to receive it. For all those who abuse others without cause, curse themselves; as Solomon saith, *As birds and sparrows fly away, so the curse causeless shall not come upon any one.* And again he saith, *Those that bring reproaches are exceeding foolish.* But as the bee, a creature as to its strength feeble, if she stingeth any one, loseth her sting, and becometh a drone; in the same manner, ye also, whatsoever injustice ye do to others, will bring it upon yourselves. *He hath excavated and digged a pit; and he shall fall into the ditch that he hath made.* And again, *He that diggeth a pit for his neighbor shall fall into it.* Let him, therefore, who would avoid a curse, not curse another. For *what thou hatest should be done to thee, do not thou to another.*

Wherefore admonish the widows that are feeble-minded, strengthen those of them that are weak, and praise such of them as walk in holiness. Let them rather bless, and not calumniate. Let them make peace, and not stir up contention. Nor let a Bishop, nor a Presbyter, nor a Deacon, nor any one else of the sacerdotal catalogue, defile his tongue with calumny, lest he inherit a curse instead of a blessing. And let it also be the Bishop's business and care, that no lay person utter a curse. For he ought to take care of the Clergy, of the Virgins, of the Widows, of the Laity.

For which reason, O Bishop, do thou ordain thy fellow-workers, the laborers for life and for righteousness,— such Deacons as are pleasing to God, such as thou provest to be worthy among all the people, and such as shall be ready for the necessities of their ministration. Ordain also a Deaconess, who is faithful and holy, for the ministrations to the women. For sometimes thou canst not send a Deacon, who is a man, to the women in certain houses, on account of the unbelievers. Thou shalt therefore send a woman, a Deaconess, on account of the imaginations of the bad.

And we stand in need of a woman, a Deaconess, for many occasions; and first in the baptism of women, the Deacon shall anoint their forehead with the holy oil, and after him the Deaconess shall anoint them. For there is no necessity that the women should be seen by the men; but only, in the laying on of hands, the Bishop shall anoint her head, as the priests and kings were formerly anointed, not because those who are now baptized are ordained priests, but as being Christians, or anointed, from Christ the Anointed; *a royal priesthood and a holy nation; the church of God, the pillar and ground of the present light;* who formerly were not a people, but now are beloved and chosen; upon whom is called his new name, as Isaiah the prophet testifieth, *And they shall call the people by his new name, which the Lord shall name for them.*

109

REGULATIONS FOR DEACONESSES, VIRGINS, WIDOWS, AND OTHER CHRISTIANS DURING THE WORSHIP SERVICE

Constitutions of the Holy Apostles II.57   4th century C.E.?

Let the Porters stand at the entries of the men, and observe them. Let the Deaconesses also stand at those of the women, like ship-men. For the same description and pattern was both in the tabernacle of the testimony and in the temple of God. But if any one be found sitting out of his place, let him be rebuked by the Deacon, as a messenger of the fore-ship, and be removed into the place proper for him. For the church is not only like a ship, but also like a sheep-fold; for as the shepherds place all the irrational animals distinctly, I mean goats and sheep, according to their kind and age; and still every one runneth together, like to his like; so is it to be in the church. Let the young persons sit by themselves, if there be a place for them; if not, let them stand up. But let those who are already stricken in years sit in order. As to the children that stand, let their fathers and mothers take them to themselves. Let the younger women also sit by themselves, if there be a place for them; but, if there be not, let them stand behind the women. Let those women who are married, and have children, be placed by themselves. But let the virgins, and the widows, and the elder women, stand first of all, or sit; and let the Deacon be the disposer of the places, that every one of those that come in may go to his proper place, and may not sit at the entrance. In like manner let the Deacon oversee the people, that no one may whisper, nor slumber, nor laugh, nor nod. For in the church all ought to stand wisely, and soberly, and attentively, having their attention fixed upon the word of the Lord.

After this, let all rise up with one consent, and, looking towards the east, after the catechumens and the penitents are gone out, pray to God eastward, *who ascended up to the heaven of heavens to the east;* remembering also the ancient situation of paradise in the east, whence the first man, when he had yielded to the persuasion of the serpent, and disobeyed the command of God, was expelled.

As to the Deacons, after the prayer is over, let some of them attend upon the oblation of the Eucharist, ministering to the Lord's body. Let others of them watch the multitude, and keep them silent. But let that Deacon who is at the High Priest's hand, say to the people, *Let no one have any quarrel against another. Let no one come in hypocrisy.* Then let the men give the men, and the women give the women, the Lord's kiss. But let no one do it with deceit, as Judas betrayed the Lord with a kiss.

After this let the Deacon pray for the whole church, for the whole world, and the several parts of it, and the fruits of it; for the priests and the rulers, for the high priest and the king, and for universal peace. After this, let the High Priest pray for peace upon the people, and bless them in these words: *The Lord bless thee, and keep thee; the Lord make his face to shine upon thee, and give thee peace.* Let the Bishop pray for the people, and say, *Save thy people, O Lord, and bless thine inheritance, which thou hast obtained with the precious blood of thy Christ, and hast called a royal priesthood and a holy nation.*

Then let the sacrifice follow, all the people standing, and praying silently; and, when the oblation hath been made, let every rank by itself partake of the Lord's body and precious blood, in order, and approach with reverence and holy fear, as to the body of their King. Let the women approach with their heads covered, as is becoming the order of women. Moreover, let the door be watched, lest there come in any unbeliever, or one not yet initiated.

New Religious Affiliation and Conversion

One of the most interesting ways to study women's religion in Greco-Roman antiquity is to consider those religious activities women consciously chose. In the Greco-Roman period a profusion of religious alternatives was available. Many old religions—the worship of Isis, Dionysus, Cybele, Mithras, and others—spread in expanded forms to the far reaches of the inhabited world. At least one new religion, Christianity, offered itself to the religiously inquiring person. There is substantial evidence about individuals who both rejected old religious allegiances and took on new ones.

Despite the plethora of evidence for religious change, how and why individuals made their religious choices in antiquity has received insufficient attention. Scholars have often remarked on the prominence of women among those commonly classed as converts, whether to Judaism, Christianity, or other Greco-Roman religions. But they have rarely offered meaningful explanations beyond such vague generalizations as an assumed proclivity of women toward foreign cults and exotic religions in general.

The materials assembled in this section present a range of evidence for women's religious choices. Livy's account of the spread of Bacchic worship to Italy and Rome in the second century B.C.E. and Josephus's report of the conversion of Queen Helena of Adiabene and other members of her household apparently represent actual historical situations. In the absence of other verification, however, it is difficult for us to determine just how accurate either source may be. *The Conversion and Marriage of Aseneth* (usually entitled *Joseph and Aseneth*)

243

and *The Acts of Thecla* present different sorts of problems. Both may be considered a form of midrash, or commentary on a biblical text: *Aseneth* clearly fills in the details of Gen. 41:45, 50; 46:20—which report that Joseph married Aseneth, daughter of Potiphera, priest of On, with whom he had two sons, Manasseh and Ephraim. The conversion of Thecla of Iconium by the apostle Paul is nowhere mentioned in Christian Scripture but seems like an expansion of Acts 14:1–7, which reports that Paul and Barnabas after successfully converting both Jews and Gentiles to Christianity were expelled from Iconium by a coalition of offended Gentiles and Jews. Although scholarly opinion considers neither text to be historically precise and reliable, both are undoubtedly paradigms of conversion experience in the minds of their readers. In that sense, they may tell us a great deal about the experiences and situations of actual newcomers to Judaism in first-century C.E. Egypt—the likely setting for *Aseneth*—and to Christianity in the second and third centuries, in a geographically diverse range of communities. While *The Conversion and Marriage of Aseneth* has no other literary counterparts, early Christian literature of the second and third centuries is replete with similar accounts of the conversion of various women by one or other apostle. In some cases, the literary dependence on *The Acts of Thecla* is manifest, but in others we can only say that such stories were widespread and widely read.

Apart from literary accounts of changes in religious affiliation, we also possess some nonliterary evidence, especially in Jewish burial inscriptions that refer to the deceased by the term "proselyte"; several are included in this section. Inscriptions referring to the deceased as one "who feared" or perhaps "who revered" God may also connote some attraction to Judaism on the part of non-Jews, although there is considerable debate on the subject. Two such inscriptions, both the epitaphs of women, are included here.[1]

My reasons for entitling this section as I have (rather than using simply the label "conversion") needs some comment. The term "conversion," particularly as it is used with reference to the ancient world, frequently carries with it value judgments about the nature of both the

---

1. There is an extensive literature on the so-called God-fearers, for which see A. Thomas Kraabel, "The Disappearance of the God-Fearers," *Numen* 28/2 (1981): 113–26 and the bibliography in his n. 7. A new inscription from Aphrodisias in Asia Minor offers new evidence for the interpretation of the term, but scholars have only begun to discuss the ramifications. See esp. Joyce M. Reynolds and Robert Tannanbaum, *Jews and Godfearers at Aphrodisias: Greek Inscriptions and Commentary*, Cambridge Philological Society supp. vol. 13 (Cambridge: Cambridge Philological Society, 1987).

new religious allegiance and the one(s) that preceded it. In the classic study *Conversion: The Old and the New in Religion from Alexander the Great to Augustine of Hippo,* Arthur Darby Nock essentially claimed that it made sense to speak of conversion only with regard to Judaism and Christianity.[2] For Nock, the distinction between conversion to either of these religions, on the one hand, and adhesion to, say, the cults of Isis or Mithras seems to revolve primarily around the possibility of multiple allegiance and the concept of dogma. True conversion, in Nock's paradigm, allows only for singular allegiance and requires not only revelation but also dogma. Although the term "conversion" is difficult to avoid, by entitling this chapter as I have, I wanted to avoid the judgmental and somewhat artificial distinctions which that terminology often bears. My purpose in assembling these texts is to allow us to begin or to continue the discussion of women's religious choices in antiquity without the modern prejudicial framework that accords some of those choices more authenticity than others.

2. A. D. Nock, *Conversion: The Old and the New in Religion from Alexander the Great to Augustine of Hippo* (Oxford: Clarendon Press, 1933), 134–37.

110

THE SPREAD OF THE BACCHIC RITES TO ROME IN 186 B.C.E., ATTRACTING WOMEN AND MEN TO THEIR FRENZIED OBSERVANCE

Livy *Annals of Rome* XXXIX.8–18   1st century B.C.E.

8. . . . . A nameless Greek came first to Etruria, possessed of none of those many arts which the Greek people, supreme as it is in learning, brought to us in numbers for the cultivation of mind and body, but a dabbler in sacrifices and a fortune-teller; nor was he one who, by frankly disclosing his creed and publicly proclaiming both his profession and his system, filled minds with error, but a priest of secret rites performed by night. There were initiatory rites which at first were imparted to a few, then began to be generally known among men and women. To the religious element in them were added the delights of wine and feasts, that the minds of a larger number might be attracted. When wine had inflamed their minds, and night and the mingling of males with females, youth with age, had destroyed every sentiment of modesty, all varieties of corruption first began to be practised, since each one had at hand the pleasure answering to that to which his nature was more inclined. There was not one form of vice alone, the promiscuous matings of free men and women, but perjured witnesses, forged seals and wills and evidence, all issued from this same workshop: likewise poisonings and secret murders, so that at times not even the bodies were found for burial. Much was ventured by craft, more by violence. This violence was concealed because amid the howlings and the crash of drums and cymbals no cry of the sufferers could be heard as the debauchery and murders proceeded.

9. The destructive power of this evil spread from Etruria to Rome like the contagion of a pestilence. At first the size of the City, with abundant room and tolerance for such evils, concealed it: at length information came to the consul Postumius in about this manner. Publius Aebutius, whose father had performed his military service with a horse supplied by the state, was left a ward, and later, on the death of his guardians, was brought under the tutelage of his mother Duronia and his stepfather Titus Sempronius Rutilus. His mother was devoted to her husband, and his stepfather, who had so administered his guardianship that he could not render an accounting, desired that the ward should either be done away with or be made dependent upon them by some tie. The one method of corrupting him was through the Bacchanalia. The mother addressed the young man: while he was sick, she said, she had vowed for him that as soon as he had recovered she would initiate him into the Bacchic rites; being compelled, by the kindness of the gods, to pay her vow, she wished to fulfil it. For ten days, she continued, he must practise continence: on the tenth day she would conduct him to the banquet and then, after ritual purification, to the shrine. There was a well-known courtesan, a freedwoman named Hispala Faecenia, not worthy of the occupation to which, while still a mere slave, she had accustomed herself, and even after she had been manumitted she maintained herself in the same way. Between her and Aebutius, since they were neighbours, an intimacy developed, not at all damaging either to the young man's fortune or to his reputation; for he had been loved and sought out without any effort on his part, and, since his own relatives made provision for all his needs on a very small scale, he was maintained by the generosity of the courtesan. More than that, she had gone so far, under the influence of their intimacy, that, after the death of her patron, since she was under the legal control of no one, having petitioned the tribunes and the praetor for a guardian, when she made her will she had instituted Aebutius as her sole heir.

10. Since there were these bonds of affection between them, and neither had any secrets from the other, the young man jestingly told her not to be surprised if he were away from her for several nights: as a matter of religious duty, he said, to free himself from a vow made for the sake of his health, he intended to be initiated in the Bacchic rites. When the woman heard this she exclaimed in great distress, "The gods forbid!" She said that it would be much better both for him and for her to die rather than do that; and she called down curses and vengeance upon the heads of those persons who had given him this counsel. Wondering both at her language and at her so manifest distress, the young man bade her spare her curses: it was his mother, he said, with the approval of his stepfather, who had ordered it. "Your stepfather, then," she replied, "is making haste—for perhaps it is not right to accuse your mother—to destroy in this way your virtue, your reputation and your life." As he marvelled the more and asked her what she meant, beseeching gods and goddesses for peace and forgiveness if, compelled by her love for him, she had declared what should be concealed, she told him that while she was a slave she had attended her mistress to that shrine, but that as a free woman she had never visited it. She knew, she said, that it was the factory of all sorts of corruptions; and it was known that for two years now no one had been initiated who had passed the age of twenty years. As each was introduced, he became a sort of victim for the priests. They, she continued, would lead him to a place which would ring with howls and the song of a choir and the beating of cymbals and drums, that the voice of the sufferer, when his virtue was violently attacked, might not be heard. Then she begged and besought him to put an end to this matter in any way he could and not to plunge into a situation where all disgraceful practices would have first to be endured and then performed. Nor would she let him go until the young man gave her his promise that he would have nothing to do with those mysteries.

11. When he came home and his mother began to tell him what he had to do that day and on the following days in connection with the rites, he informed her that he would do none of them and that it was not his intention to be initiated. His stepfather was present at the interview. Straightway the woman exclaimed that he could not do without his mistress Hispala for ten nights; infected with the enchantments and poisons of that vampire, he had no respect for his mother or his stepfather or yet the gods. Berating him thus, his mother on one side, his stepfather with four slaves on the other, drove him from the house. The young man thereupon went to his aunt Aebutia and explained to her the reason why his mother had driven him out, and on her recommendation the following day reported the affair to the consul Postumius with no witnesses present. The consul sent him away with instructions to return the third day; he himself asked his mother-in-law Sulpicia, a woman of high character, whether she was acquainted with an elderly woman, Aebutia, from the Aventine. When she replied that she knew that she was a virtuous woman of the old style, he said that he felt the need of an interview with her: Sulpicia should send her a message to come. Aebutia, summoned by Sulpicia, came, and a little later the consul, as if he had come in by chance, brought in an allusion to Aebutius, the son of her brother. Tears flowed from the woman's eyes, and she began to bewail the fate of the young man who was robbed of his estate by those who should least of all have treated him thus, and who was then at her house, driven from home by his mother because the virtuous youth—might the gods be gracious—refused to be initiated into rites which, if reports were to be believed, were full of lewdness.

12. The consul, thinking that he had learned enough about Aebutius to trust his story, sent Aebutia away and asked his mother-in-law to summon to her Hispala, also from the Aventine, a freedwoman and no stranger in the neighbourhood: he wished to ask her also certain questions. Hispala, alarmed by her message, because without knowing the reason she was summoned to so important and respected a woman, when she saw the lictors in the vestibule and the consul's retinue and the consul himself, almost swooned. Conducting her into the inner part of the house, with his mother-in-law present, the consul told her that if she could bring herself to tell the truth she had no cause to feel alarmed; she would receive a pledge either from Sulpicia, a woman of such standing, or from himself; she should state to them what rites were usually performed in the nocturnal orgies at the Bacchanalia in the grove of Stimula. When she heard this, such fear and trembling seized the woman in all her limbs that for a long time she could not open her mouth. Being at length restored, she said that when quite young and a slave she had been initiated with her mistress; that for many years after her manumission she had known nothing of what went on there. Then the consul praised her on this ground, that she had not denied that she had been initiated; but she was to tell, under the same pledge, the rest as well. When she insisted that she knew nothing more, he told her that she would not receive the same forgiveness or consideration if she were convicted by the evidence of someone else as if she had confessed of her own accord; the man, he added, who had heard it from her had told him the whole story.

13. The woman, thinking without a doubt, as was indeed the fact, that Aebutius had revealed the secret, threw herself at the feet of Sulpicia, and at first began to plead with her not to try to turn the chatter of a freedwoman with her lover into something that was not merely serious but even fatal: she had spoken thus for the purpose of frightening him, not because she knew anything. At this point Postumius, inflamed with wrath, said that she believed even then that she was jesting with her lover Aebutius, and not speaking in the house of a most respectable matron and in the presence of a consul. Sulpicia too lifted up the terror-stricken woman, and at the same time encouraged her and mollified the anger of her son-in-law. At length regaining her self-control, and complaining much of the treachery of Aebutius, who had returned such gratitude to one who deserved so well of him, she declared that she feared greatly the wrath of the gods whose hidden mysteries she was to reveal, but far more the wrath of the men who would, if she informed against them, with their own hands tear her limb from limb. Accordingly she begged Sulpicia and the consul that they would banish her somewhere outside Italy, where she could pass the rest of her life in safety. The consul bade her be of good cheer and assured her that it would be his responsibility to see that she could safely live in Rome. Then Hispala set forth the origin of the mysteries. At first, she said, it was a ritual for women, and it was the custom that no man should be admitted to it. There had been three days appointed each year on which they held initiations into the Bacchic rites by day; it was the rule to choose the matrons in turn as priestesses. Paculla Annia, a Campanian, she said, when priestess, had changed all this as if by the advice of the gods; for she had been the first to initiate men, her sons, Minius and Herennius Cerrinius; she had held the rites by night and not by day, and instead of a mere three days a year she had established five days of initiation in every month. From the time that the rites were performed in common, men mingling with women and the freedom of darkness added, no form of crime, no sort of wrongdoing, was left untried. There were more lustful practices among men with one another than among women. If any of them were disinclined to endure abuse or reluctant to commit crime, they were sacrificed as victims. To consider nothing wrong, she continued, was the highest form of religious devotion among them. Men, as if insane, with fanatical tossings of their bodies, would utter prophecies. Matrons in the dress of Bacchantes, with dishevelled hair and carrying blazing torches, would run down to the Tiber, and plunging their torches in the water (because they contained live sulphur mixed with calcium) would bring them out still burning. Men were alleged to have been carried off by the gods who had been bound to a machine and borne away out of sight to hidden caves: they were those who had refused either to conspire or to join in the crimes or to suffer abuse. Their number, she said, was very great, almost constituting a second state; among them were certain men and women of high rank. Within the last two years it had been ordained that no one beyond the age of twenty years should be initiated: boys of such age were sought for as admitted both vice and corruption.

14. Having finished her testimony, again falling at their feet, she repeated the same prayers that they should banish her. The consul asked his mother-in-law to vacate some part of the house into which Hispala might move. An apartment above the house was assigned to her, the stairs leading to the street being closed up and an approach to the house arranged. All the household goods of Faecenia were at once moved and her slaves summoned, and Aebutius was directed to move to the house of a client of the consul.

When both witnesses were thus available, Postumius laid the matter before the senate, everything being set forth in detail; first what had been reported, then what he had himself discovered. Great panic seized the Fathers, both on the public account, lest these conspiracies and gatherings by night might produce something of hidden treachery or danger, and privately, each for himself, lest anyone might be involved in the mischief. The senate, moreover, decreed that the consul should be thanked because he had investigated the affair both with great industry and without creating any confusion. Then the investigation of the Bacchanals and their nocturnal orgies they referred to the consuls, not as a part of their regular duties; they directed the consuls to see to it that the witnesses Aebutius and Faecenia did not suffer harm and to attract other informers by rewards; the priests of these rites, whether men or women, should be sought out, not only at Rome but through all the villages and communities, that they might be at the disposal of the consuls; that it should be proclaimed in addition in the city of Rome and that edicts should be sent through all Italy, that no one who had been initiated in the Bacchic rites should presume to assemble or come together for the purpose of celebrating those rites or to perform any such ritual. Before all, it was decreed that an inquiry should be conducted regarding those persons who had come together or conspired for the commission of any immorality or crime. Such was the decree of the senate. The consuls ordered the curule aediles to search out all the priests of this cult and to keep them under surveillance, in free custody for the investigation; the plebeian aediles were to see to it that no celebration of the rites should be held in secret. The task was entrusted to the *triumviri capitales* of placing guards through the City, of seeing that no night meetings were held, and of making provision against fire; as assistants to the *triumviri*, the *quinqueviri uls cis Tiberim* were to stand guard each over the buildings of his own district.

15. When the magistrates had been dispatched to these posts, the consuls mounted the Rostra and called an informal meeting of the people, and, when the consul had finished the regular formula of prayer which magistrates are accustomed to pronounce before they address the people, he thus began: "Never for any assembly, citizens, has this formal prayer to the gods been not only so suitable but even

so necessary, a prayer which reminds us that these are the gods whom our forefathers had appointed to be worshipped, to be venerated, to receive our prayers, not those gods who would drive our enthralled minds with vile and alien rites, as by the scourges of the Furies, to every crime and every lust. For my part, I do not discover what I should refrain from telling or how far I should speak out. If you are left ignorant of anything, I fear that I shall leave room for carelessness; if I lay bare everything, that I shall scatter abroad an excess of terror. Whatever I shall have said, be sure that my words are less than the dreadfulness and the gravity of the situation: to take sufficient precautions will be our task. As to the Bacchanalia, I am assured that you have learned that they have long been celebrated all over Italy and now even within the City in many places, and that you have learned this not only from rumour but also from their din and cries at night, which echo throughout the City, but I feel sure that you do not know what this thing is: some believe that it is a form of worship of the gods, others that it is an allowable play and pastime, and, whatever it is, that it concerns only a few. As regards their number, if I shall say that there are many thousands of them, it cannot but be that you are terrified, unless I shall at once add to that who and of what sort they are. First, then, a great part of them are women, and they are the source of this mischief; then there are men very like the women, debauched and debauchers, fanatical, with senses dulled by wakefulness, wine, noise and shouts at night. The conspiracy thus far has no strength, but it has an immense source of strength in that they grow more numerous day by day. Your ancestors did not wish that even you should assemble casually and without reason, except when the standard was displayed on the citadel and the army was assembled for an election, or the tribunes had announced a meeting of the plebeians, or some of the magistrates had called you to an informal gathering; and wherever there was a crowd collected they thought that there should also be a legal leader of the crowd. Of what sort do you think are, first, gatherings held by night, second, meetings of men and women in common? If you knew at what ages males were initiated, you would feel not only pity for them but also shame. Do you think, citizens, that youths initiated by this oath should be made soldiers? That arms should be entrusted to men mustered from this foul shrine? Will men debased by their own debauchery and that of others fight to the death on behalf of the chastity of your wives and children?

16. "Yet it would be less serious if their wrongdoing had merely made them effeminate—that was in great measure their personal dishonour—and if they had kept their hands from crime and their thoughts from evil designs: never has there been so much evil in the state nor affecting so many people in so many ways. Whatever villainy there has been in recent years due to lust, whatever to fraud, whatever to crime, I tell you, has arisen from this one cult. Not yet have they revealed all the crimes to which they have conspired. Their impious compact still limits itself to private crimes, since as yet it does not have strength enough to crush the state. Daily the evil grows and creeps abroad. It is already too great to be purely a private matter: its objective is the control of the state. Unless you are on guard betimes, citizens, as we hold this meeting in the day-time, summoned by a consul, in accordance with law, so there can be one held at night. Now, as single individuals, they stand in fear of you, gathered here all together in this assembly: presently, when you have scattered to your homes and farms, they will have come together and they will take measures for their own safety and at the same time for your destruction: then you, as isolated individuals, will have to fear them as a united body. Therefore each one of you should hope that all your friends have been endowed with sound minds. If lust, if madness has carried off anyone into that whirlpool, let each consider that such a person belongs, not to himself, but to those with whom he has conspired to every wickedness and wrong. I am not free of anxiety lest some even of you, citizens, may go astray through error. Nothing is more deceptive in appearance than a false religion. When the authority of the gods is put forward as a defence for crime, there steals upon the mind a fear lest in punishing human misdeeds we may violate something of divine law which became mixed up with them. From this scruple innumerable edicts of the pontiffs, decrees of the senate, and finally responses of the *haruspices* free you. How often, in the times of our fathers and our grandfathers, has the task been assigned to the magistrates of forbidding the introduction of foreign cults, of excluding dabblers in sacrifices and fortune-tellers from the Forum, the Circus, and the City, of searching out and burning books of prophecies, and of annulling every system of sacrifice except that performed in the Roman way. For men wisest in all divine and human law used to judge that nothing was so potent in destroying religion as where sacrifices were performed, not by native, but by foreign, ritual. I have thought that this warning should be given you, that no religious fear may disturb your minds when you see us suppressing the

Bacchanalia and breaking up these nightly meetings. All these things, if the gods are favourable and willing, we shall do; they, because they were indignant that their own divinity was being polluted by acts of crime and lust, have dragged these matters from darkness into the light, nor have they willed that they should be discovered in order that they might be unpunished, but that they might be coerced and suppressed. The senate has entrusted the investigation of this affair, by extraordinary assignment, to my colleague and myself. We shall zealously carry through what has to be done by ourselves; the responsibility of keeping watch through the City we have entrusted to the minor magistrates. For you too it is proper, whatever duties are assigned you, in whatever place each one is posted, to obey zealously and to see to it that no danger or confusion may arise from the treachery of criminals."

17. Then they ordered the decrees of the senate to be read and announced the reward to be paid the informer if anyone had brought any person before them or had reported the name of anyone who was absent. If anyone was named and had escaped, for him they would designate a fixed day, and, if he did not respond when summoned on that day, he would be condemned in his absence. If anyone was named of those who were at that time outside the land of Italy, they would fix a more elastic date if he wished to come to plead his cause. They next proclaimed that no one should venture to sell or buy anything for the purpose of flight; that no one should harbour, conceal, or in any wise aid the fugitives.

When the meeting was dismissed there was great panic in the whole City, nor was this confined only to the walls or the boundaries of Rome; but gradually through all Italy, as letters were received from their friends concerning the decree of the senate, concerning the assembly and the edict of the consuls, the terror began to spread. Many during the night after the day when the revelation was made in the meeting were caught trying to escape and brought back by the guards whom the *triumviri* had posted at the gates: the names of many were reported. Certain of these, men and women, committed suicide. In the conspiracy, it was said, more than seven thousand men and women were involved. But the heads of the conspiracy, it was clear, were Marcus and Gaius Atinius of the Roman *plebs,* and the Faliscan Lucius Opicernius and the Campanian Minius Cerrinius: they were the source of all wickedness and wrongdoing, the story went, and they were the supreme priests and the founders of the cult. It was seen to that at the first opportunity they were arrested. They were brought before the consuls, confessed, and asked for no delay in standing trial.

18. But so numerous were the persons who had fled from the City that, since in many instances legal proceedings and causes were falling through, the praetors Titus Maenius and Marcus Licinius were compelled, through the intervention of the senate, to adjourn court for thirty days, until the investigations should be finished by the consuls. The same depopulation, because at Rome men whose names had been given in did not respond or were not found, compelled the consuls to make the rounds of the villages and there investigate and conduct trials. Those who had merely been initiated and had made their prayers in accordance with the ritual formula, the priest dictating the words, in which the wicked conspiracy to all vice and lust was contained, but had committed none of the acts to which they were bound by the oath against either themselves or others, they left in chains; upon those who had permitted themselves to be defiled by debauchery or murder, who had polluted themselves by false testimony, forged seals, substitution of wills or other frauds, they inflicted capital punishment. More were killed than were thrown into prison. There was a large number of men and women in both classes. Convicted women were turned over to their relatives or to those who had authority over them, that they might be punished in private: if there was no suitable person to exact it, the penalty was inflicted by the state. Then the task was entrusted to the consuls of destroying all forms of Bacchic worship, first at Rome and then throughout Italy, except in cases where an ancient altar or image had been consecrated. For the future it was then provided by decree of the senate that there should be no Bacchanalia in Rome or Italy. If any person considered such worship to be ordained by tradition or to be necessary, and believed that he could not omit it without sin and atonement, he was to make a declaration before the city praetor, and the latter would consult the senate. If permission were granted to him, at a meeting where not fewer than one hundred were in attendance, he should offer the sacrifice, provided that not more than five people should take part in the rite, and that there should be no common purse or master of sacrifices or priest.

111

HELENA, QUEEN OF ADIABENE,
CONVERT TO JUDAISM

Josephus *Antiquities of the Jews* XX.17–53, 92–96   1st century C.E.

17. At the same time Helena, queen of Adiabene, and her son Izates became converts to Judaism under the following circumstances. Monobazus, surnamed Bazaeus, king of Adiabene, seized with a passion for his sister Helena, took her as his partner in marriage and got her pregnant. On one occasion as he was sleeping beside her, he rested his hand on his wife's belly after she had gone to sleep, whereupon he thought he heard a voice bidding him remove his hand from her womb so as not to cramp the babe within it, which by the providence of God had had a happy start and would also attain a fortunate end. Disturbed by the voice, he at once awoke and told these things to his wife; and he called the son who was born to him Izates. He had an elder son by Helena named Monobazus and other children by his other wives; but it was clear that all his favour was concentrated on Izates as if he were an only child. In consequence of this, Izates' half-brothers by their common father grew envious of the child. Their envy grew into an ever-increasing hatred, for they were all vexed that their father preferred Izates to themselves. Although their father clearly perceived this, he pardoned them, for he attributed their feeling not to any bad motive but rather to the desire that each of them had to win his father's favour for himself. Yet, as he was greatly alarmed for the young Izates, lest the hatred of his brothers should bring him to some harm, he gave him an abundance of presents and sent him off to Abennerigus the king of Charax Spasini, to whom he entrusted the safety of the boy. Abennerigus welcomed the lad and viewed him with such goodwill that he gave him his daughter, named Symmacho, as a wife and conferred on him a territory that would insure him a large income.

24. Monobazus, being now old and seeing that he had not long to live, desired to lay eyes on his son before he died. He therefore sent for him, gave him the warmest of welcomes and presented him with a district called Carron. The land there has excellent soil for the production of amomum in the greatest abundance; it also possesses the remains of the ark in which report has it that Noah was saved from the flood—remains which to this day are shown to those who are curious to see them. Izates, accordingly, resided in this district until his father's death. On the day when Monobazus departed this life, Queen Helena sent for all the high nobles and satraps of the realm and those who were charged with military commands. On their arrival she said to them: "I think that you are not unaware that my husband had set his heart on Izates succeeding to his kingdom and had deemed him worthy of this honour; nevertheless, I await your decision. For he is blessed who receives his realm from the hands not of one but of many who willingly give their consent." She said this to test the disposition of those whom she had called together. They, on hearing her words, first of all, according to their custom, made obeisance to the queen, and thereupon replied that they gave their support to the king's decision, and would gladly obey Izates, who, as one and all had prayed in their hearts, had been justly preferred by his father to his brothers. They added that they first wished to put his brothers and kinsmen to death in order that Izates might be seated on the throne with full security; for if they were destroyed, all fear arising from the hatred and envy that they bore towards Izates would be removed. In reply Helena expressed her gratitude for their goodwill to herself and to Izates; but she nevertheless entreated them to defer their decision about putting the brothers to death until after Izates had arrived and given his approval. Failing to persuade her to put the brothers to death as they advised, they, for their own safety, admonished her at least to keep them in custody until his arrival. They also advised her meanwhile to appoint as trustee of the realm someone in whom she had most confidence. Helena agreed to this and set up Monobazus, her eldest son, as king. Putting the diadem upon his head and giving him his father's signet ring and what they call the *sampsera*, she exhorted him to administer the kingdom until his brother's arrival. The latter, on hearing of his father's death, quickly arrived and succeeded his brother Monobazus, who made way for him.

34. Now during the time when Izates resided at Charax Spasini, a certain Jewish merchant named Ananias visited the king's wives and taught them to worship God after the manner of the Jewish tradition. It was through their agency that he was brought to the notice of Izates, whom he similarly won over with the co-operation of the women. When Izates was summoned by his father to Adiabene, Ananias accompanied him in obedience to his urgent request. It so happened, moreover, that Helena had likewise been instructed by another Jew and had been brought over to their laws. When Izates came to Adiabene to take over the kingdom and saw his brothers and his other kinsmen in chains, he was distressed at what had been done. Regarding it as impious either to kill them or to keep them in chains, and yet thinking it hazardous to keep them with him if they were not imprisoned—cherishing resentment as they must—he sent some of them with their children to Claudius Caesar in Rome as hostages, and others to Artabanus the Parthian king with the same excuse.

38. When Izates had learned that his mother was very much pleased with the Jewish religion, he was zealous to convert to it himself; and since he considered that he would not be genuinely a Jew unless he was circumcised, he was ready to act accordingly. When his mother learned of his intention, however, she tried to stop him by telling him that it was a dangerous move. For, she said, he was a king; and if his subjects should discover that he was devoted to rites that were strange and foreign to themselves, it would produce much disaffection and they would not tolerate the rule of a Jew over them. Besides this advice she tried by every other means to hold him back. He, in turn, reported her arguments to Ananias. The latter expressed agreement with the king's mother and actually threatened that if he should be unable to persuade Izates, he would abandon him and leave the land. For he said that he was afraid that if the matter became universally known, he would be punished, in all likelihood, as personally responsible because he had instructed the king in unseemly practices. The king could, he said, worship God even without being circumcised if indeed he had fully decided to be a devoted adherent of Judaism, for it was this that counted more than circumcision. He told him, furthermore, that God Himself would pardon him if, constrained thus by necessity and by fear of his subjects, he failed to perform this rite. And so, for the time, the king was convinced by his arguments. Afterwards, however, since he had not completely given up his desire, another Jew, named Eleazar, who came from Galilee and who had a reputation for being extremely strict when it came to the ancestral laws, urged him to carry out the rite. For when he came to him to pay him his respects and found him reading the law of Moses, he said: "In your ignorance, O king, you are guilty of the greatest offence against the law and thereby against God. For you ought not merely to read the law but also, and even more, to do what is commanded in it. How long will you continue to be uncircumcised? If you have not yet read the law concerning this matter, read it now, so that you may know what an impiety it is that you commit." Upon hearing these words, the king postponed the deed no longer. Withdrawing into another room, he summoned his physician and had the prescribed act performed. Then he sent for both his mother and his teacher Ananias and notified them that he had performed the rite. They were immediately seized with consternation and fear beyond measure that, if it should be proved that he had performed the act, the king would risk losing his throne, since his subjects would not submit to government by a man who was a devotee of foreign practices, and that they themselves would be in jeopardy since the blame for his action would be attributed to them. It was God who was to prevent their fears from being realized. For although Izates himself and his children were often threatened with destruction, God preserved them, opening a path to safety from desperate straits. God thus demonstrated that those who fix their eyes on Him and trust in Him alone do not lose the reward of their piety. But I shall report these events at a later time.

49. Helena, the mother of the king, saw that peace prevailed in the kingdom and that her son was prosperous and the object of admiration in all men's eyes, even those of foreigners, thanks to the prudence that God gave him. Now she had conceived a desire to go to the city of Jerusalem and to worship at the temple of God, which was famous throughout the world, and to make thank-offerings there. She consequently asked her son to give her leave. Izates was most enthusiastic in granting his mother's request, made great preparations for her journey, and gave her a large sum of money. He even escorted her for a considerable distance, and she completed her journey to the city of Jerusalem. Her arrival was very advantageous for the people of Jerusalem, for at that time the city was hard pressed by famine and many were perishing from want of money to purchase what they needed. Queen Helena sent some of her attendants to Alexandria to buy grain for large sums and others to Cyprus to bring back a cargo of dried figs. Her attendants speedily returned with these provisions, which she thereupon distributed among the needy. She has thus left a very great name that will be famous forever among our whole people for her benefaction. When her son Izates learned of the famine, he likewise sent a great sum of money to leaders of the Jerusalemites. The distribution of this fund to the needy delivered many from the extremely severe pressure of famine. But I shall leave to a later time the further tale of good deeds performed for our city by this royal pair.

92. Not long afterwards Izates passed away, having completed fifty-five years of his life and having been monarch for twenty-four; he left twenty-four sons and twenty-four daughters. His orders were that his brother Monobazus should succeed to the throne. Thus Monobazus was rewarded for faithfully keeping the throne for his brother during the latter's absence from home after his father's death. His mother Helena was sorely distressed by the news of her son's death, as was to be expected of a mother bereft of a son so very religious. She was, however, consoled on hearing that the succession had passed to her eldest son and hastened to join him. She arrived in Adiabene but did not long survive her son Izates, for, weighed down with age and with the pain of her sorrow, she quickly breathed out her last. Monobazus sent her bones and those of his brother to Jerusalem with instructions that they should be buried in the three pyramids that his mother had erected at a distance of three furlongs from the city of Jerusalem. As for the acts of King Monobazus during his lifetime, I shall narrate them later.

112

THE JEWISH PROCLIVITIES OF THE
MAJORITY OF THE WOMEN
IN DAMASCUS

Josephus *The Jewish War* II.559–61   1st Century C.E.

Meanwhile, the people of Damascus, learning of the disaster which had befallen the Romans, were fired with a determination to kill the Jews who resided among them. As they had for a long time past kept them shut up in the gymnasium—a precaution prompted by suspicion—they considered that the execution of their plan would present no difficulty whatever; their only fear was of their own wives, who, with few exceptions, had all become converts to the Jewish religion, and so their efforts were mainly directed to keeping the secret from them. In the end, they fell upon the Jews, cooped up as they were and unarmed, and within one hour slaughtered them all with impunity, to the number of ten thousand five hundred.

113

HOW THE EGYPTIAN VIRGIN ASENETH CONVERTS TO JUDAISM AND MARRIES JOSEPH

The Conversion and Marriage of Aseneth   1st Century C.E.

1.1. It happened that in the first year of the seven years of abundance, in the second month, on the fifth day, Pharaoh sent Joseph to travel around the entire land of Egypt. **1.2.** And Joseph came, in the fourth month of the first year, on the eighteenth day of the month, to the region of Heliopolis. **1.3.** And he was gathering together the corn of that area as the sands of the sea.

1.4. There was a man in that city, a satrap of Pharaoh, and he was the head of all Pharaoh's satraps and magnates. **1.5.** And this man was very wealthy, wise, and prudent; and he was Pharaoh's councilor and the priest of Heliopolis.

1.6. And the daughter of Pentephres was a virgin about eighteen years old, tall, in the bloom of youth, and beautiful, surpassing in appearance any virgin in the land. **1.7.** And she was in no way like the daughters of the Egyptians but was in all ways like the daughters of the Hebrews. **1.8.** For she was tall like Sarah, and in the bloom of youth like Rebecca, and beautiful like Rachel; and the name of this virgin was Aseneth.

1.9. And the fame of her beauty spread through the whole land, even to its borders, and all the sons of the magnates and of the satraps and of the kings, all of them young men, sought her for a wife. **1.10.** And there was much rivalry among them because of her, and they began to fight with one another on account of Aseneth.

1.11. And the firstborn son of Pharaoh heard about her, and persistently beseeched his father to give her to him as a wife. **1.12.** He said to him, "Give me Aseneth, the daughter of Pentephres, the priest of Heliopolis, as (my) wife." **1.13.** And his father said to him, "Why do you seek a wife inferior to you? Are you not king of the entire world? No, but look, the daughter of King Joakim is promised to you, and the queen is very beautiful; take her as a wife for yourself."

2.1. And Aseneth was contemptuous and disdainful of all men, and no man had ever seen her, because Pentephres had a tower in his house which was large and exceedingly high.

2.2. And at the top of the tower there was an apartment with ten rooms. **2.3.** And the first room was large and pretentiously beautiful, paved with purple stones, and its walls were faced with precious stones of many colors. **2.4.** The ceiling of this room was gold, and inside this room, the innumerable gold and silver gods of Aseneth were set up. **2.5.** And Aseneth venerated all these, and feared them, and offered sacrifices to them.

2.6. And there was a second room, containing all of Aseneth's ornaments and chests. **2.7.** And in them was much gold and silver, and garments (made) from cloth woven with gold, and choice costly stones, and fine linens. **2.8.** All the ornament of her virginity was there.

2.9. And there was a third room, containing all the good things of the earth; it was Aseneth's storehouse.

2.10. And seven virgins had the seven remaining rooms, one apiece. **2.11.** And they were in servitude to Aseneth, and were the same age, having been born in one night with Aseneth. They were very beautiful, as the stars in heaven, and no man had had contact with them, not even any male child.

2.12. And there were three windows in the large room where Aseneth's virginity was nurtured. **2.13.** There was one window looking out onto the courtyard to the east, and a second window looking out onto the street to the north, and a third looking south.

2.14. And a golden bed stood in the room looking out to the east. **2.15.** The bed was covered with purple cloth of gold, embroidered with fine linen the color of hyacinth. **2.16.** In this bed Aseneth slept alone, and no one, neither man nor woman, ever sat on it except Aseneth alone.

2.17. And there was a large courtyard beside the house encircling it, and a very high wall around the courtyard, constructed with large rectangular stones. **2.18.** And there were four gates to the courtyard, overlaid with iron, and eighteen men guarded them, strong young men, armed. **2.19.** And inside the courtyard, along the wall, all sorts of mature fruit-bearing trees were planted, and all the fruit from them was ripe, for it was the harvest season. **2.20.** And on the right side of the courtyard was an abundant spring of water, and underneath the spring a great trough received the water from this spring; from there, a river passed through the midst of the courtyard and watered all the trees of the courtyard.

3.1. And it happened that in the fourth month, on the eighteenth of the month, Joseph came to the region of Heliopolis. **3.2.** And as he approached this city, Joseph sent ten men ahead of him to Pentephres the priest, saying, **3.3.** "I will come and stay with you today, as it is noon, and the hour of the mid-day meal. The sun's heat burns greatly: I shall rest under your roof."

3.4. And Pentephres heard and was joyously happy and said, "Blessed is the Lord, the God of Joseph." **3.5.** And Pentephres called the man who managed his household and said to him, **3.6.** "Hurry and make my house ready, and prepare a great meal, because Joseph, the Powerful One of God, comes to us today."

3.7. And Aseneth heard that her father and mother had come back from the family estate, and she rejoiced and said, **3.8.** "I will go and see my father and my mother, for they have come back from the estate they have inherited."

3.9. And Aseneth hurried and put on a fine linen robe, the color of hyacinth and woven with gold, and girded herself with a gold girdle and put bracelets around her hands and feet and put on gold trousers and an ornament around her neck. **3.10.** And all around her, she had precious stones bearing the names of the gods of Egypt, everywhere on the bracelets and on the stones; and the faces of the idols were etched in relief on the stones. **3.11.** And she placed a tiara on her head and bound a diadem around her temples and covered her head with a veil.

4.1. And she hurried down the steps outside her apartment and went to her father and mother and greeted them. **4.2.** And Pentephres and his wife rejoiced in their daughter Aseneth with great gladness, for her parents beheld her adorned as a bride of God. **4.3.** And they brought out all the good things they had brought from the family estate and gave them to their daughter. **4.4.** And Aseneth rejoiced in these good things; in the fruits, and in the grapes and dates, in the doves, in the pomegranates and figs, because all these were in their prime.

4.5. And Pentephres said to his daughter, "Child." And she said, "Here I am, lord." And he said to her, "Sit down between us and I will tell you what I have to say." **4.6.** And Aseneth sat down between her father and mother. **4.7.** And her father, Pentephres, took her right hand in his right hand, and said to her, "Child." And Aseneth said, "Let my lord and my father speak."

4.8. And Pentephres said to her, "Behold, Joseph, the Powerful One of God, comes to us today; and he is the ruler of all the land of Egypt, and Pharaoh has designated him ruler of our whole land: he is the grain distributor for the whole area, and will save it from the coming famine. **4.9.** For Joseph is a man who reveres God, and is temperate and virgin, as you are today—a man strong in wisdom and knowledge—and the spirit of God is upon him, and the favor of God is with him. **4.10.** Come, my child, and I will give you to him as a wife, and you will be a bride to him, and he will be your bridegroom for eternal time."

4.11. And as Aseneth heard the words of her father, a red sweat poured from her, and great anger overcame her, and she glanced sideways at her father with her eyes and said, **4.12.** "Why does my lord and my father speak like this? Does he wish with such words to enslave me as a prisoner to a foreigner, to a fugitive who was sold into slavery? **4.13.** Is he not the son of a shepherd from the land of Canaan, and was he not abandoned by his father? **4.14.** Is he not the one who slept with the wife of his master? And didn't his master throw him into a gloomy prison, and didn't Pharaoh bring him out of the prison so that he could interpret Pharaoh's dream? **4.15.** No, but I shall marry the firstborn son of the king, because he is king of the entire earth."

4.16. Hearing this, Pentephres was ashamed to speak further with his daughter about Joseph, because she had answered him with brashness and anger.

5.1. And behold, a young man broke in from Pentephres' retinue and said, "Behold, Joseph is before the doors of our court." **5.2.** Then Aseneth fled from the presence of her father and mother and went up to her apartment, and went into her room to the great window which faced east to see the one who came to her father's house.

5.3. And Pentephres went out to meet Joseph, with his wife and his whole family.

5.4. And the gates of the courtyard which faced east were opened, and Joseph entered, seated on the chariot of Pharaoh's second-in-command. **5.5.** And four horses were yoked together, white like snow, with gold-studded bridles, and the chariot was covered in gold. **5.6.** And Joseph was clothed in an unusual white tunic, and the robe wrapped around him was fine purple linen woven with gold. He had a gold crown on his head, and around the crown were twelve precious stones, and above the stones twelve gold rays, and a royal scepter in his right hand. **5.7.** And he held an olive branch, and it had much fruit on it.

5.8. And Joseph entered the courtyard, and the gates were closed. **5.9.** But foreigners, whether man or woman, remained outside, because the guards at the gates had closed the doors. **5.10.** And Pentephres came, with his wife and his whole family, except their daughter Aseneth, and prostrated themselves before Joseph, with their faces upon the ground. **5.11.** And Joseph descended from his chariot, and gave them his right hand in greeting.

6.1. And Aseneth saw Joseph and her soul was pierced excruciatingly, and her insides dissolved and her knees became paralyzed, and her whole body trembled and she was overwhelmed with fright, and she groaned and said,

6.2. "Where will I go and where will I hide from before his face? How will Joseph, the son of God, regard me, since I have said evil things about him? **6.3.** Where will I flee and hide myself, since he sees all that is concealed, and nothing hidden escapes him, on account of the great light that is in him? **6.4.** And now, have mercy on me, O God of Joseph, because I have spoken evil words in ignorance.

6.5. "How will I regard myself now, miserable (as I am)? Did I not speak, saying, 'Joseph comes, the son of a shepherd from the land of Canaan'? And now, behold, the sun out of heaven comes toward us in his chariot and comes into our house today. **6.6.** Foolish and presumptuous was I who took no account of him and spoke evil words concerning him and did not know that Joseph is God's son. **6.7.** For who among humans will engender such beauty, and what womb will give birth to such light? Miserable and foolish am I, because I spoke evil words to my father. **6.8.** And now, let my father give me to Joseph as a servant and a slave and I will serve him for eternal time."

7.1. And Joseph entered the house of Pentephres and sat down upon a chair and washed his feet and set himself up a table by itself, because he did not eat with the Egyptians, for such was an abomination to him.

7.2. And Joseph spoke to Pentephres and his whole family, saying, "Who is that woman standing by the window of the upper story? Let her go away from this house." **7.3.** For Joseph feared that she also would attempt to seduce him, for all the wives [or, women] and the daughters of the magnates and the satraps of all Egypt sought to sleep with him.

7.4. Many of the wives [or, women] and daughters who saw Joseph suffered badly at the sight of his beauty and sent their envoys to him with gold and silver and valuable gifts. **7.5.** Joseph sent them back with threats and insults, saying, "I will not sin before the God of Israel." **7.6.** Joseph had before his eyes at all times the face of Jacob his father, and he remembered the commandments of his father, because Jacob said to Joseph and to his brothers, "Guard yourselves, children, absolutely from a foreign woman, from joining with her, for it is perdition and corruption." **7.7.** That is why Joseph had said, "Let that woman go away from this house."

7.8. And Pentephres said to him, "Lord, she whom you saw in the upper story is not a foreigner but our daughter, a virgin who detests all men, and no other man has seen her except you only today. **7.9.** And if you wish, she will come and meet with you, because our daughter is your sister." **7.10.** And Joseph rejoiced with much gladness, because Pentephres had said that the virgin detested all men.

7.11. And Joseph spoke to Pentephres and his wife, saying, "If she is your daughter, let her come, for she is my sister, and I love her from this day as my sister."

8.1. And the mother of Aseneth went up to the upper rooms, and led Aseneth to Joseph; and Pentephres said to his daughter, Aseneth, "Greet your brother, for he is a virgin as you are today, and detests all foreign women as you detest all foreign men."

8.2. And Aseneth said to Joseph, "Welcome, lord, blessed of the Most High God." And Joseph said to her, "May the God who has made all living things bless you."

8.3. And Pentephres said to Aseneth, "Come forward and kiss your brother."

8.4. And as she came forward to kiss Joseph, he stretched out his right hand and placed it on her breast and said, **8.5.** "It is not appropriate for a man who reveres God, who blesses the living God with his mouth and eats the blessed bread of life and drinks the blessed cup of immortality and is anointed with the blessed ointment of incorruptibililty, to kiss a foreign woman, one who blesses dead and deaf idols with her mouth and eats the bread of strangling from their table and drinks the cup of ambush from their libations and is anointed with the ointment of perdition. **8.6.** But a man who reveres God kisses his mother; and his sister, who is of his own tribe and family; and his wife, who shares his bed; those women who with their mouths bless the living God. **8.7.** Similarly, also, it is not appropriate for a woman who reveres God to kiss a strange man, because such is an abomination before God."

8.8. And as Aseneth heard the speech of Joseph, she grieved greatly, and wailed aloud, and gazing intently at Joseph, her eyes filled with tears.

8.9. And Joseph saw her and pitied her greatly, for Joseph was gentle and merciful, and he feared the Lord. And he raised his right hand above her head, and said,

8.10. "Lord, the God of my father Israel
The Most High, the powerful,
Who gave life to all,
and called them forth from the darkness into the light
and from error into truth
and from death into life,
You, Lord, yourself, grant life to this virgin and bless her,
And renew her by your spirit,
And re-form her by your (unseen) hand,
And revive her by your life,
And may she eat the bread of your life,
And may she drink the cup of your blessing,
    she whom you chose before she was conceived,
And may she enter into your rest,
    which you have prepared for your chosen ones."

9.1. And Aseneth rejoiced with great gladness at Joseph's blessing, and hurried up to her upper rooms, where she collapsed exhausted upon her bed, feeling joy and grief and much fear. Ceaseless sweat clung to her once she heard these words from Joseph, which he spoke to her in the name of God the Most High. **9.2.** And she wept copious, bitter tears, and repented of her gods, whom she had revered, and awaited the onset of evening.

9.3. And Joseph ate and drank and said to his servants, "Yoke the horses to the chariot, for," he said, "I must depart and tour around the entire city and the land."

9.4. And Pentephres said to Joseph, "My lord, spend the night here today, and go on your way tomorrow."

9.5. And Joseph said, "No, but I must leave today, for it is the day in which the Lord began to do his work, and on the eighth day, I will return again to you, and spend the night here."

10.1 Then Pentephres and his family went out to their estate.

10.2. And Aseneth remained alone with the virgins and was listless and cried until sunset; she did not eat bread nor drink water, but while everyone slept she alone remained awake. **10.3.** And she opened (the door) and went down to the gate, and found the gatekeeper sleeping with her children. **10.4** And Aseneth hurried and took down the leather curtain from the door and filled it with ashes and brought it up to her upper room and placed it on the floor. **10.5.** And Aseneth closed the door securely and placed the iron bar across it sideways and sighed deeply and wept.

10.6. And the virgin whom Aseneth loved the most of all her virgins heard the sigh of her mistress. She woke the rest of the virgins and went and found the door closed. **10.7.** She listened to the sighs and weeping of Aseneth and said, "Why are you sad, my lady, and what is it that grieves you? Open up for us and let us see you."

10.8. And Aseneth said to them from inside, (where she had) shut (herself) in, "I have a terrible headache, and I am lying down on my bed, and I do not have the strength to open up for you now, because I feel weak throughout my limbs, but each of you go to your chamber."

10.9. And Aseneth rose and opened the door gently and went into her second chamber where her coffers filled with ornaments were, and opened her chest and took out a staid black *chiton*. **10.10.** This was her mourning *chiton*, which she had worn when her firstborn brother died.

10.11. And Aseneth took off her royal robe and put on the black one and released her golden girdle and tied a rope around herself and took her tiara off her head, and the diadem, and the bracelets from her hands.

10.12. And she took her favorite robe, all of it, and threw it out the window for the poor.

10.13. And she took all her gold and silver gods, which were innumerable, and broke them in pieces and threw them to the beggars and the needy.

10.14. And Aseneth took her royal dinner—the fatted meats and fish and dressed meat—and all the sacrifices to her gods, and the vessels of wine for their libations, and threw all of it out the window for the dogs to eat.

10.15. And after this, she took the ashes and spread them out on the floor. **10.16.** And she took a sack and tied it about her hips and undid the braids from her head and covered herself with ashes. **10.17.** And she beat her breast frequently with both hands and fell down into the ashes and cried bitterly, moaning all night until morning.

10.18. In the morning, Aseneth rose up and looked, and behold, the ashes underneath her were like mud, from her tears. **10.19.** And

Aseneth threw herself down again on her face in the ashes until the sun set. **10.20.** And Aseneth did this for seven days, without tasting anything.

11. And on the eighth day, Aseneth lifted up her head from the floor on which she was lying, for her limbs were paralyzed from her great abasement.

12.1. And she stretched out her hands towards the east and raised her eyes to heaven and said,

12.2. "Lord, God of the ages
Who gave to all the breath of life,
Who brought into the light that which was unseen
Who made everything, and made manifest that which was
    without manifestation,

12.3. "Who raised the heaven and established the earth upon
    the waters,
Who fastened great stones on the abyss of the water,
    which shall not be immersed,
But which, until the end, do your will.

12.4. "Lord, my God, to you I cry,
Heed my prayer,
And I will confess my sins to you,
And I will reveal my lawlessness before you.

12.5. "I have sinned, Lord, I have sinned,
I have been lawless, and impious, and have spoken evil
    before you.
My mouth has been polluted by sacrifices to idols,
    and by the table of the gods of the Egyptians.

12.6. "I have sinned, Lord, before you,
I have sinned and have been impious, revering dead and
    mute idols,
And I am not worthy to open my mouth before you,
I, the wretched one.

12.7. "I have sinned, Lord, before you,
I, the daughter of Pentephres the priest,
    insolent and arrogant.
I bring my prayer before you, Lord,
    and cry unto you,
Deliver me from my persecutors,
    for unto you I have fled for refuge,
    as a child to its father and mother.

12.8. "And you, Lord, stretch forth your hands to me,
    as a father who loves his child and is affectionate,
And snatch me out of the hand of the enemy.

12.9. "For behold, the savage ancient lion pursues me,
And the gods of the Egyptians are his offspring,
Whom I cast away from myself, and destroy them,
And their father, the devil, attempts to consume me.

12.10. "But you, Lord, deliver me from his hands,
And pull me out of his mouth,
Lest he snatch me up like a wolf, and tear me apart,
And throw me into the abyss of fire,
And into the tempest of the sea,
And let not the great whale consume me.

12.11. "Save me, Lord, the desolate one,
Because my father and my mother disowned me,
Because I destroyed and broke their gods,
And now I am desolate and orphaned,
And there is no hope for me, Lord, if not with you,
For you are the father of the orphans,
And the protector of the persecuted,
And the helper of the oppressed.

12.12. "For behold, all the worldly goods of my father, Pentephres, are transitory and without substance, but the dwelling places of your inheritance, Lord, are incorruptible and eternal.

13.1. "Consider my circumstance as an orphan, Lord, because I have sought refuge before you.

13.2. "Behold, I have stripped myself of the royal robe woven with gold and have put on a black chiton.

13.3. "Behold, I have released my golden girdle and have girded myself with a sack and rope.

13.4. "Behold, I have cast off the diadem from my head and covered myself with ashes.

13.5. "Behold, the floor of my chamber, which was paved with multicolored and purple stones and sprinkled with perfume, now is sprinkled with my tears and covered with dirt.

13.6. "Behold, Lord, from the ashes and my tears, there is as much mud in my chamber as on a broad street.

13.7. "Behold, Lord, my royal dinner and fatted meats, I have given to the dogs.

13.8. "And behold, I have neither eaten bread nor drunk water for seven days and seven nights, and my mouth is parched like a drum, and my tongue is like a horn and my lips like bones; my face is wasted, and my eyes are failing from the inflammation of my tears.

13.9. "But pardon me, Lord, because I sinned against you in ignorance and spoke blasphemy against my lord Joseph.

13.10. "For I did not know, wretched as I am, that he is your son, Lord, because people told me that Joseph is the son of a shepherd from the land of Canaan, and I believed them, and I erred, and I rejected your chosen one Joseph and spoke evil concerning him, not knowing that he is your son.

13.11. "For who among human beings could engender such beauty, and who else is wise and strong like Joseph? But, my Lord, I entrust him to you, for I love him more than my own soul.

13.12. "Guard him within the wisdom of your graciousness and deliver me to him as a servant, that I may wash his feet and serve him and be a slave to him for all the rest of my life."

14.1. And as Aseneth finished confessing to the Lord, behold, the morning star rose in the heaven to the east, and Aseneth saw it and rejoiced and said, **14.2.** "The Lord God has heard me indeed, for this star is a messenger, and the herald of the light of the great day." **14.3.** And behold, the heaven split apart near the morning star, and an indescribable light appeared.

14.4. And Aseneth fell upon her face on the ashes and out of heaven a human figure came toward her. And he stood at her head and called her Aseneth.

14.5. And she said, "Who is it who calls me, since the door to my chamber is shut and the tower is high, and how is anyone able to come into my chamber?"

14.6. And the figure called to her a second time and said, "Aseneth, Aseneth." And she said, "Here I am, Lord, announce to me who you are."

14.7. And the figure said, "I am the commander of the house of the Lord and the commander of all the army of the Most High. Rise to your feet and I will speak with you."

14.8. And she raised her eyes and looked, and behold, a figure resembling Joseph in every way, with a robe and a crown and a royal scepter, **14.9.** except that his face was like lightning, and his eyes were like the light of the sun, and the hair on his head was like a burning flame, and his hands and his feet were like iron from the fire. **14.10.** And Aseneth looked and threw herself on her face before his feet in great fear and trembling.

14.11. And the figure said to her, "Take courage, Aseneth, and do not fear, but rise to your feet and I will speak to you."

14.12. And Aseneth stood up, and the figure said to her, "Take off the *chiton* which you put on, the black one, and the sack around your hips, and shake off the ashes from your head, and wash your face with living water. **14.13.** And put on a brand-new robe and gird your hips with your brilliant girdle, the double one of your virginity. **14.14.** And then come back to me and I will tell you the things I was sent to say to you."

14.15. And Aseneth went into her room where her treasure chests were and opened her chest and took out a new fine robe and took off the black robe and put on the new brilliant one, **14.16.** and released the rope and the sack around her hips and girded herself with the brilliant double girdle of her virginity, one girdle around her hips and one around her breast. **14.17.** And she shook the ashes out of her hair and washed her face with pure water and covered her head with a beautiful, fine veil.

15.1. And she went to the figure, and seeing her, he said to her, "Lift off the veil from your head, because today you are a holy virgin and your head is as a young man's." **15.2.** And Aseneth removed it from her head. And the figure said to her, "Take courage, Aseneth, for behold, the Lord has heard the words of your confession.

15.3. "Take courage, Aseneth: behold, your name is inscribed in the Book of Life and will never be erased in eternity.

15.4 "Behold, from this day you shall be made new, and formed anew, and revived, and you shall eat the bread of life and drink the cup of immortality and be anointed with the ointment of incorruptibility.

15.5. "Take courage, Aseneth: behold, the Lord has given you to Joseph as a bride, and he will be your bridegroom.

15.6. "And no longer shall you be called Aseneth, but your name shall be City of Refuge, because in you many nations shall take refuge and under your wings many peoples shall take shelter and in your fortress those who devote themselves to God through repentance shall be protected.

15.7. "For Metanoia (Repentance) is a daughter of the Most High, and she appeals to the Most High on your behalf every hour, and on behalf of all those who repent, because he is the father of Metanoia and she is the mother of virgins, and at every hour she appeals to him for those who repent, for she has prepared a heavenly bridal chamber for those who love her, and she will serve them for eternal time. **15.8.** "And Metanoia is a very beautiful virgin, pure and holy and gentle, and God the Most High loves her, and all the angels stand in awe of her.

15.9. "And behold, I will go before Joseph and speak to him concerning you, and he will come before you today and will see you and will rejoice in you and will be your bridegroom.

15.10. "So listen to me, Aseneth, and put on a wedding robe, the ancient, first robe which is in your chamber, and wrap yourself in all your favorite jewelry, and dress yourself as a bride, and prepare to meet him.

15.11. "For behold, he comes to you today, and will see you and rejoice."

15.12. And as the figure finished speaking to Aseneth, she was joyously happy and threw herself before his feet and said to him,

15.13. "Blessed is the Lord God who sent you to me to deliver me from the darkness and to lead me into the light, and blessed is his name forever.

15.14. "Let me speak now, lord, if I have found favor with you. Sit for a little while on the bed and I will prepare a table and bread, and you shall eat, and I will bring you good wine, whose perfume wafts unto heaven, and you shall drink and (then) depart on your way."

16.1. And the figure said to her, "Bring me a honeycomb also."

16.2. And Aseneth said, "I will send, lord, to the family estate, and I will bring you a honeycomb."

16.3. But the figure said to her, "Go into your chamber and you will find a honeycomb."

16.4. And Aseneth went into her chamber and found a honeycomb lying on the table, and the comb was as white as snow and full of honey, and its fragrance was like the scent of life.

16.5. And Aseneth took the comb and brought (it) to him, and the figure said to her, "Why did you say 'There is no honeycomb in my house,' and behold, you bring this to me?"

16.6. And Aseneth said, "I did not have, lord, any honeycomb in my house, but as you said, it has happened. Might it not have come from your mouth, since its fragrance is like the fragrance of perfume?"

16.7. And the figure stretched forth his hand and took hold of her head and said, "Blessed are you, Aseneth, that the secrets of God have been revealed to you; and blessed are those who devote themselves to God in repentance, for they shall eat from this comb.

16.8. "For this honey the bees of the paradise of delight have made, and the angels of God eat of it, and all who eat of it shall not die for eternity."

16.9. And the figure stretched out his right hand and broke off (a piece) from the comb and ate, and put (a piece of) the honey into Aseneth's mouth with his hand.

16.10. And the figure stretched forth his hand and put his finger on the edge of the comb facing east, and the path of his finger became like blood.

16.11. And he stretched forth his hand a second time and put his finger on the edge of the comb facing north, and the path of his finger became like blood.

16.12. And Aseneth stood to the left and observed everything the figure did.

16.13. And bees came up out of the hive of the comb, and they were white as snow, and their wings were purple and the color of hyacinth and as golden thread, and there were gold diadems on their heads and sharp stingers.

16.14. And all the bees entwined around Aseneth from [her] feet to [her] head, and other bees, as large as queen bees, attached themselves to Aseneth's lips.

16.15. And the figure said to the bees, "Go then away to your own place."

16.16. And they all left Aseneth, and all fell down to the ground and died.

16.17. And the figure said, "Arise and go back to your place." And they rose up and went away, all of them, to the courtyard adjacent to Aseneth.

17.1. And the figure said to Aseneth, "Have you perceived what was said?" And she said, "Behold, lord, I have perceived all this."

17.2. And the figure said, "So shall be the words I have spoken to you."

17.3. And the man touched the comb, and fire rose up from the table and consumed the comb. The burning honeycomb exuded a sweet odor.

17.4. And Aseneth said to the figure, "There are, lord, seven virgins with me serving me, raised with me since my childhood, born on the same night with me, and I love them. Let me call them that you might bless them as you have blessed me."

17.5. And the figure said, "Call (them)." And Aseneth called them, and the figure blessed them and said, "God, the Most High, will bless you for eternal time."

17.6. And the figure said to Aseneth, "Remove this table." And Aseneth turned to move the table, and the figure disappeared from her sight, and Aseneth saw something like a fiery chariot being taken up into the heaven to the east.

17.7. And Aseneth said, "Be merciful, Lord, to your slave, because I spoke evil in ignorance before you."

18.1. And while this was taking place, behold, a servant from Joseph's retinue came, saying, "Behold, Joseph, the Powerful One of God, comes to you today." **18.2.** And Aseneth called the steward of her house and said, "Prepare me a good dinner, for Joseph, the Powerful One of God, is coming to us."

18.3. And Aseneth went into her chamber and opened her chest and took out her first robe, which had the appearance of lightning, and put it on. **18.4.** And she girded herself with a brilliant, royal girdle. This girdle was the one with precious stones. **18.5.** And she put gold bracelets around her hands, and gold trousers about her feet, and a precious ornament about her neck, and she placed a gold crown on her head; and on the front of this crown there were very expensive stones. **18.6.** And she covered her head with a veil.

18.7. And she said to her young female attendant, "Bring me pure water from the spring." And Aseneth bent down into the water in the bowl on the conch shell. And her face was like the sun, and her eyes like the rising morning star.

19.1. And a little slave came and said to Aseneth, "Behold, Joseph [is] before the doors of our courtyard." And Aseneth went down with the seven virgins to meet him.

19.2. And when Joseph saw her, he said to her, "Come here to me, holy virgin, because I have good news concerning you from heaven, which has told me everything about you." **19.3.** And Joseph stretched out his hands and took Aseneth in his arms, and she him, and they embraced for a long time, and their spirits were rekindled.

20.1. And Aseneth said to him, "Come here, lord, come into my house." And she took his right hand and led him into her house.

20.2. And Joseph sat down upon the throne of Pentephres, her father, and she brought water to wash his feet. And Joseph said to her, "Let one of the virgins come and wash my feet."

20.3. And Aseneth said to him, "No, lord, for my hands are your hands, and your feet are my feet, and no other may wash your feet." And she constrained him and washed his feet.

20.4. And Joseph took her hand and kissed it (or: her), and Aseneth kissed his head.

20.5. And the parents of Aseneth came from the family estate and saw Aseneth sitting with Joseph and wearing a wedding robe, and they rejoiced and glorified God and ate and drank.

20.6. And Pentephres said to Joseph, "Tomorrow I will call the magnates and satraps of Egypt and make a wedding for you, and you shall take Aseneth as your wife."

20.7. And Joseph said, "First, I must report to Pharaoh concerning Aseneth, because he is my father, and he will give Aseneth to me as a wife."

20.8. And Joseph remained that day with Pentephres and did not go into Aseneth, because, he said, "It is not fitting for a man who reveres God to sleep with his wife before the wedding."

21.1. And Joseph rose up in the morning and went before Pharaoh and spoke to him concerning Aseneth. **21.2.** And Pharaoh sent and called for Pentephres and Aseneth. **21.3.** And Pharaoh was amazed at her beauty and said, "The Lord, the God of Joseph, who has chosen you to be his bride will bless you, because Joseph is the firstborn son of God and you will be called daughter of the Most High and Joseph will be your bridegroom for eternal time."

21.4. And Pharaoh took golden crowns and placed them upon their heads and said, "God the Most High will bless you and make you fruitful for eternal time."

21.5. And Pharaoh turned them toward each other, and they kissed each other.

21.6. And Pharaoh made their wedding, with feasting and much drinking for seven days.

21.7. And he called all the rulers of Egypt and made a proclamation, saying, "Everyone who works during the seven days of the wedding celebration of Joseph and Aseneth will die a bitter death."

21.8. And when the wedding and feasting were finished, Joseph went into Aseneth and Aseneth conceived by Joseph. And she gave birth to Manasseh and Ephraim his brother, in the house of Joseph.

NOTE: The Greek text of chapter 21 has been reconstructed from the Slavonic and from Greek fragments. Chapters 22–29, which are not translated here, recount the events of the seven years of famine. When Joseph departs to distribute grain, Pharaoh's son attempts to abduct Aseneth with the aid of Joseph's brothers Dan and Gad. Their treachery is attributed to their being Jacob's sons by Bilhah and Zilpah, the servants of his wives Leah and Rachel. In good romantic form, the plot is foiled by the virtuous brothers of Joseph and the miraculous intervention of God, invoked by Aseneth. Since Pharaoh's son is killed in the action, Joseph becomes the heir to the throne of Egypt and rules for forty-eight years before returning the throne to Pharaoh's grandson. Presumably Joseph and Aseneth live happily ever after, more or less.

114

THECLA OF ICONIUM, AN ASCETIC CHRISTIAN
AND THE PROTOTYPICAL CONVERT

The Acts of Thecla   2d century C.E.

7. And while Paul was speaking so in the middle of the assembly in the house of Onesiphorus, a certain virgin named Thecla (her mother was Theocleia) who was engaged to a man named Thamyris, sat at a nearby window in her house and listened night and day to what Paul said about the chaste life. And she did not turn away from the window but pressed on in the faith, rejoicing exceedingly. Moreover, when she saw many women and virgins going in to Paul she wished that she too be counted worthy to stand before Paul and hear the word of Christ, for she had not yet seen Paul in person but only heard him speak.

8. But since she did not move from the window, her mother sent to Thamyris. He came joyfully as if he were already taking her in marriage. So Thamyris said to Theocleia, "Where is my Thecla, that I may see her?" And Theocleia said, "I have something new to tell you, Thamyris. Indeed, for three days and three nights Thecla has not risen from the window either to eat or to drink but, gazing intently as if on some delightful sight, she so devotes herself to a strange man who teaches deceptive and ambiguous words that I wonder how one so modest in her virginity can be so severely troubled.

9. "Thamyris, this man is shaking up the city of the Iconians, and your Thecla too. For all the women and the young men go in to him and are taught by him that it is necessary, as he says, 'to fear one single God only and live a pure life.' And my daughter also, like a spider bound at the window by his words, is controlled by a new desire and a terrible passion. For the virgin concentrates on the things he says and is captivated. But you go and speak to her, for she is engaged to you."

10. And Thamyris went to her, loving her and yet fearing her distraction, and said, "Thecla, my fiancée, why do you sit like that? And what sort of passion holds you distracted? Turn to your Thamyris and be ashamed." And her mother also said the same thing: "Child, why do you sit like that, looking down and not answering, like one paralyzed?" And they wept bitterly, Thamyris for the loss of a wife, Theocleia for a daughter, the female servants for a mistress. So there was a great commingling of grief in the house. And while that was going on Thecla did not turn away but was concentrating on Paul's word.

11. But Thamyris jumped up and went out into the street, and carefully observed those going in to Paul and coming out. And he saw two men in a bitter quarrel with each other and said to them, "Gentlemen, tell me, who are you? And who is this man who is inside with you, the beguiling one who deceives the souls of young men and virgins that they should not marry but remain as they are? I promise now to give you a lot of money if you will tell me about him, for I am the first man of this city."

12. So Demas and Hermogenes said to him, "Who this man is we do not know. But he deprives young men of wives and virgins of husbands, saying, 'Otherwise there is no resurrection for you, unless you remain chaste and do not defile the flesh but keep it pure.'"

13. Thamyris said to them, "Come to my house, gentlemen, and rest with me." And they went away to a fabulous banquet, with lots of wine, great riches, and a splendid table. And Thamyris gave them drinks, for he loved Thecla and wished to have her for his wife. And during the banquet Thamyris said, "Tell me, gentlemen, what his teaching is, that I also may know it, for I am very anxious about Thecla because she loves the stranger so and I am deprived of my wedding."

14. But Demas and Hermogenes said, "Bring him before the governor Castellius on the ground that he is seducing the crowds with the new doctrine of the Christians, and so he will destroy him and you will have your wife Thecla. And we will teach you concerning the resurrection which he says is to come: that it has already taken place in the children whom we have and that we are risen again because we have full knowledge of the true God."

15. When Thamyris had heard this from them, he rose up early in the morning full of jealousy and wrath and went to the house of Onesiphorus, with rulers and officials and a great crowd, with clubs. He said to Paul, "You have corrupted the city of the Iconians, and my fiancée so that she does not want me. Let us go to governor Castellius!" And the whole crowd shouted, "Away with the *magus!* For he has corrupted all our women." And the crowds were persuaded.

16. And standing before the judgment seat Thamyris cried out, "Proconsul, this man—we don't know where he comes from—who does not allow virgins to marry, let him declare before you the reasons he teaches these things." And Demas and Hermogenes said to Thamyris, "Say that he is a Christian, and so you will destroy him." But the governor kept his wits and called Paul, saying to him, "Who are you and what do you teach? For they bring no light accusation against you."

17. Paul lifted up his voice and said, "If today I am interrogated as to what I teach, then listen, Proconsul. The living God, the God of vengeance, the jealous God, the God who has need of nothing has sent me since he longs for the salvation of humanity, that I may draw them away from corruption and impurity, and from all pleasure and death, that they may sin no more. Wherefore God sent his own child, the one whom I proclaim and teach that in him humanity has hope, he who alone had compassion upon a world gone astray, that humanity may no longer be under judgment but have faith, fear of God, knowledge of dignity, and love of truth. If then I teach the things revealed to me by God, what wrong do I do, Proconsul?" When the governor heard this, he commanded Paul to be bound and to be led off to prison until he could find a convenient time to give him a more careful hearing.

18. But during the night Thecla removed her bracelets and gave them to the doorkeeper, and when the door was opened for her she headed off to the prison. Upon giving a silver mirror to the jailer, she went in to Paul and sitting at his feet she heard about the mighty acts of God. And Paul feared nothing but continued to live with full confidence in God; and her faith also increased, as she kissed his fetters.

19. But when Thecla was sought by her own people and by Thamyris, they pursued her through the streets as if she were lost, and one of the doorkeeper's fellow slaves made it known that she had gone out during the night. And they questioned the doorkeeper, and he told them that she had gone to the stranger in prison. And they went just as he had told them and found her, so to speak, united with him in loving affection. And they left there, rallied the crowd about them, and relayed this to the governor.

20. He ordered Paul to be brought to the judgment seat. But Thecla rolled around in the place where Paul was teaching as he sat in the prison, so the governor commanded that she too be brought to the judgment seat. And she headed off joyfully exulting. But when Paul was brought forward again, the crowd shouted out even more, "He is a *magus!* Away with him!" But the governor gladly listened to

Paul concerning the holy works of Christ. When he had taken counsel he called Thecla, saying, "Why do you not marry Thamyris according to the law of the Iconians?" But she just stood there looking intently at Paul. And when she did not answer, Theocleia, her mother, cried out, saying, "Burn the lawless one! Burn her who is no bride in the midst of the theater in order that all the women who have been taught by this man may be afraid!"

21. And the governor was greatly moved. He had Paul whipped and threw him out of the city, but Thecla he sentenced to be burned. And immediately the governor arose and went off to the theater, and all the crowd went out to the inevitable spectacle. But Thecla, as a lamb in the wilderness looks around for the shepherd, so she sought for Paul. And looking over the crowd, she saw the Lord sitting in the form of Paul and said, "As if I were not able to bear up, Paul has come to look after me." And she looked intently at him, but he took off into the heavens.

22. Now, the young men and the virgins brought wood and straw for burning Thecla. And as she was brought in naked, the governor wept and marveled at the power in her. The executioners spread out the wood and ordered her to mount the pyre, and making the sign of the cross she mounted up on the wood pile. They put the torch underneath the pile, and although a great fire blazed up, the flame did not touch her. For God in compassion produced a noise below the earth, and a cloud above full of water and hail overshadowed (the theater), and all its contents poured out, so that many were in danger and died. The fire was extinguished, and Thecla was saved.

23. Now, Paul was fasting with Onesiphorus and his wife and the children in an open tomb on the road by which they go from Iconium to Daphne. And after many days, as they were fasting the children said to Paul, "We're hungry." And they had no means to buy bread, for Onesiphorus had left behind worldly things and followed Paul with all his house. But Paul took off his coat and said, "Go child, (sell this,) buy several loaves, and bring them (back)." But while the boy was buying bread he saw his neighbor Thecla; he was astonished and said, "Thecla, where are you going?" And she said, "I am seeking Paul, for I was saved from the fire." And the boy said, "Come, I'll take you to him, for he has been mourning for you and praying and fasting six days already."

24. Now, when she came to the tomb, Paul was kneeling in prayer and saying, "Father of Christ, do not let the fire touch Thecla, but be present with her, for she is yours!" And standing behind him, she cried out, "Father, maker of heaven and earth, the Father of your beloved child Jesus Christ, I bless you because you saved me from the fire that I might see Paul." And rising up, Paul saw her and said, "God, the knower of hearts, Father of our Lord Jesus Christ, I bless you that you have so quickly (accomplished) what I asked, and have listened to me."

25. And inside the tomb there was much love, with Paul leaping for joy, and Onesiphorus, and everyone. They had five loaves, and vegetables and water, and they were rejoicing over the holy works of Christ. And Thecla said to Paul, "I shall cut my hair short and follow you wherever you go." But he said, "The time is horrible, and you are beautiful. May no other temptation come upon you worse than the first and you not bear up but act with cowardice." And Thecla said, "Only give me the seal in Christ, and temptation will not touch me." And Paul said, "Have patience, Thecla, and you will receive the water."

26. And Paul sent away Onesiphorus with all his house to Iconium, and so taking Thecla he entered Antioch. But just as they came into town a Syrian by the name of Alexander, the first man of the Antiochenes, seeing Thecla, desired her and sought to win over Paul with money and gifts. But Paul said, "I don't know the woman of whom you speak, nor is she mine." But he, being a powerful man, embraced her on the open street; she, however, would not put up with it but sought Paul and cried out bitterly, saying, "Force not the stranger, force not the servant of God! I am the first woman of the Iconians, and because I did not wish to marry Thamyris I have been thrown out of the city." And grabbing Alexander, she ripped his cloak, took the crown off his head, and made him a laughingstock.

27. But he, partly out of love for her and partly out of shame for what had happened to him, brought her before the governor. When she confessed that she had done these things, he sentenced her to the beasts. But the women were horrified and cried out before the judgment seat, "An evil judgment! An impious judgment!" Thecla begged the governor that she might remain pure until her battle with the beasts. And a wealthy woman named Tryphaena, whose daughter had died, took her into custody and found comfort in her.

28. When the beasts were led in procession, they bound her to a fierce lioness, and the queen Tryphaena followed her. And as Thecla sat upon the lioness's back, the lioness licked her feet, and all the crowd was astounded. Now the charge on her inscription was Sacrilegious. But the women with their children cried out from above, saying, "O God, an impious judgment is come to pass in this city!" And after the procession, Tryphaena took her again, for her daughter Falconilla, who was dead, had spoken to her in a dream: "Mother, the desolate stranger Thecla you will have in my place in order that she may pray for me and I be translated to the place of the righteous."

29. So when Tryphaena received her back from the procession she was sorrowful because she was going to battle with the beasts on the following day, but at the same time she loved her dearly like her own daughter Falconilla and (she) said, "Thecla, my second child, come and pray for my child, that she may live forever; for this I saw in my dreams." And without hesitation she lifted up her voice and said, "My God, Son of the Most High, who is in heaven, give to her according to her wish, that her daughter Falconilla may live forever!" And when Thecla said this, Tryphaena grieved to think that such beauty was to be thrown to the beasts.

30. And when it was dawn, Alexander came to take her away—for he himself was arranging the hunt—and he said, "The governor has taken his seat, and the crowd is clamoring for us. Give me her who is to battle the beasts, that I may take her away." But Tryphaena cried out so that he fled, saying, "A second mourning for my Falconilla is come upon my house, and there is no one to help; neither child, for she is dead, nor relative, for I am a widow. O God of Thecla my child, help Thecla."

31. And the governor sent soldiers in order that Thecla might be brought. Tryphaena, however, did not stand aside but, taking her hand, led her up herself, saying, "My daughter Falconilla I brought to the tomb, but you, Thecla, I bring to battle the beasts." And Thecla wept bitterly and groaned to the Lord, saying, "Lord God, in whom I believe, with whom I have taken refuge, who rescued me from the fire, reward Tryphaena, who had compassion upon your servant and because she kept me chaste."

32. Then there was a clamor, a roaring of the beasts, and a shouting of the people and of the women who sat together, some saying, "Bring in the sacrilegious one!" But the women were saying, "Let the city perish for this lawlessness! Slay us all, Proconsul! A bitter spectacle, an evil judgment!"

33. Now, when Thecla was taken out of Tryphaena's hands, she was stripped, given a girdle, and thrown into the stadium. And lions and bears were thrown at her, and a fierce lioness ran to her and reclined at her feet. Now, the crowd of women shouted loudly. And a bear ran up to her, but the lioness ran and met it, and ripped the bear to shreds. And again a lion trained against men, which belonged to Alexander, ran up to her, and the lioness wrestled with the lion and perished with it. So the women mourned all the more, since the lioness that helped her was dead.

34. Then they sent in many beasts while she stood and stretched out her hands and prayed. And when she had finished her prayer, she turned and saw a great ditch full of water and said, "Now is the time for me to wash." And she threw herself in, saying, "In the name of Jesus Christ, I baptize myself on the last day!" And when they saw it, the women and the whole crowd wept, saying, "Do not throw yourself into the water!"—so that even the governor wept that such a beauty was going to be eaten by seals. So then she threw herself into the water in the name of Jesus Christ, but the seals, seeing the light of a lightning flash, floated dead on the surface. About her there was a cloud of fire so that neither could the beasts touch her nor could she be seen naked.

35. Now, the women, as other more terrible beasts were thrown in, wailed, and some threw petals, others nard, others cassia, others amomum, so that there was an abundance of perfumes. And all the beasts, overcome as if by sleep, did not touch her. So Alexander said to the governor, "I have some very fearsome bulls. Let us tie her who battles the beasts to them." Although he was frowning, the governor gave his consent, saying, "Do what you want." And they bound her by the feet between the bulls and prodded them from underneath with red-hot irons at the appropriate spot, that being the more enraged they might kill her. The bulls indeed leaped forward, but the flame that blazed around her burned through the ropes, and it was as if she were not bound.

36. But Tryphaena fainted as she stood beside the arena, so that her attendants said, "The queen Tryphaena is dead!" The governor observed this, and the whole city was alarmed. And Alexander, falling down at the governor's feet, said, "Have mercy upon me and the city, and set free her who battles the beasts, lest the city also perish with her. For if Caesar hears these things he will probably destroy both us and the city because his relative Tryphaena has died at the circus gates."

37. The governor summoned Thecla from among the beasts and said to her, "Who are you? And what have you about you that not one of the beasts touched you?" She answered, "I am a servant of the living God. As to what I have about me, I have believed in him in whom God is well pleased, his Son, on account of whom not one of the beasts touched me. For he alone is the goal of salvation and the foundation of immortal life. For to the storm-tossed he is a refuge, to the oppressed relief, to the despairing shelter; in a word, whoever does not believe in him shall not live but die for ever."

38. When the governor heard this, he ordered clothing to be brought and said, "Put on the clothing." But she said, "The one who clothed me when I was naked among the beasts, this one shall clothe me with salvation in the day of judgment." And taking the clothing, she got dressed.

And the governor issued a decree immediately, saying, "I release to you Thecla, the God-fearing servant of God." So all the women cried out with a loud voice and as with one mouth gave praise to God, saying, "One is God who has saved Thecla!"—so that all the city was shaken by the sound.

39. And when Tryphaena was told the good news, she came to meet her with a crowd. She embraced Thecla and said, "Now I believe that the dead are raised up! Now I believe that my child lives! Come inside, and I will transfer everything that is mine to you." So Thecla went in with her and rested in her house for eight days, instructing her in the word of God, so that the majority of the female servants also believed. And there was great joy in the house.

40. Yet Thecla longed for Paul and sought him, sending all around in every direction. And it was made known to her that he was in Myra. So taking male and female servants, she got herself ready, sewed her *chiton* into a cloak like a man's, and headed off to Myra. She found Paul speaking the word of God and threw herself at him. But he was astonished when he saw her and the crowd that was with her, wondering whether another temptation was not upon her. So realizing this, she said to him, "I have taken the bath, Paul, for he who worked with you for the gospel has also worked with me for my washing."

41. And taking her by the hand, Paul led her into the house of Hermias and heard everything from her, so that Paul marveled greatly and those who heard were strengthened and prayed on behalf of Tryphaena. And standing up, Thecla said to Paul, "I am going to

Iconium." So Paul said, "Go and teach the word of God!" Now, Tryphaena sent her a lot of clothing and gold, so it could be left behind for Paul for the ministry of the poor.

42. So Thecla herself headed off to Iconium and entered the house of Onesiphorus and threw herself down on the floor where Paul had sat when he was teaching the oracles of God, and wept, saying, "My God, and God of this house where the light shone upon me, Christ Jesus, the Son of God, my help in prison, my help before the governor, my help in the flame, my help among the beasts, you are God, and to you be glory for ever. Amen."

43. And she found Thamyris dead, but her mother alive. And calling her mother to her, she said to her, "Theocleia, my mother, are you able to believe that the Lord lives in the heavens? For whether you desire money, the Lord will give it to you through me, or your child, behold, I am standing beside you."

And when she had given this witness she headed off to Seleucia, and after enlightening many with the word of God, she slept with a fine sleep.

115

A ROMAN WOMAN WHO CONVERTS TO JUDAISM
AT AGE FORTY-ONE

CIJ 462   Rome, 2d/3d/4th century C.E.

Felicitas, a proselyte of six years . . . a foreigner (or: by the name of Peregrina), who lived 47 years. Her patron (erected this) to one most deserving.

116

A ROMAN WOMAN WHO CONVERTS TO JUDAISM
AT AGE SEVENTY AND ASSUMES
LEADERSHIP ROLES IN TWO SYNAGOGUES

CIJ 523   Rome, 2d/3d/4th century C.E.

Veturia Paulla . . . consigned to her eternal home, who lived 86 years, 6 months, a proselyte of 16 years, by the name of Sarah, mother of the synagogues of Campus and Volumnius. In peace (be) her sleep.

117

REFERENCES TO GOD-FEARERS IN THE
EPITAPHS OF TWO WOMEN

CIJ 73le   Rhodes, date uncertain

Euphrosyna, God-fearer, worthy, farewell.

CIJ 642   Pola, Italy, 3d/4th century C.E.

Aurelius Soter and Aurelius Stephanus to Aurelia Soteria, most pious mother, of the Jewish religion, fearing (God). Her sons placed (this monument).

Holy, Pious, and Exemplary Women

The texts in this section offer a sampling of women whose piety might be considered exemplary in some fashion. To whom, for whom, and by whom their piety is commended are not issues easily resolved. Nor is it apparent whether the virtues of these women reflect values held by men but not by women, values shared by men and women, or perhaps even values held by women alone, although this last seems least likely. It is also difficult for us to determine whether the virtues praised in these texts represent the consensus of large numbers of people even within a given community or whether they represent the values of only a small group, regardless of gender.

With a few exceptions (*The Testament of Job* and perhaps the *Lives* of Saint Pelagia and Saint Mary), I have tried to use documents reflecting actual historical women rather than hypothetical women onto whom piety exercised only in a prescriptive sense could be projected. That is, I have tried to excerpt evidence for actual women whose piety was publicly lauded but under circumstances in which such praise was not the primary intent.

So, for example, in the famous epitaph to the Roman Jewish woman Regina, her husband praises her for her devotion to Judaism, among the many virtues he enumerates, but it seems unlikely that his intent was to establish her as a public model for other women, although clearly the virtues for which he praises her may follow accepted social norms in their community of prosperous Roman Jewry.

The piety of martyrs such as Blandina, on the other hand, raises more complex problems of method. Texts such as the one from which her story is taken, as well as related documents often known as the Acts of various martyrs, often seem to report the actual records of court proceedings against Christians or the actual events of their torture in the Roman arena. Although the Romans did keep written records of legal proceedings, it is difficult for us to be sure that what we now have is in fact such documents when Christians have been the sole sources of transmission. In fact, of course, Christians do use these stories to provide examples to others, and recent scholarship suggests that early Christians may not have been above doctoring, or even fabricating, such accounts to encourage their sisters and brothers facing persecution. Not all Christians responded to the threat of persecution in ways that their coreligionists considered exemplary: many avoided martyrdom by fleeing or by recanting their Christianity (and later recanting the recantation) or by purchasing forged documents that certified to the authorities that they were law-abiding, sacrifice-performing pagans.[1] But if accounts of the martyrdom of women like Blandina may have been embellished, they nonetheless represent a communal understanding of how good Christian women should and did face torture and death for the sake of their faith. In addition, they contain the kinds of details that must reflect the social reality of some if not many Christians in the early centuries, and perhaps they report the actual experiences of real individuals.

1. An excellent, engaging discussion of this issue may be found in Robin Lane Fox's *Pagans and Christians* (New York: Alfred A. Knopf, 1987), 419–92.

118

THE EXEMPLARY SELF-DISCIPLINE AND PIETY
OF A JEWISH MOTHER FORCED TO WATCH
THE MARTYRDOM OF HER SEVEN SONS
IN THE SECOND CENTURY B.C.E.

4 Maccabees   1st century C.E.

15. O Reason of the children, master over the emotions! O religion, dearer to the mother than her sons! When two alternatives lay before her, religion, or the immediate salvation of her sons according to the tyrant's promise, she loved religion better, which preserves to eternal life according to God's promise. In what terms can I describe the passionate love of parents for their children? Upon the tender mold of the child we impress a marvellous likeness of soul and of form; and especially mothers, for by reason of their travail they are more sympathetic to offspring than fathers. For mothers are not stalwart in spirit; and in the degree that their offspring is abundant their love of children is more abounding. But of all mothers the mother of the seven sons proved most abounding in love; for by seven travails she implanted in herself a deep affection for them, and because of the manifold pains in the birth of each she was constrained to cherish a deep bond with them; yet because of her fear of God she disregarded the temporal safety of her children. Nay, more: because of her very nobility, and their ready obedience to the Law, she cherished an even deeper affection for them. For they were just, and temperate, and courageous, and great-spirited, and united by fraternal love; and so loved their mother that in obedience to her they observed the Law even unto death. Nevertheless, though so many considerations affecting maternal love drew the mother to sympathize with them, yet in the case of none of them did their manifold tortures avail to sway her reason; but each child severally and all together the mother urged on to death for religion's sake. Ah, sacred nature, charm of parental love, filial yearning, nurture, the indomitable emotions of motherhood! One by one the mother saw her sons tortured and burned—and swerved not, for religion's sake. The flesh of her children she saw disintegrating in the fire; the fingers of their hands and the toes of their feet quivering on the ground; the flesh of their heads flayed down to the cheeks, exposed like masks. O mother, who did now experience anguish more bitter than in their birth pangs! O thou woman, who alone did bring perfect religion to birth! your first-born, breathing out his life, did not turn your resolution; nor did the second, gazing pitifully upon you in his torment; nor the third, as he breathed his last; nor, when you looked at the eyes of each one, as in his torments he gazed immovable upon the same savage cruelty; nor when you perceived their nostrils revealing the forebodings of approaching death, did you wail. When you saw the flesh of your children burned over the embers of your children's flesh, and severed hands heaped on hands, and flayed skulls upon skulls, and corpses fallen upon corpses; and when you saw the place crowded with spectators of your children's torments, you did not weep. Not the sirens' melodies, nor the notes of the swan, so draw the hearers to the delight of hearing, as the voices of children in torment draw a mother's heart. How numerous, then, and how great, were the torments of the mother, as she suffered with her children as they were racked by the wheel and by fire! But devout reason gave manly courage to her heart in the midst of these emotions, and nerved her to ignore the immediate claims of maternal affection. And although she saw the destruction of seven children, and the manifold variety of their torments, that noble mother counted all these things as nought, because of her faith in God. In the tribunal of her own heart, as it were, she saw clever advocates—nature, parentage, maternal love, the torment of children; and she held in her discretion (a mother over her children!) two ballots: a doom of death, and salvation; yet she did not choose that favorable course which would bring safety to her seven sons for a brief space, but rather as a daughter of God-fearing Abraham bethought herself of Abraham's fortitude.

O mother of the nation, champion of the Law, defender of religion, and victor in the contest of the heart! O nobler than men in endurance, O more heroic than heroes in perseverance! Like the ark of Noah, which, bearing the universe in the midst of universal cataclysm, bravely endured the buffetings of the waves, so did you, guardian of the Laws, assailed on all sides in the midst of emotions' cataclysm by the powerful blasts of your sons' torments, with bold persistence withstand the tempests against religion.

16. If, then, a woman—elderly at that, and the mother of seven sons—endured seeing her children tortured to death, it must be acknowledged that religious reason is sovereign over the emotions. Thus I have demonstrated that not only men have shown mastery over the emotions, but that even a woman could despise the fiercest tortures. Not so savage were lions about Daniel; not so fiercely did Mishael's brazier burn with its greedy flame; as did innate maternal affection burn that woman, as she saw those seven sons of hers subjected to such manifold torments. But by reason which belongs to religion did the mother quench emotions so numerous and so intense.

This, too, you must consider: If the woman had been weak in spirit—being, as she was, a mother—she would have lamented over them, and perhaps have spoken as follows: "Ah, miserable woman that I am, repeatedly wretched time and again! Seven children have I borne, and I am the mother of none. In vain were my seven pregnancies; futile the ten-months burden borne seven times; fruitless the nursing, and wretched the suckling. In vain, my children, did I endure those many travails for you; and the harder anxieties of your upbringing. Alas for my sons—some unwedded, others married, but to no purpose; I shall never see your children, nor shall I ever be blessed with the title of grandmother. I had children, both numerous and handsome; and now am a woman forsaken and solitary, with many sorrows. Nor when I die, shall I have any of my sons to bury me."

Yet that holy and God-fearing mother lamented none of them with such a dirge; nor did she urge any of them to avoid death. Nor did she grieve, as they were on the point of dying. On the contrary— as though her mind were of adamant, and as though she were again giving birth to her brood of seven sons unto immortality—by her supplications she rather encouraged them to death for religion's sake. Mother, soldier of God through religion, Elder, woman! By your constancy you have vanquished even the tyrant; and by your deeds and your words discovered yourself more stalwart than a man. For when you were seized, along with your children, you stood firm, as you watched Eleazar undergoing torture; and you said to your children—speaking in Hebrew: "My sons, noble is the contest; and since you are summoned to it in order to bear testimony for your nation, strive zealously on behalf of the Law of our fathers. 'Twere shame indeed that this old man should endure agonies for the sake of religion, and you who are young should be terrified of torments. Remember that it is because of God that you have a share in the world, and have enjoyed life: for this reason you are bound to endure any hardship, for the sake of God. For His sake also was our father Abraham zealous to immolate his son Isaac, the father of a nation; nor did Isaac flinch when he saw his father's hand, armed with a sword, descending upon him. Moreover, Daniel the righteous was thrown to the lions; and Hananiah, Mishael, and Azariah were flung into the fiery furnace, and they endured for the sake of God. Do you, too, therefore, hold the same faith in God, and be not dismayed; for it would be unreasonable for you, who know religion, not to withstand suffering."

With these words the mother of the seven encouraged each of her sons, and bade them die rather than transgress the commandment of God; and they too knew well that those who die for the sake of God live with God, as do Abraham and Isaac and Jacob and all the patriarchs.

17. Certain of the guards declared that when she too was about to be seized and put to death, she flung herself into the fire, so that no one might touch her body. O mother with your seven sons, who broke the violence of the tyrant, and rendered his evil devices futile, and demonstrated the nobility of faith! Nobly set as a beam upon the pillars of your children, unswervingly did you support the earthquake of the tortures. Be of good courage, then, mother of holy soul, who keep the hope of your endurance firm with God; not so majestic stands the moon in heaven, with its stars, as you stand; lighting the way to piety for your seven starlike sons; honored by God, and with them fixed in heaven. For your childbearing was of our Father Abraham.

If it were possible for us to paint, as on a picture, the story of your religion, would not the spectators shudder when they saw the mother of seven children enduring manifold torments unto death for the sake of religion? Indeed, it would be proper to inscribe upon their very tomb the words following, as a memorial to those [heroes] of our people: **Here lie buried an aged priest, an old woman, and her seven sons, victims of the violence of a tyrant resolved to destroy the polity of the Hebrews. They vindicated their race, looking to God, and enduring torments even to death.**

Divine indeed was the contest of which they were the issue. Of that contest virtue was the umpire; and its score was for constancy. Victory was incorruptibility in a life of long duration. Eleazar was the prime contestant; but the mother of the seven sons entered the competition, and the brothers too vied for the prize. The tyrant was the adversary, and the world and humanity were the spectators. Reverence for God was the winner, and crowned her own champions. Who did not marvel at the athletes of the divine legislation, who were not astonished by them?

18. The mother of the seven children also uttered these righteous sayings to her children: "I was a chaste maiden, and did not depart from my father's house; but I kept guard over the rib fashioned into woman's body. No seducer of the desert or spoiler in the field corrupted me; nor did the seducing and deceitful serpent defile the sanctity of my chastity. All the period of my maturity I abode with my husband. When these sons were grown up, their father died. Happy was he; for he was alive to enjoy the fair season of their birth, but was not grieved at the pangs of childlessness. He, when he was still with you, taught you the Law and the Prophets. He read to you of Abel, done to death by Cain; of Isaac, offered as a holocaust; and of Joseph, in prison. He spoke to you of the zeal of Phineas; and taught you concerning Hananiah, Mishael, and Azariah in the fire. He also glorified Daniel, in the pit of lions, and called him blessed. He admonished you of the Scripture of Isaiah, which declares, 'When thou walkest through fire the flame shall not burn thee.' He chanted to you the psalm of David which says, 'Many are the ills of the righteous.' He recited the proverb of Solomon which says, 'He is a tree of life to them that do his will.' He affirmed the word of Ezekiel, 'Shall these dry bones live?' Nor indeed did he forget, in his instruction, the song that Moses taught, which says, 'I kill and I make alive; for that is thy life and the length of thy days.'"

119

THE SPIRITUAL INHERITANCE OF THE
DAUGHTERS OF JOB

The Testament of Job   2d century C.E.?

46. And they brought forth the property for distribution to the seven males. And he did not present any of the goods to the females. And they were distressed and said to their father:

> Our father, sir, it can't be that we are ⟨not⟩ also your children, can it? Why did you not give us a portion of your property?

But Job said to the females:

> Do not be upset, my daughters, for I did not forget you. For I have already selected for you an inheritance better than that of your seven brothers.

And then when he had called his daughter named Hemera, he said to her:

> Take the signet ring, go to the chamber and bring me the three golden boxes so that I may give you the inheritance.

And she went away and brought them. And he opened them and brought forth ⟨three bands⟩, shimmering, so that no man could describe their form, since they are not from earth but are from heaven, flashing with bright sparks like rays of the sun. And he gave each of the daughters one band saying,

> Place these around your breast so that it may go well with you all the days of your life.

47. And the other daughter, named Kassia, said to him:

> Father, is this the inheritance which you said was better than that of our brothers? What then is so unusual about these bands? We won't be able to sustain our life from them, will we?

And the father said to them,

> Not only will you sustain life from these, but these bands will also lead you into the better world, ⟨to live⟩ in the heavens. Are you ignorant, then, my children, of the value of these cords, of which the Lord considered me worthy on the day on which he wished to have mercy on me and remove from my body the diseases and the worms? When he called me he set before me these three bands and said to me:

Arise, gird your loins like a man!
I shall question you, and you answer me.

So I took them and girded myself, and immediately the worms disappeared from my body ⟨and the plagues as well⟩. And then, through the Lord, my body grew strong as if it had not suffered anything at all. But I could even forget the pains in my heart! And the Lord spoke to me by a powerful act, showing me things present and things to come. Now then, my children, since you have them you will not have the enemy opposing you at all, neither will you have anxieties about him in your mind, because it is a protective amulet of the Lord. Rise, then, gird them around you before I die in order that you may be able to see those who are coming for my departure, so that you may marvel at the creatures of God.

48. Thus, when the one of the three daughters ⟨called⟩ Hemera arose, she wrapped herself just as her father said. And she received another heart, so that she no longer thought about earthly things. And she chanted verses in the angelic language, and ascribed a hymn to God in accord with the hymnic style of the angels. And as she chanted the hymns, she permitted "the Spirit" to be inscribed on her garment.

49. And then Kassia girded herself and had her heart changed so that she was no longer anxious about worldly things. And her mouth received the dialect of the archons, ⟨and glorified the creation of the exalted place⟩. Wherefore if anyone wishes to know "the creation of the heavens," he will be able to find it in the "Hymns of Kassia."

50. And then the other one also, called Amaltheias-keras, girded herself and her mouth chanted verses in the dialect of those on high, since her heart also was changed by withdrawing from worldly things. And she spoke in the dialect of ⟨the⟩ cherubim, glorifying the master of virtues by exhibiting their splendor. And the one who further wishes ⟨to grasp the poetic rhythm of "the paternal splendor"⟩ will find it recorded in the "Prayers of Amaltheias-keras."

51. And after the three had stopped singing hymns, while the Lord was present as was I Nereos the brother of Job, while the holy angel was present, I was sitting near Job on the couch. And even I heard the magnificent compositions, as each [sister] noted things down for the other. And I wrote out the book ⟨of notations for most of the hymns that issued from the three daughters of my brother,⟩ so that these things would serve as a safeguard along with those, for these are the magnificent compositions of God.

52. And after three days, while Job was presumed·to be sick on the couch, without suffering or pains since suffering could not touch him because of the omen of the sash with which he was girded—and after three days he saw those who had come for his soul. And rising immediately, he took a lyre and gave it to his daughter Hemera, and gave a censer to Kassia, and gave a kettle-drum to Amaltheias-keras—so that they might praise those who had come for his soul. And when they had taken them, they praised ⟨and glorified⟩ God in the exalted dialect. ⟨And⟩ after these things, the one who sat in the great chariot came out and greeted Job, while the three daughters looked on, and their father himself looked on, but others did not see. And taking the soul, he flew up while embracing it, and made it mount the chariot, and set off for the east. But his body, wrapped for burial, was borne to the tomb as his three daughters led the way, girded about and singing hymns to God.

120

EPITAPH OF REGINA, EXTOLLED FOR
HER PIETY AND OBSERVANCE
OF JEWISH LAW

CIJ 476   Rome, 2d century C.E.

Here lies Regina, covered by such a tomb, which her husband set up as fitting to his love. After twice ten years she spent with him one year, four months and eight days more. She will live again, return to the light again, for she can hope that she will rise to the life promised, as is our true faith, to the worthy and the pious, in that she has deserved to possess an abode in the hallowed land. This your piety has assured you, this your chaste life, this your love for your people, this your observance of the Law, your devotion to your wedlock, the glory of which was dear to you. For all these deeds your hope of the future is assured. In this your sorrowing husband seeks his comfort.

121

TRIBUTE TO A PIOUS JEWISH WOMAN
FROM HER SON

CIJ 72   Date uncertain

To Julia Irene Arista, his mother, preserved through the power of God and the devotion of her family, a pious observer of the Law, Altronius Tullianus Eusebius, *vir optimus,* her son, in due tribute, aged 41.

122

THE TRIAL ACCOUNT OF CARTHAGINIAN CHRISTIAN WOMEN AND MEN

The Martyrs of Scilli   July 17, 180 c.e.

In the consulship of Praesens, then consul for the second time, and Claudian, on the 17th of July, Speratus, Nartzalus and Cittinus, Donata, Secunda, Vestia were brought to trial at Carthage in the council-chamber. The proconsul Saturninus said to them: "You may merit the indulgence of our Lord the Emperor, if you return to a right mind."

Speratus said: "We have never done harm to any, we have never lent ourselves to wickedness: we have never spoken ill of any, but have given thanks when ill-treated, because we hold our own Emperor in honours."

The proconsul Saturninus said: "We also are religious people, and our religion is simple, and we swear by the genius of our Lord the Emperor, and pray for his safety, as you also ought to do."

Speratus said: "If you will give me a quiet hearing, I will tell you the mystery of simplicity."

Saturninus said: "If you begin to speak evil of our sacred rites, I will give you no hearing; but swear rather by the genius of our Lord the Emperor."

Speratus said: "I do not recognize the empire of this world; but rather I serve that God, whom no man has seen nor can see. I have not stolen, but if I buy anything, I pay the tax, because I recognize my Lord, the King of kings and Emperor of all peoples."

The proconsul Saturninus said to the rest: "Cease to be of this persuasion."

Speratus said: "The persuasion that we should do murder, or bear false witness, that is evil."

The proconsul Saturninus said: "Have no part in this madness."

Cittinus said: "We have none other to fear save the Lord our God who is in heaven."

Donata said: "Give honour to Caesar as unto Caesar, but fear to God."

Vestia said: "I am a Christian."

Secunda said: "I wish to be none other than what I am."

The proconsul Saturninus said to Speratus: "Do you persist in remaining a Christian?"

Speratus said: "I am a Christian." And all were of one mind with him.

The proconsul Saturninus said: "Do you desire any space for consideration?"

Speratus said: "When the right is so clear, there is nothing to consider."

The proconsul Saturninus said: "What have you in your case?"

Speratus said: "The Books and the letters of a just man, one Paul."

The proconsul Saturninus said: "Take a reprieve of thirty days and think it over."

Speratus again said: "I am a Christian." And all were of one mind with him.

The proconsul Saturninus read out the sentence from his notebook: "Whereas Speratus, Nartzalus, Cittinus, Donata, Vestia, Secunda, and the rest have confessed that they live in accordance with the religious rites of the Christians, and, when an opportunity was given them of returning to the usage of the Romans, persevered in their obstinacy, it is our pleasure that they should suffer by the sword."

Speratus said: "Thanks be to God."

Nartzalus said: "To-day we are martyrs in heaven: thanks be to God!

The proconsul Saturninus commanded that proclamation be made by the herald: "I have commanded that Speratus, Nartzalus, Cittinus, Veturius, Felix, Aquilinus, Laetantius, Januaria, Generosa, Vestia, Donata, Secunda be led forth to execution."

They all said: "Thanks be to God!"

And so all were crowned with martyrdom together, and reign with the Father and Son and Holy Spirit for ever and ever. Amen.

123

THE MARTYRDOM OF THE CHRISTIAN
BLANDINA AND THREE MALE COMPANIONS
IN 177 C.E.

Letter of the Churches of Lyons and Vienne,   4th century C.E.
in Eusebius's *History of the Church* V.1.3–63

The servants of Christ who sojourn at Vienne and Lyons in Gaul to the brethren in Asia and Phrygia *who* have the same *faith* and hope *as we* of redemption: *peace and grace* and glory *from God* the Father, *and* Christ *Jesus our Lord*.

4. . . . Indeed we are unable, and it is beyond the power of pen, to state with exactitude the greatness of the affliction here, the mighty rage of the heathen against the saints, and all that the blessed martyrs endured. For the adversary fell upon us with all his might, and gave us *already* a foretaste of what *his coming* in the future without restraint would be; he left nothing undone to train and exercise beforehand his own against the servants of God, insomuch that not only were we excluded from houses and baths and market-place, but they even forbade any of us to be seen at all in any place whatsoever. Nevertheless the grace of God was our captain on the other side, rescued the weak, and ranged against the foe firm pillars, able by their endurance to draw upon themselves the whole attack of the evil one. And these joined battle, enduring every kind of reproach and punishment; yea, regarding their many trials as little, they hastened to Christ, truly showing *that the sufferings of this present time are not worthy to be compared with the glory which shall be revealed to us-ward*.

7. First of all they nobly endured the attacks which the whole mass of the people heaped upon them, clamours, blows, halings, plunderings, stonings and confinements, and all that an infuriated mob is wont to employ against foes and enemies. Then they were conducted to the market-place by the tribune and the authorities presiding over the city; and when they had been questioned before the whole multitude, and given their testimony, they were shut up in prison until the governor's arrival. But afterwards, when they were brought before the governor, who used all the usual savagery against us, Vettius Epagathus, one of the brethren, a man filled with the fulness of love towards God and his neighbour, came forward. His conduct had reached such a degree of perfection that, young though he was, his reputation equalled that of the elder Zacharias; for he had *walked in all the commandments and ordinances of the Lord blameless;* in every service to his neighbour he was untiring, *having a* great *zeal for God* and *fervent in spirit.* Such a man could not endure the passing of so groundless a judgement against us; but was exceeding angry, and requested that he himself might be heard in defence of the brethren, that there is nothing godless or impious among us. Those around the tribunal cried out against him (for he was indeed a man of note), and the governor would not listen to the just request he had thus put forward, but asked him this one question, if he too were a Christian. And having confessed in a very clear voice, he also attained to the inheritance of the martyrs, being called the advocate of Christians, but having the *Advocate in* himself, *the Spirit* of *Zacharias;* which Spirit he showed in the fulness of *his love,* in that he was *well pleased* to *lay down even* his *own life for* the defence of *the brethren.* For he was and is a true disciple of Christ, *following the Lamb whithersoever he goeth.*

11. Henceforward the rest were divided; some were manifestly ready for martyrdom, and fulfilled with all zeal the confession wherein they gave witness; but others were manifestly unready and untrained and still weak, unable to bear the strain of a mighty conflict: of which number some ten proved abortions. These last wrought in us great sorrow and immeasurable mourning, and hindered the zeal of the remainder who had not yet been seized, and who in spite of every terrible suffering nevertheless attended the martyrs and would not leave them. But then we were all greatly affrighted at the uncertainty of confession; not that we feared the punishments inflicted, but we looked to the issue and dreaded lest any should fall away. Nevertheless those who were worthy were seized day by day, thus filling up the number of the former class, so that from the two churches were gathered all the zealous members, by whose means our position here had been mainly established. And there were seized also certain of our heathen household servants, since the governor gave an official order that we should all be sought out. And they too, thanks to *the snares* of Satan, in their fear of the tortures which they saw the saints enduring, and at the instigation of the soldiers, falsely accused us of Thyestean banquets and Oedipodean intercourse, and things of which it is not right for us to speak or think, nay, not even to believe that the like was ever done by man. But these rumours spread, and all were infuriated at us, insomuch that those who had formerly acted with moderation, on the ground of friendship, were now greatly incensed and *cut* *to the heart* against us. Thus was fulfilled that which was said by the Lord: *The* time will *come, when whosoever killeth you shall think that he offereth service unto God.* From that time on the holy martyrs endured punishments beyond all description, Satan earnestly endeavouring to elicit from their lips also some of the slanders.

17. But the entire fury of the crowd, governor and soldiers fell upon Sanctus, the deacon from Vienne, and upon Maturus, a noble combatant though but lately baptized, and upon Attalus, a native of Pergamum, of which church he had been always *the pillar and ground,* and upon Blandina, through whom Christ showed that things which appear mean and unsightly and despicable in the eyes of men are accounted worthy of great glory in the sight of God, through love towards Him, a love which showed itself in power and did not boast itself in appearance. For when we were all afraid, and her mistress according to the flesh (who was herself also a combatant in the ranks of the martyrs) was in a state of agony, lest the weakness of her body should render her unable even to make a bold confession, Blandina was filled with such power that those who by turns kept torturing her in every way from dawn till evening were worn out and exhausted, and themselves confessed defeat from lack of aught else to do to her; they marvelled that the breath still remained in a body all mangled and covered with gaping wounds, and they testified that a single form of torture was sufficient to render life extinct, let alone such and so many. But the blessed woman, like a noble champion, in confession regained her strength; and for her, to say "I am a Christian, and with us no evil finds a place" was refreshment and rest and insensibility to her lot.

20. Now as for Sanctus, he also nobly endured with surpassing and superhuman courage all the torments that human hands could inflict, and though the wicked men hoped that the continuance and severity of the tortures would cause him to utter something that he ought not, he set the battle against them with such firmness that he would not state even his own name, or the people or city whence he came, or whether he were bond or free. But to every question he replied in Latin: "I am a Christian." This he confessed again and again, instead of name and city and race and all else, and no other word did the heathen hear from his lips. Hence there actually arose great contention on the part of the governor and the torturers against him, with the result that finally, when nothing else was left to inflict upon him, they applied red-hot brazen plates to the most tender parts of his body. And though these were burning, Sanctus himself remained unbending and unyielding, and firm in his confession; for he was bedewed and strengthened by the heavenly *fountain of the water of life* which issues from the bowels of Christ. But his poor body was a witness to what he had undergone—one whole wound and bruise, contracted, having lost the outward form of a man—in which body Christ suffered and accomplished mighty wonders, bringing the adversary to nought and *showing* for the *ensample* of those that remained that nothing is to be feared where the love of the Father is, nothing is painful where there is the *glory of Christ*. For the wicked men after certain days again tortured the martyr, thinking to overcome him when they applied the same instruments to limbs so swollen and enflamed that he could not bear even the hand to touch them; or that he would die under the tortures and so cause terror to the rest. Yet not only did nothing of the kind occur in this case, but, contrary to all human expectation, the poor body actually arose and became erect under the subsequent tortures, and regained its former shape and the use of its limbs. Thus by the grace of Christ the second torturing proved for him not punishment but healing. And Biblis too, one of those who had denied, *the devil* supposed that he had already *devoured;* but wishing to use her slander as a further ground of condemnation, he brought her to punishment, that he might compel an already fragile and craven woman to state impieties concerning us. She, however, regained her senses under the torture and awoke, so to speak, out of a deep sleep, when the passing retribution recalled to her mind the *eternal punishment* in hell; and she directly contradicted the slanderers, saying: "How could they eat their children, who may not eat blood even of creatures without reason?" And henceforth she confessed herself a Christian, and joined the inheritance of the martyrs.

27. Now when the tyrant's instruments of torture were brought to nought by Christ through the endurance of the blessed ones, the devil began to invent other devices: close confinement in prison, in darkness and its most noisome spot; stretching the feet in the stocks, and keeping them stretched five holes apart; and all those other torments which his servants when enraged—aye, and filled with their master—are wont to inflict upon prisoners. So that the more part were stifled in the prison, as many as the Lord willed thus to depart, that He might manifest *His glory*. For some, though tortured so cruelly that it seemed they could no longer live even with every attention, remained alive in the prison, destitute indeed of human care, but fortified afresh

by *the Lord* and *strengthened* both in body and soul, cheering on and encouraging the rest. But others who were young and just recently apprehended, whose bodies had not been previously tortured, could not endure the rigour of their confinement, and died within its walls. Now the blessed Pothinus, to whom had been committed the ministry of the bishopric at Lyons, was above ninety years of age, and very weak in body. He was scarcely breathing because of the bodily *weakness* which was laid upon him, but the earnest desire for martyrdom filled him with that renewed strength which a *willing spirit* supplies. He too was haled to the tribunal, and though his body was weakened both by age and disease, his life was preserved within him, that through it Christ might *triumph*. He was conveyed to the tribunal by the soldiers, escorted by the city authorities and *the whole multitude,* who gave utterance to all sorts of cries, as if he were Christ Himself; and so he gave *the good* witness. Being examined by the governor as to who the God of the Christians was, he replied, "If thou art worthy, thou shalt know"; and thereupon he was haled without mercy, and received blows of every kind: those close by heaped on him all manner of insult with blows of hands and feet, regardless of his age, while those at a distance made him the object of whatever missile came to their hand; and all considered it a grievous fault and impiety to be behindhand in their wanton violence to him. For thus indeed they thought to avenge their gods. Scarcely breathing he was cast into prison, and after two days gave up the ghost.

32. Then in truth a mighty dispensation of God came to pass, and the measureless compassion of Jesus was displayed, in a manner rarely vouchsafed among the brethren, but not beyond the art of Christ. For they who had denied when the Christians were first arrested were also confined with [the others] and shared their sufferings; for on this occasion their denial had profited them nothing. On the contrary, those who confessed what they really were, were confined as Christians, no other charge being brought against them; while the others were detained thenceforward as murderers and scoundrels, and were punished twice as much as the rest. For the burden of the confessors was lightened by the joy of martyrdom, the hope of the promises, their love to Christ, and the Spirit of the Father; but the others were grievously tormented by their conscience, insomuch that their countenances could be clearly distinguished from all the rest as they passed by. For they went forth with joy, great glory and grace blended on their countenances, so that even their *chains* hung around them like a

goodly ornament, as a bride adorned *with golden fringes of divers colours,* perfumed the while with the *sweet savour of Christ;* hence some supposed that they had been anointed with earthly ointment as well. But the others were dejected, downcast, unsightly and covered with every kind of confusion; reproached, moreover, by the heathen for baseness and cowardice; under the charge of murder, and having lost the one precious, glorious and life-giving Name. The rest beholding this were stablished, and those who were apprehended confessed without doubting, nor did they bestow even a thought upon the persuasion of the devil. . . . After this their martyrdoms henceforth embraced every different form of death. For having *woven* a single *crown* of divers colours and variegated flowers they offered it to the Father. And so it was fitting that the noble champions, after having endured a varied conflict and mightily conquered, should receive as their due the mighty *crown* of incorruptibility. Maturus, then, and Sanctus and Blandina and Attalus were led to contend with wild beasts to the amphitheatre, and to the public spectacle of heathen inhumanity, a day for contests with wild beasts being granted of set purpose for our benefit. And Maturus and Sanctus passed once more through every kind of torture in the amphitheatre, as if they had suffered absolutely nothing before, or rather as if they had already vanquished their antagonist in many rounds, and were now contending for the crown itself. Again they ran the gauntlet of scourges, as is the custom of the place; they were dragged by wild beasts; they endured all that the cries of a maddened populace ordered, now from this side, now from that; and last of all, the iron chair, which fried their bodies and choked them with smoke. Nor even at this point did the heathen stop, but were still further maddened, in their desire to conquer the Christians' endurance; nevertheless nothing escaped the lips of Sanctus save that word of confession which it had been his wont from the very first to utter. So then, these men, whose life had lasted long through a mighty conflict, were finally sacrificed, being *made* throughout that day *a spectacle unto the world* in place of all the varied show that single combats offered.

41. Now Blandina, suspended on a stake, was exposed as food to wild beasts which were let loose against her. Even to look on her, as she hung cross-wise in earnest prayer, wrought great eagerness in those who were contending, for in their conflict they beheld with their outward eyes in the form of their sister Him who was crucified for them, that He might persuade those who believe in Him that all who suffer for the glory of Christ have unbroken fellowship with the living God. And as none of the wild beasts then touched her, she was taken down from the stake and cast again into prison, being kept for another conflict, that she might conquer in still further contests, and so both render irrevocable the sentence passed on *the crooked serpent,* and encourage the brethren—she the small, the weak, the despised, who had *put on Christ* the great and invincible Champion, and who in many rounds vanquished the adversary and through conflict was crowned with the *crown* of incorruptibility.

43. As for Attalus, he too was loudly called for by the crowd (for he was well known), and entered the arena a ready combatant by reason of his good conscience, since he had been truly exercised in the Christian discipline, and always a *witness* among us of *truth*. He was conducted round the amphitheatre, preceded by a board, on which was written in Latin "This is Attalus the Christian," the people bursting with vehement indignation against him. But when the governor learnt that he was a Roman, he ordered him to be taken back to the prison, where also were the others concerning whom he wrote to Caesar and was awaiting his sentence.

45. But the intervening time proved *not idle nor unfruitful* in their case; nay, through their endurance the measureless compassion of Christ was displayed. For by the living the dead were quickened, and martyrs forgave those who were not martyrs, and the virgin mother rejoiced greatly to receive alive those whom her womb had brought forth dead. For by their means the more part of those who had denied were brought again to birth, were conceived again, were rekindled into life, and learnt to confess; full now of life and vigour they approached the tribunal, for their trial was made sweet by God, who *hath no pleasure in the death of the sinner,* but is kind towards *repentance;* that they might be again questioned by the governor. For Caesar had written that they should be tortured to death, but that any who denied should be set free. And as the national festival held in that place was then at its commencement—a festival largely attended by visitors from all the tribes—the governor had the blessed ones conducted to the tribunal, to make of them a spectacle, and to form a procession for the benefit of the crowds. Therefore he again examined them; and those who appeared to possess Roman citizenship he beheaded, but sent the others to the wild beasts. And Christ was mightily glorified in those who formerly denied Him, but then confessed, contrary to the expectation of the heathen. Indeed they were examined by themselves, presumably as a prelude to their release; but confessing, were added to the inheritance of the martyrs. And there remained outside those who had never even a trace of faith, or an idea of the marriage *garment,* or a thought for the fear of God, nay rather, *blaspheming the Way* by their manner of life—**49.** in fact, *the sons of perdition.* But all the rest *were added* to the Church.

While these were being examined, a certain Alexander, a Phrygian by race and a physician by profession, who had lived for many years in the Gauls, and was known almost to everyone for his love to God and *boldness* for *the word* (for he too was not destitute of the apostolic gift), stood by the tribunal and by signs encouraged them to confess. To the bystanders there he appeared to be, as it were, in travail. The crowd were enraged that those who had formerly denied should afterwards confess, and cried out against Alexander as the cause of this. Thereupon the governor summoned him and asked him who he was; and angry at his reply "A Christian," condemned him to the wild beasts. And on the following day he entered [the amphitheatre] in the company of Attalus as well; for indeed the governor, to please the crowd, had delivered Attalus too again to the wild beasts. These men experienced in turn every instrument that has been devised for torture in the amphitheatre, and, having endured a mighty conflict, at last were sacrificed like the rest. Alexander *neither groaned nor uttered* the slightest *cry,* but held converse with God in his heart. But Attalus, when he was placed in the iron chair and scorched, so that the fumes rose from his body, addressed the multitude in Latin: "Behold, this which ye do is devouring men; but we neither devour men nor practise any other wickedness." And on being asked the name of God, he replied, "God has not a name as a man has." And after all these, finally on the last day of the single combats Blandina was again brought in, in the company of Ponticus, a lad about fifteen years old. They had also been fetched in every day to view the tortures of the others. The heathen tried to force them to swear by their idols, and as they remained firm and set them at nought, the multitude was so infuriated at them that it had neither compassion for the youth of the boy nor respect for the sex of the woman. Nay, they exposed them to every cruelty and brought them through the entire round of tortures, again and again trying to force them to swear. But this they were unable to accomplish; for Ponticus, encouraged by his sister (so that the heathen themselves saw that it was she who was urging him on and strengthening him), having nobly endured every kind of torture *gave up his spirit.* But the blessed Blandina last of all, having, like a high-born mother, exhorted her children and sent them forth victorious to the King, travelled herself along the same path of conflicts as they did, and hastened to them, rejoicing and exulting at her departure, like one *bidden to* a marriage *supper,* rather than cast to the wild beasts. And after the scourging, after the wild beasts, after the frying-pan, she was at last thrown into a basket and presented to a bull. For a time the animal tossed her, but she had now lost all perception of what was happening, thanks to the hope she cherished, her grasp of the objects of her faith, and her intercourse with Christ. Then she too was sacrificed, and even the heathen themselves acknowledged that never in their experience had a woman endured so many terrible sufferings.

57. Nevertheless not even thus were their madness and cruelty towards the saints satisfied. For wild and barbarous tribes when incited by a wild beast were not easily checked; and their wanton violence found another distinct outlet with regard to the corpses. That they had been worsted did not put them out of countenance, since for them man's gift of reason did not exist; nay rather, in them as in a wild beast the fact inflamed anger, and the governor and people were at one in displaying an unjust hatred towards us, that the Scripture might be fulfilled: *He that is lawless, let him do lawlessness still; and he that is righteous, let him be accounted righteous still.* For indeed they cast those suffocated in prison to the dogs, and kept a careful guard by night and day lest any should receive funeral rites at our hands. And then they actually exposed what the wild beasts and the fire had left behind—mangled or charred, as the case might be—and the heads of the others together with their severed trunks, and guarded them likewise from burial, with a military watch, for many days. And some were moved with indignation and *gnashed on* them *with their teeth,* seeking to take still further vengeance upon them; while others laughed and jeered, at the same time exalting their own idols, to whom they attributed the punishment of the Christians; others again, of a more forbearing nature and seeming to extend to them a measure of fellow-feeling, uttered many reproaches, saying, *"Where is their god?* and what profit has their religion brought them, which they have preferred to their own life?" So varied, then, was their attitude; but as for us, we were plunged in great grief, in that we could not bury the bodies in the earth. For neither did night avail us for this purpose, nor did money persuade or prayers move them. But in every possible way they kept guard, as if the prevention of burial would bring them great gain.

62. . . . The bodies, then, of the martyrs, which for six days were displayed and exposed to the elements in every way possible, the lawless men afterwards burnt and reduced to ashes. Then they swept them down into the river Rhone which flows close by, so that not even a trace of them might remain upon the earth. And this they did, thinking that they could conquer God and deprive them of *the regeneration*, "in order," as they themselves said, "that they may not even have hope of a resurrection, in faith of which they introduce into our midst a certain strange and new-fangled cult, and despise dread torments, and are ready to go to their death, and that too with joy. Now let us see if they will rise again, and if their *god can* help them, and *deliver them out of* our *hands*."

124

A PROMINENT ROMAN OFFICIAL'S PRAISES OF
THE TRADITIONAL ROMAN PIETY
OF HIS PRIESTESS WIFE, PAULINA,
IN THEIR JOINT EPITAPH

ILS 1259–61   Rome, 384 C.E.

To the gods of the dead. Vettius Agorius Praetextatus, augur, priest
of Vesta, priest of the Sun, quindecemvir, curialis of Hercules, initiate
of Liber and the Eleusinian [mysteries], hierophant, neocorus, tauro-
boliatus, father of fathers. In public office imperial quaestor, praetor
of Rome, governor of Tuscia and Umbria, governor of Lusitania, proconsul of Achaia, praefect of Rome, senatorial legate on seven mis-
sions, prefect of the praetorian guard twice in Italy and Illyrica, consul
ordinarius elect, and Aconia Fabia Paulina, initiate of Ceres and the
Eleusinian [mysteries], initiate of Hecate at Aegina, tauroboliata,
hierophant. They lived together for forty years.

(On the right side of the tomb) Vettius Agorius Praetextatus to his
wife Paulina. (In verse) Paulina, conscious of truth and chastity, devoted to the temples and friend of the divinities, who put her husband
before herself, and Rome before her husband, proper, faithful, pure in
mind and body, kindly to all, helpful to her family gods . . . (On the
left side) Vettius Agorius Praetextatus to his wife Paulina. (In verse)
Paulina, the partnership of our heart is the origin of your propriety; it
is the bond of chastity and pure love and fidelity born in heaven. To
this partnership I entrusted the hidden secrets of my mind; it was a
gift of the gods, who bind our marriage couch with loving and chaste
bonds. With a mother's devotion, with a wife's charm, with a sister's
bond, with a daughter's modesty; with the great trust by which we are
united with our friends, from the experience of our life together, by
the alliance of our marriage, in pure, faithful, simple concord; you
helped your husband, loved him, honoured him, cared for him.

(On the back of the monument. Paulina is speaking, in verse) My
parents' distinction did nothing greater for me than that I even then
seemed worthy of my husband. But all glory and honour is my husband's name, Agorius. You, descended from noble seed, have at the
same time glorified your country, senate, and wife with your mind's
judgment, your character and your industry, with which you have
reached the highest pinnacle of excellence. For whatever has been
produced in either language by the skill of the sages to whom the gate

of heaven is open, whether songs that poets composed or writings in prose, these you make better than when you took them up to read. But these are small matters; you as pious initiate conceal in the secrecy of your mind what was revealed in the sacred mysteries, and you with knowledge worship the manifold divinity of the gods; you kindly include as colleague in the rites your wife, who is respectful of men and gods and is faithful to you. Why should I speak of your honours and powers and the joys sought in men's prayers? These you always judge transitory and insignificant, since your title to eminence depends on the insignia of your priesthood. My husband, by the gift of your learning you keep me pure and chaste from the fate of death; you take me into the temples and devote me as the servant of the gods. With you as my witness I am introduced to all the mysteries; you, my pious consort, honour me as priestess of Dindymene and Attis with sacrificial rites of the taurobolium; you instruct me as minister of Hecate in the triple secret and you make me worthy of the rites of Greek Ceres. On account of you everyone praises me as pious and blessed, because you yourself have proclaimed me as good through the whole world; though unknown I am known to all. For with you as husband how could I not be pleasing? Roman mothers seek an example from me, and think their offspring handsome if they are like yours. Now men, now women want and approve the insignia that you as teacher have given me. Now that all these have been taken away I your wife waste away in sorrow; I would have been happy, if the gods had given me a husband who had survived me, but still I am happy because I am yours and have been yours and will now be yours after my death.

(Another inscription) To Fabia Aconia Paulina, daughter of Aco Catullinus formerly prefect and consul, wife of Vettius Praetextatus prefect and consul elect, initiate at Eleusis to the god Iacchus, Ceres and Cora, initiate at Lerna to the god Liber and Ceres and Cora, initiate at Aegina to the two goddesses, tauroboliata, priestess of Isis, hierophant of the goddess Hecate, and initiate in the rites of the Greek Ceres.

(Inscription on a statue base) In honour of Coelia Concordia, chief vestal virgin, Fabia Paulina arranged that a statue be made and set up first on account of her distinguished chastity and celebrated holiness concerning the divine cult, and chiefly because [Coelia Concordia] first had set up a statue to [Paulina's] husband Vettius Agorius Praetextatus, who was a man in all ways exceptional and deserving of honour even by virgins and by priestesses of this [high] rank.

125

HOW A FORMER PROSTITUTE DEVOTES THE
REMAINDER OF HER LIFE TO
ASCETIC SOLITUDE, DISGUISED
AS A MONK

The Life of Saint Pelagia the Harlot   5th century C.E.

The Author's Preface

We ought ever to return great thanks to our Lord who desireth
not that sinners should perish in death, but would have all men turn
in penitence to life. Hear therefore the miracle that was wrought in
our time. It seemed good to me, James the sinner, to write to you,
holy brethren, that ye might come to know it, either by listening or
reading, and might lay hold on so mighty a consolation for your
souls. For God the merciful, who will have no man perish, hath
decreed that sins may be atoned for in this world, since in that which
is to come there shall be a just Judgment, wherein every man shall
receive according to his works. Now, therefore, give me silence, and
look on me with all the intent of your hearts, for my story is of a rich
repentance.

The Life

The most venerable bishop of Antioch convened all such bishops as
were his near neighbours to confer with him on a certain question:
whence it came about that eight bishops assembled, among whom
was that saintly man of God, my own bishop, Nonnus, a man marvellous great and a mighty monk of the monastery called Tabenna: but
by reason of his rare and gracious way of life, he had been reft from
the monastery and ordained a bishop. Come together as we were in
the aforenamed city, the bishop thereof appointed us our lodging in
the basilica of the Blessed Julian the Martyr. We entered, and followed
to where the other bishops sat, in front of the door of the basilica.

And as we sat, certain of the bishops besought my master Nonnus
that they might have some instruction from his lips: and straightway
the good bishop began to speak to the weal and health of all that
heard him. And as we sat marvelling at the holy learning of him, lo!
on a sudden she that was first of the actresses of Antioch passed by:
first of the dancers was she, and riding on an ass: and with all fantastic
graces did she ride, so decked that naught could be seen upon her but

gold and pearls and precious stones: the very nakedness of her feet was hidden under gold and pearls: and with her was a splendid train of young men and maidens clad in robes of price, with torques of gold about their necks. Some went before and some came after her: but of the beauty and the loveliness of her there could be no wearying for a world of men. Passing through our midst, she filled the air with the fragrance of musk and of all scents that are sweetest. And when the bishops saw her so shamelessly ride by, bare of head and shoulder and limb, in pomp so splendid, and not so much as a veil upon her head or about her shoulders, they groaned, and in silence turned away their heads as from great and grievous sin.

But the most blessed Nonnus did long and most intently regard her: and after she had passed by still he gazed and still his eyes went after her. Then, turning his head, he looked upon the bishops sitting round him. "Did not," said he, "the sight of her great beauty delight you?"

They answered him nothing. And he sank his face upon his knees, and the holy book that he held in his good hands, and his tears fell down upon his breast, and sighing heavily he said again to the bishops, "Did not the sight of her great beauty delight you?"

But again they answered nothing. Then said he, "Verily, it greatly delighted me, and well pleased was I with her beauty: whom God shall set in presence of His high and terrible seat, in judgment of ourselves and our episcopate."

And again he spoke to the bishops. "What think you, beloved? How many hours hath this woman spent in her chamber, bathing and adorning herself with all solicitude and all her mind on the stage, that there may be no stain or flaw in all that body's beauty and its wearing, that she may be a joy to all men's eyes, nor disappoint those paltry lovers of hers who are but for a day and to-morrow are not? And we who have in heaven a Father Almighty, an immortal Lover, with the promise of riches eternal and rewards beyond all reckoning, since eye hath not seen nor ear hath heard nor hath it ascended into the heart of man to conceive the things that God hath prepared for them that love Him—but what need is there of further speech? With such a promise, the vision of the Bridegroom, that great and splendid and ineffable face, whereon the Cherubim dare not look, we adorn not, we care not so much as to wash the filth from our miserable souls, but leave them lying in their squalor."

And with that, he laid hold on me, deacon and sinner, and we made our way to the hospice, where a cell had been given us. And going into his own chamber, he flung himself on the paved floor, his face to the ground; and beating his breast he began to weep, saying, "Lord Christ, have mercy on a sinful man and an unworthy, for a single day's adorning of a harlot is far beyond the adorning of my soul. With what countenance shall I look upon Thee? Or with what words shall I justify myself in Thy sight? I shall not hide my heart from Thee, Thou knowest its secrets. Woe is me, worthless and sinful that I am, for I stand at Thy altar, and offer not the fair soul that Thou askest. She hath promised to please men, and hath kept her word: I have promised to please Thee, and through my sloth have lied. Naked am I in heaven and in earth, for I have not done Thy bidding. My hope is not in any good thing that I have done, but my hope is in Thy pity, whereto I trust my salvation." Such was his prayer and such his lamenting: and vehemently did we keep the feast that day.

But on the day following, which was a Sunday, after we had finished Nocturne, the good bishop Nonnus spoke to me. "I tell thee, brother deacon, I had a dream and am mightily disturbed by it, for I cannot make sense of it." And then he told me how he had seen in his sleep a black dove, standing at the horn of the altar, stained and soiled with filth: "it kept flying round me, and I could hardly bear the stink and squalor of it. But still it kept about me, till the prayer for the catechumens was ended. And then, after the deacon had pronounced the *Procedite,* it was no more seen. But after the mass for the faithful was said and the oblation, and the congregation dismissed, and I crossing the threshold of the House of God, again came that dove in all its squalor, and again it flew about me. But I stretched out my hand and caught it and plunged it into the stoup of holy water in the porch of the church: and it left all the filth that had clung to it in the water and rose out of the water as white as snow: and flying upwards was borne into the high air and vanished from my sight." He finished telling me his dream, Nonnus, God's good bishop, and then took me with him and we came to the greater church with the other bishops and greeted the bishop of the city.

And going in, he spoke to all the clergy of the church, sitting there in their stalls: and after celebration and the reading of the Holy Gospel, the same bishop of the city, handing the Holy Gospel to the blessed Nonnus, begged him to speak to the people. And he spoke to them the wisdom of God that dwelt in him, with no alloy of artifice or of philosophy, naught unfitting, naught of human vanity: but full of the Holy Ghost, he reasoned with and admonished the people, speaking from his heart of the judgment to come and the eternal blessedness that is in store. And so stirred were all the people by the words which the Holy Ghost spake through him that the pavement of the church was wet with their tears.

Now it befell, by the guiding of the Divine compassion, that to this very church should come that harlot of whom he had spoken to us: and for a marvel, she to whom never had come a thought of her sins and who never had been inside a church door was suddenly stricken with the fear of God, as the good Nonnus reasoned with the people: and despairing of herself she fell to sorrowing, her tears falling in streams, and she in no way able to check her weeping. There and then she gave orders to two of her youths, saying, "Stay in this place: and when the good bishop Nonnus comes out, follow him and ask where he lodges and come and tell me." The young men did as their lady had bidden them: they followed us and came to the basilica of the blessed Julian the Martyr, where was our hospice or cell. And then they went back to their lady and said, "He is lodging in the basilica of the blessed Julian the Martyr." Upon this, she straightway sent a diptych by the same two, on which these words were written:

"To Christ's holy disciple, the devil's disciple and a woman that is a sinner. I have heard of thy God, that He bowed the heavens and came down to earth, not for the good men's sake, but that He might save sinners, and that He was so humble that He drew near to publicans, and He on whom the Cherubim dare not look kept company with sinners. And thou my lord, who art a great saint, although thou hast not looked with the eyes of the flesh on the Lord Christ Himself, who showed Himself to that Samaritan woman, and her a harlot, at the well, yet art thou a worshipper of Him, for I have heard the talk of the Christians. If indeed thou art a true disciple of this Christ, spurn me not, desiring through thee to see the Saviour, that through thee I may come at the sight of His holy face."

Then the good bishop Nonnus wrote back to her: "Whatsoever thou art is known unto God, thyself, and what thy purpose is, and thy desire. But this I surely say to thee, seek not to tempt my weakness, for I am a man that is a sinner, serving God. If in very deed thou hast a desire after divine things and a longing for goodness and faith, and dost wish to see me, there are other bishops with me: come, and thou shalt see me in their presence: for thou shalt not see me alone."

She read it, this harlot, and filled with joy came hurrying to the basilica of the blessed Julian, and sent word to us that she was come. On hearing it, the good Nonnus called to him all the bishops who were in the place, and bade her come to him. She came in where the bishops were assembled, and flung herself on the pavement and caught the feet of the blessed Nonnus, saying, "My lord, I pray thee to follow thy master the Lord Christ, and shed on me thy kindness and make me a Christian. My lord, I am a sea of wickedness and an abyss of evil. I ask to be baptised."

Hardly could the good bishop Nonnus prevail on her to rise from his feet: but when she had risen, "The canons of the Church," he said, "provide that no harlot shall be baptised, unless she produce certain to go surety for her that she will not fall back into her old sins."

But on hearing such a judgment from the bishop, she flung herself again on the pavement and caught the feet of the good Nonnus, and washed them with her tears and wiped them with her hair, crying, "Thou shalt answer to God for my soul and on thee shall I charge all the evil of my deeds, if thou dost delay to baptise me in my foul sin. No portion mayst thou find in God's house among the saints, if thou makest me not a stranger to my sin. Mayst thou deny God and worship idols, if thou dost not this day have me born again, bride to Christ, and offer me to God."

Then all the bishops and clergy, who were there gathered, seeing her that was so great a sinner uttering such words in her desire after God, said in wonderment that they had never seen such faith and desire for salvation as in this harlot. And straightway they sent me, deacon and sinner, to the bishop of the city to explain the matter and beg his sanctity to send back one of his deaconesses with me. And when he heard me, he rejoiced mightily, saying, "Verily, father revered, such work as this awaited thee: I know that thou wilt be as my mouth." And he sent with me the lady Romana, chief of the deaconesses.

Coming in, she found her still at the feet of the good bishop Nonnus, and hardly could he persuade her to rise from his feet, saying, "Daughter, arise, that thou mayest be shriven." And then he said to her, "Confess all thy sins."

She made answer, "If I were to search my whole heart I could find in myself no good thing. I know my sins, that they are heavier than the sands of the sea: the waters of it are too scant for the mass of my sin. But I trust in thy God, that He will loosen the load of my wrongdoing, and will look upon me."

Then said the good bishop Nonnus, "Tell me thy name." She answered, "My own name was Pelagia, that my father and mother gave me: but the townsfolk of Antioch call me Margarita, because of the pearls wherewith they did jewel my sins. For I was the devil's jewel and his armoury." Then the good bishop Nonnus again asked her, "Thine own name is Pelagia?" She answered, "Yea, lord."

And thereupon the good bishop exorcised and baptised her and set upon her the sign of the Cross, and gave her the Body of Christ. Her godmother was the holy lady Romana, chief of the deaconesses: and she took her and went to the place for the catechumens, for so long as we should remain there. Then said to me the good bishop Nonnus, "I tell thee, brother deacon, let us rejoice to-day with the angels of God, and take oil beyond our custom in our food, and drink wine with joy of heart, for the salvation of this girl."

But as we were at our meal, there came suddenly the sound of shouting as of a man to whom violence is done: it was the devil crying out, "Woe is me, for the things I suffer from this decrepit old man! Might not the thirty thousand Saracens have been enough for thee, that thou didst wrest from me and baptise, and offer to thy God? Might not Heliopolis have been enough for thee, that was mine and all the people in it worshipping me, and thou didst wrest it from me, and offer it to thy God? And now thou has stolen my greatest hope, and no longer can I endure thy machinations. O the evil this accursed wretch hath wrought upon me! Cursed be the day in which thou wast born! Rivers of tears are flooding my poor house, for my hope is lost!" All this did the devil shout aloud, lamenting up and down outside the gate, and all men heard him. And again he would come and cry out to the girl, "Hast thou done this to me, my lady Pelagia, and dost thou follow my own Judas? For he, crowned with glory and honour and appointed an apostle, betrayed his Master, and so hast thou done to me." Then said to her the good bishop Nonnus, "Sign thyself with the Cross of Christ and renounce him." So she signed herself in the name of Christ, and breathed upon the demon, and straightway he was no more seen.

Two days after, when she was asleep with her godmother the holy lady Romana in her chamber, the devil appeared by night and wakened Pelagia, God's handmaid, and said, "Tell me, my lady Margarita, wert not thou rich in silver and gold? Did I not deck thee with gold and precious stones? Tell me, did I do aught to displease thee? Tell me, that I may make thee amends, but make me not a mock to the

Christians." Then Pelagia crossed herself and breathed upon the demon and said, "My God, who snatched me from thy jaws and brought me to His heavenly couch, Himself shall fight thee for me." And straightway the devil vanished.

Now three days after the holy Pelagia had been baptised, she called to her the youth who had had charge of her house, and said to him, "Go to my tiring-room and make a list of everything that is there, gold or silver, or ornaments, or rich apparel, and bring them to me." The boy did as his lady bade him, and brought her all her substance. Then she asked the holy bishop Nonnus to come to her, sending word through her godmother, the lady Romana, and laid all her substance in his hands, saying, "These, my lord, are the riches where-with Satan endowed me: I give them to thee to do with as thou wilt, and what seems good to thee, that do: for it is the riches of the Lord Christ that I am fain of now." The bishop straightway summoned the senior treasurer of the church, and in her presence handed over to him all her substance, saying, "I adjure thee, by the indivisible Trinity, that naught of this shall go to the episcopal treasury or to the church, but rather be allotted to the widows and orphans and the poor, so that what was gotten together by ill may be dispersed to good, and the wealth of a sinner become the treasury of righteousness. But if, in contempt of thine oath, aught of this be stolen, let a curse enter either by thee or by some other, whosoever he be, into his house, and let his portion be with those who said, 'Crucify Him; crucify Him.'" But she for her part called together all her young men and her maids, and gave them all their freedom: and with her own hand she gave them golden torques saying, "Haste ye to set yourselves free from this worthless and sinful world, so that as we were together in this life, so might we abide together without sorrow in that life which is most blessed."

But on the eighth day, when she must lay aside her white robes, she rose by night, without our knowledge, and laid aside the robe of her baptism, and put on the tunic and cloak of the good bishop Nonnus: and from that day she was no more seen in the city of Antioch. The holy Romana used to weep for her with bitter tears, but the good Nonnus would comfort her, saying, "Weep not, daughter, but rejoice rather with great joy, for Pelagia hath chosen the better part, even as Mary, whom the Lord put before Martha in the Gospel." But she went to Jerusalem and built herself a cell in the Mount of Olives, where Our Lord prayed.

And after some time the bishop of the city called all the bishops together, to dismiss them each to his own place. And after a space of three or four years I, James the Deacon, took a great longing to set out to Jerusalem that I might there adore the resurrection of our Lord Jesus Christ, and I asked my bishop if he would give me leave to go. And while giving me leave, he said to me, "I tell thee, brother deacon, when thou dost reach Jerusalem, inquire there for a certain brother Pelagius, a monk and a eunuch, who has lived these many years shut up and in solitude, if so be thou mightst visit him: for thou mightst well profit by him." And all the time he spoke of God's handmaid Pelagia, but I knew it not.

So then, I arrived in Jerusalem, and I adored the holy resurrection of our Lord Jesus Christ: and the next day I made inquiry for this servant of God. And I made my way and found him in the Mount of Olives, where the Lord prayed, in a little cell closed in on every side, and it had a little window in the wall. And I knocked on the shutter of the little window, and straightway she opened to me, and she knew me: but I knew her not. And how could I know her, when she whom I had aforetime seen in beauty beyond all telling was wasted and haggard with fasting? Her eyes were trenches in her face.

"Brother," she said to me, "whence art thou come?" And I answered, "I was sent to thee by the bidding of Nonnus the bishop." Then said she, "Let him pray for me, for he is a saint of God." And therewith she closed the shutter on the window, and began to sing Tierce. And indeed I myself prayed close to the wall of her cell, and went away, much lightened by the angelic vision. And I came back to Jerusalem, and began to go here and there among the monasteries, visiting the brethren.

There was much talk among the monasteries of the fame of the holy Pelagius: and so I made up my mind to go back yet another time to visit him, and be quickened by his salutary speech. But when I had come again to his cell, and knocked, and even made bold to call upon him by name, there was no answer. I came again and waited a second day, and again a third, now and then calling, "Pelagius!" but I heard no one. So I said to myself, "Either there is no one here, or the monk who was here has gone away." And then, moved by some prompting from God, I said again to myself, "Let me make sure that he is not perhaps dead": and I opened the shutter of the window, and looked in, and I saw him dead. And I closed the shutter and carefully filled it up with clay, and came hurrying to Jerusalem and told the news that the good monk Pelagius who had wrought marvels was at peace.

Then the good fathers came with the brethren of divers monasteries, and the door of the cell was opened: and they carried out the holy little body, reckoning it as precious as gold and jewels. And when the good fathers set about anointing the body with myrrh, they found that it was a woman. They would fain have hidden the miracle, but they could not: and they cried aloud with a shout, "Glory to Thee, Lord Christ, who hast many treasures hidden on the earth, and not men only, but women also." It was told abroad to all the people, and all the convents of virgins came, some from Jericho and some from Jordan where the Lord was baptised, with candles and torches and hymns: and so the holy relics of her were buried, and the good fathers carried her to her grave.

This is the story of a harlot, this the life of a desperate sinner: and may God grant that we find with her His mercy in the day of judgment: for to Him is the glory and honour, dominion and power, world without end. Amen.

126

HOW A CHRISTIAN ORPHAN RENOUNCES HER LIFE AS A PROSTITUTE AND RETURNS TO THE ASCETICISM IN WHICH SHE WAS REARED

The Life of Saint Mary the Harlot   5th century C.E.

The blessed Abraham had a brother after the flesh: and when this brother died, he left behind him an only daughter, a child of seven. Her father's friends and acquaintances, seeing her bereft of her parents, lost no time in bringing her to her uncle. The old man saw her, and had her housed in the outer room of his cell. There was a small window between the two rooms, and through this he taught her the psalter and other passages of Holy Writ, and she kept vigil with him in praising God and would sing the Psalms along with him, and tried to copy her uncle in all abstinence. Eagerly did she seize on this way of life, and made haste to practise all the powers of the soul. And the holy man ceased not to pray with tears, that her mind might not be tangled with the cares of the doings of earth: for her father in dying had left her vast wealth: but the brother being dead, and the daughter taking refuge with him, the servant of Christ gave orders that it should be shared among the poor and the orphaned. She herself would ask her uncle every day to pray God for her, that she might be caught away from evil imaginings and the diverse traps and snares of the devil. And so she steadily followed her rule of life. Her uncle had joy to see her so swift and unhesitant in all good, in tears, in humbleness, in modesty, in quiet: and what is higher than all these, in great devotion towards God. Twenty years she lived with him in abstinence, even as an innocent lamb and an untarnished dove. But by the end of those years, the evil one began to wax violent against her, laying down his wonted snares; for let him once have her webbed in his net, and he could strike grief and anxiety into the holy man and separate some part of his mind at least from God.

Now a certain monk, but a monk in profession only, was in the habit of journeying often to visit the old man, under colour of edification. But gazing on that blessed creature through the window, he was pricked with the goads of lust: he began to long to speak with her, for wanton love had kindled his heart like a fire. For a great while he lay in ambush about her, so that a whole year went by before he had enervated her imagination by the softness of his words. But at the last she opened the window of her cell and came out to him: and forthwith he debauched and defiled her with evil and lust. But when the deed of shame was done, her heart trembled: and tearing the hair shift that clothed her, she began beating her face with her hands, and in her sorrow would have sought for death. Weighed down with anguish she could see no harbour wherein she might tarry and take thought: swayed to and fro on shifting tides of imagination, she wept that she was no longer what she had been, and her speech was broken with wailing. "From this time forward," she said, "I feel as one that has died. I have lost my days and my travail of abstinence, and my tears and prayers and vigils are brought to nothing: I have angered my God, and have destroyed myself. Sorrow upon me, with every spring of tears! I have bowed down that saint my uncle with grief most bitter: shame has gone over my soul: I am become the devil's mock. Why should such as I live on? Sorrow upon me, what have I done? Sorrow upon me, what came upon me? Sorrow upon me, what evil have I wrought? Sorrow upon me, from what have I fallen? How was my mind darkened? I know not how I fell, I know not how I was defiled, I know not what cloud darkened my heart, how I could be ignorant of what I was doing. Where shall I flee to hide? Where can I find a pit wherein to throw myself? Where was my uncle's teaching, and the counsels of Ephraem his friend, that would urge me to abide in my virginity and keep my soul unsullied for the immortal Bridegroom? For thy Bridegroom, they would say, is holy and jealous. Sorrow upon me, what am I to do? I dare not look at heaven, I that am dead to God and man. I shall not dare now to go near that window. How could I attempt ever to talk again with my good uncle, filthy as I am with all uncleanness? If I did, would not a flame leap from the window and burn me there to ashes? Better to go away to some other country where there is no one who could know me, for I am nought but a dead woman now, and there is no hope left to me any more." So she rose, and made her way to another city, and changing the garb of her youth, took refuge in a certain brothel.

Now at the time that ruin thus befell the maid, a vision came to the holy man in his sleep. For he saw a huge and monstrous dragon, most foul in its aspect and strongly hissing: it seemed to issue from a certain spot and come up to his cell, and there it found a dove and gulped it down, and again returned to its den. Wakening in heavy sadness, he began bitterly to weep, for he judged that Satan had roused up a persecution against the Church of God and that many were turned from the truth, or that some schism had been begotten in holy Church. Falling on his knees, he prayed to God, saying, "Thou that art God foreseeing all things, Lover of men, Thou knowest what this vision may mean." Again after two days he saw the same dragon come in like fashion to his cell, and it laid its head under its paws and burst asunder: but that dove which it had devoured was found alive in its belly: and he reached out his hand and took it alive. Waking from sleep, he called that blessed maid once and again, thinking that she was in her cell. "What ails thee, Mary my daughter," said he (for thus was she called), "that for two days thou hast not opened thy mouth in praise to God?" But when there was no answer, and since for two days he had not heard her singing as she was wont to do, he understood that his vision must surely touch her close. Then he sighed and wept sore. "Sorrow upon me," he said, "for a cruel wolf hath stolen my lamb, my daughter is made captive." And lifting up his voice, "Christ," he said, weeping, "Saviour of the world, send Mary my lamb back to me again, and restore her to the fold of life, that my old age go not in sorrow from the world. Despise not my beseeching, Lord, but be swift to send Thy grace to cast her forth unharmed from the dragon's mouth." Now the two days which he saw in the vision were measured by the passage of two years, wherein his niece led a wanton life, as in the belly of that monstrous dragon: but through all that time the saint not once relaxed his mind by day or night from entreating God for her.

So then, it was two years before he discovered where she was and what she did: and he asked a singular good friend of his to go to the place and find out all he could. The friend set out, and coming again he told him all the truth, and how he himself had seen her: and at the old man's asking, he brought him a military habit, and a horse to ride. So he opened his door, and dressed himself in military garb, and set a great hat upon his head, so as to cover his face: but he also took a gold piece with him, and got up on the horse, and made all haste upon the road. Even as one desirous of spying out a country or a city will put on the garb of its inhabitants lest he be recognised: so did the blessed Abraham make use of the garb of the enemy to put him to rout. Come now, brothers beloved, and marvel at this second Abraham. The first Abraham went forth to do battle with the Kings, and smote them and brought back his nephew Lot: but this second Abraham went forth to do battle with the Evil One, and having vanquished him, bring home again his niece in a greater triumph.

So then, arrived at the town, he stepped aside into the tavern, and with anxious eyes he sat looking about him, glancing this way and that in hopes to see her. The hours went by, and still no chance of seeing her appeared: and finally he spoke jestingly to the innkeeper. "They tell me, friend," said he, "that thou hast a very fine wench: if it were agreeable to thee, I should like well to have a look at her."

The innkeeper regarded the hoary head, the old frame bowed with its weight of years, and in no hope that this desire for a sight of her was prompted by lechery, made reply that it was indeed as he had heard: that she was an uncommon handsome lass. And indeed Mary in beauty of body was fair, well-nigh beyond aught that nature demandeth. The old man asked her name, and was told that they call her Mary. Then, with merry countenance, "Come now," said he, "bring her in and show her to me, and let me have a fine supper for her this day, for I have heard the praises of her on all hands." So they called her: but when she came in and the good old man saw her in her harlot's dress, his whole body well-nigh dissolved in grief. Yet he hid the bitterness of his soul behind a cheerful countenance, and checked by force of his manhood the starting tears, for fear that the girl might recognise him and take flight.

So as they sat and drank their wine, the great old man began to jest with her. The girl rose and put her arms about his neck, beguiling him with kisses. And as she was kissing him, she smelt the fragrance of austerity that his lean body breathed, and remembered the days when she too had lived austere: and as if a spear had pierced her soul, she gave a great moan and began to weep: and not able to endure the pain in her heart, she broke out into words, "Woe's me, that am alone unhappy!"

The innkeeper was dumbfounded. "What ails thee, mistress Mary," said he, "to burst out all of a sudden into this sore lamenting? It is two years to-day that thou hast been here, and no one ever heard a sigh from thee or a sad word: indeed I know not what has come over thee."

"I had been happy," said the girl, "if three years ago I had died."

At this the good old man, afraid that she might recognise him, spoke to her genially enough. "Now, now!" said he, "here am I come to make merry, art going to begin the tale of thy sins?" Marvellous is the ordering of Thy mercy, O God most high! Thinkest thou the maid did not say in her heart, How comes it that this old man's look is so like my uncle's? But Thou, that are alone the lover of men, from whom all good wisdom comes, Thou didst order it that she could not recognise him and flee in shame. It would indeed be past belief, were it not that the tears of Thy servant her uncle had come before Thee, so that Thou didst deign out of impossibility to make the possible.

So then, the good old man produced the gold piece he had brought with him and gave it to the innkeeper. "Now friend," said he, "make us a right good supper, so that I may make merry with the lass: for I am come a very long journey for love of her." O wisdom as of God! O wise understanding of the spirit! O memorable discretion in salvation! Throughout fifty years of abstinence he had never tasted bread: and now without a falter eats meat to save a lost soul. The company of the holy angels, rejoicing over the discretion of the blessed man, were mazed at that which he ate and drank, lighthearted and nothing doubting, to deliver a soul sunken in the mire. O wisdom and understanding of the wise! O discrimination of the discerning! Come, marvel at this madness, this reversal, when an upright and wise and discreet and prudent man is made a reckless fool to snatch a soul from the jaws of the lion, and set free a captive bound and thrust away from its chains and its dark prison-house.

So, when they had feasted, the girl began to provoke him to come to her room to lie with her. "Let us go," said he. Coming in, he saw a lofty bed prepared, and straightway sat gaily down upon it. What I shall call thee, O perfect athlete of Christ, I know not. Shall I say that thou art continent or incontinent, wise or foolish, discreet or reckless? For the fifty years of thy profession thou hast slept on a mat of rushes, and how dost thou indifferently climb on such a bed? But all these things thou hast done to the praise and glory of Christ, this long journey of many halting-places, this eating of flesh and drinking of wine, this turning aside to a brothel, to save a lost soul. While for our part, if we have to say but one useful word to our neighbour, we look forward to it all with sore distress.

So then, the girl says to him, as he sits there on the bed: "Come, sir, let me take off your shoes." "Lock the door carefully," said he, "and then take them off." The girl would have taken his shoes off first: but as he would not let her she locked the door and came to him.

"Come close to me, mistress Mary," said the old man. And when she was beside him he took her firmly by the hand as if to kiss her, then taking the hat from his head and his voice breaking into weeping, "Mary, my daughter," said he, "dost thou not know me? My heart, was it not I that brought thee up? What has come to thee, my child? Who was it destroyed thee? Where is that angel's garb thou didst wear, my daughter? Where is thy continence, thy tears, thy vigils, thy bed on the ground? How didst thou fall from heaven's height into this pit, my daughter? Why, when thou didst sin, didst thou not tell me? Why didst thou not come to me there and then? And indeed I would have done thy penance for thee, and my dear Ephraem too. Why didst thou act like this? Why didst thou desert me, and bring me into this intolerable sorrow? For who is without sin, save God Himself?"

This and much else he said: but all the while she stayed in his hands, motionless as a stone. Fear and shame had filled her full.

And again the old man began, weeping, "Mary, child, wilt thou not speak to me? Will thou not speak to me, half of my heart? Was it not because of thee, my child, that I came here? Upon me be this sin, O my daughter. It is I that shall answer for thee to God at the Day of Judgment. It is I that shall give satisfaction to God for this sin." And until midnight he sought to comfort her, with such words as these, encouraging her with many tears. Little by little she took courage, and at last she spoke to him, weeping, "I cannot," she said, "look on your face for shame. And how can I pour out a prayer to God, so foul as I am with the mud of this uncleanness?"

Then said the holy man, "Upon me be thy guilt, my daughter: at my hand shall God requite this sin: do but listen to me, and come, let us go home. For look you, there is our dear Ephraem grieving sore for thee, and for ever pleading with God for thee. Be not mistrustful, daughter, of the mercy of God; let thy sin be as mountains, His mercy towers above His every creature. We read that an unclean woman came to Him that was clean, and she did not soil Him, but was herself made clean by Him: she washed the Lord's feet with her tears, and dried them with her hair. If a spark can set on fire the sea, then can thy sins stain His whiteness: it is no new thing to fall in the mire, but it is an evil thing to lie there fallen. Bravely return again to that place from whence thou camest: the Enemy mocked thee falling, but he shall know thee stronger in thy rising. Have pity, I pray thee, on my old age: grieve for the travail of my white head: rise up, I implore thee, and come with me home. Fear not: mortal man is apt to slip: but if he be swift to fall, swift is he to rise again with the succour of

God who desireth not the death of a sinner, but rather that he be healed and live."

Then she said, "If you are sure that I can do penance and that God will accept my atonement, behold I shall come as you bid me: go before and I shall follow your goodness and kiss the track of your feet, you that have so grieved for me, that you would draw me out of this cesspit." And laying her head at his feet, she wept all night, saying, "What shall I render to Thee for all this, O Lord my God?"

When dawn had come, the blessed Abraham said to her, "Rise up, daughter, and let us go home to our cell." And answering him, she said, "I have a little gold here, and some clothes, what would you have me do with them?" But the blessed Abraham made answer, "Leave all those things here, for they were earned from the Evil One." And they rose up and went away. And he set her upon his horse and led it, going before, even as the good shepherd when he has found his lost sheep, carries it with joy upon his shoulder: and so the blessed Abraham, with joy in his heart, journeyed along the road with his niece. And when he had come home, he set her in the inner cell which had been his own, and himself remained in the outer. And she, clad in her hair shift, did there abide in humility of soul and in tears from the heart and the eyes, disciplining herself with vigils and stern travail of abstinence, in quiet and modesty unweariedly calling upon God, bewailing her sin but with sure hope of pardon, with supplication so moving that no man, even were he without bowels of compassion, could hear her sorrowful crying and not be stirred. For who so hardhearted as to know her weeping, and himself not weep? And who but gave God thanks for the true repentance of her heart? Indeed her repentance, compared with such prayers as ours, surpassed all measure of grief. So urgently did she pray God to pardon the thing she had done that she obtained from on high a sign that her penitence was accepted. And God the compassionate, who will have no man perish but that all should come to repentance, so accepted her atonement that after three full years He restored health to many at her prayer. For crowds flocked to her, and she would pray to God for their healing, and it was granted her.

And the blessed Abraham, after living for another ten years in his life, and seeing her blessed penitence, and giving glory to God, rested in peace in the seventieth year of his age. For fifty years in devotion and humility of heart and love unfeigned, he had fulfilled his vow. . . .

And Mary also lived another five years, yet more devoutly ruling her life, and persevering night and day in prayer to God, with lamentation and tears, so that many a one passing that place at night and hearing the voice of her grieving would himself be turned to weeping, and add his tears to hers. But when the hour of her sleeping came, wherein she was taken up from this life, all that saw her gave glory to God, for the splendour of her face.

Sorrow on me, beloved, for these fell on sleep, and with all confidence have gone their ways to God: whose minds were never set upon the business of earth, but on the sole love of God. And I unapt and reluctant in my will abide, and behold winter hath come upon me, and the infinite tempest hath found me naked and spoiled and with no perfecting of good in me.

I marvel at myself, beloved, how I daily default, and daily do repent: I build up for an hour, and an hour overthrows what I have builded. At evening I say, "To-morrow I shall repent": but when morning comes, joyous I waste the day. Again at evening I say, "I shall keep vigil all night, and I shall entreat the Lord with tears, to have mercy on my sins": but when night has come, I am full of sleep. Behold, those who received their talent along with me strive day and night to trade with it, that they may win the word of praise, and rule over ten cities: but I in my sloth hid mine in the earth, and my Lord makes haste to come; and behold my heart trembles and I weep the days of my negligence and know not what excuse to bring.

Have mercy upon me, Thou that alone art without sin, and save me, who alone art pitiful and kind: for beside Thee, the Father most blessed, and Thine only begotten Son who was made flesh for us, and the Holy Ghost who giveth life to all things, I know no other, and believe in no other. And now be mindful of me, Lover of men, and lead me out of the prison-house of my sins, for both are in Thy hand, O Lord, the time that Thou didst will me to come into this world, and the time that Thou shalt bid me go out from it elsewhere. Remember me that am without defence, and save me a sinner: and may Thy grace, that was in this world my aid, my refuge and my glory, gather me under its wings in that great and terrible day. For Thou knowest, Thou who dost try the hearts and reins, that I did shun much of evil and the byways of shame, the vanity of the impertinent and the defence of heresy. And this not of myself, but of Thy grace wherewith my mind was lit. Wherefore, holy Lord, I beseech Thee, bring me into Thy kingdom, and deign to bless me with all that have found grace before Thee, for with Thee is magnificence, adoration, and honour, Father, Son, and Holy Ghost. Amen.

The Feminine Divine

In a collection of documents on women's religion this last section may be the most difficult to justify. It presents a sampling of female representations of divinity, without being able to answer the question of whether such images are the products of women's religious perceptions or men's religious perceptions or both.

Thus, I wish to be careful of the idea that worship of feminine divinity reflects primarily or exclusively women's religiosity, when in so many cases we know this is not the case. Athena, Isis, and the virgin Mary are all cases in point. Goddesses are not per se the objects of women's devotion, nor do they by definition reflect women's perceptions of themselves and the universe in which they live.

Still, the absence of worship of feminine divinity which we see clearly in the male monotheism of Judaism and Christianity is an issue that cannot be ignored and that these texts attempt to raise. The claims of theologians over the centuries that God has no gender aside, the move to monotheism in Western religious tradition has in fact meant the promulgation of a divinity who is repeatedly and primarily referred to in masculine terminology from ancient Israel on. It is true that feminine aspects of the divine persist or recur in attenuated and often arcane forms in Jewish and Christian traditions, as in the personification of the Sabbath as a bride, the feminine Shekinah of God, the personification of Wisdom as female, the Matronit in Jewish mystical tradition, and even the virgin Mary herself. But as several feminist scholars of religion have observed, monotheism in Western religion has meant the suppression of Goddess.

Several of these texts, including the description of Metanoia in *The Conversion and Marriage of Aseneth* 15.7–9 (a text that is included in section 4, "New Religious Affiliation and Conversion") and the selections from the gnostic library at Nag Hammadi, require us to pose the difficult question, Why did some religious communities in antiquity use texts with an abundance of feminine language for the divine or for aspects of divinity while others did not? More of our evidence for this usage comes from Christian sources than from Jewish, but the figure of Metanoia in *Aseneth* compels us to concede that the phenomenon existed within some Jewish circles as well.

Can we draw any conclusions about the nature of the communities that wrote and used these texts from the religious language they used? Some scholars of Gnosticism have suggested precisely this: that gnostic use of feminine language for the divine reflected the more extensive roles women played in their communities both as leaders and as sources of revelation and authority.

Testing such a hypothesis frustrates us. We know very little about who the Gnostics were, what the social structure of their communities might have been, and so on. Descriptions of Gnostics in catalogues of heresies compiled by those antagonistic to Gnosticism lend some credence to the possibility that women played more substantial roles in gnostic groups than in nongnostic Christian communities of the same period. Regrettably, it is sometimes difficult to tell whether these descriptions accurately reflect the social composition of gnostic groups or whether heresiologists thought to discredit the gnostics by emphasizing the prominence of women among them. Of course, both could be true: women may have figured significantly among gnostic communities, and heresiologists may have seen that as one manifestation of the communities' heretical nature.

On the other hand, the dilemma remains. Those texts which come to be called orthodox, whether canonical (within Scripture) or extra-canonical but still acceptable, use predominantly male language not only for God but also for angels, demons, prophets, priests, messiahs, and virtually all the key players in the religious sphere. Texts found at Nag Hammadi and a relatively small number of others in contrast envision a cosmos populated by both male and female superhuman figures as well as male and female prophets and recipients of revelation. If this is not to be explained by some difference in the social environment of the communities that wrote and used these texts, what alternative explanation accounts for the distinction? Or, to put it another way, in communities in which women do have public religious authority and are seen as recipients of revelation, what kind of gender language for the divine occurs? If women are the ones who formulate, write, or transmit religious expression, do they use the overwhelmingly male metaphors that pervade most of Jewish and Christian tradition or do they use different language? Certainly in our own time both Jewish and Christian women have brought about the revision of religious language. (The Reform Jewish *Gates of Prayer* and the *Inclusive Language Lectionary* published by the National Council of the Churches of Christ constitute two instances of this.) Whether the agency of women accounts for the presence of female language in some ancient religious texts and whether the absence of that agency accounts for the absence of that language in the majority of other texts remain two sides of a tantalizing and critical question.

127

THE PRINCIPAL VERSION OF THE
MYTH OF DEMETER

The Homeric Hymn to Demeter   7th century B.C.E.

1. I begin my song of the holy goddess, fair-haired Demeter, and of her slim-ankled daughter whom Aidoneus snatched away; and Zeus the loud-crashing, the wide-voiced one, granted it. She was playing with the deep-bosomed daughters of Ocean, away from Demeter of the golden weapon and glorious fruit, and she was gathering flowers throughout the luxuriant meadow—roses, saffron, violets, iris, hyacinth, and a narcissus which was a trap planted for the blossoming maiden by Earth in accord with Zeus's plans, a favor to Hades the receiver of many guests; it was radiantly wonderful, inspiring awe in all who saw it, whether immortal god or mortal man; a hundred stems grew from its root; and the whole wide heaven above, the whole earth, and the salt surge of the sea smiled for joy at its fragrance. The girl was charmed by it, and reached out both hands to pluck the pretty plaything—suddenly, the earth split open wide along the plain and from it the lord host of many, Kronos' son of many names, darted out on his immortal horses. He grabbed her, resisting and screaming, and took her away in his golden chariot. She lifted her voice in a cry, calling upon father Zeus, the almighty and good. But no one, god or mortal, heard her voice, not even the glorious-fruited olive-trees, except the childish daughter of Perses, Hecate of the glistening veil, who—from her cave—heard, and so did Lord Helios the glorious son of Hyperion, as the maiden calling upon father Zeus, though he was sitting, removed from the other gods, in his much-besought temple, receiving fine sacrifices from mortal men.

30. Her, all unwilling, with the approval of Zeus, he took away on his immortal horses, Kronos' son of many names, brother of her father, designator of many, host of many. As long as the goddess could see the earth and the starry sky, the flowing, fish-filled sea and the rays of the sun, she still had hope that her holy mother and the race of the immortal gods would see her, and there was still much hope in her heart in spite of her distress. . . . The peaks of the mountains and the depths of the sea echoed back the immortal voice, and her blessed mother heard her. Then sharp grief seized the mother's heart; she tore the head-dress upon her ambrosial hair, and threw her dark veil down from both her shoulders; and like a bird she darted over land and sea, searching. None of the gods or of mortal men would give her a true report, nor would any of the birds come to her as a true messenger.

47. For nine days then lady Deo wandered the earth, holding blazing torches in her hands; in her grief she touched neither ambrosia nor the sweetness of nectar, nor did she bathe her body with water. But when the tenth day dawned Hecate, bearing light in her hands, encountered her and spoke to her this message: "Lady Demeter, bringer of seasons and glorious gifts, who of the gods of heaven or of mortal men has taken Persephone and pained your own heart? I heard her voice, but did not see who it was. I am telling you everything promptly, and accurately."

59. So spoke Hecate. The daughter of fair-haired Rheia did not answer a word, but she immediately darted off with her, holding blazing torches in her hands, and they came to Helios, the viewer of gods and men. They stood before his horses and the divine goddess said, "Helios, as a god, respect me, as a goddess, if ever in word or deed, I have warmed your heart. The maiden whom I bore—sweetest blossom— beautiful—I heard her voice, sobbing, as if she were being raped, but I did not see her. But you survey from the bright heaven all the earth and the sea with your rays; tell me accurately whether you have seen who of gods or mortal men has forced her and taken her away, all unwillingly, in my absence."

74. So she spoke, and the son of Hyperion answered her: "Lady Demeter, daughter of fair-haired Rheia, you will know all: I have great respect for you and pity you in your grief for your slim-ankled child: none of the immortals is responsible except Zeus the cloud-gatherer, who has granted to Hades his own brother that she be called his tender wife; and he has taken her, screaming a loud cry, away on his horses down into the misty darkness. So, goddess, stop your loud lament; you should not rashly hold on to this boundless anger; Aidoneus, the designator of many, is after all not an unsuitable son-in-law for you, since you have the same mother and father; and his honor he gained when at the beginning a division into three parts was made; and he dwells with those over whom the lot made him king." When he had said this he called to his horses, and at his command they bore the swift chariot like broad-winged birds.

90. Then grief still more horrible and oppressive came upon her heart, and in her anger at Zeus, shrouded in clouds, she deserted the gatherings of the gods and went far from Olympus to the cities and farms of men and for a long time disguised her appearance. No man, no woman who saw her recognized her, until she arrived at the home of clever Keleos, who was the king of fragrant Eleusis at the time. At the Spring Parthenion where the citizens draw water in the shade of a towering olive tree she sat by the side of the road in the guise of an old woman, one who is beyond the age of childbearing and the gifts of Aphrodite who bears the garland of love, one who might be a nurse of royal children or governess of important households. The daughters of Keleos of Eleusis saw her as they came to draw water and carry it in bronze vessels to their father's house. There were four of them, like goddesses in youthful bloom—Kallidike, Klesidike, lovely Demo and Kallithoe, the eldest of them all. They did not recognize her, for gods are hard for mortals to see. They approached her and said, "Old woman, who are you? Why have you kept away from the city and not approached the settlement? There in the dusky houses there are women as old as you and younger, who would treat you kindly in word and deed."

118. So they spoke, and the goddess mistress said in answer, "Dear children, daughters of womanly mothers, be of good cheer, and I will tell you, for it is right to tell you the truth. The name my lady mother gave to me is Doso. I have just come across the sea from Crete, forced by pirate men who abducted me against my will. They brought their swift ship to shore at Thorikos, and a crowd of women came on board from the land and they all prepared their dinner by the ship's stern-cables. But my heart had no desire for a pleasant supper; instead I got up secretly and escaped those arrogant overlords across the dark countryside, so that they might not enjoy any profit from selling me. I wandered about until I arrived here; but I do not know what land it is nor which people dwell here. May all the gods who dwell on Olympus grant you vigorous husbands and all the progeny they want; but pity me, maidens; dear children, help me come propitiously to some home of a man and woman where I may provide the services of an aged woman for them: I could hold their infant child in my arms and nurse it well, I could keep house, make the master's bed in the inmost chamber, and instruct the women in their tasks."

145. So said the goddess, and the maiden Kallidike, most beautiful of Keleos' daughters, answered her, "Mother, we humans endure the gifts of the gods, even under grievous compulsion, for they are much mightier. I will explain it all to you clearly, and tell you the men who hold the power of authority here, and who stand out in the government and direct the defense of the city with their counsels and decisions. There are Triptolemos the clever, Dioklos, Polyxeinos, Eumolpos the blameless, Dolichos, and our father the manly one. Their wives manage everything in their households, and not one of them would dishonor you at first sight by making you depart from their houses. They will receive you, for you are godlike. If you wish, wait here while we go to our father's house and tell Metaneira our deep-belted mother all these things, and see whether she bids you come to our house and not search for another's. A favorite son, born to her late, is being nursed in the strongly built palace; she prayed much for him, and rejoiced in him. If you would nurse him and he would reach adolescence, any woman would envy the sight of you, for she [Metaneira] would give you so great a reward for nursing him."

169. So she spoke, and she nodded her head, and then they filled their shining jugs with water and carried them proudly. Soon they reached their father's great house, and quickly told their mother what they had seen and heard. She told them to go quickly and bid her come, at a vast wage. As deer or heifers frolic across the meadow eating to their heart's content, so they darted along the road down the gulley, holding up the folds of their lovely gowns, and their hair streamed along their shoulders like saffron blossoms. They reached the spot near the road where they had left the glorious goddess, and they led her to their father's house. She, grieved at heart, walked behind them with her head veiled, and the dark robe trailed along around the slender feet of the goddess.

184. Soon they reached the house of Zeus-descended Keleos, and went through the portico to the place where their lady mother was sitting beside a column of the carefully made chamber, holding her new baby in her lap. The girls ran to her, but Demeter trod upon the threshold, and her head reached the roof-beam, and she filled the doorway with a divine radiance. At this awe, reverence and pale fear seized the woman. She rose from her chair and urged her to be seated, but Demeter the bringer of seasons and glorious gifts did not wish to be seated on the gleaming chair, but silently cast down her beautiful eyes and waited until Iambe understood and set a jointed stool out for her, and threw a shining white fleece upon it. She sat down, holding her veil in front with her hands. For a long time she sat there on the stool sorrowfully, without speaking; and made no contact with anyone in word or gesture. Without smiling, without touching food or drink she sat, consumed with yearning for her daughter, until Iambe understood and made plenty of jokes and jests and made the holy Lady smile with kindly heart, and ever afterward she continues to delight her spirit. Then Metaneira filled a cup of sweet wine and offered it to her, but she refused it, for she said it was not right for her to drink red wine. Instead, she asked her to give her barley groats and water mixed with crusted pennyroyal to drink. She made the compound, the *kykeon,* as she commanded, and offered it to the goddess. Deo the greatly revered accepted it for the sake of the ceremony. . . . Fair-belted Metaneira began with these words, "Be of good cheer, woman; I do not expect that you are sprung from base stock, but from good; dignity and grace are manifest in your eyes, like those of kings, stewards of the right. But we humans endure the gifts of the gods, even under grievous compulsion, for a yoke lies upon our neck. But now that you have come here, all that is mine shall be yours. Nurse this child for me, whom the immortals have given me, late-born and unexpected, but much prayed for. If you would nurse him and he would reach adolescence, any woman would envy the sight of you, for I would give you so great a reward for nursing him."

224. Then Demeter of the fair crown said to her, "May you also be of good cheer, woman, and may the gods grant you all good things; I willingly accept the child, as you bid me. I will nurse him, and I do not expect that he will be injured by nurse's incompetence, supernatural attacks nor magical cuttings, for I know an antidote more mighty than the woodcutter, and I know a fine preventative against malignant attacks."

231. When she had said this she received him with her immortal hands in her fragrant lap, and the mother's heart rejoiced. So she nursed the glorious son of clever Keleos, Demophon, whom fair-belted Metaneira bore, and he grew like a god, eating no food, being suckled on no milk, for Demeter would [feed and] anoint him with *ambrosia,* like the progeny of a god, and she breathed sweetly on him and held him in her lap. At night she would hide him like a fire-brand within the might of the flame, without his parents' knowledge. It made them wonder greatly how he was so precocious, and why his appearance was like the gods'. She would have made him ageless and deathless, if it had not been that fair-belted Metaneira foolishly kept watch one night and watched her from her fragrant bed-chamber. She screamed and struck both her thighs in fear for her child and in a frenzy of mindlessness. Wailing, she said, "My child Demophon, the stranger woman is hiding you in the blazing fire, and is making grief and bitter sorrow for me."

250. So she spoke, lamenting, and the divine goddess heard her. Demeter of the beautiful crown was amazed at her; with her immortal hands she put from her the dear child whom [Metaneira] had borne, all unexpected, in the palace, and threw him at her feet, drawing him out of the fire, terribly angry at heart, and at the same time she said to fair-belted Metaneira, "Humans are short-sighted, stupid, ignorant of the share of good or evil which is coming to them. You by your foolishness have hurt him beyond curing. Let my witness be the oath of the gods sworn by the intractable water of Styx, that I would have made your son deathless and ageless all his days, and given him imperishable honor. But now it is not possible to ward off death and destruction. Still he will have imperishable honor forever, since he stood on my knees and slept in my arms; in due season, as the years pass around, the children of the Eleusinians will conduct in his honor war (games) and the terrible battle-cry with each other for ever and ever. I am Demeter, the Venerable, ready as the greatest boon and joy for immortals and mortals. So now, let the whole people build me a great temple, and an altar beneath it, below the city and the towering wall, above Kallirhoe on the ridge which juts forth. I myself will establish rites so that henceforth you may celebrate them purely and propitiate my mind."

275. With these words the goddess altered size and form and sloughed off old age; beauty wafted about her. A lovely fresh smell radiated from her lovely gown and the radiance from the skin of the immortal goddess shone afar. Her blonde hair flowed down over her shoulders, and the sturdy house was filled with light like a flash of lightning. She went out through the palace. As for the other, her knees gave way, and for a long time she was speechless. She did not even remember the child, her favorite, to pick him up from the floor. His sisters heard his piteous crying, and they leapt down from their well-covered beds. Then one of them took the child in her hands and put him in her lap, one kindled a fire, and another hurried on gentle feet to rouse her mother out of the fragrant chamber. Crowding around they washed him, covering him with love as he squirmed; his heart was not comforted, however, for less skillful nurses and nurse maids were holding him now.

292. All night long the women, quaking with fear, propitiated the glorious goddess. As soon as dawn appeared they gave a full report to wide-ruling Keleos, as Demeter of the beautiful garlands commanded. He summoned the people from their many boundaries and ordered them to build an elaborate temple to fair-haired Demeter and an altar on the ridge which juts forth. They obeyed him straightway, and hearkened to him as he spoke, and started to build as he commanded. And it grew at the dispensation of the divinity. When they finished and ceased from their toil, each person went back to his home. Blonde Demeter stayed there, seated far from all the blessed gods, wasting with grief for her deep-belted daughter.

305. She made the most terrible, most oppressive year for men upon the nourishing land, and the earth sent up no seed, as fair-garlanded Demeter hid it. Cattle drew the many curved plows in vain over the fields, and much white barley seed fell useless on the earth. By now she would have destroyed the entire race of men by grievous famine, and deprived those who dwell on Olympus of the glorious honor of offerings and sacrifices, if Zeus had not taken notice and taken counsel with his mind. First he roused gold-winged Iris to summon fair-haired Demeter, of the very desirable beauty. So he spoke, and she obeyed Zeus wrapped in clouds, the son of Kronos. She rushed down the middle and arrived at the citadel of fragrant Eleusis. In the temple she found Demeter dark-clad, and addressed her with winged words. "Demeter, father Zeus who understands imperishable things summons you to come among the race of the immortal gods. So come, and let my message from Zeus not be fruitless."

324. So she spoke in supplication, but her heart was not persuaded. Therefore the Father sent out the blessed, ever-living gods one after another, and they went in turn and implored her, and offered her many fine gifts and whatever honors she might choose among the immortal gods. None, however, was able to persuade the heart and mind of the angry goddess. She rejected their speeches firmly, and claimed that she would never set foot upon fragrant Olympus, nor allow any fruit to grow on the earth, until she saw with her eyes the beautiful face of her daughter.

334. When Zeus the loud-crashing, the wide-voiced one, heard this he sent Hermes the slayer of Argos with his golden wand to Erebos, to use smooth words on Hades and lead pure Persephone out of the misty darkness into the light to join the deities, in order that her mother might see her with her eyes and turn from her anger. Hermes obeyed, and eagerly rushed down under the recesses of the earth, leaving the seat of Olympus. He found the Lord inside his house, seated on couches with his modest and very unwilling wife, yearning for her mother. . . .

346. The mighty slayer of Argos came near and said, "Dark-haired Hades, ruler of the departed, Father Zeus has ordered me to lead glorious Persephone out of Erebos to join them, in order that her mother might see her with her eyes and cease from her anger and terrible wrath, since she is contriving a tremendous deed, to destroy the fragile race of earth-born men, hiding the seed under the earth and obliterating the honors of the immortals. Her anger is terrible, she has no contact with the gods, but sits apart inside her fragrant temple, holding the rocky citadel of Eleusis."

357. So he spoke, and Aidoneus the lord of the underworld smiled with his brows, and did not disobey the injunctions of Zeus the king. Promptly he gave the command to diligent Persephone: "Go, Persephone, to your dark-clad mother, and keep gentle the strength and heart in your breast. Do not be despondent to excess beyond all others. I shall not be an inappropriate husband for you among the immortals; I am a brother of Father Zeus. Being there, you will rule over all that lives and moves, enjoying the greatest honors among the immortals. And there shall be punishment forever on those who act unjustly and who do not propitiate your might with sacrifices, performing the pious acts and offering appropriate gifts."

370. So he spoke, and Persephone the discreet was glad, and swiftly leapt up for joy. But he gave her a honey-sweet pomegranate seed to eat, having secretly passed it around [himself?], so that she might not stay forever there by modest dark-clad Demeter. Aidoneus, designator of many, harnessed the immortal horses in front of the golden chariot, and she stepped on the chariot; beside her the mighty slayer of Argos took the reins and a whip in his hands and drove out of the palace. The pair of horses flew willingly. They finished the long journey quickly. Neither sea nor rivers nor grassy glens nor mountain peaks held back the rush of the immortal horses; they went above them, and cut through the high air. He drove them where Demeter of the fair crown waited in front of her fragrant temple, and he stopped them there. Seeing them, she darted up like a maenad in the woods on a thick-shaded mountain.

387. [Demeter asked Persephone if she had eaten anything in the underworld. If not,] "you will come up and dwell with me and Zeus of the dark clouds, and be honored by all the immortals. But if you have tasted anything, then you shall go back down and dwell there for the third part of the season, and for the other two, here with me and the other immortals. Whenever the earth blossoms with all the sweet-smelling flowers of spring, then you will come back up from the misty darkness, a great wonder to gods and to mortal men. But what trick did the powerful host of many use to deceive you?"

405. Persephone, the exceedingly beautiful, gave her this response: "I will tell you, Mother, everything accurately. When the swift slayer of Argos came to me from Father Zeus and the others in heaven with the message to come out of Erebos, so that seeing me with your eyes you might cease from your anger and terrible wrath, I leapt up for joy. But he secretly insinuated a pomegranate seed, honey-sweet food, and though I was unwilling, he compelled me by force to taste it. How he snatched me away through the clever plan of Zeus and carried me off, down into the recesses of the earth, I will tell you and I will go through it all as you ask. We were all there in the lovely meadow—Leukippe, Phaino, Elektre, Ianthe, Melite, Iache, Rhodeia, Kallirhoe, Melobosis, Tyche, Okyrhoe of the flowering face, Chryseis, Ianeira, Akaste, Admete, Rhodope, Plouto, charming Kalypso, Styx, Ouranie, lovely Galaxaure, Pallas the inciter of battles, Artemis the shooter of arrows—playing and picking the lovely flowers, a profusion of gentle saffron blossoms, iris, hyacinth, rose birds and lilies, a marvel to see, and narcissus, which the broad land grew like saffron. Full of joy, I was picking them, but the earth under me moved, and the powerful Lord, the host of many, leapt out. And he took me under the earth on his golden chariot, against my will, and I screamed loudly with my voice. Grieved though I am, I am telling you the whole truth."

434. Then with minds in concord they spent the whole day warming their hearts and minds, showering much love on each other, and her mind found respite from its griefs, as they gave and received joys from each other. And there came near them Hecate of the glistening veil, and she also showered much love on the daughter of holy Demeter, and ever since she has been her attendant and Lady-in-waiting.

441. Zeus the land-crashing, the wide-voiced one, sent fair-haired Rheia as a messenger to them, to bring dark-gowned Demeter among the race of the gods; he promised to give her whatever honors she might choose among the immortal gods. He granted that her daughter should spend the third portion of the year in its cycle down in the misty darkness, but the other two with her mother and the other immortals.

448. So he spoke, and the goddess obeyed the biddings of Zeus. Promptly she darted along the peaks of Olympus, and came to the Rarian plain, the life-bringing udder of plough-land formerly, but at that time not life-bringing at all, as it stood all barren and leafless. The white barley was concealed according to the plans of fair-ankled Demeter, but at this time it was about to grow shaggy with waves of grain as it became spring. In the field the rich furrows were to be loaded with the grain, and they were to be bound in sheaves. Here she first alighted from the boundless aether, and they saw each other gladly, and rejoiced in their hearts.

459. Rheia of the glistening veil said to her, "Come here, child. Zeus the loud-crashing, the wide-voiced one, summons you to come among the race of the immortal gods, and he has promised to give whatever honors you might choose among the immortal gods. He has granted that your daughter will spend the third portion of the year in its cycle down in the misty darkness, but the other two with you and the other immortals. So has he promised, and nodded his head in affirmation. Go, now, my child, and obey; do not be obdurately angry at Zeus of the dark clouds but give prompt increase to the fruit, bringer of life to men."

470. So she spoke, and Demeter of the fair crown obeyed. Promptly she sent up fruit on the rich-soiled fields, and the whole broad land was loaded with leaves and flowers. She went to the royal stewards of the right and to Triptolemos, Diokles the driver of horses, mighty Eumolpos and Keleos the leader of the people. She showed the tendance of the holy things and explicated the rites to them all, to Triptolemos, to Polyxeinos and to Diokles—sacred rites, which it is forbidden to transgress, to inquire into, or to speak about, for great reverence of the gods constrains their voice. Blessed of earth-bound men is he who has seen these things, but he who dies without fulfilling the holy things, and he who is without a share of them, has no claim ever on such blessings, even when departed down to the moldy darkness.

483. When the divine goddess had ordained all this, she went to Olympus among the assembly of the other gods. And there they dwell, sacred and reverent, with Zeus who revels in thunder. Greatly blessed of earth-bound men is he whom they propitiously love: to him they promptly send to the hearth of his great house Ploutos [Wealth], who gives abundance to mortal men.

490. Now, ye that hold the people of fragrant Eleusis, and sea-girt Paros and rocky Antron, Lady mistress Deo, bringer of seasons and glorious gifts, thou thyself and Persephone, the exceedingly beautiful, do ye bestow a heartwarming livelihood in exchange for my song. Now I shall recall thee, and also another song.

128

TWO ACCOUNTS OF THE ORIGINS OF THE WORSHIP OF THE GREAT MOTHER AT ROME

Ovid *Fasti* IV.247–348   1st century B.C.E./C.E.

"Instruct me, too, I pray, my guide, whence was she fetched, whence came? Was she always in our city?" "The Mother Goddess ever loved Dindymus, and Cybele, and Ida, with its delightful springs, and the realm of Ilium. When Aeneas carried Troy to the Italian fields, the goddess almost followed the ships that bore the sacred things; but she felt that fate did not yet call for the intervention of her divinity in Latium, and she remained behind in her accustomed place. Afterwards, when mighty Rome had already seen five centuries, and had lifted up her head above the conquered world, the priest consulted the fateful words of the Euboean song. They say that what he found ran thus: 'The Mother is absent; thou Roman, I bid thee seek the Mother. When she shall come, she must be received by chaste hands.' The ambiguity of the dark oracle puzzled the senators to know who the Parent was, and where she was to be sought. Paean was consulted and said, 'Fetch the Mother of the Gods; she is to be found on Mount Ida.' Nobles were sent. The sceptre of Phrygia was then held by Attalus; he refused the favour to the Ausonian lords. Wonders to tell, the earth trembled and rumbled long, and in her shrine thus did the goddess speak: ''Twas my own will that they should send for me. Tarry not: let me go, it is my wish. Rome is a place meet to be the resort of every god.' Quaking with terror at the words Attalus said, 'Go forth. Thou wilt still be ours. Rome traces its origin to Phrygian ancestors.' Straightway unnumbered axes fell those pine-woods which had supplied the pious Phrygian with timber in his flight: a thousand hands assemble, and the Mother of the Gods is lodged in a hollow ship painted in encaustic colours. She is borne in perfect safety across the waters of her son and comes to the long strait named after the sister of Phrixus; she passes Rhoeteum, where the tide runs fast, and the Sigean shores, and Tenedos, and Eetion's ancient realm. Leaving Lesbos behind, she came next to the Cyclades and to the wave that breaks on the Carystian shoals. She passed the Icarian Sea also, where Icarus lost his wings that slipped, and where he gave his name to a great water. Then she left Crete on the larboard and the

Pelopian billows on the starboard, and steered for Cythera, the sacred isle of Venus. Thence she passed to the Trinacrian Sea, where Brontes and Steropes and Acmonides are wont to dip the white-hot iron. She skirted the African main, and beheld astern to larboard the Sardinian realms, and made Ausonia.

"She had arrived at Ostia, where the Tiber divides to join the sea and flows with ampler sweep. All the knights and the grave senators, mixed up with the common folk, came to meet her at the mouth of the Tuscan river. With them walked mothers and daughters and brides, and the virgins who tended the sacred hearths. The men wearied their arms by tugging lustily at the rope; hardly did the foreign ship make head against the stream. A drought had long prevailed; the grass was parched and burnt; the loaded bark sank in the muddy shallows. Every man who lent a hand toiled beyond his strength and cheered on the workers by his cries. Yet the ship stuck fast, like an island firmly fixed in the middle of the sea. Astonished at the portent, the men did stand and quake. Claudia Quinta traced her descent from Clausus of old, and her beauty matched her nobility. Chaste was she, though not reputed so. Rumour unkind had wronged her, and a false charge had been trumped up against her: it told against her that she dressed sprucely, that she walked abroad with her hair dressed in varied fashion, that she had a ready tongue for gruff old men. Conscious of innocence, she laughed at fame's untruths; but we of the multitude are prone to think the worst. When she had stepped forth from the procession of the chaste matrons, and taken up the pure water of the river in her hands, she thrice let it drip on her head, and thrice lifted her palms to heaven (all who looked on her thought that she was out of her mind), and bending the knee she fixed her eyes on the image of the goddess, and with dishevelled hair uttered these words: 'Thou fruitful Mother of the Gods, graciously accept thy suppliant's prayers on one condition. They say I am not chaste. If thou dost condemn me, I will confess my guilt; convicted by the verdict of a goddess, I will pay the penalty with my life. But if I am free of crime, give by thine act a proof of my innocency, and, chaste as thou art, do thou yield to my chaste hands.' She spoke, and drew the rope with a slight effort. My story is a strange one, but it is attested by the stage. The goddess was moved, and followed her leader, and by following bore witness in her favour: a sound of joy was wafted to the stars. They came to a bend in the river, where the stream turns away to the left: men of old named it the Halls of Tiber.

Night drew on; they tied the rope to an oaken stump, and after a repast disposed themselves to slumber light. At dawn of day they loosed the rope from the oaken stump; but first they set down a brazier and put incense on it, and crowned the poop, and sacrificed an unblemished heifer that had known neither the yoke nor the bull. There is a place where the smooth Almo flows into the Tiber, and the lesser river loses its name in the great one. There a hoary-headed priest in purple robe washed the Mistress and her holy things in the waters of Almo. The attendants howled, the mad flute blew, and hands unmanly beat the leathern drums. Attended by a crowd, Claudia walked in front with joyful face, her chastity at last vindicated by the testimony of the goddess. The goddess herself, seated in a wagon, drove in through the Capene Gate; fresh flowers were scattered on the yoked oxen. Nasica received her. The name of the founder of the temple has not survived; now it is Augustus; formerly it was Metellus."

Livy *Annals of Rome* XXIX.14   1st century B.C.E./C.E., in reference to
                                                204 B.C.E.

Although Africa had not been openly assigned as a province, while the senators kept the matter dark, I believe, for fear the Carthaginians might know in advance, nevertheless the people were aroused to hope that the war would be waged that year in Africa, and that the end of the Punic war was at hand. That situation had filled men's minds with superstitious fears and they were inclined both to report and to believe portents. All the greater was the number of them in circulation: that two suns had been seen, and that at night there had been light for a time; and that at Setia a meteor had been seen shooting from east to west; that at Tarracina a city-gate had been struck by lightning, at Anagnia a gate and also the wall at many points; that in the temple of Juno Sospita at Lanuvium a noise was heard with a dreadful crash. To expiate these there was a single day of prayer, and on account of the shower of stones nine days of rites were observed. In addition they deliberated on the reception of the Idaean Mother, in regard to whom not only had Marcus Valerius, one of the ambassadors, arriving in advance, reported that she would be in Italy very soon, but also there was recent news that she was already at Tarracina. It was no unimportant decision that occupied the senate—the question who was the best man in the state. At any rate every man would have preferred a real victory in that contest to any high commands or magistracies, whether conferred by vote of the senators or of the people. Publius Scipio, son of the Gnaeus who had fallen in Spain, was the young man not yet of an age to be quaestor, whom they judged to be the best of good men among all the citizens. If writers who lived nearest in time to men who remembered those days had handed down by what virtues the senate was led to make that judgment, I should indeed gladly hand it on to posterity. But I shall not interject my own opinions, reached by conjecture in a matter buried by the lapse of time. Publius Cornelius was ordered to go to Ostia with all the matrons to meet the goddess, and himself to receive her from the ship, and carrying her to land to turn her over to the matrons to carry. After the ship had reached the mouth of the river Tiber, in compliance with the order he sailed out into open water on a ship, received the goddess from her priests and carried her to land. The foremost matrons in the state, among whom the name of one in particular, that of Claudia Quinta, is conspicuous, received her. Claudia's repute, previously not unquestioned, as tradition reports it, has made her purity the more celebrated among posterity by a service so devout. The matrons passed the goddess from hand to hand in an unbroken succession to each other, while the entire city poured out to meet her. Censers had been placed before the doors along the route of the bearers, and kindling their incense, people prayed that gracious and benignant she might enter the city of Rome. It was to the Temple of Victory, which is on the Palatine, that they carried the goddess on the day before the Ides of April, and that was a holy day. The people thronged to the Palatine bearing gifts for the goddess, and there was a banquet of the gods, and games also, called the Megalesia.

129

IMAGERY OF LACTATION AND CHILDBEARING
IN A CHRISTIAN ODE

The Odes of Solomon 19   1st/2d century C.E.?

1. A cup of milk was offered to me,
   and I drank it in the sweetness of the Lord's kindness.
2. The Son is the cup,
   and the Father is he who was milked;
   and the Holy Spirit is she who milked him;
3. Because his breasts were full,
   and it was undesirable that his milk should be released without
   purpose.
4. The Holy Spirit opened her bosom,
   and mixed the milk of the two breasts of the Father.
5. Then she gave the mixture to the generation without their
   knowing,
   and those who have received (it) are in the perfection of the
   right hand.
6. The womb of the Virgin took (it),
   and she received conception and gave birth.
7. So the Virgin became a mother with great mercies.
8. And she labored and bore the Son but without pain,
   because it did not occur without purpose.
9. And she did not seek a midwife,
   because he caused her to give life.
10. She bore as a strong man with desire,
    and she bore according to the manifestation,
    and possessed with great power.
11. And she loved with salvation,
    and guarded with kindness,
    and declared with greatness.

   Hallelujah.

131

A VERSION OF THE
MYTH OF ISIS

Plutarch *On Isis and Osiris* 355–358   1st/2d century C.E.

They say that the Sun, when he became aware of Rhea's intercourse with Cronus, invoked a curse upon her that she should not give birth to a child in any month or any year; but Hermes, being enamoured of the goddess, consorted with her. Later, playing at draughts with the moon, he won from her the seventieth part of each of her periods of illumination, and from all the winnings he composed five days, and intercalated them as an addition to the three hundred and sixty days. The Egyptians even now call these five days intercalated and celebrate them as the birthdays of the gods. They relate that on the first of these days Osiris was born, and at the hour of his birth a voice issued forth saying, "The Lord of All advances to the light." But some relate that a certain Pamyles, while he was drawing water in Thebes, heard a voice issuing from the shrine of Zeus, which bade him proclaim with a loud voice that a mighty and beneficent king, Osiris, had been born; and for this Cronus entrusted to him the child Osiris, which he brought up. It is in his honour that the festival of Pamylia is celebrated, a festival which resembles the phallic processions. On the second of these days Arueris was born whom they call Apollo, and some call him also the elder Horus. On the third day Typhon was born, but not in due season or manner, but with a blow he broke through his mother's side and leapt forth. On the fourth day Isis was born in the regions that are ever moist; and on the fifth Nephthys, to whom they give the name of Finality and the name of Aphroditê, and some also the name of Victory. There is also a tradition that Osiris and Arueris were sprung from the Sun, **356** Isis from Hermes, and Typhon and Nephthys from Cronus. For this reason the kings considered the third of the intercalated days as inauspicious, and transacted no business on that day, nor did they give any attention to their bodies until nightfall. They relate, moreover, that Nephthys became the wife of Typhon; but Isis and Osiris were enamoured of each other and consorted together in the darkness of the womb before their birth. Some say that Arueris came from this union and was called the elder Horus by the Egyptians, but Apollo by the Greeks.

One of the first acts related of Osiris in his reign was to deliver the

Egyptians from their destitute and brutish manner of living. This he did by showing them the fruits of cultivation, by giving them laws, and by teaching them to honour the gods. Later he travelled over the whole earth civilizing it without the slightest need of arms, but most of the peoples he won over to his way by the charm of his persuasive discourse combined with song and all manner of music. Hence the Greeks came to identify him with Dionysus.

During his absence the tradition is that Typhon attempted nothing revolutionary because Isis, who was in control, was vigilant and alert; but when he returned home Typhon contrived a treacherous plot against him and formed a group of conspirators seventy-two in number. He had also the co-operation of a queen from Ethiopia who was there at the time and whose name they report as Aso. Typhon, having secretly measured Osiris's body and having made ready a beautiful chest of corresponding size artistically ornamented, caused it to be brought into the room where the festivity was in progress. The company was much pleased at the sight of it and admired it greatly, whereupon Typhon jestingly promised to present it to the man who should find the chest to be exactly his length when he lay down in it. They all tried it in turn, but no one fitted it; then Osiris got into it and lay down, and those who were in the plot ran to it and slammed down the lid, which they fastened by nails from the outside and also by using molten lead. Then they carried the chest to the river and sent it on its way to the sea through the Tanitic Mouth. Wherefore the Egyptians even to this day name this mouth the hateful and execrable. Such is the tradition. They say also that the date on which this deed was done was the seventeenth day of Athyr, when the sun passes through Scorpion, and in the twenty-eighth year of the reign of Osiris; but some say that these are the years of his life and not of his reign.

The first to learn of the deed and to bring to men's knowledge an account of what had been done were the Pans and Satyrs who lived in the region around Chemmis, and so, even to this day, the sudden confusion and consternation of a crowd is called a panic. Isis, when the tidings reached her, at once cut off one of her tresses and put on a garment of mourning in a place where the city still bears the name of Kopto. Others think that the name means deprivation, for they also express "deprive" by means of "koptein." But Isis wandered everywhere at her wits' end; no one whom she approached did she fail to address, and even when she met some little children she asked them about the chest. As it happened, they had seen it, and they told her the mouth of the river through which the friends of Typhon had launched the coffin into the sea. Wherefore the Egyptians think that little children possess the power of prophecy, and they try to divine the future from the portents which they find in children's words, especially when children are playing about in holy places and crying out whatever chances to come into their minds.

They relate also that Isis, learning that Osiris in his love had consorted with her sister through ignorance, in the belief that she was Isis, and seeing the proof of this in the garland of melilote which he had left with Nephthys, sought to find the child; for the mother, immediately after its birth, had exposed it because of her fear of Typhon. And when the child had been found, after great toil and trouble, with the help of dogs which led Isis to it, it was brought up and became her guardian and attendant, receiving the name of Anubis, and it is said to protect the gods just as dogs protect men.

Thereafter Isis, as they relate, learned that the chest had been cast up by the sea 357 near the land of Byblus and that the waves had gently set it down in the midst of a clump of heather. The heather in a short time ran up into a very beautiful and massive stock, and enfolded and embraced the chest with its growth and concealed it within its trunk. The king of the country admired the great size of the plant, and cut off the portion that enfolded the chest (which was now hidden from sight), and used it as a pillar to support the roof of his house. These facts, they say, Isis ascertained by the divine inspiration of Rumour, and came to Byblus and sat down by a spring, all dejection and tears; she exchanged no word with anybody, save only that she welcomed the queen's maidservants and treated them with great amiability, plaiting their hair for them and imparting to their persons a wondrous fragrance from her own body. But when the queen observed her maidservants, a longing came upon her for the unknown woman and for such hairdressing and for a body fragrant with ambrosia. Thus it happened that Isis was sent for and became so intimate with the queen that the queen made her the nurse of her baby. They say that the king's name was Malcander; the queen's name some say was Astartê, others Saosis, and still others Nemanûs, which the Greeks would call Athenaïs.

They relate that Isis nursed the child by giving it her finger to suck instead of her breast, and in the night she would burn away the mortal portions of its body. She herself would turn into a swallow and flit about the pillar with a wailing lament, until the queen who had been watching, when she saw her babe on fire, gave forth a loud cry and thus deprived it of immortality. Then the goddess disclosed herself and asked for the pillar which served to support the roof. She removed it with the greatest ease and cut away the wood of the heather which surrounded the chest; then, when she had wrapped up the wood in a linen cloth and had poured perfume upon it, she entrusted it to the care of the kings; and even to this day the people of Byblus venerate this wood which is preserved in the shrine of Isis. Then the goddess threw herself down upon the coffin with such a dreadful wailing that the younger of the king's sons expired on the spot. The elder son she kept with her, and, having placed the coffin on board a boat, she put out from land. Since the Phaedrus river toward the early morning fostered a rather boisterous wind, the goddess grew angry and dried up its stream.

In the first place where she found seclusion, when she was quite by herself, they relate that she opened the chest and laid her face upon the face within and caressed it and wept. The child came quietly up behind her and saw what was there, and when the goddess became aware of his presence, she turned about and gave him one awful look of anger. The child could not endure the fright, and died. Others will not have it so, but assert that he fell overboard into the sea from the boat that was mentioned above. He also is the recipient of honours because of the goddess; for they say that the Maneros of whom the Egyptians sing at their convivial gatherings is this very child. Some say, however, that his name was Palaestinus or Pelusius, and that the city founded by the goddess was named in his honour. They also recount that this Maneros who is the theme of their songs was the first to invent music. But some say that the word is not the name of any person, but an expression belonging to the vocabulary of drinking and feasting: "Good luck be ours in things like this!", and that this is really the idea expressed by the exclamation "maneros" whenever the Egyptians use it. In the same way we may be sure that the likeness of a corpse which, as it is exhibited to them, is carried around in a chest, is not a reminder of what happened to Osiris, as some assume; but it is to urge them, as they contemplate it, to use and to enjoy the present, since all very soon must be what it is now and this is their purpose in introducing it into the midst of merry-making.

As they relate, Isis proceeded to her son Horus, who was being reared in Buto, and bestowed the chest in a place well out of the way;

but Typhon, who was hunting by night in the **358** light of the moon, happened upon it. Recognizing the body he divided it into fourteen parts and scattered them, each in a different place. Isis learned of this and sought for them again, sailing through the swamps in a boat of papyrus. This is the reason why people sailing in such boats are not harmed by the crocodiles, since these creatures in their own way show either their fear or their reverence for the goddess.

The traditional result of Osiris's dismemberment is that there are many so-called tombs of Osiris in Egypt; for Isis held a funeral for each part when she had found it. Others deny this and assert that she caused effigies of him to be made and these she distributed among the several cities, pretending that she was giving them his body, in order that he might receive divine honours in a greater number of cities, and also that, if Typhon should succeed in overpowering Horus, he might despair of ever finding the true tomb when so many were pointed out to him, all of them called the tomb of Osiris.

Of the parts of Osiris's body the only one which Isis did not find was the male member, for the reason that this had been at once tossed into the river, and the lepidotus, the sea-bream, and the pike had fed upon it; and it is from these very fishes the Egyptians are most scrupulous in abstaining. But Isis made a replica of the member to take its place, and consecrated the phallus, in honour of which the Egyptians even at the present day celebrate a festival.

Later, as they relate, Osiris came to Horus from the other world and exercised and trained him for the battle. After a time Osiris asked Horus what he held to be the most noble of all things. When Horus replied, "To avenge one's father and mother for evil done to them," Osiris then asked him what animal he considered the most useful for them who go forth to battle; and when Horus said, "A horse," Osiris was surprised and raised the question why it was that he had not rather said a lion than a horse. Horus answered that a lion was a useful thing for a man in need of assistance, but that a horse served best for cutting off the flight of an enemy and annihilating him. When Osiris heard this he was much pleased, since he felt that Horus had now an adequate preparation. It is said that, as many were continually transferring their allegiance to Horus, Typhon's concubine, Thueris, also came over to him; and a serpent which pursued her was cut to pieces by Horus's men, and now, in memory of this, the people throw down a rope in their midst and chop it up.

Now the battle, as they relate, lasted many days and Horus prevailed. Isis, however, to whom Typhon was delivered in chains, did not cause him to be put to death, but released him and let him go. Horus could not endure this with equanimity, but laid hands upon his mother and wrested the royal diadem from her head; but Hermes put upon her a helmet like unto the head of a cow.

Typhon formally accused Horus of being an illegitimate child, but with the help of Hermes to plead his cause it was decided by the gods that he also was legitimate. Typhon was then overcome in two other battles. Osiris consorted with Isis after his death, and she became the mother of Harpocrates, untimely born and weak in his lower limbs.

132

THE EXPERIENCES OF A MALE
INITIATE OF ISIS

Apuleius *Metamorphoses* 11   2d century C.E.

Introduction

[Book XI opens with an auspicious note of mystery. Lucius is spending the night asleep on the warm sand of the seashore.]

About the first watch of the night, I awoke in sudden terror; the full moon had risen and was shining with unusual splendor as it emerged from the waves. All about me lay the mysterious silence of the night. I knew that this was the hour when the goddess [Isis] exercised her greatest power and governed all things by her providence—not only animals, wild and tame, but even inanimate things were renewed by her divine illumination and might; even the heavenly bodies, the whole earth, and the vast sea waxed or waned in accordance with her will.

The Epiphany of Isis

[Lucius decides to make his appeal to Isis for release from his asinine disguise, and the goddess responds. His prayer in §2 recounts her titles as Queen of Heaven, Ceres, Proserpina, celestial Venus.]

3. So I poured out my prayers and supplications, adding to them much pitiful wailing, and once more fell sound asleep on that same bed of sand. Scarcely had I closed my eyes when lo! from the midst of the deep there arose that face divine to which even the gods must do reverence. Then a little at a time, slowly, her whole shining body emerged from the sea and came into full view. I would like to tell you all the wonder of this vision, if the poverty of human speech does not prevent, or if the divine power dwelling within that form supplies a rich enough store of eloquence.

First, the tresses of her hair were long and thick, and streamed down softly, flowing and curling about her divine neck. On her head she wore as a crown many garlands of flowers, and in the middle of her forehead shone white and glowing a round disc like a mirror, or rather like the moon; on its right and left it was bound about with the furrowed coils of rising vipers, and above it were stalks of grain. Her tunic was of many colors, woven of the finest linen, now gleaming with snowy whiteness, now yellow like the crocus, now rosy-red like a flame. But what dazzled my eyes more than anything else was her cloak, for it was a deep black, glistening with sable sheen; it was cast about her, passing under her right arm and brought together on her left shoulder. Part of it hung down like a shield and drooped in many a fold, the whole reaching to the lower edge of her garment with tasseled fringe. **4.** Here and there along its embroidered border, and also on its surface, were scattered sequins of sparkling stars, and in their midst the full moon of midmonth shone forth like a flame of fire. And all along the border of that gorgeous robe there was an unbroken garland of all kinds of flowers and fruits.

In her hands she held emblems of various kinds. In her right hand she carried a bronze rattle [the sistrum] made of a thin piece of metal curved like a belt, through which were passed a few small rods; this gave out a tinkling sound whenever she shook it three times with a quivering pulsation. In her left hand was a golden cup, from the top of whose slender handle rose an asp, towering with head erect and its throat distended on both sides. Her perfumed feet were shod with sandals woven of the palm of victory.

Such was the vision, and of such majesty. Then, breathing forth all the blessed fragrance of happy Arabia, she deigned to address me with voice divine: **5.** "Behold, Lucius, I have come, moved by thy prayers! I, nature's mother, mistress of all the elements, earliest offspring of the ages, mightiest of the divine powers, Queen of the dead, chief of them that dwell in the heavens, in whose features are combined those of all the gods and goddesses. By my nod I rule the shining heights of heaven, the wholesome winds of the sea, and the mournful silences of the underworld. The whole world honors my sole deity [*numen unicum*] under various forms, with varied rites, and by many names. There the Phrygians, firstborn of men, call me the Mother of the Gods, she who dwells at Pessinus; there the Athenians, sprung from their own soil, know me as Cecropian Minerva; there the sea-girt Cyprians call me Paphian Venus; the Cretans, who are archers, call me Diana Dictynna [of the hunter's net]; the Sicilians, with their three languages, call me Stygian Proserpina; the Eleusinians, the ancient goddess Ceres. Others call me Juno, others Bellona, others Hecate, while still others call me the Rhamnusian. But those on whom shine the first rays of the Sun-God as daily he springs to new birth, the Arii and the Ethiopians, and the Egyptians mighty in ancient lore, honoring me with my peculiar rites, call me by my true name, *Isis the Queen*.

"I have come in pity for thy woes. I have come, propitious and ready to aid. Cease from thy weeping and lamentation, and lay aside thy grief! For thee, by my providence, the day of salvation is dawning! Therefore turn thy afflicted spirit, and give heed to what I command. The day, even the very day that follows this night, is dedicated to me by an everlasting dedication; for on this day, after I have laid to rest the storms of winter and stilled the tempestuous waves of the sea, my priests shall dedicate to the deep, which is now navigable once more, a new boat, and offer it in my honor as the first fruits of the year's seafaring. Thou must await this festival with untroubled heart and with no profane thoughts."

[*The goddess tells Lucius that he must mingle with the crowd at the Ploiaphesia and edge his way up to the priest, who will be wearing a garland of roses. Having been forewarned by the goddess in a vision, the priest will be prepared for what is to happen, namely, that Lucius (still the ass) will seize the priest's garland and eat it, whereupon he will be restored to human form. And so it takes place. Transformed once more into human shape, Lucius is exhorted by one of the priests, "whose smiling face seemed more than mortal":*]

15. "O Lucius, after enduring so many labors and escaping so many tempests of Fortune, you have now at length reached the port and haven of rest and mercy! Neither your noble lineage nor your high rank nor your great learning did anything for you; but because you turned to servile pleasures, by a little youthful folly you won the grim reward of your hapless curiosity. And yet while Fortune's blindness tormented you with various dangers, by her very malice she has brought you to this present state of religious blessedness. Let Fortune go elsewhere and rage with her wild fury, and find someone else to torment! For Fortune has no power over those who have devoted themselves to serve the majesty of our goddess. For all your afflictions—robbers, wild beasts, slavery, toilsome and futile journeys that ended where they began, and the daily fear of death—all these brought no advantage to wicked Fortune. Now you are safe, under the protection of that Fortune who is not blind but can see, who by her clear light enlightens the other gods. Therefore rejoice and put on a more cheerful countenance, appropriately matching your white robe, and follow with joyful steps the procession of this Savior Goddess. Let all such as are not devout followers of the goddess see and acknowledge their error[, saying]: 'See, here is Lucius, freed from his former miseries by the providence of the great goddess Isis, and rejoicing in triumph over his Fortune!' And in order that you may live even more safely and securely, hand in your name to this sacred militia [i.e., join the Isiac order]—for it is only a little while ago that you were asked to take the oath—and dedicate yourself to obey our religion and take upon yourself the voluntary yoke of ministry. For when you have begun to serve the goddess, then will you realize more fully the fruits of your liberty."

The Initiation of Lucius

[And so the priest prophesied and made his appeal to Lucius, and Lucius consented and joined the procession, amid the jeers of the unbelievers. But his conversion, like that of many others, was a slow process, and only gradually did he come to identify himself with the Isiac priests; for, like many another, he believed the strict profession of religion was something too hard for him: "The laws of chastity and abstinence are not easy to obey" (19). And yet he continued to frequent the services of worship (21), and eventually came to desire earnestly to be admitted to the mysteries of Isis. This took place on "the night that is sacred to the goddess."]

22. The priest finished speaking, and I did not mar my obedience by any impatience, but with a quiet and gentle and edifying silence I rendered attentive service at the daily observance of the sacred rites. Nor did the saving grace of the mighty goddess in any way deceive me or torture me with long delays, but in the dark of night, by commands that were not in the least dark, she clearly signified to me that the day so long desired had come, in which she would grant the fulfillment of my most earnest prayers. She also stated what amount I must provide for the supplications, and she appointed Mithras himself, her high priest, to administer the rites to me; for his destiny, she said, was closely bound up with mine by the divine conjunction of the stars.

These and other gracious admonitions of the supreme goddess refreshed my spirit, so that even before it was clear day I shook off sleep and hastened at once to the priest's lodging. I met him just as he was coming out of his bedchamber, and saluted him. I had decided to request with even more insistence that I should be initiated, now that it was due me. But he at once, as soon as he saw me, anticipated me, saying, "Lucius, you happy, you greatly blessed man, whom the august deity deigns to favor with such good will! But why," he asked, "do you stand here idle, yourself delaying? The day you have so long asked for by your unwearied prayers has come, when by the divine commands of the goddess of many names you are to be admitted by my hands into the most holy secrets of the mysteries." Then, taking my right hand in his, the gentle old man led me to the very doors of the huge temple; and after celebrating with solemn ritual the opening of the gates and completing the morning sacrifice, he brought out from a hidden place in the temple certain books whose titles were written in undecipherable letters. Some of these [letters] were shaped like all kinds of animals and seemed to be brief ways of suggesting words; others had their extremities knotted or curved like wheels, or intertwined like the tendrils of a vine, which was enough to safeguard them from the curiosity of profane readers. At the same time he told me about the various preparations it was necessary to make in view of my initiation.

23. I lost no time, but promptly and with a liberality even beyond what was required I either bought these things myself or had my friends buy them for me. And now, the time drawing near and requiring it, as he said, the priest conducted me with an escort of the religiously-minded to the nearest baths; and when I entered the bath, where it is customary for the neophytes to bathe, he first prayed to the gods to be gracious to me and then sprinkled me with purest water and cleansed me. He then led me back to the temple, and since the day was now more than half over he placed me at the feet of the goddess herself; then, after confiding certain secret orders to me, those which were too holy to be spoken, he openly, before all who were present, bade me for ten successive days to abstain from all pleasures of the table, to eat no meat and drink no wine. All these requirements I observed with scrupulous care. And at last came the day designated by the divine guarantee. The sun was sloping downward and bringing on the evening when lo! from everywhere came crowds of the initiates, flocking around me, and each of them, following the ancient rite, presented me with various gifts. Finally, all the uninitiated having withdrawn, they put on me a new linen robe, and the priest, seizing me by the hand, led me to the very inmost recesses of the holy place.

It may be, my studious reader, that you would very much like to know what was said there and what was done. I would tell you if it were lawful for me to tell, and you would know all if it were lawful for you to hear. But both tongue and ear would be infected as the consequence of such rash curiosity! Yet it may of course be a pious longing that torments you, and so I will torture you no longer. Hear then and believe, for what I tell you is true. I drew near to the confines of death, treading the very threshold of Proserpine. I was borne through all the elements and returned to earth again. At the dead of night, I saw the sun shining brightly. I approached the gods above and the gods below, and worshiped them face to face. See, I have told you things which, though you have heard them, you still must know nothing about. I will therefore relate only as much as may, without committing a sin, be imparted to the understanding of the uninitiate.

24. As soon as it was morning and the solemn rites had been completed, I came forth clothed in the twelve gowns that are worn by the initiate, apparel that is really most holy, but about which no sacred ban forbids me to tell, since at that time there were many who saw me wearing it. For in the very midst of the holy shrine, before the image of the goddess, there was a wooden platform on which I was directed to stand, arrayed in a robe which, although it was only of linen, was so richly embroidered that I was a sight to behold. The precious cape hung from my shoulders down my back even to the ground, and it was adorned, wherever you looked, with the figures of animals in various colors. Here were Indian dragons, there griffins from the Hyperborean regions, winged like birds, but out of another world. This cape the initiates call the Olympian. In my right hand I carried a flaming torch, and my head was decorated with a crown made of white palm leaves, spread out to stand up like rays. After I had been thus adorned like the sun and set up like an image of a god, the curtains were suddenly withdrawn, and the people crowded around to gaze at me.

Thereafter I celebrated this most joyful birthday of my initiation, and there were feasts and gay parties. The third day was likewise celebrated with formal ceremonies, with a solemn breaking of my fast, and the due consummation of my initiation. I remained a few days longer, enjoying the ineffable delight of being near the image of the goddess, to whom I was now pledged by blessings which I could never repay. But at length being admonished by the goddess, I offered up my humble thanks—not indeed in the full measure of my debt to her, but to the best of my poor abilities—and made a tardy preparation for my homeward journey; but it was hard to break the bonds of burning desire that held me back. At last I entered into the presence of the goddess and prostrated myself before her; and after I had for a long time wiped her feet with my face, I spoke, though there were tears in my eyes and my voice was so broken with sobs that my words were swallowed up:

25. "O holy and eternal guardian of the human race, who dost always cherish mortals and bless them, thou carest for the woes of miserable men with a sweet mother's love. Neither day nor night, nor any moment of time, ever passes by without thy blessings, but always on land and sea thou watchest over men; thou drivest away from them the tempests of life and stretchest out over them thy saving right hand, wherewith thou dost unweave even the inextricable skein of the Fates; the tempests of Fortune thou dost assuage and restrainest the baleful motions of the stars. Thee the gods above adore, thee the gods below worship. It is thou that whirlest the sphere of heaven, that givest light to the sun, that governest the universe and tramplest down Tartarus. To thee the stars respond, for thee the seasons return, in thee the gods rejoice, and the elements serve thee. At thy nod the winds blow, the clouds nourish [the earth], the seeds sprout, and the buds swell. Before thy majesty the birds tremble as they flit to and fro in the sky, and the beasts as they roam the mountains, the serpents hiding in the ground, and the monsters swimming in the deep. But my skill is too slight to tell thy praise, my wealth too slender to make thee due offerings of sacrifice. Nor has my voice that rich eloquence to say what I feel would suffice for thy majesty—no, not even had I a thousand mouths, a thousand tongues, and could continue forever with unwearied speech! Therefore the only thing one can do, if one is devout but otherwise a pauper, that I will strive to do. Thy face divine and thy most holy deity—these I will hide away deep within my heart; thine image I shall treasure forever!"

Having thus pleaded with the mighty deity, I embraced Mithras the priest, now my spiritual father, and hanging upon his neck with many a kiss I begged his forgiveness, since I could make no proper return for all the great benefits that he had conferred upon me. **26.** Then, after many words of thanks, long drawn out, I finally set out for home by the shortest route . . . a few days later, led on by the mighty goddess, I reached Rome on the eve of the Ides of December.

133

THE TITLES OF THE
GODDESS ISIS

P. Oxy. XI.1380   Early 2d century C.E.

[I invoke thee, who at Aphrodito]polis [art called] One- . . . ; in the
House of Hephaestus . . . chmeunis; who at . . . ophis art called
Bubastis . . . ; at Letopolis Magna, one . . . ; at Aphroditopolis in the
Prosopite nome, fleet-commanding, many-shaped, Aphrodite; at
Delta, giver of favors; at Calamisis, gentle; at Carene, affectionate; at
Niciu, immortal, giver; at Hierasus . . . athroichis; at Momemphis,
ruler; at Psochemis, bringer to harbor; at Mylon, ruler . . . ; at Her-
mopolis, of beautiful form, sacred; at Naucratis, fatherless, joy, savior,
almighty, most great; at Nithine in the Gynaecopolite nome, Aphro-
dite; at Pephremis, Isis, ruler, Hestia, lady of every country; . . . in
Asia, worshiped at the three ways; at Petra, savior; at Hypsele, most
great; at Rhinocolura, all-seeing; at Dora, friendship; at Stratonos
Pyrgos Hellas, good; at Ascalon, mightiest; at Sinope, many-named;
at Raphia, mistress; at Tripolis, supporter; at Gaza, abundant; at
Delphi, best, fairest; at Bambyce, Atargatis; among the Thracians and
in Delos, many-named; among the Amazons, warlike; among the
Indians, Maia; among the Thessalians, moon; among the Persians,
Latina; among the Magi, Kore, Thapseusis; at Susa, Nania; in Sy-
rophoenicia, goddess; in Samothrace, bull-faced; at Pergamum, mistress; in Pontus, immaculate; in Italy, love of the gods; in Samos,
sacred; at the Hellespont, mystic; at Myndus, divine; in Bithynia,
Helen; in Tenedos, name of the sun; in Caria, Hecate; in the Troad
and at Dindyma . . . , Palentra [?], unapproachable, Isis; at Berytus,
Maia; at Sidon, Astarte; at Ptolemaïs, understanding; at Susa in the
district by the Red Sea, Sarkounis; thou who expoundest by the
fifteen commandments, first ruler of the world; guardian and guide of
seas, and Lady of the mouths and rivers; skilled in writing and calcula-
tion, understanding; who also bringest back the Nile over every
country; the beautiful animal [i.e., cow] of all the gods; the glad face
in Lethe; the leader of the muses; the many-eyed; the comely goddess
in Olympus; ornament of the female sex and affectionate; providing
sweetness in assemblies; the lock of hair [? or bunch of grapes] in
festivals; the prosperity of observers of lucky days; Harpocratis [i.e.,
the darling] of the gods; all-ruling in the processions of the gods,

enmity-hating; true jewel of the wind and diadem of life; by whose command images and animals of all the gods, having . . . of thy name, are worshiped; O Lady Isis, greatest of the gods, first of names, Io Sothis; thou rulest over the mid-air and the immeasurable; thou devisest the weaving of . . . ; it is also thy will that women in health come to anchor with men; all the elders at E . . . ctus sacrifice; all the maidens who . . . at Heracleopolis turn [?] to thee and dedicated the country to thee; thou art seen by those who invoke thee faithfully; from whom . . . in virtue of the 365 combined days; gentle and placable is the favor of thy two ordinances; thou bringest the sun from rising unto setting, and all the gods are glad; at the risings of the stars the people of the country worship thee unceasingly and the other sacred animals in the sanctuary of Osiris; they become joyful when they name thee; the . . . daemons become thy subjects; . . . [the next few lines are very fragmentary] and thou bringest decay on what thou wilt and to the destroyed bringest increase, and thou purifiest all things; every day thou didst appoint for joy; thou . . . having discovered all the . . . of wine providedst it first in the festivals of the gods . . . ; thou becamest the discoverer of all things wet and dry and cold [and hot], of which all things are composed; thou broughtest back alone thy brother, piloting him safely and burying him fittingly; . . . thou didst establish shrines of Isis in all cities for all time; and didst deliver to all men observances and a perfect year; . . . thou didst establish thy son Horus Apollo everywhere, the youthful Lord of the whole world and . . . for all time; thou didst make the power of women equal to that of men; . . . thou hast dominion over winds and thunders and lightnings and snows; thou, the Lady of war and rule, easily destroyest tyrants by trusty counsels; thou madest great Osiris immortal, and deliveredst to every country . . . religious observances; likewise thou madest immortal Horus who showed himself a benefactor . . . and good; thou art the Lady of light and flames. . . .

The Kyme Aretalogy   Recension, 2d/3d century C.E.

[*Demetrius, son of Artemidorus, and Thraseas, the Magnesian from the Maeander, crave the blessing of Isis. The following was copied from the stele which is in Memphis, where it stands before the temple of Hephaestus:*]
I am Isis, the mistress of every land, and I was taught by Hermes, and with Hermes I devised letters, both the sacred [hieroglyphs] and

the demotic, that all things might not be written with the same [letters].

I gave and ordained laws for men, which no one is able to change.
I am eldest daughter of Kronos.
I am wife and sister of King Osiris.
I am she who findeth fruit for men.
I am mother of King Horus.
I am she that riseth in the Dog Star.
I am she that is called goddess by women.
For me was the city of Bubastis built.
I divided the earth from the heaven.
I showed the paths of the stars.
I ordered the course of the sun and the moon.
I devised business in the sea.
I made strong the right.
I brought together woman and man.
I appointed to women to bring their infants to birth in the tenth month.
I ordained that parents should be loved by children.
I laid punishment upon those disposed without natural affection toward their parents.
I made with my brother Osiris an end to the eating of men.
I revealed mysteries unto men.
I taught [men] to honor images of the gods.
I consecrated the precincts of the gods.
I broke down the governments of tyrants.
I made an end to murders.
I compelled women to be loved by men.
I made the right to be stronger than gold and silver.
I ordained that the true should be thought good.
I devised marriage contracts.
I assigned to Greeks and barbarians their languages.
I made the beautiful and the shameful to be distinguished by nature.
I ordained that nothing should be more feared than an oath.
I have delivered the plotter of evil against other men into the hands of the one he plotted against.
I established penalties for those who practice injustice.
I decreed mercy to suppliants.
I protect [or honor] righteous guards.

With me the right prevails.

I am the Queen of rivers and winds and sea.

No one is held in honor without my knowing it.

I am the Queen of war.

I am the Queen of the thunderbolt.

I stir up the sea and I calm it.

I am in the rays of the sun.

I inspect the courses of the sun.

Whatever I please, this too shall come to an end.

With me everything is reasonable.

I set free those in bonds.

I am the Queen of seamanship.

I make the navigable unnavigable when it pleases me.

I created walls of cities.

I am called the Lawgiver [Thesmophoros, a classical epithet of Demeter].

I brought up islands out of the depths into the light.

I am Lord [note masculine form] of rainstorms.

I overcome Fate.

Fate harkens to me.

Hail, O Egypt, that nourished me!

134

ASPECTS OF FEMALE DIVINITY IN
THREE GNOSTIC TEXTS

The Thunder, Perfect Mind   Date uncertain

I was sent forth from [the] power,
    and I have come to those who reflect upon me,
    and I have been found among those who seek after me.
Look upon me, you (pl.) who reflect upon me,
    and you hearers, hear me.
    You who are waiting for me, take me to yourselves.
And do not banish me from your sight.
    And do not make your voice hate me, nor your hearing.
    Do not be ignorant of me anywhere or any time. Be on
      your guard!
    Do not be ignorant of me.
For I am the first and the last.
I am the honored one and the scorned one.
I am the whore and the holy one.
I am the wife and the virgin.
I am ⟨the mother⟩ and the daughter.
I am the members of my mother.
I am the barren one
    and many are her sons.
I am she whose wedding is great,
    and I have not taken a husband.
I am the midwife and she who does not bear.
I am the solace of my labor pains.
I am the bride and the bridegroom,
    and it is my husband who begot me.
I am the mother of my father
   and the sister of my husband,
   and he is my offspring.
I am the slave of him who prepared me.
I am the ruler **14** of my offspring.
    But he is the one who [begot me] before the time
      on a birthday.
    And he is my offspring [in] (due) time,
      and my power is from him.

The Feminine Divine   371

I am the staff of his power in his youth,
   [and] he is the rod of my old age.
   And whatever he wills happens to me.
I am the silence that is incomprehensible
   and the idea whose remembrance is frequent.
I am the voice whose sound is manifold
   and the word whose appearance is multiple.
I am the utterance of my name.

Why, you who hate me, do you love me,
   and you hate those who love me?
You who deny me, confess me,
   and you who confess me, deny me.
You who tell the truth about me, lie about me,
   and you who have lied about me, tell the truth about me.
You who know me, be ignorant of me,
   and those who have not known me, let them know me.

For I am knowledge and ignorance.
I am shame and boldness.
I am shameless; I am ashamed.
I am strength and I am fear.
I am war and peace.
Give heed to me.
I am the one who is disgraced and the great one.

Give heed to my **15** poverty and my wealth.
Do not be arrogant to me when I am cast out upon the
      earth,
   [and] you will find me in [those that] are to come.
And do not look [upon] me on the dung-heap
   nor go and leave me cast out,
   and you will find me in the kingdoms.
And do not look upon me when I am cast out among those
      who
   are disgraced and in the least places,
   nor laugh at me.
And do not cast me out among those who are slain in
      violence.
But I, I am compassionate and I am cruel.

Be on your guard!
Do not hate my obedience
    and do not love my self-control.
In my weakness, do not forsake me,
    and do not be afraid of my power.
For why do you despise my fear
    and curse my pride?
But I am she who exists in all fears
    and strength in trembling.
I am she who is weak,
    and I am well in a pleasant place.
I am senseless and I am wise.

Why have you hated me in your counsels?
For I shall be silent among those who are silent,
    and I shall appear and speak. 16
Why then have you hated me, you Greeks?
    Because I am a barbarian among [the] barbarians?
For I am the wisdom [of the] Greeks
    and the knowledge of [the] barbarians.
I am the judgment of [the] Greeks and of the barbarians.
[I] am the one whose image is great in Egypt
    and the one who has no image among the barbarians.
I am the one who has been hated everywhere
    and who has been loved everywhere.
I am the one whom they call Life,
    and you have called Death.
I am the one whom they call Law,
    and you have called Lawlessness.
I am the one whom you have pursued,
    and I am the one whom you have seized.
I am the one whom you have scattered,
    and you have gathered me together.
I am the one before whom you have been ashamed,
    and you have been shameless to me.
I am she who does not keep festival,
    and I am she whose festivals are many.
I, I am godless,
    and I am the one whose God is great.

I am the one whom you have reflected upon,
  and you have scorned me.
I am unlearned,
  and they learn from me.
I am the one whom you have despised,
  and you reflect upon me.
I am the one whom you have hidden from,
  and you appear to me. **17**
  But whenever you hide yourselves,
    I myself will appear.
  For [whenever] you [appear],
    I myself [will hide] from you.
Those who have [. . .] to it [. . .] senselessly [. . .].

Take me [. . . understanding] from grief,
  and take me to yourselves from understanding [and]
    grief.
And take me to yourselves from places that are ugly and in
    ruin,
  and rob from those which are good even though in
    ugliness.
Out of shame, take me to yourselves shamelessly;
  and out of shamelessness and shame, upbraid my
    members in yourselves.
And come forward to me, you who know me
    and you who know my members,
  and establish the great ones among the small first
    creatures.
Come forward to childhood,
  and do not despise it because it is small and it is little.
And do not turn away greatnesses in some parts from the
    smallnesses,
  for the smallnesses are known from the greatnesses.

Why do you curse me and honor me?
You have wounded and you have had mercy.
Do not separate me from the first **18** ones whom you have
  [known].
[And] do not cast anyone [out nor] turn anyone away

[. . .] turn you away and [. . . know] him not.
[. . . him].
What is mine [. . .].
I know the [first ones] and those after them [know] me.

But I am the mind of [. . .] and the rest of [. . .].
I am the knowledge of my inquiry,
    and the finding of those who seek after me,
    and the command of those who ask of me,
    and the power of the powers in my knowledge
        of the angels, who have been sent at my word,
        and of gods in their seasons by my counsel,
        and of spirits of every man who exists with me,
           and of women who dwell within me.
I am the one who is honored, and who is praised,
    and who is despised scornfully.
I am peace,
    and war has come because of me.
And I am an alien and a citizen.
I am the substance and the one who has no substance.

Those who are without association with me are ignorant of
      me,
    and those who are in my substance are the ones who
      know me.
Those who are close to me have been ignorant of me,
    and those who are far away from me are the ones who
      have
        known me.
On the day when I am close to **19** [you],
    [you] are far away [from me],
[and] on the day when I [am far away] from you,
    [I am close] to you.

[I am . . .] within.
[I am . . .] of the natures.
I am [. . .] of the creation of the [spirits].
[. . .] request of the souls.
[I am] control and the uncontrollable.

I am the union and the dissolution.
I am the abiding and I am the dissolving.
I am the one below,
    and they come up to me.
I am the judgment and the acquittal.
I, I am sinless,
    and the root of sin derives from me.
I am lust in (outward) appearance,
    and interior self-control exists within me.
I am the hearing which is attainable to everyone
    and the speech which cannot be grasped.
I am a mute who does not speak,
    and great is my multitude of words.

Hear me in gentleness, and learn of me in roughness.
I am she who cries out,
    and I am cast forth upon the face of the earth.
I prepare the bread and my mind within.
I am the knowledge of my name.
I am the one who cries out,
    and I listen. **20**
I appear and [. . .] walk in [. . .] seal of my [. . .].
I am [. . .] the defense [. . .].
I am the one who is called Truth,
    and iniquity [. . .].

You honor me [. . .] and you whisper against [me].
[. . .] victorious over them.
Judge them before they give judgment against you,
    because the judge and partiality exist in you.
If you are condemned by this one, who will acquit you?
    Or if you are acquitted by him, who will be able to
        detain you?
For what is inside of you is what is outside of you,
    and the one who fashions you on the outside
        is the one who shaped the inside of you.
    And what you see outside of you,
        you see inside of you;
        it is visible and it is your garment.

Hear me, you hearers,
  and learn of my words, you who know me.
I am the hearing that is attainable to everything;
  I am the speech that cannot be grasped.
I am the name of the sound
  and the sound of the name.
I am the sign of the letter
  and the designation of the division.
And I [. . .].
[. . .] **21** light [. . .].
[. . .] hearers [. . .] to you
[. . .] the great power.
And [. . .] will not move the name.
[. . .] to the one who created me.
  And I will speak his name.

Look then at his words
  and all the writings which have been completed.
Give heed then, you hearers
  and you also, the angels and those who have been sent,
  and you spirits who have arisen from the dead.
For I am the one who alone exists,
  and I have no one who will judge me.

For many are the pleasant forms which exist in
  numerous sins,
  and incontinencies,
  and disgraceful passions,
  and fleeting pleasures,
    which (men) embrace until they become sober
    and go up to their resting-place.
And they will find me there,
  and they will live,
  and they will not die again.

The Thought of Norea   3d century C.E.?

Father of the All, [Ennoia] of the Light, Nous [dwelling] in the
heights above the (regions) below, Light dwelling [in the] heights,

Voice of Truth, upright Nous, untouchable Logos, and [ineffable] Voice, [incomprehensible] Father!

It is Norea who [cries out] to them. They [heard], (and) they received her into her place forever. They gave it to her in the Father of Nous, Adamas, as well as the voice of the Holy Ones, **28** in order that she might rest in the ineffable Epinoia, in order that ⟨she⟩ might inherit the first mind which ⟨she⟩ had received, and that ⟨she⟩ might rest in the divine Autogenes, and that she (too) might generate herself, just as he himself [has] inherited the [living] Logos, and that she might be joined to all of the Imperishable Ones, and [speak] with the mind of the Father.

And [again], speaking with words of [Life], ⟨she⟩ remained in the [presence] of the Exalted One, [possessing that] which she had received before the world came into being. [She has] the [great mind] of the Invisible One, [and she gives] glory to ⟨her⟩ Father, [and she] dwells within those who [. . .] within the Pleroma, [and] she beholds the Pleroma.

There will be days when she will [behold] the Pleroma, and she will not be in deficiency, for she has the four holy helpers who intercede on her behalf with the Father of the All, Adamas, the one **29** who is within all of the Adams that possess the thought of Norea, who speaks concerning the two names which create a single name.

The Hypostasis of the Archons   3d century C.E.?

On account of the reality (hypostasis) of the Authorities, (inspired) by the Spirit of the Father of Truth, the great apostle—referring to the "authorities of the darkness" (Colossians 1:13)—told us that "our contest is not against flesh and [blood]; rather, the authorities of the universe and the spirits of wickedness" (Ephesians 6:12). [I have] sent (you) this because you (sing.) inquire about the reality [of the] Authorities.

Their chief is blind; [because of his] Power and his ignorance [and his] arrogance he said, with his [Power], "It is I who am God; there is none [apart from me]."

When he said this, he sinned against [the Entirety]. And this speech got up **87** to Incorruptibility; then there was a voice that came forth from Incorruptibility, saying, "You are mistaken, Samael"—which is, "god of the blind."

His thoughts became blind. And, having expelled his Power—that is, the blasphemy he had spoken—he pursued it down to Chaos and the Abyss, his mother, at the instigation of Pistis Sophia (Faith-Wisdom). And she established each of his offspring in conformity with its power—after the pattern of the realms that are above, for by starting from the invisible world the visible world was invented.

As Incorruptibility looked down into the region of the Waters, her Image appeared in the Waters; and the Authorities of the Darkness became enamored of her. But they could not lay hold of that Image, which had appeared to them in the Waters, because of their weakness—since beings that merely possess a soul cannot lay hold of those that possess a Spirit—; for they were from Below, while it was from Above.

This is the reason why "Incorruptibility looked down into the region (etc.)": so that, by the Father's will, she might bring the Entirety into union with the Light. The Rulers (Archons) laid plans and said, "Come, let us create a man that will be soil from the earth." They modelled their creature as one wholly of the earth.

Now the Rulers . . . body . . . they have . . . female . . . is . . . face(s) . . . are . . . bestial. . . . They took some [soil] from the earth and modelled their [Man], after their body and [after the Image] of God that had appeared [to them] in the Waters.

They said, "[Come, let] us lay hold of it by means of the form that we have modelled, [so that] it may see its male counterpart [. . .], **88** and we may seize it with the form that we have modelled"—not understanding the force of God, because of their powerlessness. And he breathed into his face; and the Man came to have a soul (and remained) upon the ground many days. But they could not make him arise because of their powerlessness. Like storm winds they persisted (in blowing), that they might try to capture that image, which had appeared to them in the Waters. And they did not know the identity of its power.

Now all these (events) came to pass by the will of the Father of the Entirety. Afterwards, the Spirit saw the soul-endowed Man upon the ground. And the Spirit came forth from the Adamantine Land; it descended and came to dwell within him, and that Man became a living soul.

It called his name Adam since he was found moving upon the ground. A voice came forth from Incorruptibility for the assistance of Adam; and the Rulers gathered together all the animals of the earth and all the birds of heaven and brought them in to Adam to see what

Adam would call them, that he might give a name to each of the birds and all the beasts.

They took Adam [and] put him in the Garden, that he might cultivate [it] and keep watch over it. And the Rulers issued a command to him, saying, "From [every] tree in the Garden shall you (sing.) eat; yet—[from] the tree of recognizing good and evil do not eat, nor [touch] it; for the day you (pl.) eat [from] it, with death you (pl.) are going to die."

They [. . .] this. They do not understand what [they have said] to him; rather, by the Father's will, **89** they said this in such a way that he might (in fact) eat, and that Adam might ⟨not⟩ regard them as would a man of an exclusively material nature.

The Rulers took counsel with one another and said, "Come, let us cause a deep sleep to fall upon Adam." And he slept.—Now the deep sleep that they "caused to fall upon him, and he slept" is Ignorance.—They opened his side like a living Woman. And they built up his side with some flesh in place of her, and Adam came to be endowed only with soul.

And the spirit-endowed Woman came to him and spoke with him, saying "Arise, Adam." And when he saw her, he said, "It is you who have given me life; you will be called 'Mother of the Living.'—For it is she who is my mother. It is she who is the Physician, and the Woman, and She Who Has Given Birth."

Then the Authorities came up to their Adam. And when they saw his female counterpart speaking with him, they became agitated with great agitation; and they became enamored of her. They said to one another, "Come, let us sow our seed in her," and they pursued her. And she laughed at them for their witlessness and their blindness; and in their clutches, she became a tree, and left before them her shadowy reflection resembling herself; and they defiled [it] foully.—And they defiled the form that she had stamped in her likeness, so that by the form they had modelled, together with [their] (own) image, they made themselves liable to condemnation.

Then the Female Spiritual Principle came [in] the Snake, the Instructor; and it taught [them], saying, "What did he [say to] you (pl.)? Was it, 'From every tree in the Garden shall you (sing.) eat; yet—from [the tree] **90** of recognizing evil and good do not eat'?"

The carnal Woman said, "Not only did he say 'Do not eat,' but even 'Do not touch it; for the day you (pl.) eat from it, with death you (pl.) are going to die.'"

And the Snake, the Instructor, said, "With death you (pl.) shall not die; for it was out of jealousy that he said this to you (pl.). Rather your (pl.) eyes shall open and you (pl.) shall come to be like gods, recognizing evil and good." And the Female Instructing Principle was taken away from the Snake, and she left it behind merely a thing of the earth.

And the carnal Woman took from the tree and ate; and she gave to her husband as well as herself; and these beings that possessed only a soul, ate. And their imperfection became apparent in their lack of Acquaintance; and they recognized that they were naked of the Spiritual Element, and took fig leaves and bound them upon their loins.

Then the chief Ruler came; and he said, "Adam! Where are you?" —for he did not understand what had happened.

And Adam said, "I heard your voice and was afraid because I was naked; and I hid."

The Ruler said, "Why did you (sing.) hide, unless it is because you (sing.) have eaten from the tree from which alone I commanded you (sing.) not to eat? And you (sing.) have eaten!"

Adam said, "The Woman that you gave me, [she gave] to me and I ate." And the arrogant Ruler cursed the Woman.

The Woman said, "It was the Snake that led me astray and I ate." [They turned] to the Snake and cursed its shadowy reflection, [. . .] powerless, not comprehending [that] it was a form they themselves had modelled. From that day, **91** the Snake came to be under the curse of the Authorities; until the All-powerful Man was to come that curse fell upon the Snake.

They turned to their Adam and took him and expelled him from the Garden along with his wife; for they have no blessing, since they too are beneath the curse.

Moreover they threw Mankind into great distraction and into a life of toil so that their Mankind might be occupied by worldly affairs, and might not have the opportunity of being devoted to the Holy Spirit.

Now afterwards, she bore Cain, their son; and Cain cultivated the land. Thereupon he knew his wife; again becoming pregnant, she bore Abel; and Abel was a herdsman of sheep. Now Cain brought in from the crops of his field, but Abel brought in an offering (from) among his lambs. God looked upon the votive offerings of Abel; but he did not accept the votive offerings of Cain. And carnal Cain pursued Abel his brother.

And God said to Cain, "Where is Abel your brother?"

He answered, saying, "Am I, then, my brother's keeper?"

God said to Cain, "Listen! The voice of your brother's blood is crying up to me! You have sinned with your mouth. It will return to you: anyone who kills Cain will let loose seven vengeances, and you will exist groaning and trembling upon the earth."

And Adam [knew] his female counterpart Eve, and she became pregnant, and bore [Seth] to Adam. And she said, "I have borne [another] man through God, in place [of Abel]."

Again Eve became pregnant, and she bore [Norea]. And she said, "He has begotten on [me a] virgin **92** as an assistance [for] many generations of mankind." She is the virgin whom the Forces did not defile.

Then Mankind began to multiply and improve.

The Rulers took counsel with one another and said, "Come, let us cause a deluge with our hands and obliterate all flesh, from man to beast."

But when the Ruler of the Forces came to know of their decision, he said to Noah, "Make yourself an ark from some wood that does not rot and hide in it—you and your children and the beasts and the birds of heaven from small to large—and set it upon Mount Sir."

Then Orea came to him wanting to board the ark. And when he would not let her, she blew upon the ark and caused it to be consumed by fire. Again he made the ark, for a second time.

The Rulers went to meet her intending to lead her astray. Their supreme chief said to her, "Your mother Eve came to us."

But Norea turned to them and said to them, "It is you who are the Rulers of the Darkness; you are accursed. And you did not know my mother; instead it was your female counterpart that you knew. For I am not your descendant; rather it is from the World Above that I am come."

The arrogant Ruler turned, with all his might, [and] his countenance came to be like (a) black [. . .]; he said to her presumptuously, "You must render service to us, [as did] also your mother Eve; for . . . [. . .]."

But Norea turned, with the might of [. . .]; and in a loud voice [she] cried out [up to] the Holy One, the God of the Entirety, **93** "Rescue me from the Rulers of Unrighteousness and save me from their clutches—forthwith!"

The (Great) Angel came down from the heavens and said to her, "Why are you crying up to God? Why do you act so boldly towards the Holy Spirit?"

Norea said, "Who are you?"

The Rulers of Unrighteousness had withdrawn from her. He said, "It is I who am Eleleth, Sagacity, the Great Angel, who stands in the presence of the Holy Spirit. I have been sent to speak with you and save you from the grasp of the Lawless. And I shall teach you about your Root."

—Now as for that angel, I cannot speak of his power: his appearance is like fine gold and his raiment is like snow. No, truly, my mouth cannot bear to speak of his power and the appearance of his face!

Eleleth, the Great Angel, spoke to me. "It is I," he said, "who am Understanding. I am one of the Four Light-givers, who stand in the presence of the Great Invisible Spirit. Do you think these Rulers have any power over you (sing.)? None of them can prevail against the Root of Truth; for on its account he appeared in the final ages (text corrupt); and these Authorities will be restrained. And these Authorities cannot defile you and that generation; for your (pl.) abode is in Incorruptibility, where the Virgin Spirit dwells, who is superior to the Authorities of Chaos and to their universe."

But I said, "Sir, teach me about the [faculty of] these Authorities—[how] did they come into being, and by what kind of genesis, [and] of 94 what material, and who created them and their force?"

And the Great Angel Eleleth, Understanding, spoke to me: "Within limitless realms dwells Incorruptibility. Sophia, who is called Pistis, wanted to create something, alone without her consort; and her product was a celestial thing.

"A veil exists between the World Above and the realms that are below; and Shadow came into being beneath the veil; and that Shadow became Matter; and that Shadow was projected apart. And what she had created became a product in the Matter, like an aborted fetus. And it assumed a plastic form molded out of Shadow, and became an arrogant beast resembling a lion." It was androgynous, as I have already said, because it was from Matter that it derived.

"Opening his eyes he saw a vast quantity of Matter without limit; and he became arrogant, saying, 'It is I who am God, and there is none other apart from me.'

"When he said this, he sinned against the Entirety. And a voice came forth from above the realm of absolute power, saying, 'You are mistaken, Samael'—which is, 'god of the blind.'

"And he said, 'If any other thing exists before me, let it become visible to me!' And immediately Sophia stretched forth her finger and introduced Light into Matter; and she pursued it down to the region of Chaos. And she returned up [to] her light; once again Darkness [. . .] Matter.

"This Ruler, by being androgynous, made himself a vast realm, **95** an extent without limit. And he contemplated creating offspring for himself, and created for himself seven offspring, androgynous just like their parent.

"And he said to his offspring, 'It is I who am the god of the Entirety.'

"And Zoe (Life), the daughter of Pistis Sophia, cried out and said to him, 'You are mistaken, Sakla!'—for which the alternate name is Yaltabaoth. She breathed into his face, and her breath became a fiery angel for her; and that angel bound Yaldabaoth and cast him down into Tartaros below the Abyss.

"Now when his offspring Sabaoth saw the force of that angel, he repented and condemned his father and his mother Matter.

"He loathed her, but he sang songs of praise up to Sophia and her daughter Zoe. And Sophia and Zoe caught him up and gave him charge of the seventh heaven, below the veil between Above and Below. And he is called 'God of the Forces, Sabaoth,' since he is up above the Forces of Chaos, for Sophia established him.

"Now when these (events) had come to pass, he made himself a huge four-faced chariot of cherubim, and infinitely many angels to act as ministers, and also harps and lyres.

"And Sophia took her daughter Zoe and had her sit upon his right to teach him about the things that exist in the Eighth (Heaven); and the Angel [of] Wrath she placed upon his left. [Since] that day, [his right] has been called **96** Life; and the left has come to represent the unrighteousness of the realm of absolute power above. It was before your (sing.) time that they came into being (text corrupt?).

"Now when Yaldabaoth saw him in this great splendor and at this height, he envied him; and the envy became an androgynous product; and this was the origin of Envy. And Envy engendered Death; and Death engendered his offspring and gave each of them charge of its heaven; and all the heavens of Chaos became full of their multitudes.

"But it was by the will of the Father of the Entirety that they all came into being—after the pattern of all the things Above—so that the sum of Chaos might be attained.

"There, I have taught you (sing.) about the pattern of the Rulers; and the Matter in which it was expressed; and their parent; and their universe."

But I said, "Sir, am I also from their Matter?"

—"You, together with your offspring, are from the Primeval Father; from Above, out of the imperishable Light, their souls are come. Thus the Authorities cannot approach them because of the Spirit of Truth present within them; and all who have become acquainted with this Way exist deathless in the midst of dying Mankind. Still that Sown Element will not become known now.

"Instead, after three generations it will come to be known, and free them from the bondage of the Authorities' error."

Then I said, "Sir, how much longer?"

He said to me, "Until the moment when the True Man, within a modelled form, reveals (?) the existence of [the Spirit of] Truth, which the Father has sent. 97

"Then he will teach them about every thing: And he will anoint them with the unction of Life eternal, given him from the undominated generation.

"Then they will be freed of blind thought: And they will trample under foot Death, which is of the Authorities: And they will ascend into the limitless Light, where this Sown Element belongs.

"Then the Authorities will relinquish their ages: And their angels will weep over their destruction: And their demons will lament their death.

"Then all the Children of the Light will be truly acquainted with the Truth and their Root, and the Father of the Entirety and the Holy Spirit: They will all say with a single voice, 'The Father's truth is just, and the Son presides over the Entirety': And from everyone unto the ages of ages, 'Holy—Holy—Holy! Amen!'"

The Reality
of the Rulers

135

THE FALL AND DELIVERANCE OF THE SOUL, WHICH IS FEMININE

The Exegesis on the Soul   3d century C.E.?

Wise men of old gave the soul a feminine name. Indeed she is female in her nature as well. She even has her womb.

As long as she was alone with the Father, she was virgin and in form androgynous. But when she fell down into a body and came to this life, then she fell into the hands of many robbers. And the wanton creatures passed her from one to another and [. . .] her. Some made use of her [by force], while others did so by seducing her with a gift. In short, they defiled her, and she [. . .] **128** virginity.

And in her body she prostituted herself and gave herself to one and all, considering each one she was about to embrace to be her husband. When she had given herself to wanton, unfaithful adulterers, so that they might make use of her, then she sighed deeply and repented. But even when she turns her face from those adulterers, she runs to others and they compel her to live with them and render service to them upon their bed, as if they were her masters. Out of shame she no longer dares to leave them, whereas they deceive her for a long time, pretending to be faithful, true husbands, as if they greatly respected her. And after all this they abandon her and go.

She then becomes a poor desolate widow, without help; not even a measure of food was left her from the time of her affliction. For from them she gained nothing except the defilements they gave her while they had sexual intercourse with her. And her offspring by the adulterers are dumb, blind, and sickly. They are feeble-minded.

But when the Father who is above visits her and looks down upon her and sees her sighing—with her sufferings and disgrace—and repenting of the prostitution in which she engaged, and when she begins to call upon [his name] so that he might help her, [. . .] all her heart, saying, "Save me, my Father, for behold I will render an account [to thee, for I] abandoned my house and **129** fled from my maiden's quarters. Restore me to thyself again." When he sees her in such a state, then he will count her worthy of his mercy upon her, for many are the afflictions that have come upon her because she abandoned her house.

Now concerning the prostitution of the soul the Holy Spirit prophesies in many places. For he said in the prophet Jeremiah (3:1–4),

If the husband divorces his wife and she goes and takes another man, can she return to him after that? Has not that woman utterly defiled herself? "And you (sing.) prostituted yourself to many shepherds and you returned to me!" said the Lord. "Take an honest look and see where you prostituted yourself. Were you not sitting in the streets defiling the land with your acts of prostitution and your vices? And you took many shepherds for a stumbling block for yourself. You became shameless with everyone. You did not call on me as kinsman or as father or author of your virginity."

Again it is written in the prophet Hosea (2:2–7),

Come, go to law with your (pl.) mother, for she is not to be a wife to me nor I a husband to her. I shall remove her prostitution from my presence, and I shall remove her adultery from between her breasts. I shall make her naked as on the day she was born, and I [shall] make her desolate like a land without [water], and I shall make her [longingly] childless. [I] shall show her children no pity, for they are children of prostitution, since their mother prostituted herself and [put her children to shame]. **130** For she said, "I shall prostitute myself to my lovers. It was they who gave me my bread and my water and my garments and my clothes and my wine and my oil and everything I needed." Therefore behold I shall shut them up so that she shall not be able to run after her adulterers. And when she seeks them and does not find them, she will say, "I shall return to my former husband, for in those days I was better off than now."

Again he said in Ezekiel (16:23–26),

It came to pass after much depravity, said the Lord, you built yourself a brothel and you made yourself a beautiful place in the streets. And you built yourself brothels on every lane, and you wasted your beauty, and you spread your legs in every alley, and you multiplied your acts of prostitution. You prostituted yourself to the sons of Egypt, those who are your neighbors, men great of flesh.

But what does "the sons of Egypt, men great of flesh" mean if not the domain of the flesh and the perceptible realm and the affairs of the earth, by which the soul has become defiled here, receiving bread from them, as well as wine, oil, clothing, and the other external nonsense surrounding the body—the things she thinks she needs.

But as to this prostitution the apostles of the Savior commanded (cf. Acts 15:20, 29; 21:25; 1 Thessalonians 4:3; 1 Corinthians 6:18; 2 Corinthians 7:1),

Guard yourselves against it, purify yourselves from it,

speaking not just of the prostitution of the body but especially of that of the soul. For this [reason] the apostles [write to the churches] of God, that such [prostitution] might not occur among [us].

Yet the greatest [struggle] has to do with the prostitution **131** of the soul. From it arises the prostitution of the body as well. Therefore Paul, writing to the Corinthians (1 Corinthians 5:9), said,

> I wrote you in the letter, "Do not associate with prostitutes," not at all (meaning) the prostitutes of this world or the greedy or the thieves or the idolators, since then you would have to go out from the world.

—here he is speaking spiritually—

> For our struggle is not against flesh and blood—as he said (Ephesians 6:12)—but against the world rulers of this darkness and the spirits of wickedness.

As long as the soul keeps running about everywhere copulating with whomever she meets and defiling herself, she exists suffering her just deserts. But when she perceives the straits she is in and weeps before the Father and repents, then the Father will have mercy on her and he will make her womb turn from the external domain and will turn it again inward, so that the soul will regain her proper character. For it is not so with a woman. For the womb of the body is inside the body like the other internal organs, but the womb of the soul is around the outside like the male genitalia, which are external.

So when the womb of the soul, by the will of the Father, turns itself inward, it is baptized and is immediately cleansed of the external pollution which was pressed upon it, just as [garments, when] dirty, are put into the [water and] turned about until their dirt is removed and they become clean. And so the cleansing of the soul is to regain the [newness] **132** of her former nature and to turn herself back again. That is her baptism.

Then she will begin to rage at herself like a woman in labor, who writhes and rages in the hour of delivery. But since she is female, by herself she is powerless to beget a child. From heaven the Father sent her her man, who is her brother, the first-born. Then the bridegroom came down to the bride. She gave up her former prostitution and cleansed herself of the pollutions of the adulterers, and she was renewed so as to be a bride. She cleansed herself in the bridal chamber; she filled it with perfume; she sat in it waiting for the true bridegroom. No longer does she run about the market place, copulating with whomever she desires, but she continued to wait for him— (saying) "When will he come?"—and to fear him, for she did not know what he looked like: she no longer remembers since the time she fell from her Father's house. But by the will of the Father ⟨ . . . ⟩. And she dreamed of him like a woman in love with a man.

But then the bridegroom, according to the Father's will, came down to her into the bridal chamber, which was prepared. And he decorated the bridal chamber.

For since that marriage is not like the carnal marriage, those who are to have intercourse with one another will be satisfied with that intercourse. And as if it were a burden they leave behind them the annoyance of physical desire and they do not [separate from] each other, but this marriage [. . .], but [once] they unite [with one another], they become a single life. **133** Wherefore the prophet said (Genesis 2:24) concerning the first man and the first woman,

> They will become a single flesh.

For they were originally joined to one another when they were with the Father before the woman led astray the man, who is her brother. This marriage has brought them back together again and the soul has been joined to her true love, her real master, as it is written (cf. Genesis 3:16; 1 Corinthians 11:1, Ephesians 5:23),

> For the master of the woman is her husband.

Then gradually she recognized him, and she rejoiced once more, weeping before him as she remembered the disgrace of her former widowhood. And she adorned herself still more so that he might be pleased to stay with her.

And the prophet said in the Psalms (45:10–11),

> Hear, my daughter, and see and incline your ear and forget your people and your father's house, for the king has desired your beauty, for he is your lord.

For he requires her to turn her face from her people and the multitude of her adulterers, in whose midst she once was, to devote herself only to her king, her real lord, and to forget the house of the earthly father, with whom things went badly for her, but to remember her Father who is in the heavens. Thus also it was said (Genesis 12:1) to Abraham,

Come out from your country and your kinsfolk and from your father's house.

Thus when the soul [had adorned] herself again in her beauty [. . .] enjoyed her beloved, and [he also] loved her. And when she had intercourse with him, she got **134** from him the seed that is the life-giving Spirit, so that by him she bears good children and rears them. For this is the great, perfect marvel of birth. And so this marriage is made perfect by the will of the Father.

Now it is fitting that the soul regenerate herself and become again as she formerly was. The soul then moves of her own accord. And she received the divine nature from the Father for her rejuvenation, so that she might be restored to the place where originally she had been. This is the resurrection that is from the dead. This is the ransom from captivity. This is the upward journey of ascent to heaven. This is the way of ascent to the Father. Therefore the prophet said (Psalm 103: 1–5),

> Praise the Lord, O my soul, and, all that is within me, (praise) his holy name. My soul, praise God, who forgave all your sins, who healed all your sicknesses, who ransomed your life from death, who crowned you with mercy, who satisfies your longing with good things. Your youth will be renewed like an eagle's.

Then when she becomes young again she will ascend, praising the Father and her brother, by whom she was rescued. Thus it is by being born again that the soul will be saved. And this is due not to rote phrases or to professional skills or to book learning. Rather it [is] the grace of the [. . . , it is] the gift of the [. . .]. For such is this heavenly thing. Therefore the Savior cries out (John 6:44), **135**

> No one can come to me unless my Father draws him and brings him to me; and I myself will raise him up on the last day.

It is therefore fitting to pray to the Father and to call on him with all our soul—not externally with the lips but with the spirit, which is inward, which came forth from the depth—sighing; repenting for the life we lived; confessing our sins; perceiving the empty deception we were in, and the empty zeal; weeping over how we were in darkness and in the wave; mourning for ourselves, that he might have pity on us; hating ourselves for how we are now. Again the Savior said (cf. Matthew 5:4, 6; Luke 6:21),

> Blessed are those who mourn, for it is they who will be pitied; blessed, those who are hungry, for it is they who will be filled.

Again he said (cf. Luke 14:26),

> If one does not hate his soul he cannot follow me.

For the beginning of salvation is repentance. Therefore (cf. Acts 13:24),

> Before Christ's appearance came John, preaching the baptism of repentance.

And repentance takes place in distress and grief. But the Father is good and loves humanity, and he hears the soul that calls upon him and sends it the light of salvation. Therefore he said through the Spirit to the prophet (cf. 1 Clement 8:3),

> Say to the children of my people, "[If your] sins extend [from earth to] heaven, and if they become [red] like scarlet and blacker than [sackcloth and if] **136** you return to me with all your soul and say to me, 'My Father,' I will heed you as a holy people."

Again another place (Isaiah 30:15),

> Thus says the Lord, the Holy One of Israel: "If you (sing.) return and sigh, then you will be saved and will know where you were when you trusted in what is empty."

Again he said in another place (Isaiah 30:19–20),

> Jerusalem wept much, saying, "Have pity on me." He will have pity on the sound of your (sing.) weeping. And when he saw he heeded you. And the Lord will give you (pl.) bread of affliction and water of oppression. From now on those who deceive will not approach you (sing.) again. Your eyes will see those who are deceiving you.

Therefore it is fitting to pray to God night and day, spreading out our hands towards him as do people sailing in the middle of the sea: they pray to God with all their heart without hypocrisy. For those who pray hypocritically deceive only themselves. Indeed it is in order that he might know who is worthy of salvation that God examines the inward parts and searches the bottom of the heart. For no one is worthy of salvation who still loves the place of deception. Therefore it is written in the poet (Homer, *Odyssey* I, 48–59),

> Odysseus sat on the island weeping and grieving and turning his face from the words of Calypso and from her tricks, longing to see his village and smoke coming forth from it. And had he not [received] help from heaven, [he would] not [have been able to] return to his village.

Again [Helen] ⟨ . . . ⟩ saying (*Odyssey* IV, 260–261),

[My heart] turned itself from me. **137** It is to my house that I want to return.

For she sighed, saying (*Odyssey* IV, 261–264),

> It is Aphrodite who deceived me and brought me out of my village. My only daughter I left behind me, and my good, understanding, handsome husband.

For when the soul leaves her perfect husband because of the treachery of Aphrodite, who exists here in the act of begetting, then she will suffer harm. But if she sighs and repents, she will be restored to her house.

Certainly Israel would not have been visited in the first place, to be brought out of the land of Egypt, out of the house of bondage, if it had not sighed to God and wept for the oppression of its labors. Again it is written in the Psalms (6:6–9),

> I was greatly troubled in my groaning. I will bathe my bed and my cover each night with my tears. I have become old in the midst of all my enemies. Depart from me, all you who work at lawlessness, for behold the Lord has heard the cry of my weeping and the Lord has heard my prayer.

If we repent, truly God will heed us, he who is long-suffering and abundantly merciful, to whom is the glory for ever and ever. Amen.

The Expository Treatise on the Soul

About the Authors
and Sources

This section is intended to equip the reader to delve further into the primary sources themselves. It also introduces authors and sources to those not previously acquainted with them. For the abbreviations used in this section, see the list at the beginning of the book.

Where we know the author of a particular text, I have included some basic biographic information, together with a brief indication of the significance of that author for the study of women's religion in the Greco-Roman world. In many cases, however, we do not know the identity of the text's author, either because the text has come down to us anonymously (e.g., *The Conversion and Marriage of Aseneth*) or because modern scholarship for whatever reasons considers the ascribed authorship inaccurate or pseudepigraphic (e.g., *The Odes of Solomon*). Whereas materials representing the full range of Greco-Roman religions have been transmitted anonymously, pseudepigraphic works tend to be Jewish and Christian, although not exclusively. With sources whose authorship is unknown to us, or where we know nothing about the author beyond the information available in the documents themselves, I have provided brief pertinent background.

In all cases, I have included references to editions of the materials in their original languages and to English translations. Wherever possible I have cited editions, translations, and commentaries accessible to students as well as scholars. Given the nature of these sources, though, that has not always been possible, especially in the case of inscriptions and papyri.

In the bibliography accompanying most entries, I have limited myself to studies that consider the implications of the sources for the study of women, especially women's religion. The bibliography on women's studies in antiquity and women's studies in religion has been growing rapidly. My bibliographic essay "Women in the Religions of the Greco-Roman World" (*Religious Studies Review* 9 [1983]: 127–39) contains some additional references not included here, but many of the references below update that bibliography. Especially valuable is "Selected Bibliography on Women in Classical Antiquity," by Sarah B. Pomeroy (with Ross S. Kraemer and Natalie Kampen), in *Women in the Ancient World: The Arethusa Papers*, ed. J. Peradotto and J. P. Sullivan (Albany: State Univ. of New York Press, 1984), 317–72. It too is already in need of updating. Other sourcebooks (see footnotes to the Introduction) also contain useful bibliography. Finally, three recent works on antiquity devote considerable attention to women and contain many useful primary and secondary references: Robin Lane Fox, *Pagans and Christians* (New York: Alfred A. Knopf, 1987), Paul Veyne, ed., *A History of Private Life: From Pagan Rome to Byzantium* (Cambridge: Harvard Univ. Press, 1987), and Aline Rousselle, *Porneia: On Desire and the Body in Antiquity* (Oxford and New York: Basil Blackwell, 1988).

Many of the sources included here have been the subject of extensive general research. Basic bibliographic references may be found in the reference works listed below, as well as through the usual bibliographic sources such as *L'Annee Philologique; Religion Index One: Periodicals; Religion Index Two: Multi-Author Works; New Testament Abstracts; Old Testament Abstracts; Bibliographica Patristica; Elenchus Bibliographicus Biblica;* and so forth.

NOTE: Asterisks identify the translations used in this volume. Except as noted, sources without an asterisk have been translated by the editor. All translations are used by permission or in accordance with the laws of fair use and are acknowledged at the beginning of this volume.

GENERAL REFERENCES

Altaner, Berthold. *Patrology*. Trans. Hilda C. Graef. New York: Herder & Herder, 1958.

Cross, F. L., and E. A. Livingstone, eds. *The Oxford Dictionary of the Christian Church*. 2d ed. London/New York/Toronto: Oxford Univ. Press, 1974.

Geerard, M. *Clavis Patrum Graecorum*. 5 vols. Brussels: Turnhout, 1974–87.

Goodspeed, Edgar. *A History of Early Christian Literature*. Rev. and enl. Robert M. Grant. Chicago: Univ. of Chicago Press, 1966.

Gordon, A. *Illustrated Introduction to Latin Epigraphy*. Berkeley/Los Angeles/London: Univ. of California Press, 1983.

Hadas, M. *A History of Greek Literature*. New York: Columbia Univ. Press, 1950.

———. *A History of Latin Literature*. New York: Columbia Univ. Press, 1952.

Hammond, N. G. L., and H. H. Scullard, eds. *The Oxford Classical Dictionary*. 2d ed. Oxford: Clarendon Press, 1970.

Nickelsburg, G. W. E. *Jewish Literature Between the Bible and the Mishnah*. Philadelphia: Fortress Press, 1981.

Quasten, Johannes. *Patrology*. 4 vols. Westminster, Md: Christian Classics, 1951–86.

Reynolds, L. D. *Texts and Transmission: A Survey of Latin Classics*. Oxford: Clarendon Press, 1983.

Stern, M. *Greek and Latin Authors on Jews and Judaism*. 3 vols. Jerusalem: Israel Acad. of Sciences and Humanities, 1976–84.

Stone, Michael E., ed. *Jewish Writings of the Second Temple Period*. Compendia Rerum Iudaicarum ad Novum Testamentum 2/2. Philadelphia: Fortress Press; Assen, Neth.: Van Gorcum, 1984.

Turner, E. G. *Greek Papyri: An Introduction*. 2d ed. Princeton: Princeton Univ. Press, 1980.

Wace, H., and W. Smith. *Dictionary of Christian Biography*. 4 vols. London, 1877–87. Reprint. New York: AMS Press, 1968.

Woodhead, A. *The Study of Greek Inscriptions*. 2d ed. Cambridge: Cambridge Univ. Press, 1981.

SOURCES WITH
KNOWN AUTHORSHIP

Apuleius. 2d century C.E. Born in Madaurus, North Africa, in 123 C.E., Apuleius is probably best known for his Latin *Metamorphoses,* also known as *The Golden Ass,* which recounts the adventures of one unfortunate Lucius who turns into an ass through the misuse of magic and is ultimately restored to his proper form by the goddess Isis. Apuleius's depiction of Lucius's initiations into the worship of the Egyptian goddess and her consort Osiris may be autobiographical. Most of Apuleius's other works are not extant.

Metamorphoses

   TEXT: Budé (D. S. Robertson, 1940–45); Teubner (R. Helm, 1931).

   TRANSLATION: J. Gwen Griffiths, *The Isis-Book (Metamorphoses XI): Apuleius of Madauros,* EPRO 39 (1975); LCL (W. Adlington and S. Gaselee, 1915); *F. C. Grant, *Hellenistic Religions: The Age of Syncretism* (New York: Liberal Arts Press, 1953).

   BIBLIOGRAPHY: F. Dunand, *Le culte d'Isis dans le bassin oriental de la Mediterranee,* 3 vols., EPRO 26 (1973); S. Heyob, *The Cult of Isis among Women,* EPRO 51 (1975).

Demosthenes. 384–322 B.C.E. Thought by many to be the greatest of the Athenian orators, Demosthenes is the author of *On the Crown,* which is considered by some to be his greatest oration. The oration was written as a defense against the accusations of his longstanding opponent Aeschines concerning Demosthenes' actions during the wars with Philip of Macedon. Although most of Demosthenes' orations similarly address the military-political situation, he did argue some private cases. One oration attributed to him, *Against Neaera,* has received considerable discussion by feminist classicists. As is often the case with passages that shed light on women, the excerpt from *On the Crown* is only incidentally concerned with women: Demosthenes' intent is to impugn Aeschines by demonstrating his participation in his mother's questionable religious activities.

On the Crown

   TEXT: OCT (S. H. Butcher, [1903] 1966, 1:221–332).

   TRANSLATION: LCL (C. A. Vince and J. H. Vince, 1926).

   BIBLIOGRAPHY: Ross S. Kraemer, "'Euoi Saboi' in Demosthenes' *De Corona:* In Whose Honor Were the Women's Rites?" *SBLSP* 20 (1981): 229–36.

Diodorus Siculus. 1st century B.C.E. Originally from Agyrium, Diodorus remains an enigmatic figure. The exact dates of his life are not known, but his works are thought to date from 60–30 B.C.E. His forty-volume history of the world drew extensively on the works of various earlier historians and annalists. Although his work has been considered undistinguished by modern scholars, it contains some intriguing references to the religious activities of women, including the one excerpted here. Regrettably, because he depended so heavily on other authors, it is particularly difficult to determine the reliability of his information.

Library

TEXT: Teubner (F. Vogel, C. T. Fisher, and L. Dindorf [1887] 1970–85, 6 vols.).

TRANSLATION: *LCL (C. H. Oldfather, C. L. Sherman, R. M. Geer, and F. R. Walton, 1933–67, 12 vols.).

Dionysius of Alexandria. 3d century C.E. The child of wealthy pagan parents, Dionysius studied with Origen of Alexandria and ultimately became the Christian bishop of that city in 247 C.E. During the persecutions by the emperor Decius he went into hiding rather than suffer. Although Dionysius was hardly alone in his response to the persecutions, fleeing torture and martyrdom was highly controversial among Christians in North Africa in the mid–third century, and Dionysius's actions may explain, in part, why his writings were preserved only in fragments, mostly in Eusebius. His *Letter to Basilides* was preserved in a larger collection of epistles of the Greek church which served as one of the sources of that church's canon law.

Letter to Basilides

TEXT: C. L. Feltoe. *Dionusiou Leipsana: The Letters and Other Remains of Dionysius of Alexandria* (Cambridge, 1904), 91–105; PG 10, 1272–77.

TRANSLATION: *ANF 6:94–96.

Epiphanius. 4th century C.E. Born in Eleutheropolis in Palestine in the early fourth century C.E., Epiphanius founded one of the early Christian monasteries there ca. 335. Eventually bishop of Salamis in Cyprus, he is best known for his lengthy *Panarion,* or the *Medicine Box* (sometimes also called the *Refutation of All Heresies*), a work that describes eighty Christian heresies as illnesses and prescribes antidotes for the afflicted and preventives for potential victims. A significant number of the heresies concern the activities of women. Until recently, there has been no published English translation at all, and many sections that describe the activities of women are still untranslated.

Medicine Box

TEXT: GCS 25 (1915; *Medicine Box* 1–33); GCS 31 (1980; *Medicine Box* 34–64); GCS 37 (1985; *Medicine Box* 65–80); PG 41, 156–1200; 42, 9–832.

TRANSLATION: Frank Williams, *The Panarion of Epiphanius of Salamis: Book I (Sects. 1–46)*. NHS 35 (1987). The sourcebook translations are by Carolyn Osiek (nos. 29, 30) and by the editor (nos. 105, 106).

Euripides. ca. 485–406 B.C.E. One of the most famous of the Athenian playwrights, Euripides wrote a significant number of plays that treat the figures of

Greek women: *Medea; Andromache; Hecuba; Helen; Electra; Iphigenia in Aulis;* and *Iphigenia in Tauris.* Some scholars have suggested that Euripides' often unflattering portraits reflect his personal hostility to women, but others consider his generalizations about feminine evil to be conventional rhetoric.

Euripides devoted one of the last of his plays, *The Bacchae* (which posthumously brought him victory at the Dionysia in 406 B.C.E.), to the origins and character of women's worship of the Thracian god Dionysus. The dramatic nature of the text makes it difficult to tell how accurately Euripides portrays Bacchic worship, either in his own Athens or in Thrace, where some scholars think he may have witnessed Bacchic rites similar to those he ascribes to his characters. Much of Euripides' description is not significantly at odds with other ancient evidence.

Bacchae

TEXT: OCT (G. Murray, 1901–13); E. R. Dodds, *Euripides Bacchae,* 2d ed. (Oxford: Clarendon Press, 1970).

TRANSLATION: LCL (Arthur S. Way, 1912, vol. 3); *W. Arrowsmith, *The Bacchae,* in *Greek Tragedies,* ed. David Grene and Richmond Lattimore, vol. 3 (Chicago: Univ. of Chicago Press, 1960); G. S. Kirk, *The Bacchae* (Englewood Cliffs, N.J.: Prentice-Hall, 1970); P. Vellacott, *The Bacchae and Other Plays* (Harmondsworth, Eng.: Penguin Books, 1954).

BIBLIOGRAPHY: Susan Guettel Cole, "New Evidence for the Mysteries of Dionysos," *GRBS* 21 (1980): 223–38; A. Henrichs, "Greek Maenadism from Olympias to Messalina," *HSCP* 82 (1978): 121–60; E. Keuls, *The Reign of the Phallus* (New York: Harper & Row, 1985), 349–80; Ross S. Kraemer, "Ecstasy and Possession: The Attraction of Women to the Cult of Dionysos," *HTR* 72 (1979): 55–80; Charles Segal, "The Menace of Dionysus: Sex Roles and Reversal in Euripides' *Bacchae,*" in *Women in the Ancient World: The Arethusa Papers,* ed. J. Peradotto and J. P. Sullivan (Albany: State Univ. of New York Press, 1984), 195–212.

Eusebius. ca. 260–340 C.E. Bishop of Caesarea, Eusebius is best known as the major ancient historian of the early churches in the eastern portion of the Roman Empire. His extensive *History of the Church* is often our only source for certain ancient texts, which Eusebius often quoted uncritically and at great length. As with most ancient authors, Eusebius did not have a particular interest in women's history and religious life, but now and again he preserves significant evidence for women in early Christianity. Of his other works, two of the better known are *The Preparation for the Gospel* and *The Demonstration of the Gospel.* The former is especially important for its preservation of quotations from classical sources now otherwise lost.

History of the Church

TEXT: *PG* 19–24; GCS 9 (E. Schwartz and T. Mommsen, 1903–9).

TRANSLATION: *LCL (K. Lake, 1926; J. E. L. Oulton and H. J. Lawlor, 1932); FC 19, 29 (R. J. Deferrari, 1953–55); G. A. Williamson, *The History* of the Church from Christ to Constantine [by] Eusebius (Baltimore: Penguin Books, 1965).

Gellius, Aulus. 2d century C.E. Born ca. 130 C.E., Gellius is the author of *Attic Nights,* a collection of short chapters on philosophy, history, law, grammar, literary criticism, and the like. The collection was explicitly written to entertain and instruct his children. Because he relied so heavily on quotations from earlier Greek and Latin sources, his work is a major source for later writers and historians both ancient and modern.

Attic Nights
    TEXT: editio maior (M. Hertz, Berlin, 1883–85, 2 vols.); Budé (R. Marache, books 1–4, 1967; 5–10, 1978); OCT (P. K. Marshall, 1968, 2 vols.); Teubner (C. Hosius, 1903).
    TRANSLATION: *LCL (J. C. Rolfe, 1927, 3 vols.).

Hippolytus. 170–236 C.E. Little is known about the life of this Roman presbyter, perhaps because he spent much of his life opposing the leadership of the Roman church, especially Callistus, bishop of Rome (217–22). He died in Sardinia during the persecution of Maximinus. Portions of works attributed to him have survived, although their authorship has been debated. His principal work seems to have been the *Refutation of All Heresies,* which attempts to demonstrate that all Christian heresies derive from Greek philosophical systems. In Hippolytus, as in other antiheretical writers, women figure prominently in the beliefs and practices opposed.

Refutation of All Heresies
    TEXT: *PG* 10, 16/3; GCS 26 (P. Wendland, 1916).
    TRANSLATION: *ANF 5:9–153.

Jerome. ca. 342–420 C.E. A prominent biblical scholar in his time, Jerome is best known for his translation of most of the Bible into Latin, in an edition known as the Vulgate. Adopting the ascetic life by his early thirties, he spent a number of years in the Syrian desert as a hermit and there learned Hebrew. He arrived in Rome in 382 C.E. an ordained priest and developed such close ties with a small circle of ascetic and aristocratic Christian women that he was forced to leave Rome three years later under suspicion of having had inappropriate relationships with them. Relocating in Bethlehem, he founded a monastery for men while his Roman friend and pupil Paula, together with her daughter Eustochium, ran a nearby monastery for women. His letter to Eustochium on the death of her mother is one of his most famous, and an important source for the study of Roman Christian ascetic women in the fourth century. Jerome wrote many letters to women both known and unknown to him, urging them to adopt and maintain an ascetic life. Not surprisingly, many of his letters have survived, while none of theirs to him remain.

Letters

TEXT: *PL* 22–30; SC (Jerome Labourt, 1949–63, 8 vols.).

TRANSLATION: *NPNFC ser. 2, vol. 6; ACW (C. C. Mierow and T. C. Lawler, 1963–); selected letters in LCL (F. A. Wright, 1933).

BIBLIOGRAPHY: Elizabeth A. Clark, "Friendship between the Sexes: Classical Theory and Christian Practice," in *Jerome, Chrysostom, and Friends,* SWR 2 (1979), 35–106; idem, "Ascetic Renunciation and Feminine Advancement," in *Ascetic Piety and Women's Faith: Essays on Late Ancient Christianity,* SWR 20 (1986), 175–208 (= *Anglican Theological Review* 63 (1981): 240–57); Anne E. Yarbrough, "The Christianization of Rome: The Example of Roman Women," *Church History* 45 (1976): 149–65.

John Chrysostom. ca. 354–407 C.E. A prolific preacher who had earned the epithet Chrysostom, "golden-mouthed," by the sixth century, John Chrysostom is a particularly important source for the life of Olympias, his devoted friend and benefactor. Seventeen of his letters to her are still extant, although none of hers to him have survived.

Like many Christians of his time, Chrysostom was not born to Christian parents. He converted at age 18. His father died while he was an infant, and his mother, to whom he was apparently greatly attached, provided his early education. He spent six years in monastic seclusion, during which he became seriously ill. Returning to Syrian Antioch in 381, he became a deacon and then a priest in 386. Eleven years later he was abducted to Constantinople by the emperor's order and elected bishop, a post he held from 397 until 404. His criticisms of the powerful empress Eudoxia ultimately led to his banishment: he was exiled to Cucusus and died of the stresses of an enforced march in 407.

Among his many surviving sermons are those entitled *Against Judaizing Christians,* of whom women seem to have been a substantial number, as the selections included in this volume suggest. He also wrote several treatises advocating asceticism and virginity.

Against Judaizing Christians

TEXT: *PG* 48:843–942.

TRANSLATION: *FC (Paul Harkins, 1977).

Letters to Olympias

TEXT: SC 13 (A.-M. Malingrey, 1968, 2d ed.).

TRANSLATION: *NPNFC ser. 1, vol. 9.

BIBLIOGRAPHY: Elizabeth A. Clark, "John Chrysostom and the Subintroductae," in *Ascetic Piety and Women's Faith,* 265–90 (= *Church History* 46 [1977]: 171–85); idem, "Introduction to John Chrysostom *On Virginity, Against Remarriage,* in *Ascetic Piety and Women's Faith,* 229–64; idem, "Sexual Politics in the Writings of John Chrysostom," *Anglican Theological Review* 59 (1977): 3–20. For translations of some of Chrysostom's other works on women (not excerpted in this sourcebook), see Elizabeth A. Clark, *Instruction and Refutation Directed against Those Men Cohabiting with Virgins,* and *On the*

Necessity of Guarding Virginity, in *Jerome, Chrysostom, and Friends: Essays and Translations,* SWR 2 (1979), 164–208, 209–48; and Sally R. Shore, *John Chrysostom: On Virginity; Against Remarriage,* SWR 9 (1983).

Josephus. ca. 37–100 C.E. The writings of the historian Flavius Josephus constitute our major source for Jewish history in the first century C.E. During the Jewish war with Rome (66–73 C.E.), he reluctantly led Jewish forces in Galilee, ultimately surrendering to Vespasian, whose favor he claims to have won by predicting Vespasian's elevation to the position of emperor. After the war, he settled in Rome, where under Flavian patronage (hence the name Flavius) he wrote an account of the war, a history of the Jews, an apologia for Judaism, and a defense of his behavior during the war. It is interesting and significant that although Josephus spent many years living in Rome, he tells us nothing about the Jewish community there.

As we might expect, Josephus shows no particular concern for the history of Jewish women per se. Nevertheless, his writings contain significant evidence for Hellenistic Jewish queens, a lengthy account of the conversion of Helena, queen of Adiabene, excerpted here, and many occasional references that shed light on Jewish women in the first century.

Antiquities of the Jews; The Jewish War

TEXT: B. Niese ([1887–89] 1955); S. A. Naber (1888–96).
TRANSLATION: *LCL (H. St. J. Thackeray, R. Marcus, A. Wikgren, and L. H. Feldman, 1926–65). The sourcebook translation of selection 112 is the editor's.

Juvenal. 1st–2d centuries C.E. Little is known of the life of the Roman satirist Juvenal, including the dates of his birth and death. His earliest extant satire dates to ca. 100–110 C.E., and he was still writing ca. 127 C.E. He was not well known during his lifetime, and his works did not acquire any popularity until the late fourth century. His sixteen extant satires present a nasty critique of Roman society. The excerpt in this collection is taken from his sixth satire, a vicious indictment of Roman wives and the only one that substantially concerns women.

Satires

TEXT: OCT (W. V. Clausen, *Persius and Juvenal: Satires,* 1959); John Ferguson, *Juvenal: The Satires* (New York: St. Martins Press, 1979).
TRANSLATIONS: LCL (C. G. Ramsay, 1918); *H. Creekmore (New York: Mentor Books, 1963).

Livy, Titus. 1st century B.C.E.–1st century C.E. We know little about the life of one of the most important ancient Roman historians except the approximate dates of his life, the place of his birth (Patavium, modern Padua), and his work itself. His magnum opus was a 142-volume history of Rome written in annalistic fashion, according to which the official business of the state was set forth in a formal arrangement, year by year. In compiling his history, Livy relied heavily on other sources and has been criticized by modern scholars for his less than careful use of those sources.

Only about a quarter of the books of the *Ab urbe condita libri* or *Annals of Rome* have survived (1–10, 21–45). Concerned exclusively with a presentation of public history, Livy is an important source on the involvement of Roman women in public life, if a problematic one, as we see in the selection here on the importation of Bacchic rites into Rome and their subsequent banning.

Annals of Rome

TEXT: Budé (P. Bayet, 1940–54, 5 vols.; 1967–86, 33 vols.); OCT (R. S. Conway and C. F. Walters, 1914–65, 5 vols.).

TRANSLATION: *LCL (B. O. Foster, F. G. Moore, E. T. Sage, A. C. Schlesinger, and R. M. Geer, 14 vols.).

BIBLIOGRAPHY: E. E. Best, "Cicero, Livy, and Educated Roman Women," *Classical Journal* 65 (1970): 199–204; see also references under Euripides, especially the articles by Kraemer and Henrichs.

Ovid. 43 B.C.E.–17 C.E. A prolific writer, Ovid abandoned public service to take up poetry, eventually becoming the leading Roman poet of his time. For reasons still undetermined, he fell out of favor with the emperor Augustus and was banished to Tomis on the Black Sea. He is probably best known for his *Metamorphoses* and his love poems *Amores* and *Ars Amatoria (The Art of Love)*. The latter contains three books on the arts of seduction, two written for men, and a third added for women. His *Fasti* or *Festival Calendar,* which covers January through June, is the work of most interest to scholars of religion, containing a number of references to women's religious activities.

Fasti (Festival Calendar)

TEXT: Teubner (D. E. W. Wormell and E. Courtney, 1978).

TRANSLATION: *LCL (J. G. Frazer, 1929).

BIBLIOGRAPHY: D. Porte, "Claudia Quinta et le problème de la lavatio de Cybele en 204 av. JC," *Klio* 66 (1984): 93–103.

Palladius. 4th century C.E. Born in Galatia ca. 363, Palladius took up the monastic life in his mid-twenties but modified his ascetic rigor because of poor health. His *Lausiac History* was dedicated to Lausus, chamberlain in the court of Theodosius II. Originally written in Greek in 419–20 and subsequently translated into Latin, it represents a major source for early monasticism in Egypt, Palestine, Syria, and Asia Minor. Though the bulk of the work describes male monastics and their communities, the work also contains important references to early women's monasteries and anecdotes about female ascetics.

Lausiac History

TEXT: PG 34, 991–1262; CTS 6 (C. Butler, 1904); CSCO (R. Draguet, 1978, 389–90, 398–99). Draguet also provides corrections to Butler's text in various articles, for which see M. Geerard, *Clavis Patrum Graecorum* 3:169.

TRANSLATION: W. K. L. Clarke, *The Lausiac History of Palladius* (London: SPCK, 1918); *A. Veilleux, *Pachomian Koinonia*, vol. 2, *Pachomian Chronicles and Rules*, Cistercian Studies 45 (Kalamazoo, Mich.: Cistercian Pubs., 1981).

BIBLIOGRAPHY: Alanna Emmett, "Female Ascetics in the Greek Papyri," *Jahrbuch der österreichischen Byzantinistik* 32/2 (1982): 507–15; idem, "An Early Fourth-Century Female Monastic Community in Egypt?" in *Maistor: Classical, Byzantine, and Renaissance Studies for Robert Browning*, ed. A. Moffatt, Byzantina Australiensia 5 (Canberra: Australian Assn. for Byzantine Studies, 1984), 77–83.

Pausanias. ca. mid–second century C.E. We have little biographic information on the author of the ten-volume *Description of Greece*, an extensive travelogue. Pausanias was particularly fascinated by religious monuments—temples, statues, and the like—and by religious beliefs and rituals. His work is filled with reports of local mythologies and worship, including many accounts of the activities of women.

Description of Greece
TEXT: Teubner (Maria Helena Rocha-Pereira, 1973–81, 3 vols.).
TRANSLATION: *LCL (W. H. S. Jones, 1918–35, 5 vols.).

Perpetua. ca. 181–203 C.E. Everything we know about the woman martyred along with several other Christians at the beginning of the third century C.E. in Carthage comes from the account of her martyrdom. According to the text, Perpetua herself composed the account of her detainment and visions, which was joined together with the account of another martyr, Saturus, and given a narrative framework by an anonymous author. More and more scholars have come to accept this as reasonable, making Perpetua one of the few known women authors from the early Christian period. There is some speculation that Tertullian (see below) wrote the additional narrative, possibly while a Montanist.

The Martyrdom of Saints Perpetua and Felicitas
TEXT: C. J. M. van Beek, *Passio Sanctarum Perpetuae et Felicitatis* (Nijmegen, 1936); H. Musurillo, *Acts of the Christian Martyrs* (Oxford: Clarendon Press, 1972), 106–31; J. A. Robinson, *The Passion of Perpetua, with an Appendix on the Scillitan Martyrdom*, CTS 1, 2 (1891).
TRANSLATION: *Musurillo, *Acts of the Christian Martyrs*; Rosemary Rader, in *A Lost Tradition: Women Writers of the Early Church*, ed. P. Wilson-Kastner et al. (Lanham, Md.: Univ. Press of America, 1981), 1–32; ANF.
BIBLIOGRAPHY: Mary F. Lefkowitz, "The Motivation for St. Perpetua's Martyrdom," *Journal of the American Academy of Religion* 44 (1976): 417–21; idem, *Women in Greek Myth* (Baltimore: Johns Hopkins Univ. Press, 1986), esp. 95–111.

Philo Judaeus. ca. 20 B.C.E.–50 C.E. Little is known about Philo, the child of a prosperous Jewish family in Alexandria, beyond the few biographical hints we can extract from his writings (e.g., that he was well schooled in the Greek philosophical tradition). Most of his works are lengthy allegorical interpretations of the Greek translation of Jewish Scriptures, although one of them *(On the Embassy to Gaius)* describes an embassy he undertook with other Jewish leaders to plead the cause of the Jews before Caligula, and several of his writings describe Jewish ascetic communities. Philo's allegorical method was extremely attractive to later generations of Alexandrian Christian biblical exegetes. Ultimately, Philo was preserved not by Jewish communities but by Christians.

Very little social and historical information can be deduced from the writings of Philo, although occasional observations about Jewish life are interspersed among his writings, and his description of the female members of the Therapeutic sect is fascinating. Also of interest is his allegorical interpretation of female figures in the Jewish Scriptures—such as Sarah, Rachel, and Rebecca—and his occasional use of feminine language for aspects of the divine.

On the Contemplative Life; On the Special Laws

TEXT: editio maior (Cohn, Wendland, and Reiter, 1896–1930, 7 vols.).

TRANSLATION: *LCL (F. H. Colson, G. H. Whitaker, W. Earp, and R. Marcus, 1929–53, 12 vols.); D. Winston, *Philo of Alexandria: The Contemplative Life, the Giants and Selections.* Classics of Western Spirituality (New York: Paulist Press, 1981).

BIBLIOGRAPHY: Richard Baer, *Philo's Use of the Categories Male and Female* (Leiden: E. J. Brill, 1970); Ross S. Kraemer, "Ecstatics and Ascetics: Studies in the Functions of Religious Activities for Women in the Greco-Roman World" (Ph.D. diss., Princeton Univ., 1976), 203–19; idem, "Monastic Jewish Women in Greco-Roman Egypt: Philo of Alexandria on the Therapeutae and Therapeutrides," *Signs: Journal of Women in Culture and Society,* forthcoming; Judith Romney Wegner, "The Image of Woman in Philo," *SBLSP* 21 (1982): 551–63.

Plutarch. ca. 50–120 C.E. A noted philosopher and biographer, Plutarch of Chaeronea was particularly interested in religious matters, to which many of his treatises are devoted. His works are now generally divided into two categories, the *Moralia* (essays of varying length on a wide range of topics) and the *Lives.* Although he rarely sets out to tell us positive things about women in antiquity, he appears much more sympathetic to women than most of his contemporaries, and a few of his works, such as *On the Bravery of Women,* laud the actions of women.

He was apparently close friends with a priestess at Delphi named Clea, for whom he wrote not only *On The Bravery of Women* but also his well-known *On Isis and Osiris,* both of which are excerpted in this volume. References to women's religion are also scattered throughout his other writings, as in the passage from his *Life of Alexander.* As with all ancient literary sources, modern scholars must use Plutarch's testimony cautiously, but his kinder attitude toward women makes his material all the more intriguing.

Moralia: On the Bravery of Women
TEXT: Teubner (W. R. Paton and I. Wegehaupt, [1929] 1971, vol. 2, fasc. 1, 225–72).
TRANSLATION: *LCL (F. C. Babbitt, 1936, vol. 4).

Moralia: On Isis and Osiris
TEXT: Teubner (W. R. Paton and I. Wegehaupt, [1929] 1971, vol. 2, fasc. 3, 1–80).
TRANSLATION: *LCL (F. C. Babbitt, 1936, vol. 5).

Life of Alexander
TEXT: Budé (R. Flacelière, E. Chambry, and M. Juneaux, 1975, vol. 9); J. R. Hamilton, *Vies: Plutarque* (Paris: Les Belles Lettres, 1968).
TRANSLATION: *LCL (B. Perrin, 1919, vol. 7).

Life of Numa Pompilius
TEXT: Budé (R. Flacelière, E. Chambry, and M. Juneaux, 1957, vol. 1).
TRANSLATION: *LCL (B. Perrin, 1914, vol. 1).
BIBLIOGRAPHY: F. LeCorsu, *Plutarch et les femmes dans les Vies parallels* (Paris: Les Belles Lettres, 1981). For bibliography on Isis, see references under Apuleius.

Shenoute. 4th–5th centuries C.E. Shenoute of Atripe was born in the latter part of the fourth century and entered the Pachomian White Monastery in Egypt as a young boy. After the death of his uncle Pgol, he assumed the leadership of the monastery, ruling it until his death in 466. According to his pupil Besa he lived 118 years. The White Monastery was a large complex of buildings and land extending about twenty square miles. The Arabic *Life of Shenoute* states that twenty-two hundred monks and eighteen hundred nuns were under Shenoute's authority in this complex. The *Letter to Tachom* implies that there was a separate community of women having some kind of connection with the White Monastery. In the Pachomian system, separate communities of men and women in the area around Egyptian Thebes were all supervised by the abbot at the chief monastery, Pbow. Shenoute writes as though he occupied a similar position of authority relative to Tachom's community.

Nothing is known about Tachom herself except her name (which is the feminine form of Pachom/Pachomius) and her leadership of the women's community.

Letter to Tachom
TEXT: CSCO 41:21–22 (J. Leipoldt and W. E. Crum, 1906).
The sourcebook translation is by Janet Timbie.
BIBLIOGRAPHY: See references under Palladius.

Tertullian, Quintus Septimius Florens. ca. 160–225 C.E. Many of Tertullian's writings have survived to the present, but little is known about the details of his life. A native of Carthage, he converted to Christianity before 197 C.E. Though the chronology of his career as a Christian is disputed, it is known that at some point he joined the Montanists, a charismatic sect led by two women, Maximilla and Priscilla, and a man named Montanus, from whom the movement took its name. After some years, Tertullian separated from the community for reasons that remain unknown to us. In a work dated ca. 203 *(On Baptism)* he disparaged the *Acts of Thecla* (see below), or a similar text, on the grounds that some people used it inappropriately to legitimate baptism by women. This may suggest that Montanist attitudes toward the leadership roles of women were one of his points of contention with Montanism.

A significant number of his extant works concern appropriate behavior for Christian women: *On the Dress of Women; On the Veiling of Virgins; On Modesty; On Monogamy; On the Exhortation to Chastity.* Married himself, he nevertheless advocated celibacy and chastity as the ideal Christian life. He was the author of numerous polemics against those he considered heretics, including Marcionites and Valentinians.

On the Soul

TEXT: CSEL 20 (A. Reifferscheid and G. Wissowa, 1890); J. H. Waszink, *Tertullianus: De Anima* (Amsterdam, 1947).

TRANSLATION:*ANF 3:181–235; FC 10: 179–309 (E. A. Quain, 1950).

Texts of his other works, including many pertinent to the study of Christian women, may be found in *PL* 1–2; editio maior (F. Oehler, *Tertulliani Opera Omnia,* 3 vols. [Leipzig, 1851–54]); editio minor (1854); CSEL 20, 47, 69, 70–; CCSL (E. Dekkers, 1954). All are translated in ANF 3, 4.

BIBLIOGRAPHY: F. Forrester Church, "Sex and Salvation in Tertullian," *HTR* 68 (1975): 83–101; C. Tibiletti, "La Donna in Tertulliano," in *Misoginia e maschilismo in Grecia e in Roma* (Genoa: Istituto di filologia classica e medievale, 1981), 69–95.

Theocritus. ca. 300–260 B.C.E. A bucolic poet from Syracuse in Sicily who eventually won the admiration of Ptolemy Philadelphus, Theocritus is not a major source for women's religion, except for his *Idyll,* excerpted here. The poem, on the worshipers of Adonis, is set in Alexandria, where Theocritus lived for some time: its reliability warrants discussion. Many of Theocritus's other poems concern the vicissitudes of romantic love.

Idylls

TEXT AND TRANSLATION: *A. S. F. Gow, *Theocritus,* 2 vols. (Cambridge: Cambridge Univ. Press, 1950).

BIBLIOGRAPHY: Frederick T. Griffiths, "Home before Lunch: The Emancipated Woman in Theocritus," in *Reflections of Women in Antiquity,* ed. Helene P. Foley (New York: Gordon & Breach, 1981), 247–73.

SOURCES WITH ANONYMOUS OR
PSEUDONYMOUS AUTHORSHIP

The Acts of Thecla. 2d century C.E. Written before the beginning of the third century C.E., and possibly as early as the mid–second century C.E., the work usually called *The Acts of Paul and Thecla* is found within a larger composite work, *The Acts of Paul,* although it may have circulated independently at first. It might more properly be called simply *The Acts of Thecla,* since it is only tangentially concerned with Paul: the central theme is the conversion and subsequent life of Thecla of Iconium. Originally written in Greek, it exists in Latin, Syriac, and Ethiopic as well, testimony to its broad popularity.

The work engendered controversy early, in part because Thecla's self-baptism was apparently used by some Christians to legitimate women's performance of the rite of baptism on others. Tertullian denounced the work (or a similar text) in 203 C.E., arguing that it could not be used to give women the authority to baptize, since it was a fraudulent work written by a presbyter in Asia Minor who had in fact admitted the forgery. With the exception of D. MacDonald, Tertullian's testimony has not been given much credence by twentieth-century scholarship, which still considers the author unknown. In the past few years, some scholars have begun to pay serious attention to the possibility that the text was authored by a woman, but the evidence remains inconclusive.

Was there ever a Thecla? Scholars have generally assumed that the story in its present form is untrue—that Paul did not convert a woman named Thecla of Iconium. Rather, they have tended to see the story as an enlargement on the few biblical hints of Paul's activity in that area, none of which would account for the development of the Thecla legend. Later Christians, however, were firmly convinced of her reality, and a cult developed around her figure. *The Acts of Thecla* are clearly the literary prototype for other similar stories such as *The Acts of Xanthippe* and are probably the prototype for similar stories about women converts in the Acts of other apostles. In any case, the text— many of whose characters, especially the more admirable ones, are women—is rich evidence for the kinds of stories told about ascetic Christian women.

TEXT: M. Bonnet and R. A. Lipsius, *Acta Apostolorum Apocrypha* (reprint, Darmstadt: Wissenschaftliche Buchgesellschaft, 1959), 1:235–72.

TRANSLATION: *NTA* 2:353–64; *ANT* 272–281; ANF 8:487–92

BIBLIOGRAPHY: Gail P. Corrington, "Propaganda and the Power of Chastity in the New Testament Apocrypha," in *Rescuing Creusa: New Methodological Approaches to Women in Antiquity,* ed. Marilyn B. Skinner (*Helios* 13/2 [1986]: 151–62); Stevan L. Davies, *The Revolt of the Widows: The Social World of the Apocryphal Acts* (Carbondale: Southern Illinois Univ. Press, 1980); Ross S. Kraemer, "Ecstatics and Ascetics: Studies in the Functions of Religious Activities for Women in the Greco-Roman World" (Ph.D. diss., Princeton Univ., 1976), 134–84; idem, "The Conversion of Women to

Ascetic Forms of Christianity," *Signs: Journal of Women in Culture and Society* 6 (1980): 298–307; Dennis R. MacDonald, *The Legend and the Apostle: The Battle for Paul in Story and Canon* (Philadelphia: Westminster Press, 1983); idem, "The Role of Women in the Production of the Apocryphal Acts of the Apostles," *Iliff Review* 41 (1984): 21–38.

The Constitutions of the Holy Apostles. 4th century C.E.? A lengthy work that purports to set down the regulations of the apostles for appropriate Christian behavior, the *Constitutions* contains much material on women, although how accurately it reflects the beliefs, attitudes, and practices of actual Christian women has not been studied. In addition to including chapters on evil women and the subjugation of wives to husbands, book 1 contains a passage on why women should not bathe with men. Book 3, concerning widows, is for the most part a commentary on 1 Timothy and other biblical texts on widows. It also contains arguments against baptizing by women, on the grounds that Christ could have authorized women to baptize but did not, as well as arguments against teaching by women. Book 8 contains prayers for the ordination of deaconesses, including one that cites the spiritual replenishment of Miriam, Deborah, Anna, and Huldah.

TEXT: SC 320, 329 (Marcel Metzger, 1985–86).
TRANSLATION: *Irah Chase, *The Work Claiming to Be the Constitutions of the Holy Apostles, Including the Canons* (New York: D. Appleton, 1848).
BIBLIOGRAPHY: Carolyn Osiek, "The Widow As Altar: The Rise and Fall of a Symbol," *The Second Century* 3 (1983): 159–69.

The Conversion and Marriage of Aseneth. 1st century C.E.?
The Conversion and Marriage of Aseneth purports to explain how it was that Joseph married Aseneth, the daughter of an Egyptian priest (Gen. 41:45), by recounting in great detail the circumstances of her conversion to the God of Joseph. Ostensibly a tale of ancient Egypt, *Aseneth* is quite clearly a Greco-Roman Jewish romance whose true social setting is Hellenistic Egypt. Long thought to be a Christian or Christianized text, and considered of minor significance, it has recently begun to receive more detailed attention, which has emphasized its significance as a text in which a woman occupies center stage, and which is conspicuously lacking in misogynist language or implications. It is one of the few Jewish texts of this period to use some compelling feminine imagery for the divine.

Although the work is usually titled *Joseph and Aseneth* in contemporary editions, the ancient manuscripts give it a variety of titles, such as *The Prayer and Confession of Aseneth*. The modern choice of *Joseph and Aseneth* has been favored for its similarity to the titles of other Hellenistic romances, which are usually called by the name of the hero and heroine. Since the manuscript traditions do not conclusively support any one name, I have taken the liberty of retitling the work, choosing one that is descriptive and at the same time reflective of the centrality of Aseneth herself.

Although nothing is known about the author, there has been some speculation that *Aseneth* might have been written by a member of the Therapeutic community that Philo describes (see above). It is certainly not out of the question that the author was female, but there is no conclusive evidence.

In recent years there has been considerable debate over the text. A French scholar, Marc Philonenko, has favored a shorter version, which is the basis for the translation here; the German scholar Christoph Burchard has argued in detail for a longer text. His translation in *OTP* is based on his preliminary Greek text.

TEXT: M. Philonenko, *Joseph et Aseneth: Introduction, texte critique, traduction, et notes*, Studia Post Biblica (Leiden: E. J. Brill, 1968), including French translation; Christoph Burchard, *Joseph und Aseneth*, Judische Schriften aus hellenistisch-romischer Zeit (Gütersloh, 1983); editio minor forthcoming in PVTG.

TRANSLATION: D. Cook in *AOT* 465–503, using the text of Philonenko; C. Burchard in *OTP* 2:177–247, with introduction and notes.

Homeric Hymn to Demeter. 7th century B.C.E. One of the only selections in this volume to antedate the fourth century B.C.E., the so-called Homeric Hymn to Demeter contains the classic legend of the seizure of Persephone by Hades, Demeter's subsequent revengeful famine, Zeus's eventual compromise solution of restoring Persephone to her mother for a portion of the year, and the establishment of the rites of Demeter and Persephone at Eleusis. Although Demeter was worshiped by both women and men, her religion was of particular import for women, which recent feminist scholarship has fruitfully examined. Since the rites of Demeter at Eleusis and elsewhere played a central part in Greek religion for centuries, well into the Greco-Roman period, I have included the text here despite its clear violation of my chronological boundaries.

TEXT AND TRANSLATION: N. J. Richardson, *The Homeric Hymn to Demeter* (Oxford: Clarendon Press, 1974).
OTHER TRANSLATIONS: LCL (Hugh G. Evelyn-White, 1914); *David G. Rice and John E. Stambaugh, *Sources for the Study of Greek Religion*, SBLSBS 14 (Missoula, Mont.: Scholars Press, 1979), 171–83.
BIBLIOGRAPHY: Marylin B. Arthur, "Politics and Pomegranates: An Interpretation of the Homeric Hymn to Demeter," *Arethusa* 10 (1977): 7–35; Allaire Chandor Brumfield, *Attic Festivals of Demeter and the Agricultural Year* (New York: Arno Press, 1981); J. Prytz Johansen, "The Thesmophoria as a Women's Festival," *Temenos* 11 (1975): 78–87; Bruce Lincoln, "The Rape of Persephone: A Greek Scenario of Women's Initiation," *HTR* 72 (1979): 223–35; G. E. Skov, "The Priestess of Demeter and Kore and Her Role in the Initiation of Women at the Festival of the Haloa at Eleusis," *Temenos* 11 (1975): 136–47.

Inscriptions and Papyri. Some of the most important evidence for women's lives, including their religious lives, comes from nonliterary sources—everything from burial epitaphs to private letters to tax registers. Although the preservation of this material is subject to the vagaries of time and weather, among other things, it is less susceptible to the gender bias that affects literary sources, which come principally from male authors and are transmitted and translated principally by men. Once engraved on stone or marble, a woman's donative or burial inscription is considerably less dependent on copying to survive to modern times. Similarly, the special combination of the Egyptian climate and the characteristics of writing material made from the papyrus plant have enabled ordinary correspondence and documents to survive two thousand years, to emerge from archaeological discoveries in the last century. Inscriptions and papyrus documents have often been neglected by scholars of early Judaism and early Christianity in favor of literary texts, and the disciplines of epigraphy and papyrology are highly intimidating to the uninitiated. Nevertheless, they are well worth the effort for students of women in antiquity.

Because scholars often favor literary evidence, many inscriptions and papyrus documents from the Greco-Roman period are available only in esoteric collections, and often they have not been translated into English. An important exception to this is the Jewish papyri and inscriptions from Egypt.

TEXTS: The Greek and Latin inscriptions and the Greek papyri included in this volume may be found in the editions indicated for each entry: the full bibliography may be found in the abbreviations section at the beginning of the book.

SOURCEBOOK TRANSLATIONS

Inscriptions. Translations of Christian burial and donative inscriptions are the editor's, except for a few inscriptions from Gibson 1975 and Gibson 1978. Translations of pagan burial and donative inscriptions are taken from Fant and Lefkowitz, except for selection 55, which is the editor's. Translations of women Jewish leaders are mostly from Bernadette J. Brooten's *Women Leaders in the Ancient Synagogues,* BJS 19 (Chico, Calif.: Scholars Press, 1982); translations of selections 115, 120, and 121 are from Harry J. Leon's *The Jews of Ancient Rome* (Philadelphia: Jewish Publication Society, 1960). Translation of selection 54 is by Richard Lim.

Papyri. All translations of Jewish papyri are from *CPJ*. Translations of the Greek magical papyri are from *The Greek Magical Papyri in Translation, Including the Demotic Spells,* ed. Hans Dieter Betz (Chicago and London: Univ. of Chicago Press, 1986).

BIBLIOGRAPHY: Any novice in the study of inscriptions and papyri might begin with the entries and bibliography in the *OCD*. In addition, the following bibliography on the study of inscriptions and papyri as it pertains to women's history and religion in antiquity may be helpful: Brooten, *Women Leaders in the Ancient Synagogues;* Ross S. Kraemer, "Non-literary Evidence for Jewish Women in Rome and Egypt," in *Rescuing Creusa: New Methodological Approaches to Women in Antiquity,* ed. Marilyn B. Skinner (*Helios* 13/2

[1986]: 85–101); idem, "Hellenistic Jewish Women: The Epigraphical Evidence," *SBLSP* 25 (1986): 181–200; idem, "A New Inscription from Malta and the Question of Women Elders in the Diaspora Jewish Communities," *HTR* 78 (1985): 431–83; Sarah B. Pomeroy, "Women in Roman Egypt (A Preliminary Study Based on Papyri)," in *Reflections of Women in Antiquity,* ed. Helene B. Foley (New York: Gordon & Breach, 1981), 303–22; idem, *Women in Hellenistic Egypt: From Alexander to Cleopatra* (New York: Schocken Books, 1984). See also the studies by A. Emmett listed above under Palladius.

On the inscriptions for Artemis at Brauron, see Lilly Kahil, "Le 'Craterisque' d'Artemis et le Brauronion de l'Acropole," *Hesperia: Journal of the American School of Classical Studies of Athens* 50 (1981): 253–63; idem, "L'Artemis de Brauron, rites et mystère," *Antike Kunst* 20 (1977): 86–98; Paula Perlman, "Plato *Laws* 833C–834D and the Bears of Brauron," *Greek, Roman, and Byzantine Studies* 24 (1983): 115–30; Christiane Sourvinou, "Aristophanes, *Lysistrata,* 641–647," *Classical Quarterly* 21 (1971): 339–42; T. C. W. Stinton, "Iphigeneia and the Bears of Brauron," *Classical Quarterly* 26 (1972): 12–14; M. B. Walbank, "Artemis Bear-Leader," *Classical Quarterly* 31 (1981): 276–81.

Kyme Aretalogy. 2d century C.E. Found in Kyme in Asia Minor, this version of the virtues of Isis is probably a Hellenistic revision of an Egyptian hymn extolling the goddess. The first-person format is typical though by no means the only one used in aretalogies. Nothing is known about the person or persons who composed the hymn in this form, which attributes to Isis characteristics of Greek deities such as Demeter in addition to her native Egyptian traits.

TEXT: W. Peek, *Der Isishymnus von Andros und verwandte Texte* (Berlin, 1930), 123–25.

TRANSLATION: *F. C. Grant, *Hellenistic Religions: The Age of Syncretism* (New York: Liberal Arts Press, 1953).

BIBLIOGRAPHY: See references under Apuleius.

Letter of the Churches of Lyons and Vienne. 2d century C.E. Our only evidence for this account of the martyrs of Lyons and Vienne in ancient Gaul comes from the fourth-century Eusebius, who presents it as a letter written from those communities to Christians in Asia Minor, from where many of the Christians at Lyons and Vienne had emigrated. If it is in fact that, it describes events of 177 C.E. Although there is some internal evidence that the text may have been reworked before Eusebius, and there are questions about the accuracy of the original writers, it is generally considered to be important testimony to the experiences of Christian women and men.

TEXT: Eusebius *Church History* V.1.

TEXT AND TRANSLATION: *H. Musurillo, *The Acts of the Christian Martyrs* (Oxford: Clarendon Press, 1972), 62–85; see also above, under Eusebius.

The Life of Olympias. 5th century C.E. While virtually nothing is known about the anonymous author of this work, numerous ancient texts testify to the person of Olympias. Born to a family recently promoted to nobility under Constantine, she was orphaned at an early age and apparently educated by a woman named Theodosia, who was associated with a group of pious Christian women. After her husband of only a brief time left her a widow, she chose the ascetic life. Well connected in Constantinople, she became the benefactor of the bishop Nectarius, who ordained her a deaconess. When Nectarius died and John Chrysostom came to Constantinople, she became his friend and supporter, in a relationship that endured until his death.

TEXT: SC 13 (A.-M. Malingrey, 1968).
TRANSLATION: *Elizabeth A. Clark, *Jerome, Chrysostom, and Friends,* SWR 2 (1979), 127–42.
BIBLIOGRAPHY: See references under Chrysostom.

The Life of Saint Mary the Harlot. 5th century C.E. Extracted from the *Life of Abraham,* which is about a fourth-century monk and uncle of the protagonist, the tale was extremely popular, circulating in Syriac, Greek, and Latin. Eventually it was dramatized by the tenth-century nun Hroswitha, who also drew upon the Apocryphal Acts of the Apostles for her plays. Historians of ancient religion must consider whose perspective this text, and similar texts such as *The Life of Saint Pelagia,* represent, but it offers an intriguing source for women's asceticism in late antiquity.

TEXT: *BHO* 16–17; T. J. Lamy, *Sancti Ephraem Syri Hymni et Sermones* (Malines, 1902), 4:cols. 1–84; Greek in *Bibliotheca Hagiographica Graeca,* ed. F. Halkin, 3d ed. (Brussels, 1957), 5–8.
TRANSLATION: *H. Waddell, *Sayings of the Desert Fathers* (London: Constable & Co., 1936), 189–201 (from the Latin); S. Brock and S. Harvey, *Holy Women of the Syrian Orient* (Berkeley and Los Angeles: Univ. of California Press, 1987), 27–39 (from the Syriac).
BIBLIOGRAPHY: See references on Palladius; see also Brock and Harvey, *Holy Women,* 185–86.

The Life of Saint Pelagia the Harlot. 5th century C.E. Purportedly the work of one Jacob, deacon to a bishop called Nonnus and the agent of Pelagia's conversion to Christianity, *The Life of Saint Pelagia* recounts the repentance of a prostitute in Antioch, presumably in the late fourth century. To maintain her chastity and solitude, Pelagia disguises herself as a man. The motif of disguise occurs in other Christian texts as well—*The Acts of Thecla* and the *Martyrdom of Perpetua* being only two earlier examples, although in both those cases the disguise is only temporary, whereas Pelagia lives out the remainder of her life incognito. Some scholars suggest that Pelagia, or women like her, may very well have adopted masculine dress and identity to live as monastics.

TEXT: *BHO* 919; J. Gildemeister, *Acta sanctae Pelagiae syriace* (Bonn, 1879); variants in A. Smith Lewis's *Select Narratives of Holy Women,* Studia Sinaitica 9, 1:306–25.

TRANSLATION: Waddell, *Sayings of the Desert Fathers,* 173–88 (from the Latin); Brock and Harvey, *Holy Women,* 40–62 (from the Syriac).

BIBLIOGRAPHY: See references under Palladius; see also Brock and Harvey, *Holy Women,* 186–87.

4 Maccabees. 1st century C.E. In the first half of the second century B.C.E., Antiochus IV Epiphanes, king of Syria, desecrated the Jewish temple in Jerusalem, compelled Jews to perform sacrilegious acts, and martyred a considerable number of those who resisted. The Jewish festival of Chanukah commemorates Antiochus's ultimate defeat by Judah the Maccabee, the restoration of the temple, and the establishment of a politically independent Judea that lasted until the advent of the Romans. A work called 2 Maccabees—which together with 1 Maccabees chronicles the events of this period, if problematically—briefly describes Antiochus's sadistic martyring of a woman who is forced to watch her seven sons put to death before she also is butchered. Fourth Maccabees, an anonymous work praising Jewish martyrs of the Maccabean period, greatly enlarges on that account. The author takes great pains to demonstrate the triumph of reason over emotion exemplified in the courage and fortitude of martyrs, notably the unnamed mother, her seven tortured sons, and the priest Eleazar. The emphasis on philosophical concerns has led most scholars to look for the origins of this text in a Diaspora Jewish community such as Antioch or Alexandria.

TEXT: A. Rahlfs, *Septuaginta* 1:1157–84 (Stuttgart, 1935); W. Baars, *Septuaginta,* Vetus Testamentum Supplements 9.4 (Göttingen: Vandenhoeck & Ruprecht).

TRANSLATION: *OTP* 2:531–64; *M. Hadas, *The Third and Fourth Books of Maccabees* (New York: Ktav, 1953); B. Metzger, ed., *RSV Apocrypha Expanded Edition.*

The Martyrs of Scilli. 2d century C.E. The oldest dated Latin Christian document from North Africa, *The Acts of the Martyrs of Scilli,* belongs to the genre of Acts that have traditionally been considered court records, as opposed to *passiones* or *martyria,* the reports of eyewitnesses or just legends about martyrs. As such, they are often thought to be reliable accounts of the court proceedings against Christian martyrs. Recent scholarship, however, acknowledges that Christians apparently processed such accounts and even fabricated them from whole cloth, and Musurillo's introduction to these Acts points out some internal obstacles to their being considered verbatim court reports. Although the skepticism about the reliability of such documents seems well taken, the Acts offer important information to scholars studying Christian women since many of them report on the martyrdom of women as well as men.

These martyrdom accounts were, and are, typically read on the anniversary of the martyrdom, and they are collected in calendrical formats. The location of Scilli is unknown.

TEXT: Acta Sanctorum (Antwerp, 1643); Analecta Bollandiana (Brussels, 1882–).
TEXT AND TRANSLATION: H. Musurillo, *The Acts of the Christian Martyrs* (Oxford: Clarendon Press, 1972), 86–89; J. A. Robinson, *The Passion of Perpetua, with an Appendix on the Scillitan Martyrdom*, CTS 1, 2 (1891); *J. Stevenson, *A New Eusebius* (London: SPCK, 1957), 41–43.

The Mishnah. ca. 200 C.E. A compilation of Jewish rabbinical commentary on the Torah arranged into tractates by subject and codified at the end of the second century C.E., the Mishnah contains oral traditions dating back generations in many cases.

Comparable in some ways to a combination of case law and theoretical legal discussion, the Mishnah is extremely problematic as a source of Jewish social and religious history. Although the Mishnah is still viewed in many quarters as evidence for normative Judaism in late antiquity, there is increasing sensitivity to the possibility that many Jews in the first two centuries C.E. did not share its world view. This seems particularly true for the Mishnaic references to women, which may tell us much more about what some Jewish rabbis thought about women than about what women did or thought themselves.

Nevertheless, the Mishnah remains a major source for Judaism in late antiquity, and the difficulties of extracting reliable historical information from it do not excuse us from examining its commentary on women closely.

TEXT: *Mishnayoth* (Wilna: Widow Romm and Brothers, 1922); P. Blackman (London, 1951–56).
TRANSLATION: H. Danby, *The Mishnah* (Oxford: Clarendon Press, 1933); *Jacob Neusner, *History of the Mishnaic Law*, SJLA.
BIBLIOGRAPHY: Judith Baskin, "The Separation of Women in Rabbinic Judaism," in *Women, Religion, and Social Change*, ed. E. Findly and Y. Haddad (Albany: State Univ. of New York Press, 1985), 3–18; Shaye J. D. Cohen, "The Origins of the Matrilineal Principle in Rabbinic Law," *Association for Jewish Studies Review* 10 (1985): 19–53; Anne Goldfeld, "Women as Sources of Torah in the Rabbinic Tradition," in *The Jewish Woman: New Perspectives*, ed. Elizabeth Koltun (New York: Schocken Books, 1976), 257–71 (= *Judaism* 24 [1975]: 245–56); Judith Hauptman, "Images of Women in the Talmud," in *Religion and Sexism: Images of Women in Jewish and Christian Tradition*, ed. Rosemary Radford Ruether (New York: Schocken Books, 1974), 248–56; Jacob Neusner, "From Scripture to Mishnah: The Origins of Tractate Niddah," *Journal of Jewish Studies* 29 (1978): 135–48; idem, "From Scripture to Mishnah: The Origins of Mishnah's Division of Women," *Journal of Jewish Studies* 30 (1979): 138–53; idem, "Thematic or Systemic Description: The Case of Mishnah's Division of Women," in *Method and*

Meaning in Ancient Judaism (Chico, Calif.: Scholars Press, 1979); idem, *A History of the Mishnaic Law of Women,* SJLA (1980), part 5.

Nag Hammadi Library. At the end of 1945, two Egyptian peasants from an area called Nag Hammadi stumbled upon an ancient jar containing thirteen Coptic codices that had been hidden for about fifteen hundred years. The Nag Hammadi Library, as these codices have come to be called, contains an assortment of works believed to have been read, if not also written, by gnostic Christians no later than the fifth century C.E. Together with the Dead Sea Scrolls found in Israel in 1947, these Coptic translations of Greek originals constitute the most exciting discoveries for the study of ancient religion in this century.

Of particular interest for the study of women's religion is the plethora of female aspects of the divine in these texts, as well as traditions about women as the sources of divine revelation and power. Unfortunately, very little is known about the individuals and communities that produced and transmitted the texts, making the precise correlations between religious language and social reality difficult to determine.

Thunder, Perfect Mind. Codex VI, 2. date uncertain.

TEXT: *FENHC;* NHS 11 (G. W. MacRae and D. M. Parrott, 1979).

The Thought of Norea. Codex IX, 2. late 2d century C.E.?

TEXT: *FENHC;* NHS 15 (S. Giversen and B. A. Pearson, 1981).

Hypostatis of the Archons. Codex II, 4. 3d century C.E.?

TEXT: *FENHC;* NHS 20 (B. Layton, 1988); R. A. Bullard (Berlin, 1970).

Exegesis on the Soul. Codex II, 6. ca. 200 C.E.

TEXT: *FEHNC;* NHS 21 (B. Layton, forthcoming); J. M. Sevrin, *L'exégèse de l'âme,* Bibliothèque copte de Nag Hammadi (Quebec, 1983).

TRANSLATIONS (OF ALL):*J. Robinson, ed., *The Nag Hammadi Library in English* (San Francisco: Harper & Row; Leiden: E. J. Brill, 1977). See also Bentley Layton, *The Gnostic Scriptures: A New Translation with Annotations and Introductions* (Garden City, N.Y.: Doubleday & Co., 1987).

BIBLIOGRAPHY: Rose H. Arthur, *The Wisdom Goddess: Feminine Motifs in Eight Nag Hammadi Documents* (Lanham, Md.: Univ. Press of America, 1984); Karen King, ed., *Images of the Feminine in Gnosticism,* Studies in Antiquity and Christianity (Philadelphia: Fortress Press, 1988); Elaine Pagels, "What Became of God the Mother? Conflicting Images of God in Early Christianity," *Signs: Journal of Women in Culture and Society* 2 (1976): 293–303; idem, "God the Father/God the Mother," in *The Gnostic Gospels* (New York: Random House, 1979), chap. 3; David Scholer, *Nag Hammadi Bibliography 1948–1969* (Leiden: E. J. Brill, 1971), with periodic supplements, "Bibliographica gnostica," in *Novum Testamentum;* Maddalena Scopello, *L'exégèse de l'âme: Nag Hammadi codex II, 6—introduction, traduction, et commentaire,* NHS 25 (1985).

Odes of Solomon. late 1st–early 2d centuries C.E.? Little is known about the authorship or original language of the Odes, which are extant primarily in Syriac. In their present form, they are explicitly Christian. Of particular interest is their use of feminine imagery for the divine.

TEXT: J. H. Charlesworth, *The Odes of Solomon* (Oxford: Clarendon Press, 1973).

TRANSLATION:*OTP* 2:725–71; *AOT* 683–731.

BIBLIOGRAPHY: Susan Ashbrook Harvey, "Women in Early Syrian Christianity," in *Images of Women in Antiquity,* ed. Averil Cameron and Amelie Kuhrt (Detroit: Wayne State Univ. Press, 1983), 288–98.

Sayings of the Desert Fathers. 4th–5th centuries C.E. Sayings attributed to the ascetics who lived in the Egyptian desert in the fourth and fifth centuries have come down to us in several forms, interspersed with anecdotes about the monastic life. Extant in Latin and in Greek, and arranged sometimes by subject and sometimes alphabetically by the hermit's name, the vast majority of the sayings are attributed to men. A handful, however, are given in the names of women, and a few stories are told about pious ascetic women, although the collections also contain many misogynist remarks and warnings about the dangers women pose to monastic males.

TEXT: *PG* 65, 71–440; J. B. Cotelier, *Ecclesiae Graecae Monumenta* 1:338–712 (1677), supplemented by F. Nau's "Histoires des solitaires égyptiens," *Revue de l'orient chrétien* (Paris, 1907–); *PL* 73, 855–1022; H. Rosweyde (Antwerp, 1615).

TRANSLATION: H. Waddell, *Sayings of the Desert Fathers* (London: Constable & Co., 1936); *Benedicta Ward, *The Sayings of the Desert Fathers: The Alphabetical Collection* (London: A. R. Mowbray, 1981); Owen Chadwick, ed., *Western Asceticism,* LCC (Philadelphia: Westminster Press, 1958).

The Talmud. 5th century C.E. The classic compilation of Jewish law, the Talmud contains both the Mishnah (see above) and commentary on the Mishnah known as the Gemara. The Babylonian Talmud, usually referred to as *the* Talmud, contains the commentary of Babylonian rabbis on the Mishnah; the Jerusalem Talmud contains the commentary of rabbis living in the land of Israel on a not always identical text of the Mishnah. Although the Babylonian Talmud was not codified until the fifth century C.E., both it and the Jerusalem Talmud contain much earlier material. It is not easy for scholars to determine the precise age of any given tradition within the Talmud.

As evidence for the beliefs and practices of Jewish women the Talmud must be used with extreme caution, for as Jacob Neusner has demonstrated in his studies on the Mishnah, the rabbinic discussions of women focus primarily on those instances in which women jeopardized the ritual purity and religious obligations of Jewish men. Nonetheless, particularly in the haggadic portions of the Talmud, those concerned not with the law itself (Halakah) but with illustrative material, we find possible evidence for real or representative Jewish women.

TEXT: Talmud Babli (Wilna, 1880–86); Talmud Jerushalmi (Wilna, 1922).
TRANSLATION: I. Epstein, ed., 35 vols. of the Babylonian Talmud (London: Soncino, 1935–52); Jacob Neusner, *The Talmud of Babylonia: An American Translation*, BJS (1980–84); idem, *The Talmud of the Land of Israel: A Preliminary Translation and Explanation* (Chicago: Univ. of Chicago Press, 1982–). The sourcebook translators are Neusner for *Sukkah,* the Soncino translators for all other texts.
BIBLIOGRAPHY: See references under Mishnah.

The Testament of Job. date uncertain, perhaps 2d century C.E. Virtually nothing is known about the origins of this elaboration of the biblical story of Job. There are no clear references to it in ancient sources, and there is little scholarly consensus about authorship beyond the recognition that the author knew the canonical Book of Job in the Greek Jewish translation of the Hebrew Scriptures known as the Septuagint. Some scholars have argued for an Egyptian provenience, but no one really knows.

What is particularly compelling about the work is its attention to women, which is far in excess of anything found in the canonical Job. The wife of Job, who remains nameless and all but speechless in the canonical work, obtains a name, plays a significant part in the drama, and speaks frequently. Excerpted in this volume is the account of Job's legacy to his three daughters, all of whom receive great spiritual powers. The account is a fascinating expansion on the Biblical narrative and a significant aspect of the *Testament of Job* which until recently had gone unnoticed by scholars.

TEXT: M. R. James, *Apocrypha Anecdota* (Cambridge, 1899), 2:lxxii–cii, 103–37; S. Brock, *Testamentum Iobi*, PVTG (1967), 1–60; *R. A. Kraft et al., *The Testament of Job: Greek Text and English Translation*, SBLTT 5, Pseudepigrapha Series 4 (Missoula, Mont.: Scholars Press, 1974).
TRANSLATION: *AOT* 617–48; *OTP* 1:829–68.
BIBLIOGRAPHY: P. van der Horst, "The Role of Women in the Testament of Job," *Nederlands Theologisch Tijdschrift* 40 (1986): 273–89.

Index of Sources

Selection numbers for this volume are given in parentheses, followed by page numbers in bold type.

419

Index of Personal Names

Includes the names of all female persons and the names of selected males mentioned in the sources and introductory sections. References from "About the Authors and Sources" are not indexed. Since many women are nameless in ancient texts, not all women who figure in these sources can be identified through this index, for example, the woman who is identified only as the martyred mother of seven sons in 4 Maccabees (selection 118). Different persons bearing the same name are not distinguished in the index except in the case of well-known figures such as Mary Magdalen and so forth.

Aurelia Soteria, 289
Aurelia Syncletica, 111
Aurelia Tation, 114
Aurelia Tryphaina, 110
Aurelios Onesimos, 115
Aurelios Papylos, 115
Aurelios Zosimos, 111
Aurelius . . . , 93
Aurelius Dioskoros, 93
Aurelius Justus, 93
Aurelius Theon, 93
Autonoe, 12
Auxanon, 114

Babata, 79
Bar Kochba, 79
Baubo, 21
Berenice, 18, 217
Berenike, 81
Beroneikiane, 112
Beronike, 219
Biblis, 307
Bilhah, 279
Blaesilla, 139, 140
Blandina, 291–92, 306, 309, 311

Callippe, 17
Candida, 108–9
Canuleia, 212
Capitolina, 113
Celsus, 8
Chaerippe, 17
Chrysis, 211
Claudia Quinta, 349–51
Cleopas, 143
Colonis, 116
Cosco, 21

Demo, 339
Demophon, 21, 341–42
Dinah, 132
Dinocrates, 100–101
Diocleidas, 19
Diogenis, 116
Domitiana, 108–9
Domna, 114, 222
Domnina, 116

Donata, 302–3
Dorcas, 143, 166
Dosarion, 91
Duronia, 247

Egeria, 77 n. 1
Eirene, 84, 88
Elisanthia, 198, 201
Epiphanius, 7–8, 141–42, 158,
    182, 202
Erotion, 91–92
Eucoline, 17
Eugenia, 115
Eulogia, 220
Euphrosyna, 289
Eupithis, 116
Eusebis, 114
Eusthatis, 116
Eustochiane, 205
Eustochium, 131, 136, 139–40,
    142, 150, 152, 164–68, 181
Euterpe, 91, 205
Euthychiane, 115
Eve, 51–52, 56–57, 71, 226–27,
    382
Eythycheianes, 114

Faustina, 219
Felicitas, 77 n. 1, 78, 96, 103,
    105–6, 289
Flavia Domitilla, 142
Flavia Vibia Sabina, 217

Gaudentia, 220
Gegania, 212
Generosa, 303
Glukianos, 110
Gorgo, 18–19

Hannah, 128, 137
Helen, 95
Helena, 143, 243, 257–58, 260–61
Hemera, 298–300
Herais, 91, 95
Herakleia, 81–82
Hermiones, 114
Hesychion, 116

Pentheus, 7, 13, 26
Peregrina, 289
Peristeria, 218
Perpetua, 77 n. 1, 78, 96, 98, 101–7
Persis, 202
Pheidylla, 17
Phile, 17
Philous, 91
Philumene, 17
Phoebe, 221
Physcoa, 35–36
Praxinoa, 18–19
Principia, 178, 186
Priscilla, 51, 225–26, 228, 230
Proba, 77 n. 1
Protous, 91–92
Ptollas, 91
Ptollous, 91
Pythias, 17

Quintilla, 51, 226

Rachel, 263, 279
Rachelis, 85
Rebecca, 263
Rebeka, 219
Regina, 301
Retibi, 49
Revocatus, 97, 105–6
Romana, 320–22
Rufina, daughter of Paula, 140–41
Rufina of Smyrna, 218

Salome, 56, 234
Sambathion (feminine), 91
Sambathion (masculine), 88, 90
Sambous, 91
Saosis, 356
Saprikia, 116
Sara, 220, 219
Sarah, 117, 146, 263, 289
Sarapias, 95
Saturninus, 97, 102, 105
Saturus, 98, 102–3, 105–7
Saufeia, 39
Secunda, 302–3
Secundulus, 97, 103

Seleucia, 190
Septimia Maria, 94
Serapion, 150
Seuthes, 91–92
Shenoute, 125
Sophia, 218, 221
Sophronia, 181
Sulpicia, 249–51
Symmacho, 257
Syncletica, 118, 121

Tachom, 125
Tarpeia, 212
Tata, 207, 216
Tatia, 111
Tation, 112
Tertullian, 78, 208
Thamyris, 280–84, 288
Thases, 90
Thaumasis, 116
Thecla, 54, 195, 208, 244, 280–88
Theocleia, 280, 283, 288
Theodora, 123–24
Theodote, 86–87
Theopempte, 218
Thermoutharin, 95
Thettale, 21
Theudous, 91
Thyaene, 17
Toxotius the elder, 127, 137, 140
Toxotius the younger, 140, 141, 155, 164
Trophimas, 115
Tryphaena, 202, 284–88
Tryphaina, 91
Tryphosa, 202
Tyche, 86–87

Urbana, 108–9
Urbanus, 108–9

Verenia, 212
Vestia, 302–3
Veturia Paulla, 289

Zilpah, 279

Index of Divine Names

Includes the names of all ancient non-mortal beings, both male and female, mentioned in the sources or in the introductory sections. God, Jesus, and Christ are not indexed, nor are any references from "About the Authors and Sources."

Fortuna, 57
Fortune, 25, 362
Furies, 253

Gabriel, 132
Galaxaure, 345
Good Goddess, 39

Harpocrates, 359
Hecate, 314–15, 337–38, 345, 361, 367
Helen, 367
Helios, 337–38
Hera, 35, 207, 216
Hercules, 23, 314
Hermes, 95, 343, 354, 359, 368
Hestia, 367
Horus, 354, 357–59, 368–69
Hyperion, 337–38

Iacchus, 13, 315
Iache, 345
Ianeira, 345
Ianthe, 345
Iao, 108–9
Idaean Mother, 350
Io, 41, 368
Iris, 343
Isis, 41, 134, 243, 245, 315, 333, 354–62, 367–68

Juno, 22, 350, 361
Jupiter, 22

Kallirhoe, 345
Kalypso, 345
Kore, 217, 367
Kronos, 337, 343, 369

Latina, 367
Leucothea, 22–23
Leukippe, 345
Liber, 314–15

Maia, 367
Marnas, 128
Mars, 41, 214

Matronit, 333
Melobosis, 345
Metanoia, 209, 275, 334
Minerva, 361
Mithras, 128, 243, 245
Mother Matuta, 22–23
Mother of the Gods, 110, 348–49, 361

Nania, 367
Nephthys, 354, 356
Norea, 377–78, 382–83

Okyrhoe, 345
Orpheus, 174
Oserapis, 95
Osiris, 41, 354–59, 368–69
Ourante, 345

Palaemon, 22–23
Pallas, 345
Persephone, 338, 343–45, 347
Phaino, 345
Pistis Sophia, 379, 383–84
Plouto, 345
Ploutos, 347
Portunus, 23
Priapus, 39
Proserpina, 360–61
Proserpine, 365

Queen of Heaven, 57, 360

Rhea, 354
Rheia, 338, 345–46
Rhodeia, 345
Rhodope, 345

Sabaoth, 384
Sabos, 15
Sakla, 283
Sarkounis, 367
Samael, 378, 384
Saturn, 23, 105
Semele, 11, 22
Serapis, 128
Shekinah, 333

Sipulenes, 110
Sophia, 209, 383–84
Sosipolis, 37
Sothis, 368
Stimula, 22, 250
Styx, 345

Thapseusis, 367
Thueris, 358
Tithonus, 22
Tyche, 345
Typhon, 354–56, 358–59

Venus, 25, 260–61
Vesta, 214, 314

Wisdom, 333

Yaldabaoth, 384
Yaltabaoth, 384

Zeus, 11, 13, 19, 26, 337, 338,
    343–46, 354
Zoe, 384